THE SUNDAY TIMES
Book of the Countryside

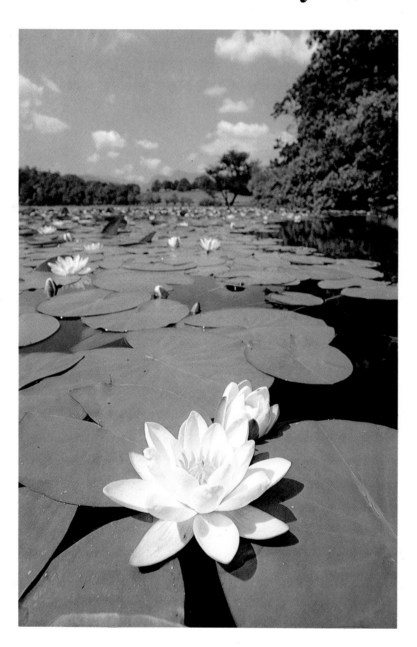

THE SUNDAY TIMES
Book of the Countryside

EDITORS

Philip Clarke

Brian Jackman

Derrik Mercer

ART DIRECTOR
Clive Crook

PEERAGE BOOKS

CONTRIBUTORS

Rosemary Atkins
Alec Clifton-Taylor
A.W. Coysh
Barry Dennis, editor, *Angling Times*
Professor David Dineley, Professor of Geology, University of Bristol
Andrew Gilg, lecturer in geography, University of Exeter
Richard Girling, editor, Scene, *The Sunday Times*
Mark Girouard, formerly Slade Professor of Art, University of Oxford
Anthony Greenbank
Francesca Greenoak
Christopher Hall, director, Council for the Protection of Rural England
Arthur Hellyer, formerly editor of *Gardening Illustrated* and *Amateur Gardening*
Suzanne Hodgart
Roy Milward, reader in geography, University of Leicester
John Prizeman
Dr Adrian Robinson, reader in geography, University of Leicester
Graham Rose, agricultural and gardening correspondent, *The Sunday Times*
Bryan Silcock, science correspondent, *The Sunday Times*
Robert Troop, property correspondent, *The Sunday Times*
John Watney
Dr John Whittow, senior lecturer in geography, University of Reading
Geoffrey Young, director, WATCH Trust for Environmental Education

The books which have helped to establish the reputation
of many of our contributors are detailed in the bibliography on page 235;
the names of other contributors appear in the
acknowledgements on page 233.

CONSULTANTS

Professor T.W. Freeman, Emeritus Professor of Geography, University of Manchester
Sir Emrys Jones, formerly Principal, Royal Agricultural College and Chief Scientific Adviser to
the Minister of Agriculture
Professor H.H. Lamb, Emeritus Professor, Climatic Research Unit, University of East Anglia
Grenville Lucas, deputy keeper, Herbarium, Royal Botanic Gardens, Kew
Graham Moss, director, Community Resources and Planning Group

In addition to the consultants named above, several contributors acted also as consultants,
notably Alec Clifton-Taylor, Roy Milward, Dr Adrian Robinson and Dr John Whittow. Many
organisations were also particularly helpful and our debt to these sources, along with other
acknowledgments, appears on page 233

DESIGNER
Pedro Silmon

PICTURE EDITOR
June Stanier

First published in Great Britain in 1980 by
Macdonald Futura Publishers

This edition published in 1986 by
Peerage Books
59 Grosvenor Street
London W1

ISBN 1 85052 072 0

Printed in Hong Kong

Contents

Foreword

Forewords are supposed to sing praises, but
wine like this needs no bush. A look at the formidably
distinguished list of contributors, at the wealth
of illustration and subject-matter, and not least at the price, is
recommendation enough. Such a comprehensive
introduction to the pleasures of rural and 'wild' Britain – and Ireland –
has long been needed. But now I am going to break rules,
because I suspect the book's very excellence and attractiveness requires
a warning to the unwary. The greatest threat to our countrysides
is less the physical harm we do them than our growing detachment from
their reality. For two centuries now we have become
increasingly an urban culture, increasingly in exile from
what exists outside our cities. A major danger of such exile is
that one can fall in love with pictures of things.
But pictures of things, as Henry VIII found with some of his brides,
can be insidiously more seductive than things in the flesh.
Real countrysides are sometimes much more secretive and 'difficult'
than they may appear from an armchair.
The essential passport to all things rural is patience,
and patience is not a town virtue. Much urban ingenuity
is devoted to artificially concentrating pleasure in time and space.
But this is a trick nature never learnt.
Rarities never occur there as in a film, one crowding on another,
all in perfect close-up. Very little yields to the passing glance,
nothing is displayed and labelled as in a zoo or a museum.
The wild will always stay closed to those who cannot learn to wait,
and to see the commonplace with fresh eyes.
I am a heretic too about the labelling. Never be brainwashed
into thinking that the countryside is like
some fiendish identification test, which you fail if you cannot
name everything you meet. Seeing and feeling
are just as important, and too many names act like blinkers:
they narrow vision. Truly knowing any form of life –
or way of life – is always as much an art as a science. In this we are all
amateurs, and start equal. Of course some names and explanations,
such as this book will give you, are necessary for the hard knowledge
that must underlie genuine feeling and affection, as opposed to
mere sentiment. What you have here is a key to a door, behind which lies
a secret land; it will let you in, but it is not the land itself.
No book, however thorough, however well-intentioned,
can be that. Once beyond the door, only you can find it –
its place in you, your place in it. Discovering this, one's own nature
in the mirror of nature, remains one of the most rewarding
experiences that life has to give, as strange and fertile as a journey to
another, and greener, planet. You may read
this invitation to it, and still decline; but you cannot claim it
was not handsomely offered.

John Fowles

Chapter One
The Making of the Countryside: the Natural Landscape

The British Isles possess a diversity of landscape which is unsurpassed; nowhere of comparable size has such variety. This scenic richness is a reflection of a complex, immensely long and, at times, mysterious geological history. To build the land has taken 3000 million years in which there were periods of convulsive upheaval, unceasing attrition and undisturbed calm. Only in the last 26 million years has this group of islands acquired the shape we know today. The sweep and scale of these great episodes is described here. So are the major Earth movements and Earth processes which have determined the scenery we see today, such as this view of Langdale in the Lake District

The British Isles do not go in for brash extremes. There are no deserts, no glaciers; no Niagaras nor Matterhorns (though it was not always so). But that is not to say the landscape lacks drama. For a demonstration of elemental savagery, walk out along any Cornish headland when a heavy sea is running. When heavy rollers charge the bays head on, and the shock of their fall, the suck and grind of pebbles swept up in their terrible undertow booms in the zawns and chasms of the shaken cliffs, then the entire coast from Hartland to Sennen seems the wildest place on earth.

And there are other places, as in the Black Cuillins of Skye, where even on a calm day, the silence of those implacable summits, the feeling of being watched by unseen eyes, is overpoweringly eerie.

The same prickle of unease can be felt among the lonely plains of Mayo, where bleached skeletons of long dead tree trunks protrude forlornly from the peat bogs, like the relics of a lost world.

Mostly, though, the face of the land responds to gentler rhythms. Its variations are more subtle, its contours softer. Connoisseur's country, often secretive, its sweet surprises walled about by hedgerow trees or lost in a fold of the hills. Then, just as you feel you are getting the measure of a particular stretch of countryside it suddenly changes pace, throws up some topographical *trompe l'oeil* that stops you in your tracks: Cheddar Gorge, the Wrekin, the Wye from Symonds Yat, the cliffs of Moher falling sheer into the sea.

Often it is a man-made feature which dominates the view; Bamburgh's hoary sea castle crouched on its rock above the Northumbrian dunes; or the Uffington White Horse, that free-flowing piece of pagan graffiti carved in the turf of the Berkshire Downs. It could hardly be otherwise in islands where man has been tilling, building, scratching and burrowing since the last Ice Age.

The much-maligned British climate has also played a vital part in the shaping of the landscape (see Chapter 9). The ice has been gone 10,000 years but, as will be explained later, the insidious forces of wind, frost and rain are still chipping away at the land, splintering the mountain summits, punching holes in the sea cliffs and carrying sediment down to the estuaries.

This temperate climate on the edge of Europe has determined the range of plant and animal habitats which can survive (see Chapter 4). Some localities within the British Isles have their own micro-climates. For instance, what could be more different than the sub-arctic tundra of the Cairngorm plateau and the Gulf Stream gardens of Tresco in the Isles of Scilly? But overall, it is a climate of moderation. The prevailing south-westerlies that sweep in from the Atlantic give a rain-washed, water-colour landscape, but it sparkles between the showers, matching its moods to the skies.

What we see when we look at the British Isles is a countryside of man's making. But to understand what is happening on the surface, to read the landscape and unravel its mysteries, you must first look to the rocks beneath.

The land underfoot is a rock hound's paradise, a complex mosaic running right through the geological spectrum (see p 18) from volcanic magmas forged in the crucible of the Earth's core (Edinburgh Castle is built on the plug of an eroded volcano which belched its last some 350 million years ago), to Ice Age moraines dumped by dying glaciers.

Fire and ice, and in between the slow laying down of the sedimentary rocks; downland chalk, red Devon sandstone; the clays and marls of the Midland vales; Pennine gritstone, cornbrash, limestone; each layer an epitaph to its own epoch, the burying ground of long dead seas and lost continents going back to the age of dinosaurs and beyond.

And all this time the part of the Earth's crust we call the British Isles was slowly drifting around the globe. Some 300 million years ago, when the coal forests were growing, it was a tropical Everglade straddling the Equator. Since then it has been nudged slowly north all the way to the present latitude, a pawn in the battle of the restless continents.

It was not a smooth ride. The land rose and fell, tilted, bent and buckled as it lurched from one geological era to the next. At one point, some 400 million years ago, the ponderous jockeying of the great land masses threw up a mountain chain that stretched across Scotland into Northern Ireland and down into Cumbria and Snowdonia. In their prime these peaks rivalled the Himalayas, but weather and the slow drip of time has ground them down to mere stumps of their former grandeur.

Even the most cursory glance at the structure of these islands reveals the scars of those cataclysmic spasms – fault, fold and fracture – in all their terrifying beauty (see p 14). It was a violent birth, subjected to unimaginable forces which

The oldest rocks in the British Isles are in north-west Scotland. Suilven (above) is a hulking 1000-million-year-old mountain of Torridonian sandstone. It sits upon even older rock, the Lewisian gneiss, which pre-dates it by a further 1800 million years

split Scotland from coast to coast, creating the Great Glen in which Loch Ness lies, and caused entire seas to vanish.

In southern Britain rocks of igneous origin are rare. They crop up as no more than a few pre-Cambrian hiccups among the Midland clays; Charnwood Forest in Leicestershire, Shropshire's Long Mynd, the switchback humps of the Malvern Hills (see p 12), each with its own distinctive micro-landscape flung up in sharp relief above the encircling vales.

But in the far south-west of Britain it is a different story. There, erosion and ancient earth movements have laid bare the cupolas of a plutonic underworld formed 290 million years ago (see illustration), and the dark glitter of granite is everywhere. From the tors of the Dartmoor skyline to the natural rock castles of the Penwith peninsula, this toughest of rocks adds its own obdurate qualities to the West Country landscape.

Granites also make distinctive contributions to the Scottish and Irish skylines. The bare summit plateaux of the Cairngorms are matched by the rolling Wicklow Mountains south of Dublin; the lonely Scottish heights of Arran are echoed by the Mountains of Mourne.

Elsewhere, the British Isles are mostly an accumulation of mud, sand and shell, a huge spoil heap stuffed with the residue of the vanished deserts, oceans and deltas in which life evolved and whose countless dead, themselves turned to stone long ago, lie buried in deep swathes from Durham to Dorset. Under the skin, much of the land is little more than a boneyard (see p 26).

Life in its earliest forms appeared in Cambrian times 570 million years ago,

Devon and Cornwall owe much of their scenic appeal to the huge 'stocks' of granite which rise from a single elongated core, or batholith, which reaches down to unknown depths beneath the surface. The upper parts of these 'stocks' appear as rugged coastal and moorland areas like Land's End and Dartmoor. The white areas indicate the proportions of surface exposure. These granite masses were pushed up and intruded into the overlying sedimentary rocks 290 million years ago. Dartmoor is the largest of the five shown. The Isles of Scilly are the surviving remnants of a sixth

slowly evolving in the warm Ordovician and Silurian seas which then covered much of eastern Ireland, southern Scotland, Wales and the Welsh border country. Relics of those primeval seas are the Silurian coral reefs and fossil trilobites – primitive crustaceans – of Wenlock Edge and Ludlow.

In the Devonian period 400 million years ago the British Isles became a prehistoric Arizona, a sandstone furnace of desolate badlands and painted deserts whose fierce red colours still glow from the sea-cliffs and fields of Devon and the mountains above Killarney. This was the age of fishes, barbaric creatures with armour-plated snouts and bony scales, who evolved in warm lagoons and left their fossil remains in the sandstone beds of the Caithness cliffs.

In time the deserts were drowned by invading seas which laid down the limestone carcass of the Pennines, added the gaunt Millstone Grits of the High Peak and gave rise to the Coal Measures, fossil relics of the world's first forests. These were the Carboniferous rocks, whose limestones form almost two-thirds of Ireland's present surface, including the rocky wilderness of the Burren in County Clare.

Then followed the Mesozoic era, the day of the dinosaur, when fierce ichthyosaurs surged through Britain's tropical seas, and the primitive life forms which had crawled from the Devonian ooze now walked the earth in the shape of giant reptiles.

The ichthyosaurs left their skeletons, entombed among myriads of coiled ammonite shells in the crumbling Blue Lias clays of Lyme Regis, and the dinosaurs

their footprints embedded in the Purbeck ledges. But the richest treasure of the epoch was the great stripe of Jurassic limestone that runs from Dorset through the Cotswolds and on up to Yorkshire. This is the stone, sometimes silvery grey, sometimes weathered to a deep honeygold, whose mellow beauty embellishes a long line of towns from Chipping Campden to Stamford.

During the final 60 million years of Mesozoic time, further subsidence led to deep inroads of the Cretaceous seas, their waters teeming with tiny marine organisms whose shelly skeletons fell like an endless snowstorm to build the English chalklands.

Where they fell they buried other corpses, including shoals of primitive sponges which, in the fullness of time became the flint nodules from which early man would fashion his tools.

The Tertiary era, which had tiptoed in after the Cretaceous to the whisper of drifting silt, went out to the apocalyptic crunch of the 'Alpine Storm', the global shudder which lasted 20 million years and which created the Alps and raised a crumpled England from the waves.

By now another remarkable change had taken place. Gone at last were the great reptiles, the primitive tree-ferns and giant horsetails of the coal forests. In their place came plants and animals more closely related to the flora and fauna of today.

In Northern Ireland and Western Scotland volcanoes were still pouring out lava which contracted as it cooled, forming in places the strange pencil columns of the Giant's Causeway and Fingal's Cave. But elsewhere Britain was becom-

ing more docile in old age. London was laying down the clays from which so many of her houses would be dug; and sabre-toothed tigers roamed the Home Counties.

The two or three million years of the Pleistocene period, which ended only 10,000 years ago, form the last chapter in the natural shaping of the British Isles, and in many ways it is the most important.

This was the period during which these islands lay deep frozen in the grip of the Great Ice Age which made several forays far into Western Europe. Glaciers gouged out the Lakeland dales and scalloped cwms and corries from the summits of Snowdon and Helvellyn; ice sheets disgorged their debris in vast outpourings of sands and gravels like those which now cover parts of Cheshire and the Norfolk Breckland (see p 15).

The power of the ice planed smooth the mountainsides, its meltwaters fed a 240ft (73m) high Niagara in Yorkshire where Malham Cove's grey cliffs now rise, and its presence diverted the Thames, which used to flow across East Anglia.

This, then, was the finishing touch, nature's final polish to the landscape we see today. When the ice retreated for the last time, the climate improved. The sealevel rose, creating the drowned *rias* or river valleys of Milford Haven, the Fal and Bantry Bay, and forests spread north as if to blot out the bleak memory of the post-glacial permafrost. And in the wake of the woods, as we shall see in Chapter 2, came man.

Forging of a landscape.
Six hundred million years to make it
The Malvern Hills are one of the few places in the British Isles where much of the story of landscape can be seen in a single, explicit 'georama'. The view looking south-south-eastwards from Worcestershire Beacon (1394ft, 425m), highest point on the hump-backed crest line of the Malverns, takes the eye over the middle reaches of the River Severn and the Vale of Gloucester to the distant limestone escarpment of the Cotswolds.

To the east, fertile and fruitful, lie the Vales of Worcester and Evesham and the north-eastern extension of the escarpment with its isolated outlying hills; to the north the red rocks and soils of the Midland Plain; and to the west a swathe of undulating country which runs beyond Hereford to the hills of Wales.

From this one point the viewer, turn-

Millstone grit country. The strange shapes of Yorkshire's Brimham Rocks weathered by rain and frost into a landscape which suggests an alien world

ing full circle, sees scenery which is based on rocks of almost every geological period, except for the chalk and a few younger formations; which has been subjected to the spasms and turbulence of huge earth movements; and which has been fashioned by the unremitting work of natural forces. All this represents a time span of 540 million years, 90 per cent of the Earth history of southern Britain.

Here the rich, rolling farmlands of the English Midlands, with neatly hedged fields and water-threaded meadows, epitomise the landscapes of lowland Britain. Rivers like the Severn have, over the past few million years, gradually etched the gently tilted land surface into a series of scarps and vales. At the same time the red sandstones and clays of the Midlands have been slowly exposed and lowered by the constant incision of running water.

The same forces of erosion and weathering have caused the Cotswold escarpment to retreat slowly south-eastwards, leaving behind the outlier (see opposite) of Bredon Hill to show something of its former extent.

In contrast to these lowlands the Malvern Hills rise dramatically from the Midland Plain, a rugged exposure of Britain's primeval skeleton which was once blanketed by younger rocks. This narrow line of hills, running north to south, possessed of a complicated geology of its own and made from ancient and harder rocks, belongs to the oldest of the great geological ages, the Pre-Cambrian.

The Malverns are a bony massif of ancient lavas and granite-like materials which protrudes through layers of younger calcareous muds, sands and clays laid down in the tranquil seas which once covered the country.

These venerable foundation stones of basement Britain were forged in the fires of early Earth over 600 million years ago.

The Malvern Hills. Here older rocks of basement Britain protrude through the lowland floor. Snow on the summits is a reminder that these are the first foothills of the mountain land

Chalk country. The rounded, rolling green of Wiltshire downland with a farm set in a sheltering fold in the hill and woods marching the crest above

Since then they have been crushed, folded and faulted by gigantic earth movements which punctuated the quieter episodes when sedimentary layers were gently accumulating.

Like their Welsh, Scottish and Irish counterparts, the Malverns are mere shadows of their former selves; no more than stumps of an ancient mountain chain worn down by the same forces – water, sun, wind and ice – which are still inexorably at work, fashioning the scenery of the British Isles.

Yet still they stand, by man's time scale permanent and enduring, geological milestones upon the Midland Plain, providing a scenic boundary between lowland and highland Britain – the first foothills of the mountain land.

The hill that was left behind.
Remnant of the Cotswold scarp

Bredon Hill (961ft, 293m), to the north of the A435 road between Evesham and Tewkesbury, is an outlier of the main Cotswold escarpment. An outlier is a mass of rock separated from its main outcrop, the intervening strata having been destroyed by weathering and stream erosion (see illustration below).

The scarp summit is of hard limestone. Beneath are softer clays which are worn away more rapidly. Rain, and spring water rising along the junction of the two rocks carries the clay downhill.

This action undercuts the limestone to form a steep scarp slope. As it is undermined portions slip down and are gradually broken up. The process is repeated unceasingly, but faster in some places than others, to give an uneven scarp line. As new surfaces are attacked the scarp edge retreats, slowly and irregularly.

The Bredon bastion, isolated from the main escarpment several million years ago, is now being reduced more rapidly as it is assaulted on all sides by the forces of erosion. One day it will disappear.

This stretch of countryside has been in the making for 540 million years, a span of geological time which nearly covers the complete Earth history of southern Britain. The scenery, based on rocks of almost every geological age, has been shaped by natural forces. Thus Bredon Hill is an isolated remnant of the Cotswold Scarp which has retreated (marked by dotted line) before the continuous onslaught of rain and stream erosion

The land in spasm. How violent upheaval changed the terrain

The Great Glen slashes through the highlands of Scotland for almost a hundred miles (160km) from Inverness to the island of Lismore near Oban. It is one of the most remarkable topographical boundaries in the British Isles. To one side are the North-West Highlands, to the other the Grampians. Within it, between Loch Linnhe and the Moray Firth, runs a chain of lochs – long, straight and deep. One is Loch Ness.

The Glen's scenery is outstanding, its mysteries compelling. Whatever it is which is supposed to lurk in the depths of Loch Ness has excited the interest of investigators for years. Geologists, however, are trying to unravel a different mystery. The Great Glen (also known as Glen Mor and the Great Glen of Albyn) is a major landscape feature which is the product of one of those periods in the geological past when scenery changed dramatically in relatively short spans of time. The gigantic fractures which have cracked the rocks of the British Isles are legacies of these great periods of flux. Of these fractures, or faults, the Great Glen is the most notable.

How was it formed? Periodically the world's tectonic plates shift position (see map below). The plates are major structural elements of the Earth's crust. They are like enormous floes of pack-ice which move in relation to each other.

Sometimes, as they shift, they collide head on. Such collisions which cause considerable crumpling or folding of the rocks are the very stuff of mountain building. At other times the plates grind slowly past each other along so-called tear, or wrench faults. The Great Glen is the best example in the British Isles of this sort of large scale lateral movement (see opposite). In this instance it began during an earlier phase of plate tectonics, some 350 million years ago, when the plate boundaries were quite different (see map below).

How much movement there has been, or even in what direction, is a matter of argument. The most likely case is that the North-West Highlands have been moving slowly south-westwards relative to the Grampians for the past 350 million years. In that time they have travelled about 65 miles (104km). Then, of course, the shape of Scotland was totally different to what it is today, and the country was part of a continent which included Greenland and Newfoundland. So the idea of Inverness once sitting somewhere near to where Wick is now may be amusing but is misleading. An even larger movement, up to 200 miles (320km), has been suggested by some authorities. Others argue a movement of 60-odd miles (100km) in the opposite direction, north-eastwards. Whatever the answer, the line of the fault is now lost beneath a chain of lochs.

The largest faults in the British Isles are found in Scotland. So are all the main types of fault which geologists identify. Indeed, it was here that one of these types was first discovered. The Moine Thrust in the North-West Highlands follows a line from Skye to Loch Eriboll on the north coast. This line marks the north-west edge of a huge block of the Earth's crust which was driven bodily over another, along an oblique plane of sliding called a thrust fault (see opposite).

To the west of the Moine Thrust is the oldest landscape in the British Isles where mountains of sandstone rise abruptly from a lake-dotted, ice-scoured basement of Lewisian gneiss. To the east is a landscape of hills and plateaux built upon Moinian rocks, dark coloured, flaky schists produced by the action of intense heat and pressure on sands and muds.

Here, a century ago, geologists were puzzled because the normal order in which beds of rock appear, lying in sequence according to their age, with the oldest at the bottom and the most recently formed at the top, was reversed. It was the search for an answer to this apparent anomaly which led to the discovery and understanding of the thrust fault, one of the fundamental principles of structural geology. The complexities of this can be seen and more easily understood at the Nature Conservancy Council's Knockan Cliff Geological Trail between Ullapool and Inchnadamph.

Farther south, near Stirling, another major Scottish fracture, the Ochil Fault, has brought tough, resistant volcanic lavas hard up against relatively soft rocks. This happened when there was a large displacement, or downthrow, of rocks towards the south which left a cliff-like formation. This has been accentuated by erosion and weathering, the softer rocks being worn away at a faster rate than the harder ones. The result is the fault line escarpment of the Ochil Hills which runs from Blairlogie eastwards to beyond Dollar. It extends for some 20 miles (30 km) and viewed from the south appears as a straight mountain-front rising steeply from the Clackmannan plain. This type of fracture is described as a normal fault (see illustration opposite).

Earth movements such as these are not completed. Minor earth tremors still occur along the Great Glen and Ochil Faults. In the last 200 years sixty have been recorded along the Great Glen.

In other parts of the British Isles the rocks, instead of fracturing, have crumpled under pressure. The main forms of this crumpling, or folding, are shown on the opposite page. There have been three

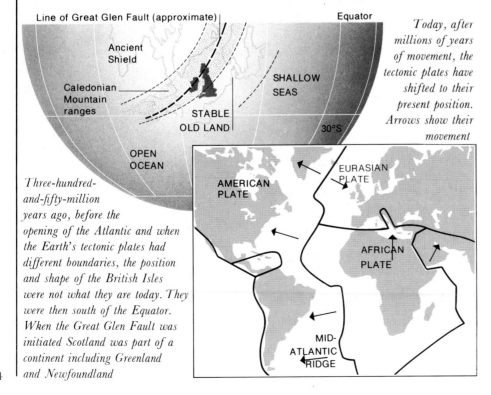

Today, after millions of years of movement, the tectonic plates have shifted to their present position. Arrows show their movement

Three-hundred-and-fifty-million years ago, before the opening of the Atlantic and when the Earth's tectonic plates had different boundaries, the position and shape of the British Isles were not what they are today. They were then south of the Equator. When the Great Glen Fault was initiated Scotland was part of a continent including Greenland and Newfoundland

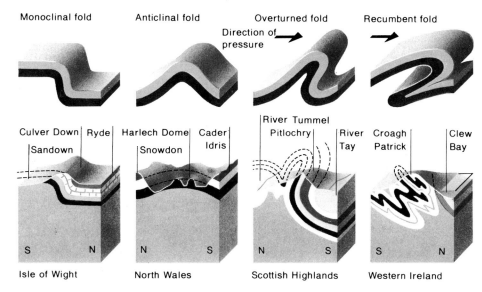

Monoclinal fold   Anticlinal fold   Overturned fold   Recumbent fold

Direction of pressure

Culver Down | Ryde   Harlech Dome | Cader Idris   River Tummel / Pitlochry | River Tay   Croagh Patrick | Clew Bay

Sandown   Snowdon

Isle of Wight   North Wales   Scottish Highlands   Western Ireland

The mechanics of mountain building: folding. Folds occur when layers of rock are crumpled and buckled into a series of wave-like structures. They are usually produced by horizontal compression and result in a variety of forms which influence scenery. The simple syncline, where rock layers are folded downwards, is not illustrated. The last period of British Folding was 90 million years ago

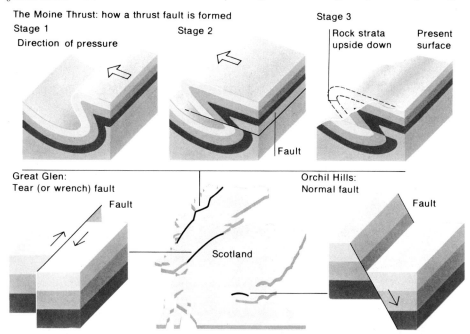

The Moine Thrust: how a thrust fault is formed

Stage 1 — Direction of pressure

Stage 2

Stage 3 — Rock strata upside down | Present surface

Fault

Great Glen: Tear (or wrench) fault — Fault

Orchil Hills: Normal fault — Fault

Scotland

The mechanics of mountain building: faulting. Faults are fractures produced by pressure and tension in the Earth's crust which cause rocks to be displaced. They have a marked influence on landscape. Scotland's Moine Fault, Great Glen and Ochil Hills are examples of three different types of fault

major episodes of this. Episode one, 400 million years ago, formed the fold mountains of Scotland (the Grampians and Southern Uplands), the Lake District, North Wales and Northern Ireland.

Episode two, 300 million years ago, created the spectacular folding of Munster in Southern Ireland, the tight folds of Pembrokeshire and South-West England and those of the Pennines.

Episode three, a mere 30 million years ago, represented the outer ripples of the maelstrom which threw up the European Alps and also folded the sedimentary rocks of Dorset and stood the chalk and its neighbouring rocks on end in the Isle of Wight.

Scotland's Great Glen. A 100-mile-long (160km) fault which has made one of the most dramatic boundaries in the British Isles

The mighty power of ice. A major force in moulding scenery

On the seashore at Porthleven, Cornwall, stands a block of rock. It is estimated to weigh 60 tons. How it came to be there is a geological puzzle. For it is entirely foreign to its surroundings, unlike any other rocks in the vicinity. Geologists think it may have originated from Scotland since it is a form of very ancient material called gneiss which is common to the North-West Highlands and the Hebrides.

Only ice sheets, with their immense power, seem to have the capability to have transported it to Cornwall's Channel coast. In successive ice ages they did move enormous quantities of material from the highlands to the lowlands. Ice carried rocks from North Wales to Birmingham and from Scandinavia to East Anglia and Yorkshire. Boulders and pebbles from Cumbria's Shap Granite have been found far to the south and east in lowland boulder clays and gravels. It has even been suggested that the famous blue-stones of Stonehenge were transported from Pembrokeshire, not by men, but by ice sheets!

These alien rocks, or erratics as geologists call them, are useful in helping map the routes of the ice sheets. The examples mentioned are located in areas which were within the southern limits of the ice. Porthleven, however, lies south of the generally accepted line of the great glaciations (see map overleaf).

How then did its large erratic rock, the Giant's Block, get there? The most likely explanation is that it was 'rafted' there on a floating iceberg and then dumped as the iceberg melted. Other erratics along the Channel coast are thought to have been transported in the same way. Ice rafting is a process common in higher latitudes and can be seen happening in Canada's Gulf of St Lawrence today.

In the British Isles the legacy of the Ice Age, which lasted, with warmer interruptions, for two million years, is seen almost everywhere. The rugged magnificence of highland scenery, the smooth lowland spreads of clays, gravels and sands and even some features of chalk downland can be explained in terms of this cold period. Although the last ice caps disappeared 10,000 years ago, this in geological time is only yesterday.

To understand the Ice Age imagine British winters, such as that of 1962–63 or 1978–79, becoming commonplace

Extent of last ice sheets
Maximum extent of ice sheets
Areas not covered by ice

The British Isles under ice. In the last 2½ million years there have been periods of intense arctic cold when glaciers formed in the mountains, later coalesced and spread out, across the lowlands. The map shows how the earliest glaciations reached farthest south. The ice sheets also filled the basins of the Irish and North Seas. It was over 3000ft (914m) thick

and even more prolonged. Eventually the heavy snowfalls survive the shorter, cooler summers. Glaciers begin to form in the Scottish, Welsh and Irish mountains. Ultimately these combine to form ice sheets completely burying even the highest mountain tops (as in Greenland today). They then surge outwards into the British and Irish lowlands.

Ireland had two such ice caps, a large one in the north and a smaller one centred on the mountains of Kerry and Cork, but their coalescence just failed to submerge the highest peaks of the Dingle Peninsula and the Galty Mountains.

All Scotland and Wales disappeared as ice lobes reached as far south as the Thames, the Bristol Channel and the Isles of Scilly. In front of the ice sheets, in unglaciated southern England, a severe climate prevailed, similar to that of Canada's modern Arctic. For most of the year the ground was frozen and snow covered, even in summer still frozen just beneath the surface.

In what is now Devon and Cornwall frost action helped fashion the distinctive moorland tors. These granite rocks were sharpened by frost splitting them along their joints; and the fallen blocks, or clitters, were moved down the gentle slopes by solifluxion, a movement which occurs with the continuous freezing and thawing of the ground.

The seasonal surface melting of the frozen terrain sent surface water coursing over the barren landscape. This was swollen by the meltwaters of nearby ice sheets and streams were able to flow across the frozen subsoil of the formerly permeable chalk. The chalk downlands were therefore quite drastically modified. Most of the dry valleys of the chalklands are thought to have been formed in this way.

The main river valleys were quickly filled with a detritus of chalky mud, sands and gravels, which was later carved by rivers into river terraces such

as those of the Thames and the River Severn.

Elsewhere the glacial meltwaters either left spreads of sandy gravel in places such as Thetford Chase in Norfolk or they carved out gorges across hill barriers. Of these the Ironbridge Gorge in Shropshire, now followed by the River Severn, is the most spectacular although the streamless Valley of the Rocks, near Lynton, North Devon, and winding Newtondale on the North Yorkshire Moors are also noteworthy.

In Ireland the dumping ground of the ice sheets was the Central Plain where spreads of boulder clay, sand and gravel totally buried the solid rocks. These, in turn, have been mantled by post-glacial peat bogs.

The effects of the Ice Age are more marked in Ireland than in Britain, so much so that Irish terminology has been adopted internationally to describe certain glacial landforms, such as eskers and drumlins.

The first are sinuous gravelly ridges marking the former courses of glacial streams which ran in tunnels beneath the ice. The second are low, whale-backed

U-shaped glacial trough
Horn peak
Pinnacle ridge (Arête)
Corrie moraine
Corrie lake
Hanging valley
Corrie
Truncated spurs
Perched blocks

How ice shapes the land surface. At the peak of the last Ice Age, 50,000 to 30,000 years ago, a glacier bulldozed down a highland valley (see inset) carving out a U-shaped trough. When the ice melted it left behind this and other distinctive features of glacial erosion. Today ice and frost are still at work in winter cutting back the corries and sharpening the high ridges

At the lower end of Snowdonia's Llyn Ogwen (above) the waters of the lake escape down a high cliff where the Nant Ffrancon pass makes a sharp bend. Beyond is a typical glaciated valley, U-shaped, with truncated spurs and ice-smoothed rocks. Some have ice scratch marks, like those shown (top left) from the Lake District. Here the huge Bowder Stone (above left) was carried down valley by ice

hills of boulder clay, fluted by the over-riding ice and likened to a basket of eggs. There are superb examples of these in the Central Plain, and in Antrim and Armagh. Drumlins can also be seen in north Anglesey, Cumbria's Vale of Eden and in the Tweed Valley.

At the close of the Ice Age, glaciers in the mountains of Scotland, Ireland, Wales and the Lake District bulldozed remorselessly from their rocky, arm-chair-shaped hollows, known as cor-ries or cwms, into the adjoining valleys (see illustration). The erosive power of these ice streams is exemplified by the ice-polished and scratched rocks of many Scottish glens and the overdeepened U-shaped troughs of Cumbria's Langdale, Snowdonia's Nant Ffrancon and

Ireland's Glendalough.

In the Llanberis Pass in North Wales truncated spurs – spurs which have been partly shaved off by the glacier as it moved down the valley – testify to the amount of rock that has been removed. Here, too, perched blocks, erratics which have been left in an exposed position, teeter on the edge of the abyss. The height from the floor of the pass to their precarious resting place shows how thick the ice was.

Some large blocks, such as the Bowder Stone on the lower slopes of the fell overlooking the entrance to Borrowdale in the Lake District, were moved far down the valleys. This block is estimated to weigh nearly 2,000 tons.

Sometimes these blocks are associated with piles of hummocky, glacial 'rubbish' termed moraines. These mark the termi-nation or recessional stages of a valley glacier.

The majority of moraines, however, are found high up in the corries. They are remnants of the very last cold phase 10,000 years ago and frequently these bouldery ridges impound circular lakes beneath the rocky headwalls of the

corrie. Snowdonia's Llyn Idwal and Cumbria's Stickle Tarn are among the best known.

Other waters occupy the long, gla-cially overdeepened hollows of the neigh-bouring valleys. Cumbria's lakes, Scotland's numerous lochs, especially Skye's Loch Coruisk and Loch Avon in the Cairngorms, and the renowned Lakes of Killarney are outstanding examples.

On the mountain tops the work of frost is everywhere: in the splintered summits, the ever-growing cliff-foot screes and the knife-edged ridges or arêtes. When the headwalls of adjoining corries retreat, eaten back by glacial plucking, the pul-ling away of rock by moving ice, the intervening ridges are narrowed or even breached. The pinnacle ridges of The Cuillins, the Crib Goch ridge of Snowdon and Helvellyn's Striding Edge testify to the sharpness of these almost Alpine landforms. Although most of the frost shattering took place in the Ice Age the highest summits in the British Isles still experience an Alpine climate, so that plateau tops like the Cairngorms are mantled with freshly broken rock waste.

How they were formed

The look of a piece of landscape is determined largely by the nature of the rocks beneath it. In the British Isles the variety of scenery reflects the presence of rocks of almost every age in the Earth's history. Geologically, these islands are almost a museum model.

The three main groups of rocks are all present. The igneous rocks are formed from molten rock or magma brought up from deep below the Earth's surface. When magma cools slowly beneath the surface it forms rocks with large crystals such as granite. When it cools rapidly on the surface – as, for example, volcanic lava – it forms finely crystalline rocks such as basalt.

The sedimentary rocks have their beginnings in the weathering or breaking down of the other rocks by frost, rain, sun, wind and chemical processes. The weathered material is transported by water and deposited in rivers, lakes and the sea. As these loose sediments are cemented together by mineral matter, or are compressed by the pressure of overlying material, sedimentary rocks are formed. Some like coal and limestone are the remains of once living organisms. Others form from chemicals dissolved in water. Shales and sandstones are other examples of sedimentary rocks. All these rocks are layered.

Metamorphic rocks are those igneous or sedimentary rocks which have been changed from their original form by heat, pressure and chemical action. This happens most commonly when molten magma is intruded into layers of sedimentary rocks. Limestone, for example, becomes marble. Shale is compacted into slate.

How to recognise rocks
Sedimentary

Oolitic limestone. This is a build-up of small calcareous spheres like fish roe, cemented together. Its creamy colour and durability has led to its popularity as an English building stone.

Chalk. Probably the best known of all rocks, and the material which makes up the White Cliffs of Dover. It is a pure form of limestone. Dazzling white when freshly exposed. Fine grained and permeable. Often has flints and fossils.

Sandstone. Composed of small rounded glassy quartz granules plus some reddish feldspar minerals cemented together. The commonest red and brown sandstones are stained by iron oxides but there are white and grey varieties.

Conglomerate. Composed of rounded pebbles derived from all rock types in a fine grained matrix of sand or silt cemented by silica or calcite. These consolidated pebble or gravel beds are formed mainly along sea and lake shores.

Shale. A fine-grained rock of silty or muddy particles, characterised by the ease with which it splits along its thin bedding planes. In section it appears like the pages of a closed book.

Journeys through geological time

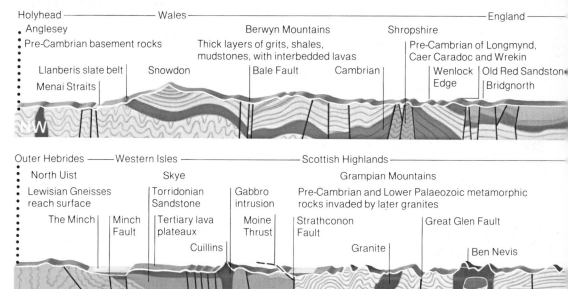

Holyhead ———— Wales ———— England

- Anglesey
- Pre-Cambrian basement rocks
- Llanberis slate belt | Snowdon
- Menai Straits

Berwyn Mountains
Thick layers of grits, shales, mudstones, with interbedded lavas
Bale Fault | Cambrian

Shropshire
Pre-Cambrian of Longmynd, Caer Caradoc and Wrekin
Wenlock Edge | Old Red Sandstone | Bridgnorth

NW

Outer Hebrides ———— Western Isles ———— Scottish Highlands

- North Uist
- Lewisian Gneisses reach surface
- The Minch | Minch Fault

Skye
Torridonian Sandstone
Tertiary lava plateaux
Cuillins

Gabbro intrusion
Moine Thrust

Grampian Mountains
Pre-Cambrian and Lower Palaeozoic metamorphic rocks invaded by later granites
Strathcanon Fault
Granite
Great Glen Fault
Ben Nevis

NW

Old Head of Kinsale ———— Munster ———— Leinster

- Munster Uplands
- Carboniferous limestone, shales and grits. Old Red Sandstone forms ridges
- Cork | Nagles Mts | Fermoy

Palaeozoic grits and shales
Galtymore | Tipperary

Central Plain
Limestone blanketed with glacial deposit and peat

Lower Carboniferous shales |
Old Red Sandstone |
Devilsbit Mt

Carboniferous limestone

S

Igneous

Basalt. This is a black fine-grained rock, created by the solidification of a former lava. Often weathers into hexagonal columns, as at the Giant's Causeway and Fingal's Cave.

Rhyolite. Is a yellowish-buff coloured, fine grained lava. This rock is found especially in Snowdonia.

Granite. The most common igneous rock. Distinguished by its large crystalline grains of mica, quartz and feldspar. Formed at very great depths and exposed only in the highlands of Britain and Ireland and as Dartmoor's tors.

Metamorphic

Mica Schist. Rocks which have silvery or bronze flakes of mica are found in the north-west of Scotland and western Ireland. They split easily but unlike slates their splitting surfaces are often irregular not flat.

Slate. A stone produced by metamorphism of shales and mudstones. Can be black or shades of blue, green, brown or buff. Easily splits into slabs and very thin sheets, but unlike a shale it splits obliquely across the bedding planes.

Gneiss. Rocks which have undergone considerable change by heat and pressure. Is often striped into black and white or black and red crystalline layers which sometimes occur draped around glassy aggregates or 'eyes' of quartz.

Quartzite. Occurs when great pressure closes up the pore spaces of a sandstone. It thus becomes very hard and because of its almost 100% silica is usually white or light-coloured and medium grained.

Journey 1 cross-section labels:
London — Warwickshire — Cotswolds — Chilterns — Thames Valley
New Red Sandstone — Gently dipping scarp and vale — Tertiary clays and sands
West Midlands coalfield — Broadway — Oolitic limestone — Chalk — Lias ironstone
Oxford
SE

Journey 2 cross-section labels:
Scottish Lowlands — Gretna Green
Midland Valley — Southern Uplands
Highland Boundary Fault — Grits, shales and mudstones — Permian Sandstone
Old Red Sandstone — Southern Uplands Fault — Solway Firth
Lavas
Carboniferous Basin
SE

Journey 3 cross-section labels:
Ulster — Torr Head
Antrim Plateau — Pre-Cambrian rocks with Tertiary igneous intrusions
Grits and shales — Chalk beneath lavas
Monaghan — Basin of New Red Sandstone — Tertiary lava — Lough Neagh — North Channel

Journey 1. London–Holyhead. Following this 230 mile (370km) line the traveller cuts across the grain of the country (see geological map below). The cross-section shows how after leaving the young clays and sands of the London Basin the surface rocks get progressively older north-westwards until the ancient metamorphics of Anglesey are reached. In the south, limestone scarp and clay vale succeed each other as far as the red sandstone plain of The Midlands. The ancient rocks of Shropshire break up the orderly progression but beyond the Border, Welsh grits and mudstones form a rolling, dissected plateau which rises gently to the high peaks of Snowdonia.

Journey 2. Gretna Green–Outer Hebrides. Here the line, 260 miles (418km) long, (see map) crosses from one of Scotland's youngest rocks – the New Red Sandstone of the Solway – to Britain's oldest rocks, the Lewisian gneiss of the Outer Hebrides. In between lie the rolling hills of the Southern Uplands, the coalfields and the sandstones and limestones of the Central Valley, the gentler scenery of which is punctuated by scarps of tougher, interbedded lavas. To the north lie the incomparable Highlands where ice has worked on a variety of old igneous and metamorphic rocks to create a landscape of deep glens and rugged mountains. Skye's mountains and plateaux are built from much younger igneous rocks.

Journey 3. Old Head of Kinsale–Torr Head. From south to north the line of the section (see map) is 270 miles (434km). The well folded sandstones and limestones of southern Ireland have been greatly denuded – enough to uncover the underlying Silurian grits and shales which form some of Ireland's highest mountains. Lying to the north the gently folded Carboniferous limestone, with its blanket of glacial drift and peat, creates the featureless, lake-dotted Central Plain which rises northwards to the older hill country of Northern Ireland. Here some younger clays, sandstones and even chalk occur but they have been almost swamped by thick basalt lava flows – now forming the Antrim Plateau in the central hollow of which is Lough Neagh.

Geological map of British Isles. This shows sedimentary rocks classified according to their age of deposition and igneous rocks according to their mode of origin. The map is simplified. At this scale it is not possible to show the detail which appears in the geological sections above. This is why the colour coding on it is different to that used in the sections. The lines on the map correspond to the sections. Following these lines on the ground, even approximately, takes the traveller on three incredible journeys through geological time. The figures indicate age in millions of years.

Shetlands
Edinburgh
Belfast
Dublin
Manchester
London

Sedimentary rocks
Cenozoic
Tertiary and marine Pleistocene. Mainly clays and sands. Glacial drift not shown... up to 65

Mesozoic
Cretaceous. Mainly chalk, clays and sands 65–140

Jurassic. Mainly limestones and clays 140–195

Triassic. Marls, sandstones and conglomerates 195–230

Palaeozoic
Permian. Mainly magnesian limestones, marls and sandstones 230–280

Carboniferous. Limestones, sandstones, shales and coal seams 280–345

Devonian. Sandstones, shales, conglomerates (Old Red Standstone); slates and limestones.. 345–395
Silurian. Shales, mudstones, greywacke, limestones 395–445

Ordovician. Mainly shales and mudstones; limestone in Scotland 445–510

Cambrian. Mainly shales, slate and sandstones; limestone in Scotland 510–570

Upper Proterozoic
Late Pre-Cambrian. Mainly sandstones, conglomerates and siltstones 600–1000

Metamorphic rocks
Lower Palaeozoic and Proterozoic. Mainly schists and gneisses 500–1000

Early Pre-Cambrian (Lewisian). Mainly gneisses 1500–3000

Igneous rocks
Intrusive. Mainly granite, gabbro and dolerite } .... { Rocks of all ages
Volcanic. Mainly basalt, rhyolite, andesite and tuffs }

A pattern of rivers. Their waters lend beauty to the land

The University of Keele in North Staffordshire, is both a well of learning and a watershed. Perched at 600ft (183m) on its sandstone ridge, it is in a remarkable location on one of England's major drainage divides (see map below).

Water from a bucket emptied upon its campus will have as its final destination the sea. But which sea? For Keele sits at the hub of three great river systems. Northwards the streams drain towards the River Mersey and thence to the Irish Sea; the south-east flowing streams are the headwaters of the River Trent which empties into the North Sea; and to the south-west they are part of the River Severn system which carries water to the Bristol Channel.

These three great rivers, like others in the British Isles, are part of a drainage pattern which is the product of a long and complex evolution. No less important to the overall pattern are other substantial rivers: the Thames, the longest river wholly in England; Fenland's Witham, Welland, Nene and Great Ouse, a run of rivers which drain one of the most singular of landscapes; the Tyne, Tees and Wear, the flows of which are soon to be regulated by man with the 2,700 acre reservoir of the Kielder Water Scheme in the North Tyne Valley; Scotland's Forth, Tay, Clyde and fast flowing Spey; and the Shannon which drains a vast tract of Ireland.

There is no sensible answer to how old these rivers are. For throughout the geological history of the British Isles rivers have existed whenever there was land. Some flow today following a pattern which was broadly set millions of years ago. Others follow courses the carving of which can be counted in mere thousands of years. The latter only flow where they do because of the Ice Age; and the sweeps and curves they follow on their inevitable downhill journey to the sea may bear little relation to the paths they took before the ice sheets over-whelmed their courses.

The Thames, although there is argument about it, is thought to have followed a more northerly course across Essex and Suffolk than it does today. At one time, perhaps, its mouth was at the Wash; at another where the estuary of the River Blackwater is now. But the ice sheets and their debris pushed it south, deflecting it to its present course.

The Severn also has had a dramatic and permanent change of route. It used to flow northwards from near Shrewsbury, possibly taking the Dee as a tributary, and emptying into the Irish Sea where the Dee estuary is now.

Then, during one of the Ice Age's recessional phases when the ice sheets retreated northwards they uncovered a rocky ridge near to Shropshire's Wrekin. The melt waters, trapped between ice and ridge, were unable to escape. A lake formed and its level rose until it over-flowed, cutting through the ridge to form the Ironbridge Gorge, the waters moving southwards to the Bristol Channel. Eventually the lake was emptied but the Severn never regained its previous course. For now it was blocked by mounds of debris left by the ice sheets.

These are two dramatic instances of Ice Age river diversion. There were many changes to river scenery in that period which were only superficial. Often meltwater channels were cut beneath or alongside the ice. Temporary lakes formed, grew in depth and made their own overflow channels. Many of these channels are now dry. The streams which trickle through them are so small that they are obviously incapable of having carved out the wide deep valleys in which they flow. Newtondale in North Yorkshire is an example.

In fact most of the major scenic features of England and Wales, rivers included, have developed in the last 26 million years since Miocene times. The rivers then were beginning to adopt the lines they occupy at present, The Miocene marked the climax of the Alpine storm which had great influence on Britain, among other things creating the newly formed trough which is now known as the London Basin. Into this the drainage of the lower Thames was collected. It is also thought to have given the Lake District the domed form on which its rivers were developed, the very earliest stages in the making of a marked radial drainage pattern. Much, much later Wordsworth, in his '*Description of the Scenery of the Lakes*', was to write of a number of valleys diverging 'like spokes from the nave of a wheel'.

Before the onset of the Ice Age, many coastal areas which had been cut into wide, level platforms by both rivers and the sea, were uplifted. This gave the rivers which flowed across them a new lease of life enabling them once more to cut down, incising new and deeper valleys. This rejuvenation created many gorge-like valleys and meanders like those on the River Wye.

It has given the Wye outstanding scenic appeal. The river swings in big curves up to four miles in amplitude, and in several it almost forms a complete loop, as at Symond's Yat and the great turn under Wynd Cliff, near Chepstow. Here the river's progress to the sea is through a narrow, steep-sided gorge.

The Wye works to shape the landscape in its own particular way. Equally the character of the river itself, its vigour and power, depends upon the kind of land surface across which it flows. The Wye is a river which belongs to the western hills and mountains, where the coastal plains, unlike those of the south and east, are narrow or missing altogether. Rivers and streams are fast flowing, often short, plunging directly into the sea.

In most of eastern, lowland Britain very broad plains intervene between the hills and the sea. Rivers now seem larger but lazier, gliding through broad valleys and far-spreading flood plains, giving a very different texture to the landscape. Nowhere is this more apparent than in the vast shallow basin of the Fenlands.

Here the Fenland rivers concentrate an enormous volume of fresh water; and man since Roman times has been trying to temper its worst excesses with large and impressive drainage schemes. The soil, the economy and the history of Fenland stem from one salient, natural phenomenon – an excess of water. As Daniel Defoe put it: 'All the water of the middle part of England which does not run into the Thames or Trent comes down into these fens'.

It is a happy benefit that a river's work

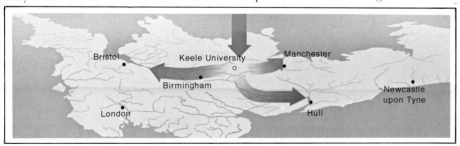

Where the water flows. One of England's great drainage divides is centred on Keele University, North Staffordshire, which is at the hub of three major river systems

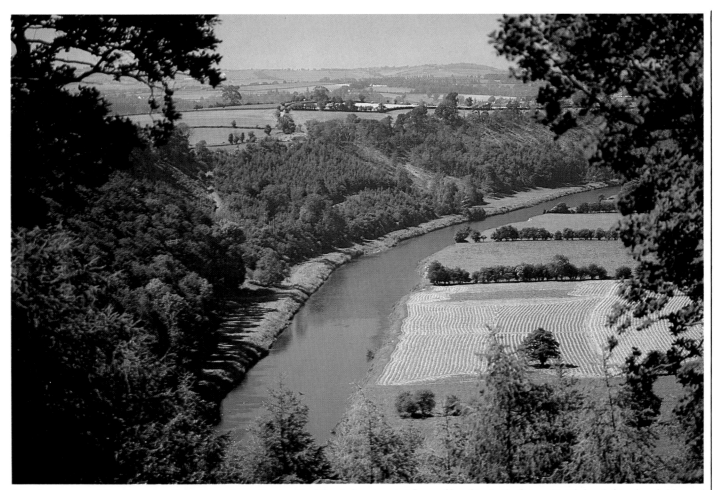

Running water enriches the green of meadow and woodland on the Wye (above) and at Lower Slaughter in the Cotswolds (below left) where bridge and buildings are of local stone. At High Force (below right) the peaty waters of the Tees foam against dark blue-grey Whin Sill rock

enhances and nourishes the visual appeal of the landscape. Constable painting by the Stour understood this well. The opportunities for paint and canvas are rich and varied: the Thames making its spectacular cut through the hills at Goring Gap, the only river crossing a six-mile wide (9.6km) belt of waterless chalk; the coalescence at Dartmeet of the East and West rivers to make one incomparable Dart; the surprise of a tiny tributary of Scotland's river Dee called

Vat Burn cutting a deep gorge and gigantic circular pothole 50ft (15m) into solid granite.

History, of course, is much lubricated by rivers. Their banks have served as settlement sites, their running waters as power for mills, their broad expanses as barriers and boundaries.

Yet their greatest work is that which springs from their power as natural forces. There is no better example than the valley of the Severn seen from the

Cotswolds or the Malverns.

When the Severn started the work, which lasted millions of years, of making this great vale it is unlikely that much of a depression existed. Now the immensity of the valley is so impressive that it is hard to believe that it and its tributaries have been able to carry away the vast amount of material which once filled it. It is a panorama which helps one grasp the astonishing power of rivers in shaping the land.

How running water shapes the countryside

Despite its apparent tranquillity and sense of permanence the scenery of the British Isles is constantly changing. The clatter of a pebble bouncing along a river bed is a reminder of this dynamic quality of landscape. Indeed, it is running water, among all the agents engaged in shaping scenery, which is the most effective. It whittles away mountains and hills and carries away the loosened material.

Thus a river is a powerful work-horse – and the work it does is demonstrated by these powers of erosion, transport and deposition. The load of transported material it carries, either by rolling or bouncing, as in the case of the pebble, or as fine particles suspended in the water, depends on its energy.

In its upper course a river is engaged primarily in erosion. In these steep upper gradients boulders, cobbles and pebbles are quickly dumped, to be moved again only in times of flood. But the fine sands and clays stay with the river longer, constantly being carried downstream to the lowlands, or swept out to sea.

Therefore it is easy to distinguish between the cascading clear waters of the boulder-strewn Scottish, Welsh and Cumbrian streams and the slow, muddy waters of the Thames in London.

Because of the geological diversity of the British Isles, rivers rarely complete their journeys without encountering rock strata of differing hardness. So instead of a theoretical smooth curve a river's long profile – what its slope looks like in section from source to sea – is really a succession of gentle reaches interspersed with rapids or even falls.

Many of these steps occur where the river flows over a band of hard rock such as that which creates the High Force falls in Upper Teesdale. Some waterfalls occur at fault-lines. The Clyde Falls and the Pennine stream of Gordale Scar are two of the finest examples.

In the mountains the majority of waterfalls result from the severe over-deepening of the main trunk valleys by ice. This leaves subsidiary streams to plummet from the high, hanging tributary valleys. Lodore Falls in the Lake District is a good example and so is the Powerscourt Fall, near Dublin.

The rivers of the limestone and chalklands possess special features. These rocks are so permeable that surface drainage is generally absent unless the rock is mantled with boulder clay, as in Ireland's Central Plain.

In the Pennines the drainage of Ingleborough disappears underground when it crosses from impervious rocks on to the Carboniferous limestone. Ireland's famous Burren has virtually streamless landscapes for the same reason, although it possesses miles of subterranean channels (see illustration below).

The chalk downlands of England are also notoriously waterless. Nevertheless they have a remarkable network of dry valleys probably formed in the Ice Age.

The latter are called bournes. The amount of water flowing in them fluctuates according to seasonal rainfall. They are drainage features which have given distinctive names, such as Winterbourne, to chalk localities.

Limestone is riddled with vertical and horizontal cracks through which water percolates. The water, which falls as rain, picks up carbon dioxide which turns it into weak carbonic acid. This dissolves the limestone creating cavities and caves. On the surface this produces a limestone 'pavement' like that at Malham (left)

Scarp
Acidic rainwater trickles through joints in limestone enlarging them
Underground stream
Cave
Syphon
Swallow-hole or pot-hole
Stalactites form as drops of water evaporate
Stalagmites form as drops of water fall on cave floor
Older, harder impervious rock
Underground stream re-emerges
Clints (blocks of rock) and grikes (dissolved joints) form limestone 'pavement'

Waterfall
The river is running over hard rock. Beneath this are softer rocks. The falling water wears back these softer layers leaving the hard rock unsupported. Fragments break away and slowly the fall recedes, leaving a gorge

Gorge | Plunge pool | Hard rock | Softer rocks

Ox-bow lake
Floodplain
Tidal estuary | Shingle spur | Salt marsh

Anatomy of a river. Its journey from source to sea

In the hills a river is born. Water rises from a spring. Or trickles as meltwater from snow and ice. Or runs in tiny runnels down a rain-lashed slope.

From such modest beginnings great rivers flow. But, in the course of their journeys from source to sea, they change their character dramatically. As they do so, they also change the character of the landscape.

As the youthful stream tumbles through the mountains, instead of following a straight course, it winds round minor obstacles, then between overlap-

Incised meanders

Interlocking spurs

Gorge

Waterfall

Glacial corrie

Interlocking spurs

Reservoir

River terraces

Meanders

First and oldest terrace

Second terrace

Meandering river on bed of alluvium it has deposited

Third terraces: most recent and lowest

River terraces
These are formed when a river gets a new lease of life. This rejuvenation gives the river new energy to cut down into the alluvium it has deposited thus creating terraces

Protecting sea walls

Meanders
This shows the formation of a meander and its development into an ox-bow lake. In 1 the current (direction is shown by solid arrows) heaps up water on the outside of the bend, cutting into the bank. But a return bottom current (broken arrows) flows to the inside bank causing deposition of sand and shingle. As the process continues the meander becomes more pronounced 2. The meander neck is ultimately breached 3 thus straightening the course of the river. The old meander is left abandoned as an ox-bow lake 4. The meander stage is shown in more detail in 5

Erosion | Deposition
Meander neck
River course straightens
Ox-bow lake
Sand and shingle | River cliff

1　2　3　4　5

ping or interlocking hill spurs. This happens because some of the rocks it encounters are more resistant than others to the wearing action of running water.

All the time the river cuts deeper into the land surface, but as it does so it may encounter a formerly buried, tough band of rock. It cuts through this as well, but takes longer. Then steep-sided gorges are formed. Their shape is influenced by the well-jointed hard rocks which make their walls. The beautiful wooded Dove Dale in the Peak District, Scotland's lonely Corrieshalloch Gorge Near Ullapool and the romantic Fairy Glen on the Conwy River in Wales are examples.

On leaving the mountains the river's volume increases as the number of its tributaries grows. It now begins to swing from side to side in its ever-widening valley. These swings become meanders.

Meanders are clearly visible on most of our major rivers: the Severn near Shrewsbury, the Trent at Nottingham, the Forth at Stirling.

Sometimes the river acquires a new lease of life. This happens when earth movements uplift the land, or when the level of the sea falls. The re-energised river then cuts down deep into its existing valley creating incised meanders. These can be seen on the Wye above Chepstow or on the Dee near Llangollen.

At the same time the river cuts down into its former valley deposits, the thick layers of mud, sand and gravel, or alluvium, which it laid down in its lower reaches, thus creating a series of terraces above the newly entrenched channel. Without such re-energising much of the load it is carrying would be deposited, as downcutting has virtually ceased.

A river's lower reaches are the widest part of its valley and are very susceptible to floods since the floodplain is protected only by artificial embankments built following early inundations.

Finally the river arrives at the seawalls of the estuary where there are wide, sweeping mudflats and tidal marshes. Here its work is taken over by the sea.

Birth of the lakes. Ice gouged the hollows, meltwater filled them

Lough Neagh in Northern Ireland is the oldest and largest sheet of fresh water in the British Isles. Yet, seen for the first time, it seems unspectacular. Its very size, 155sq miles (40,145 hectares), its lack of islands and woodlands, its regular shape and the low levels of the surrounding countryside scarcely produce a scenic triumph. It is fascinating, however, for other reasons. It is the only lake in the British Isles which has its origin in a major earth movement.

Forty million years ago the basalt rocks of the central part of the Antrim Plateau gradually sank. This great down-sagging is thought to have brought the basalt surface some 2000ft (610m) below the surrounding rim of the basalt plateau. In this great hollow Lough Neagh was formed. Since then the basin has been substantially filled with sand, gravel and clay sediments. Lough Neagh itself, with eight rivers draining into it but only one flowing out, is now quite shallow, only 40–50ft (12–15m) deep.

Unlike Lough Neagh, the majority of British lakes were created in the last 50,000 years as a result of glacial activity. Even the lakes of Scotland's Great Glen (Lochs Ness, Oich and Lochy) and Lake Bala in Wales, although influenced in their direction by geological faults, occupy glacier-deepened troughs.

Elsewhere the mountainsides are dotted with hundreds of llyns (Welsh) or tarns (English) formed where corrie glaciers have scooped out rocky hollows. Where ice has scoured and over-deepened the valleys into glacial troughs, rock basin lakes occur. Loch Coruisk, below the main ridge of the Cuillins in the Isle of Skye, is a spectacular example. The rocky hollow of Loch Morar, south of Mallaig, contains Britain's deepest lake (1017ft, 310m). Yet its surface, like that of Loch Coruisk, is only a few feet above sea level.

Sometimes lakes impose curious patterns on the landscape. In the Western Highlands of Scotland and the Lake District they exhibit a radial formation. These areas were former centres of ice caps from which glaciers streamed out in all directions. Some of the long, narrow finger-lakes such as Windermere, Wastwater and Loch Lomond have been in part impounded behind terminal moraines of the last valley glaciers, but they all occupy ice-deepened rock basins.

In other places some smaller lakes

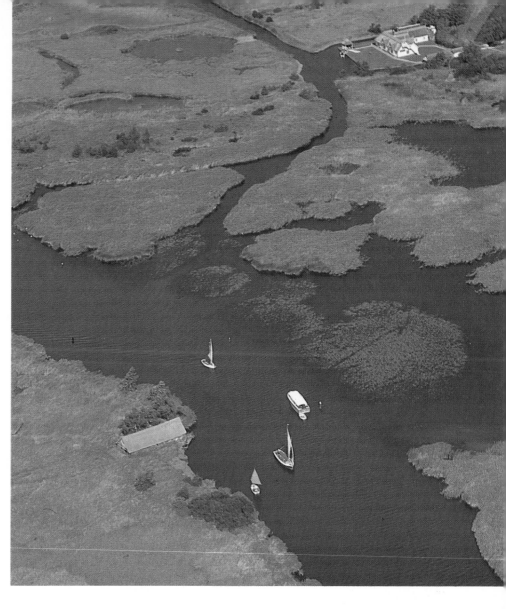

have formed in what are described as kettle holes. These occurred when large blocks of stagnant ice, buried in the tumultuous outwash sands and gravels and moraines of glaciers, finally melted, creating an enclosed hollow. The material which lay above the ice collapsed and the hollow was filled by water. Shropshire's meres at Ellesmere were formed in this way.

The curious shapes of Ireland's Lough Oughter and Upper Lough Erne reflect the fact that they have partly submerged a drumlin landscape. Of all the landscapes in the British Isles Ireland's is the richest in lakes.

Here the presence of Carboniferous limestone has had a profound influence on lake formation, for some of the largest lakes occupy enormous solution hollows. These are hollows produced by the solvent action of water on limestone. Because the level of groundwater – water below the surface stored in openings, spaces and cavities in the rocks – is high, the subterranean limestone is waterlogged and surface water does not drain through it. So Loughs Derg, Mask and Corrib and Lower Lough Erne are all

permanent features.

Some of the largest bodies of water in the British Isles are man-made, either as sources of drinking water or to serve hydro-electric schemes. The Lackan Reservoir in Ireland's Wicklow Mountains, Scotland's Blackwater Reservoir, Hawes Water in Cumbria and the Elan, Vyrnwy and Trawsfynydd lakes in Wales all fall into these categories. The Kielder Water Scheme, in the North Tyne Valley, will create when completed one of the biggest man-made lakes in Western Europe.

Other waters have been created inadvertently – subsidence lakes in the coalfields or the Cheshire 'flashes' of the Northwich salt mining area. The Thames valley is scarred with lakes in old gravel workings. Even the famous Norfolk Broads are man-made.

Norfolk's Broadland with its marshes, meandering, reed-fringed rivers and wide, shallow lakes – the 'Broads' themselves – is one of the best known and most unusual areas of East Anglia.

For many years it was thought of as the remains of a large river estuary which was gradually silting up. Some Broads have disappeared since the first Ordnance Survey map of the area was published; others are getting smaller. Now the combined researches of historian, geographer, archaeologist and botanist have resulted in the spectacular discovery that these large lakes are the works of man – flooded medieval peat diggings. Their scale makes them one of the more astonishing modifications to a natural landscape.

There was a time when Broadland was indeed a wide open estuary with exits to the sea near Horsey and at Yarmouth and Lowestoft. This estuary probably existed as late as Roman and Anglo-Saxon times. Silting must have taken place in the quieter waters within it, especially at the seaward end. This produced brackish, swampy conditions with thick vegetation. Over the years this led to the formation of thick layers of peat.

Norwich, a thriving city in medieval times, provided a ready market for peat fuel. Digging started in the 11th century and lasted about 200 years. In this time over 2500 acres of peat were excavated. The diggings were possible because at this time there was a rise in the land

relative to sea level which produced drier conditions.

But from the 13th century this changed. There was a gradual rise in sea level, possibly coupled with a downward tilting of the land surface. This caused the flooding, over a long period, of the old peat workings. This process, still continuing today, formed the Broads as we know them.

Norfolk's Broadland (above left) represents one of man's more remarkable unplanned modifications to the landscape. In contrast Loch Coruisk (above) in the Isle of Skye owes its genesis to natural forces, to the enormous erosive power of ice. The wholesale excavation of the valley in which the loch lies is the work of a glacier on a grand scale. Lake Vyrnwy (below) in Wales is an example of a man-made lake created to ensure a supply of drinking water

Fossils. Once living organisms, now date-stamps of geological time

Fossils, so common in many British rocks, are links with the unimaginably distant past. They are the remains of things once living, mostly the hard parts of animals or the woodier tissues of plants, which became entombed in sand and mud.

In time these soft sediments were compressed and hardened into stone; and fragments of bone, shell, leaves or wood within them were permeated by mineral matter. This resulted in fossils being formed, sometimes as large as a dinosaur skeleton or so small as to be invisible to the eye.

Once buried, a sedimentary rock and its fossils may not be returned to the surface of the Earth for millions of years, perhaps washed out from the face of a sea cliff, or revealed by quarrying.

Fossil-rich sea cliffs near Charmouth, Dorset. For many miles on this coast the cliffs are cut in nearly horizontal rocks, limestones and shales in blue and yellow. Storms wash fossils from them

During the time it is buried the world evolves new forms of life and the whole face of the Earth and its climate change. Many living things become extinct, and the only remaining evidence of their existence may be fossils. The geological map of the British Isles, with its complicated arrangement of rock strata, reflects the immense series of changes which have gone on over the last 600 million years.

Many of the British rock formations have been adopted as 'milestones' along the geological way, and the time they represent is marked by the kind of fossils they contain. By using various fossils as 'date stamps' geologists are able to correlate rocks of the same age over wide geographical areas.

Thousands of different species of fossils have been found in the British Isles. The small selection shown here are fairly common and represent a time span of 400 million years.

All the drawings are produced at half scale except for those of *Trinucleus* and *Atrypa* which are to size.

Trinucleus (*Trinucleus fimbriatus*). Age: 425 to 465 million years. Common in Ordovician period.
One of a large diverse group known as trilobites of which woodlice and king crabs are among recent living relatives. *Trinucleus* had a large, three-lobed head, segmented body and tail. Its many pairs of legs on underside of body are rarely preserved. Trilobites swam, floated, crawled on the bottom or burrowed. Some, like *Trinucleus*, were blind, probably scavengers and browsers. As trilobites grew, they shed their tough skins and these are frequently found as fossils. The earliest trilobites are found in Lower Cambrian rocks, the last in Permian rocks, so they lasted perhaps 355 million years.
Where found: this one at Builth Wells. They occur in north and south Wales, the Welsh Borderlands, the Lake District and south Scotland.

Atrypa (*Atrypa reticularis*). Age: 400 to 435 million years. Abundant in Silurian period.
This is the shell of a brachiopod, a small marine creature, shaped rather like a nut, which lived in shallow warm water and fed by collecting tiny particles of food from the water drawn into the space within the shells. It is often associated with fossil corals. It suffered an eclipse 225 million years ago when many kinds of bivales (cockles, mussels, clams) began to colonise the sea floors. Since then brachiopods seem to have survived only in deeper and cooler parts of the seas and oceans, usually firmly attached to seaweed or the sea floor.
Where found: common in the Wenlock and associated rocks of the Welsh Borderlands and West Midlands.

Dictyoclostus (*Dictyoclostus semireticulatus*). Age: 325 to 370 million years. Flourished in early Carboniferous period.
A large, relatively thick-shelled and robust brachiopod shellfish recognised by its almost hemi-

spherical shape and the regular pattern of surface lines and ridges. It lived in the shallow, clear, warm waters of the early Carboniferous period, building up shell banks and spreads of shell debris.
Where found: typical member of fossil assemblages in Carboniferous limestones of Wales, the Pennines, Ireland and parts of Scotland.

Gryphaea (*Gryphaea arcuata*). Age: about 200 million years. Common in the Jurassic period.
Known in some localities as Devil's Toenail, this is a distant relative of the oysters. It is a bivalve with one very curved shell and one less so.

As the animal grew the left valve became curved and developed into a form of cup in which the soft parts lay, covered by the small right valve. Conspicuous growth ridges emphasise the curvature. *Gryphaea* abounded on the relatively shallow sea floor over much of Britain in Jurassic times. In adult life it lay free on the silty clay or silt. By the end of the Jurassic period it was replaced by the early true oysters. This was about 140 millions years ago.
Where found: in the grey shales, clays and limestones of the Liassic rocks from Dorset to Yorkshire.

Dactylioceras (*Dactylioceras commune*). Age: about 170–180 million years. Also of the Jurassic period.
This coiled and chambered shell is typical of one of the most common British ammonites, extinct

sea animals akin to living squid and nautilus. It floated in open water and probably fed on small invertebrate creatures, and in its turn, may have been eaten by fish, ichthyosaurs or plesiosaurs. When the animal died gas in the chambers of the shell may have kept it floating for some time, but very large numbers of these shells accumulated on the sea floor. Sediment there was rich in partially decomposed organic matter and in due course this became bituminous black shale. *Dactyliocera* shells in it are beautifully preserved, commonly in full relief rather than squashed flat. Many have been replaced by iron pyrite (iron sulphide) and appear to be made of brass.
Where found: in the Upper Liassic rocks of Yorkshire around Whitby.

Micraster (*Micraster cor-anguincum*) Age: about 75 million years. Common in the Cretaceous period.
This inhabitant of the Chalk sea is not unlike some modern sea-urchins found round the shores of the British Isles today. It belongs to a group known as the echinoids and is rather bun-shaped, covered in small spines like its modern relatives and has the five-rays or feeding grooves that most echinoids have. It lived on, and burrowed just below, the soft chalky surface mud of the sea floor, feeding on a rich supply of microscopic organic debris. Being buried so much in life, it was well placed to become a fossil. Many were preserved by the replacement of their shell and the chalk mud within it by silica (flint). Flint echinoids occur in soils over much of the chalk land of the British Isles long after the chalk itself has been eroded away.
Where found: in the Upper Chalk from southern England to Yorkshire. Also in Northern Ireland.

Cardita (*Cardita planicosta*). Age: about 60 million years. Lived in the Tertiary period.
To all intents and purposes *Cardita* is a modern bivalve but more conspicuous with a thick shell and robust hingeing of the two valves. The shell was not only a protection from the waves and currents but also from shellfish-eating sharks and rays. *Cardita* was shallow burrowing and fed on small food particles in the water which it drew into its shell. It lived, with a large population of other bivalves, all looking remarkably like living species, not far from shore and probably in sub-tropical conditions, on the silty floor of the Eocene sea which covered south east England. Also present in the sea were snails, tusk shells, limpets and other forms of shellfish.
Where found: in the Bracklesham Beds of Sussex and the Isle of Wight.

Great British landscapes

This guide to the classic landscapes of the British Isles shows the underlying rocks which makes them what they are; how natural forces have fashioned them; and the way man has modelled them to his particular purpose

Glaciated Nant Ffrancon valley, Snowdonia

Ice eroded
U-shaped valley

Slate quarries

Rugged cliffs and
crags carved from
lavas and grits

Artificial lake
supplies
hydro-electricity
station on
valley floor

Granite

Interbedded lavas

Cambrian slates

Older rocks

Snowdonia, North Wales

Snowdonia, where grey peaks rise dramatically above the coastal plains of Gwynedd, is one of the best-known mountain lands in the British Isles. A great variety of rocks has helped build a complex massif which has been folded, faulted and uplifted on countless occasions.

The most spectacular peaks, with ice-eroded cliffs and jagged pinnacle ridges, are generally found where volcanic rocks abound. These often came from sub-marine volcanoes and the lavas and ashes are interbedded with coarse grits and finer-grained mudstones of the former sea bed sediments. Later earth-movements, accompanied by enormous pressures, created the slaty rocks. It is these more easily weathered rocks which build the smoother, dome-like mountains.

Because of the Ice Age few deep soils have survived. Some of the earlier valley lakes, however, have been slowly filled with peaty sediments in post-glacial times, allowing some rudimentary farming on the valley floors at lower altitudes. Elsewhere, the countryside is given over to rough grassland, scattered broadleaf woodlands in the sheltered hollows and conifer plantations on the plateaux.

But the works of industrial man are also apparent. Slate quarrying has left gigantic scars in certain valleys.

☐ Where to see similar scenery: also in Wales in the vicinity of Cader Idris and in the area of Tal-y-llyn.

The Highlands of Scotland

The Highlands of Scotland are composed of a great variety of rocks, most of which are extremely old, highly fractured, tightly folded and altered by numerous intrusive igneous rocks such as granite. The Outer Hebrides are the home of the oldest rocks in the British Isles.

Gashed by deep, often fault-guided corridors, the upland massifs offer towering cliffs and sweeping ice-steepened slopes to challenge climber and skier. Less adventurous travellers will be content to marvel at waterfalls, beautiful lochs and seemingly endless forests. Many of the glens have been so deepened by glaciers that they are now occupied by Britain's deepest waters, such as Loch Ness and Loch Morar. In places the sea has flooded some of the western valleys to create long, winding fjords which penetrate far into the mountains.

Scattered remnants of the once-ubiquitous Scots pine forests survive. But in the far north birchwoods predominate and newly-planted ranks of exotic conifers now clothe many of the formerly open moorlands. These contrasting habitats harbour a rich wild life.

Amid the generally barren and rocky terrain, good farming land is at a premium – except for the widely dispersed crofting communities of the northwest who cling to the small pockets of productive land, particularly on the shelly, sandy soils of the old uplifted shorelines.

☐ Where to see similar scenery: the Highlands have a character all their own.

The Craven Uplands of the Pennines

Some of the highest summits in the Pennine backbone of England occur in the Craven Uplands where such peaks as Ingleborough, Penyghent and Whernside rear their flat-topped heads above the surrounding limestone moorlands and the intervening valleys. Few other uplands exist with such contrasts of colour. The limestone cliffs, or 'scars', gleam white in the sunshine with a mantle of bright green grassland. The peaks, however, are built of terraced layers of hard gritstone and softer shales. These weather to dark aprons of scree and give thin, barren soils below the black, peat-crowned summit plateaux.

Streams rise on these windswept upper slopes, then plunge rapidly into great vertical shafts once they cross on to the permeable limestone.

The uplands are sometimes terminated abruptly by escarpments which may have been fashioned along a geological fracture or fault. Contrasting rocks and different soils on the lower side of the fault lead to a different type of land use. The Craven Lowlands, for example, are an area of improved farming land with trees, scattered farms and villages, very different from the treeless uplands.

☐ Where to see similar scenery: in Derbyshire at Matlock and on the border with Staffordshire at Dovedale. Also isolated examples in the Mendips, at Llandudno (The Great Orme) and the Marble Arch area of County Fermanagh.

The Highlands of Scotland

Ice eroded corrie with lake and waterfall

Glacial over-steepening forms cliffs sought by rock climbers

Red deer herds in lonely corrie

Forestry plantations on lower slopes

Sea loch in glacial valley

Granite

Crofting settlement on coastal terraces

Table top summits of Millstone Grit on peaty moorlands

Stone-walled fields on streamless plateau of Carboniferous limestone

Limestone scarp with spring-line of emergent streams

Fault

Highly folded and faulted metamorphic rocks

Surface streams of upper slopes disappear down 'swallow holes' on reaching limestone

Exposed limestone joints make bare pavement pattern

Farm land of Yorkshire Dales

The Craven Uplands

Alternating bands of shale and grits

Carboniferous limestone

Carboniferous limestone

Older rocks

Limestone gorge formed by roof collapse of underground stream

The Wessex Heathlands

Rolling chalk downlands of North Dorset

Conifer forests on poorer soils

Heathland on sands, clays and gravels

Broadleaf woodland of New Forest

Holiday resorts along coast

Drowned coastline forms natural harbour

Chalk ridge and sea stack

Wealden Beds

Tertiary sands, clays and gravels

Chalk

Cotswold landscape: stone-walled fields and scattered farms

Scarp-foot, stone-built village at spring line

Steep, wooded limestone escarpment

Kimmeridge clays

Portland and Purbeck limestones

Outlying hill capped with oolitic limestone

Orchards and market gardens of Vale

Brick-built market town of the Vale

Oolitic limestones

Upper Lias clay

Middle Lias marlstone

Triassic marls

The Cotswold Escarpment

Lower Lias clays and limestones

The Cotswold Escarpment and Vale of Evesham

The mellow, creamy-coloured stone villages of the Cotswolds reflect the excellence of the locally-quarried building material. The Cotswolds are formed of limestones which are older than chalk and different in character. The most important are the Great and Inferior Oolitic limestones – the harder rocks which create the prominent escarpment and include the famous Bath Stone, one of England's foremost free-stones, fine grained and easily sawn. Oolitic limestone consists of minute, tightly-cemented spheres of calcium carbonate, resembling the roe of a fish, from which it derives its name.

As with chalk, limestone allows rainwater to permeate rapidly. Uplands are virtually streamless and only the deepest valleys and the scarp-foot springlines provide sufficient surface water to maintain permanent settlements. Underlying the limestones are thick beds of marlstone and clay. Surface water abounds in the clay vale where these gently tilted older rocks emerge from beneath the limestone escarpment. The escarpment is generally too steep for farming and is either left in rough grassland and scrub or planted in thick woodlands.

The chestnut brown soils of the limestone terrain give way rapidly to the grey and red soils of the vale, with extensive fruit orchards and market gardens adding variety to the field patterns.

☐ Where to see similar scenery: the Stone Belt extends north-east to Oxfordshire and Northants.

The Wessex Heathlands

The heathlands of Dorset and Hampshire occupy a lowland basin which has been partly flooded by the sea to form the landlocked harbour of Poole. They are bounded on the north by the rolling chalk downlands of Dorset's Cranbourne Chase and on the south by the open grassland plateaux and ridges of the Isle of Purbeck.

To the layman the sands, clays and gravels of the heathlands hardly merit the term 'rocks', but they were laid down as some of Britain's youngest rocks within the last 70 million years. Their acid soils can maintain only a heathland flora of heather, gorse and occasional clumps of Scots pine, which are unusual in the well-farmed English Lowlands. Only in the more fertile east – in the New Forest – are there remnants of primeval oakwoods. Elsewhere, the Forestry Commission has utilised the poorer soils for extensive conifer plantations.

The sandy heathlands have a remoteness and charm of their own, for this is Thomas Hardy country where Puddletown Heath has been immortalised as the famous 'Egdon Heath'. At Poole Harbour the heathlands reach the coast. This is the habitat of the red squirrel and such rare birds as the Dartford warbler and the red-backed shrike. Here, too, are sandy beaches and coastal resorts.

The impact of modern man and the implicit threat to wildlife and lonely beauty is beginning to change the Wessex heathlands. The pipeclays of Poole have long been the basis of a pottery but the Winfrith atomic energy station and the recently discovered oilfield of the Arne peninsula pose new hazards to the heathlands.

☐ Where to see similar scenery: around Aldershot and Bagshot. London's Hampstead Heath is a watered-down version of this type of landscape.

South West Ireland

Former valley now drowned by sea

Isolated mountains of Old Red Sandstone

Carboniferous Limestone

Irregular patchwork of fields

Old Red Sandstone

Fault

Old Red Standstone

Iron Age hill fort

Bronze Age earthworks

Neolithic ʼRidgeway

Thickly wooded chalk escarpment

Hilltop beech plantation

Large arable fields on rolling downland

Hill figure of White Horse

Chalk dry valley with beechwoods

Sandstones and clays

Lower chalk

Chalk Downlands

Middle chalk

Upper chalk

Chalk Downlands of Southern England

The Chalk Downlands are often taken as the epitome of Lowland England. They stretch from the Channel coast of Devon, eastwards to Kent, and north-eastwards to beyond the Wash.

Although some of its beds are harder than others, chalk is soft by comparison with its flints, but resistant when compared with its neighbouring clay rocks. Thus, where it has been gently folded or tilted, chalk creates distinctive hills and escarpments overlooking the clay vales.

Chalk's permeability means that surface water is rarely found on the downlands, although the rocks act like a giant sponge by retaining subterranean water and releasing it slowly at springs which mark the 'water table'.

Largely due to the scarcity of water, villages are dotted along the spring-line in the valley bottoms, while flint-built farms are scattered on the downs. Impressive prehistoric earthworks and standing stones, linked by ancient trackways, such as The Ridgeway, illustrate the former importance of chalk uplands at a time when the clay vales were too marshy and forested for easy settlement.

The short, springy grassland was the basis of extensive sheep farming in the Middle Ages, but today it has frequently been ploughed, so that large, hedgeless fields of corn have replaced much of the livestock. Except where younger clays mantle the surface, woodland is generally confined to the steeper slopes of the dry valleys and scarps.

☐ Where to see similar scenery: the Chilterns, for a chalk landscape with a thick covering of clay supporting beechwoods. For open downland, the North and South Downs, the Berkshire Downs, Salisbury Plain, Cranbourne Chase.

South West Ireland

The sea-girt mountainlands of Kerry and west Cork have long been famed for their scenery. Atlantic rollers bite deeply into the fertile valleys, leaving the bony fingers of the gaunt hills as intervening peninsulas. Geology and scenery are at their most simple here, for the Old Red Sandstone survives in the 300 million year-old upfolds (anticlines) while the less resistant Carboniferous shales and limestones of the downfolds (synclines) are picked out by the linear valleys, now partially submerged by the sea.

Ice sheets have scoured the uplands, leaving the massive red, purple and green grits as bare slabs and crags along the crestlines. These are pitted with glacial hollows and dotted with lakes, such as the beautiful Barley Lake. Some of the sheltered valleys, especially Glengarriff, support thick woodlands, but in the main these windswept coasts are treeless, with the heather and gorse-strewn slopes of the sandstone giving way to the brighter green fields of the shale and limestone valleys floors. Here, surrounded by fuchsia hedges, are the few scattered farms and the tiny market towns, some of which have become modern tourist centres. The deep waters of Bantry Bay are famed not only as a text book example of a ria (drowned river valley) but also for their value as an oil tanker terminal.

On the headlands good farming land is at a premium, especially near Kenmare which was the centre of a former ice cap. Here soils have been swept away from the ice-scrubbed hills. Only Mizen Head (the Land's End of Ireland) appears less barren than its neighbouring peninsulas, partly due to its lower elevation and its less glaciated terrain.

☐ Where to see similar scenery: geological structures and related topography of this kind are rare in the British Isles, but ria coastlines typify south-west England and Pembrokeshire.

Dartmoor

Dartmoor is made of granite, just one exposure of a gigantic, subterranean, dome-shaped mass of granite which stretches laterally for 120 miles beneath Devon and Cornwall. Its various outcrops also form Bodmin Moor, St Austell, Falmouth, Land's End and the Isles of Scilly granites.

Some 300 million years ago this granite, then molten rock, or magma, was forced up from within the earth, into the existing slates and sandstones. Since then the forces of erosion have stripped away the overlying rocks to reveal the granite rising above the surrounding lowlands. Despite its hardness, granite weathers in a particular way, along its planes of weakness, to form weirdly-shaped grey tors, such as Haytor, which crown the skyline.

According to season these dark peaty moors, with their dangerous bright-green mires, are carpeted with purple heather or golden gorse. In a few remote river valleys remnants of ancient oakwoods, such as Wistman's Wood, survive. Coniferous plantations cover many lower slopes.

The moorlands are almost devoid of modern settlement, although prehistoric earthworks testify to the presence of early man. Today villages are tucked in sheltered valleys around the perimeter of the moor, leaving the trackless uplands to buzzard, curlew, fox and deer.

☐ Where to see similar scenery: in Galloway, Southern Scotland. Granite also produces higher mountain areas in the Isle of Arran, the Cairngorms, Cheviots and Mountains of Mourne.

The Antrim Coast, Northern Ireland

The north-eastern corner of Northern Ireland boasts scenery which is uncommon in the British Isles, for here layer upon layer of basaltic lavas, poured out some 60 million years ago, have buried a landscape of chalk. Where the two rocks are exposed in juxtaposition at the coast the contrasts of black and white cliff scenery are startling.

Unlike the deep-seated, intrusive granites, the dark basalts cooled quickly as they were forced out from surface fissures. Thus, their crystals are smaller and their columnar jointing much more marked owing to the different rates of cooling. Nowhere are the basaltic columns as well displayed as at the Giant's Causeway. Here the hexagons are so perfectly fashioned that in 1694 a paper read to the Royal Society acknowledged that they were not man-made owing to the lack of mortar between the columns!

Inland from the coastal cliffs there are deep valleys in the rolling, moorland-covered surface of the plateau. These valleys, known as the Glens of Antrim, bring bright green farmland into the sombre bog landscapes of the interior where the dark peat cuttings contrast with the white painted cottages and farms. The narrow walled fields climb the slopes with such regularity that their patterns have been referred to as 'ladder farms'.

Underlying the extensive peat bogs are thick layers of boulder clay deposited by former ice-sheets. In places this clay has been fahioned by the glacier ice into streamlined hillocks known as drumlins.

☐ Where to see similar scenery: on a smaller scale there are columnar basalts in Scotland on the Isle of Staffa (Fingal's Cave) and on Mull.

Dartmoor

Natural broadleaf woodland surviving in remote valley

Summit tors on granite

Mire

Treeless moorlands

Conifer plantations on lower slopes

Rich farming country of lowland Devon

Stepped landforms created by layers of basaltic lava

Basalt columns on coast

'Ladder' farms of Antrim glens

Fault

Devonian slates and sandstones

Granite

Peat cuttings in extensive bogs

Whaleback hills in boulder clay known as drumlins

The Antrim Coast

Clays

Sandstones

Older rocks

Chalk

Boulder clay

Basaltic lavas

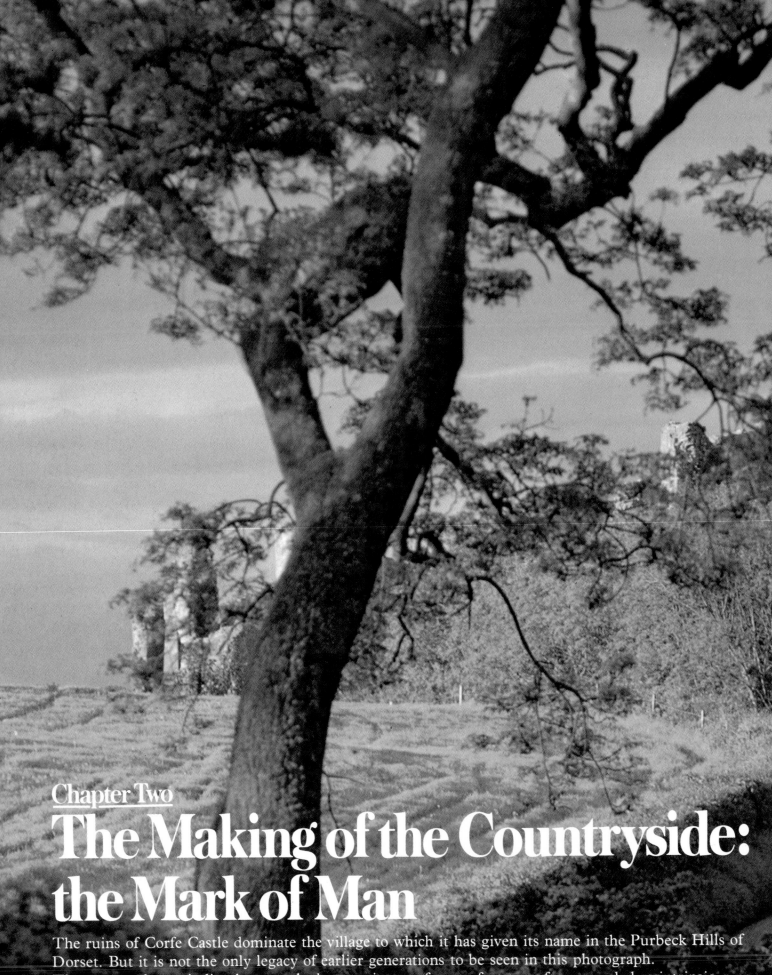

Chapter Two
The Making of the Countryside: the Mark of Man

The ruins of Corfe Castle dominate the village to which it has given its name in the Purbeck Hills of Dorset. But it is not the only legacy of earlier generations to be seen in this photograph.
The country lane winding between hedgerows is one of many features often regarded as intrinsic elements of traditional or 'unspoilt' countryside which originate from the work of man moulding the landscape. How man contributed to the diversity of the British Isles through six broad periods of history is the theme of this chapter

Prehistoric Britain: Man begins to change the natural landscape

Man arrived late in the British Isles, barely yesterday in a geological calendar that measures time in millions of years. And it is only in the last 5000 years that he has been able to shape the landscape. Up to then the forces of nature, the long-term processes of geology and the rhythms of climatic change, discussed elsewhere in this book, were the dominant factors. It was they that determined the topography, soils and vegetation which combined to form the habitat of this relative newcomer to Earth, *homo sapiens*.

The first human evidence of Man's life in the British Isles came from a gravel pit at Swanscombe in the Thames valley 20 miles (32km) from what is now the heart of London. Three fragments of a skull and thousands of flint tools dating back around 150,000 years ago to the Palaeolithic Age (see panel, opposite) were found there.

Even older worked flints have been found indicating that man was living in the British Isles possibly 200,000 years ago. Palaeolithic Man seems most likely to have lived primarily in the lowlands of southern Britain, although the absence of flints in upland areas could also be a consequence of the Ice Age obliterating evidence of earlier cultures in northern Britain. Archaeologists simply do not know for certain. But wherever he lived it was a life of hunting, fishing and food-gathering that continued well into the Mesolithic era.

It was in Neolithic or the New Stone Age, from about 3250 BC, that the first dramatic change occurred: forest dwellers – hunters and fishermen – turned to the first primitive forms of farming. The first communities of farmers still hunted animals for food but they also began to cultivate grain crops such as wheat and barley. And botanists, who have analysed the pollen preserved in peat bogs and muds gathered over the centuries on lake beds, have shown that the Neolithic farmers made the first inroads into the great forests which had covered most of Britain since the Ice Age finally ended around 10,000 BC. Thus, for the first time, man became an intrusive force in shaping the landscape.

Man's exploitation of the land grew through the Bronze and Iron Ages which preceded the Roman occupation and the first *written* account of the British Isles – prehistoric is so-called where there is

Chysauster in Cornwall is one of the few Iron Age villages in Britain to survive in anything like its original form – largely because it was built of local stone. It was occupied from 100 BC to 300 AD

only archaeological rather than written evidence of the past. By the time of the late Iron Age, when the Romans first set eyes on Britain, considerable areas had been cleared of their original woodland.

The complex succession of cultures that existed in Britain during those final prehistoric eras also left their mark in ways which, although faint and indistinct, can still be seen today. Outlines of ancient field patterns pick out areas of earliest settlement; disturbed ground along the Downs and the heathlands of southern England betray sites of ancient flint workings; and, most striking of all, burial places, stone circles and hill forts remain as testimony to societies whose complexity is still far from understood.

Clearing the forests

Over most of the British Isles the continuous farming of the last 1,000 years or more has erased all traces of prehistoric agriculture from the countryside. Yet aerial photography and botanical analysis have proved that the first farmers had altered the landscape substantially by the time of the Roman conquest.

After the end of the Ice Age forests grew to cover all but the highest mountain tops. But when the Romans first encountered the ancient areas of settlement on Salisbury Plain and its neighbouring chalk uplands, for instance, they saw not woodland but a patchwork pattern of fields and extensive pastures for the grazing of cattle and, to a lesser extent, sheep.

The same process of forest clearances – accomplished mainly by burning and maintained by the grazing of livestock – has been traced through pollen analysis in the lake muds and peat bogs of the Lake District. There it has been proved that extensive tracts of moorland, particularly above the 1000ft (305m) contour, had come into being as early as the later centuries of the Bronze Age. Likewise the mantle of forest had been pushed back in the limestone upland of the Peak District ever since the intrusion of the first Neolithic farmers to whose presence, almost 5000 years ago, the landscape of Derbyshire still bears silent witness in the ruined monoliths of their burial places at Five Wells and Minninglow.

How prehistoric man actually farmed can be seen through aerial photography which has revealed patterns of ancient fields still inscribed upon the contemporary designs of arable and pasture land. For instance, in the chalk lands of southern England, especially in the South Downs, fields are visible which have been dated back 3000 years to the early Bronze Age. These small fields have even smaller rectangular or oblong plots separated from each other on sloping ground by lynchets – see below right.

But in highland Britain, at places ranging from the hill masses of southwest England to the Shetlands, abundant proof of land clearing and cultivation as well as settlement can still be detected by the human eye. Most of this evidence, on the fringes of Bodmin Moor and Dartmoor, for instance, survives at heights above the present levels of farming. Clusters of cairns, low overgrown heaps of stone on what are today heather-covered moors, are a legacy of the original stone-by-stone clearance of the land. And on the ground faint markings of hut circles show where the Bronze Age cultivators of such upland field systems in the North Yorkshire Moors lived and worked.

From the Bronze Age onwards man's primitive farming was greatly aided by more efficient tools. Archaeological investigation of ancient field sites at Overton Down, Wiltshire, and Gwithian, Cornwall, has even revealed the marks of prehistoric ploughing. In the downland of Wiltshire the ploughlines are scored into the chalk subsoil while wind-blown sand has preserved a whole series of ploughing layers at Gwithian.

Small and irregular fields thus seem to have been part of the rural economy of the British Isles from the earliest Neolithic farmers through to the Iron Age. But the fragmentary and widely scattered evidence suggests that these early landscape elements have played little part in the subsequent evolution of field patterns – even in Ireland.

There it was long believed that the present pattern of fields was largely a legacy of the Celtic world, linked with ancient pastoral traditions. It is certainly true that in western Ireland archaeologists have traced more than 30 prehistoric field boundaries of stones that had been preserved under thick growths of peat. But recent research has shown that the patterns of the Irish rural landscape have evolved largely since the 17th century.

However there may be one small area where the honeycomb pattern of tiny fields has survived virtually intact since Iron Age times – around the hamlets of the Penwith peninsula in Western Cornwall. Otherwise it was through the first clearing of the forests that the prehistoric farmers most effectively put their stamp on the face of the British Isles.

Five Ages of Prehistoric Britain

Palaeolithic: before 8000 BC. Man lived by hunting, fishing and food gathering (eg nuts, roots and berries), often dwelling in caves. Much evidence destroyed by Ice Age, but many animals known to have existed that are now extinct in the British Isles such as bison, bear, rhinoceros and hyaena. No firm evidence of any settlement in Ireland.

Mesolithic: 8000 to 3250 BC. Man still practised a shifting culture, not strictly nomadic but no permanent settlement. Increasing evidence of population in northern England, Scotland and Ireland. First evidence of temporary woodland clearances in areas such as Dartmoor and the Cleveland Hills.

Neolithic: 3250 to 1700 BC. Forest clearances became more widespread as man began to farm the land with grain crops. Settlements were generally on high ground where many long barrow burial chambers can still be found. Extensive trade in stone axes around Britain. Early embanked sanctuaries or 'henges', sometimes with stone, although these were mostly of a later period.

Bronze Age: 1700 to 500 BC: Metallurgical skills developed sufficiently to make bronze weapons and ornamental objects, but stone and wooden implements (including a primitive plough in the late Bronze Age) were still used in agriculture. More forest clearing. Stone circles tend to date from this period, as do round barrows (*tumuli*) and cairns. Ireland's gold brought new settlers and trade, not only with Britain but with continental Europe. Increasing evidence of lowland settlements, notably in the English Midlands.

Iron Age: 500 BC to 43 AD. Many hilltop settlements were developed into hill 'forts', often defended by vast ramparts and serving as tribal capitals. Settlement patterns become more varied with farmsteads and small villages or hamlets as well as the larger communities associated with the biggest hill-forts. Cattle and sheep grazing became more common and trade routes expanded. Much of Scotland and Ireland remained in the Bronze Age for several centuries, but may have entered the Iron Age with the builders of hill forts, possibly about 200 BC. Many facets of Iron Age or Celtic society survived the Roman centuries, particularly in highland Britain and Ireland which were largely or totally unaffected by Roman influences.

☐ All dates are approximate and there were often important regional variations from the generalised summaries above.

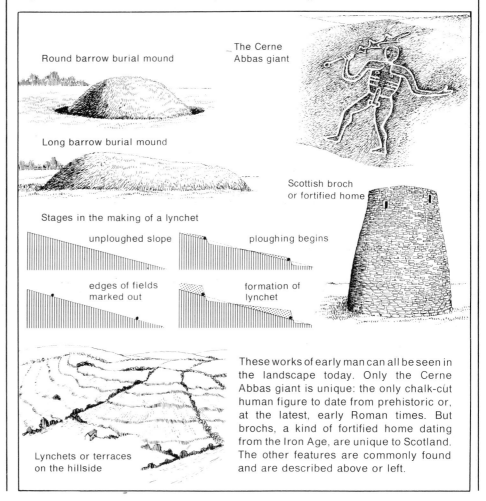

Round barrow burial mound

Long barrow burial mound

The Cerne Abbas giant

Scottish broch or fortified home

Stages in the making of a lynchet

unploughed slope

ploughing begins

edges of fields marked out

formation of lynchet

Lynchets or terraces on the hillside

These works of early man can all be seen in the landscape today. Only the Cerne Abbas giant is unique: the only chalk-cut human figure to date from prehistoric or, at the latest, early Roman times. But brochs, a kind of fortified home dating from the Iron Age, are unique to Scotland. The other features are commonly found and are described above or left.

Above: Pentre Ifan cromlech in Dyfed, South Wales. Originally the large capstone, so elegantly poised on the supporting slabs, formed the roof of a Neolithic burial chamber but the covering mound of earth has eroded away. Cromlechs are also known as quoits or dolmens

Left: Hambledon Hill Iron Age hill fort in Dorset. The long and winding double ramparts enclose earlier fortifications and a substantial Neolithic long barrow can be seen clearly on the hilltop
Right: Long Meg and Her Daughters stone circle in Cumbria. Long Meg herself is a standing stone 12ft (3.6m) high just outside this Bronze Age circle of 59 stones which represents 'her' daughters. There were originally 70 stones and of those which survive only 27 are still standing upright

Prehistoric Man's first settlements

Many of the most striking examples of the prehistoric centuries surviving in the present landscapes are monuments to the dead: the Neolithic burial chambers, or long barrows, sometimes guarded at their entrance by massive stones that each weigh several tons. They have survived long after the mud-and-wattle stockades of the earliest settlements disintegrated. But their locations, as well as their size, give the first clues as to where early man lived. Where these burial chambers were also near great stone monuments, such as at Avebury and Stonehenge in Wiltshire and Callanish on the Isle of Lewis, we may take it that these were areas of abiding settlement

even in times of shifting agriculture when people were neither strictly nomadic nor settling permanently in one particular location within an area.

Burial chambers date from not only the Neolithic Age but also the Bronze Age when most of the many barrows on Salisbury Plain were constructed. There may once have been more circles of standing stones but these survive only where they are elaborate, as at Stonehenge and Avebury, or remote, as at Castlerigg in the Lake District.

It is in the more remote parts of the British Isles that the relics of earlier centuries have best escaped plundering and destruction. In the heart of Mainland, the chief island of Orkney, for instance, stand three relics all gathered

together close to the shores of an inland loch: the Ring of Brodgar, the gaunt stones of Stenness and the severe formal architecture of Maes Howe, a chambered tomb. Together they must have formed an important core of population in this far outpost of northern Britain.

Other great monuments from the prehistoric ages include the tombs of Newgrange, north-west from Dublin in the central plain of Ireland. These predate Stonehenge by around 1000 years, indicating an advanced and sizeable settlement for that time. And Arbor Low, the great 'henge' monument of recumbent stones whose site forms a focal point for the limestone country of the Peak District near Buxton, may well have acted as a ritual centre for the prehistoric population of the southern Pennines.

It is only possible to surmise that this might be so since few relics of actual living accommodation survive anywhere from prehistoric times. Those that do, such as the clusters of stone huts and paved courtyards at Chysauster in Cornwall and Skara Brae in the Orkneys, were small farming or fishing communities which survive because they were built in local stone rather than the more common timber. However, Skara Brae's remarkable quality of preservation is also due to being buried beneath sand-dunes until these were exposed by a gale in the 19th century.

More numerous, however, are the hill forts which developed during the Iron Age. Altogether, if small examples are

excluded, no fewer than 600 such forts have been found in England and Wales alone. To some extent the name 'fort' is misleading. Some were simply places on exposed hill-tops where cattle and sheep were penned, probably overnight to give protection from wild animals during the summer months when upland pastures were grazed. Many hill forts contained only a single farm and thus were entirely rural in their functions.

But many were the true precursors of towns with a pattern of streets, evidence of industries such as metal-working and pottery and temples in a few sites. Some were very large – 100 acres (40 hectares) or more – and, surrounded by vast ramparts, served as tribal capitals. In Ireland forts were built with more elab-

orate defences in the west than the east of the country and, as in Scotland, some sites are coastal promontories as well as hill tops. Notable examples are Maiden Castle and Hambledon Hill (above, left) in Dorset: Tre'r Ceiri on Llyn peninsula, North Wales: An Sgurr on the island of Eigg in the Inner Hebrides; and Dun Aengus on Inishmore, one of the Aran islands in Galway Bay.

Even now the work (genius, perhaps) of prehistoric man, whether it be barrows, stone circles or hill forts, manages to convey the feeling of earlier cultures – of nameless people whose engineering knowledge and skills have been discerned only in the most recent research and whose work survives to be a marvel even in the Space Age.

The first industrial revolution

If prehistoric farmers contributed to the making of the landscape, it is equally true that the earliest industries – stone quarrying and the extraction of metallic ores – have left their marks on the countryside.

Rocks which could be shaped to give hard cutting edges to tools and weapons were exploited with increasing effect through prehistoric times. The chief sources for these earliest industries were: 1. Flint which was abundant in the chalklands of southern and eastern Britain and also on the coast of Antrim, in glacial deposits and on the beaches; 2. Volcanic rocks among the ancient uplands of the north and west of the British Isles.

Probably the most impressive and exciting of the early industrial sites is Grimes Graves near Thetford, Norfolk. Here 35 acres (14 hectares) of tumbled ground, hollows and hillocks of chalk waste, conceal the entrances to mine shafts that were worked for at least 500 years in the extraction of flint. More than 800 separate pits have been counted, some 30 or 40ft (9 12m) deep while, at the surface, 100 'chipping' floors where the raw material was shaped into tools have been recognised.

More than 4000 years ago the area around Grimes Graves was suffering from the side-effects of mining more commonly associated with the last industrial revolution: its shafts and underground galleries had caused subsidence, its waste materials had buried good pastureland to create the first derelict land and maybe the first tips of waste.

So far it has been impossible to trace the extent of the traffic in implements made from the Norfolk flint, although it doubtless extended all over southern Britain and perhaps to the continent. But tools made from igneous rocks, whose sources are clearly established under microscopic analysis, have shown that there was widespread and long-distance trade from the 'axe-factories' in western and northern Britain.

Such factories have been found as far apart as Land's End and Shetland while high up on the Langdale Pikes in the Lake District, a distinctive grey-green volcanic rock was quarried for more than 1000 years in order to make stone axes. Langdale axes have been found in archaeological investigations in the Peak District, the East Midlands and Hampshire to name but a few places.

Their discovery bears witness to widespread trade that helped to establish the first lines of communication across the British Isles. It is likely that the earliest tracks from the valleys into the hills were traced by Neolithic farmers following their livestock in the annual migrations to the summer pastures. By the early Bronze Age several long-distance routes had been established.

Many of these tracks were often used centuries later, in Tudor and Stuart times, by the cattle drovers making their way to the lush fattening pastures and cattle fairs of the Midlands. The most famous prehistoric road is the Icknield Way – also known as the Ridgeway for part of its course – which follows the long belt of the chalk hills from Salisbury Plain across the Chilterns into the flint rich Norfolk Breckland around Grime's Graves described above.

Roman Britain: the legacy of conquest and civilisation

The Roman occupation of the British Isles lasted just under 400 years. It began with the invasion of south-east England in AD 43 and ended about 410 when the last of the Roman armies withdrew to continental Europe. Their conquest had never been complete. Ireland had always remained outside the sphere of the Empire, while many costly military expeditions had failed to achieve an effective and lasting occupation of Scotland.

Agricola's invasion of northern Britain in the last quarter of the 1st century brought the Romans as close as ever they came to the incorporation of Caledonia. His army reached as far north as the lowlands flanking the Moray Firth and it is believed that a fleet was based in Orkney. Agricola established a series of forts between the Forth and the Clyde, a line of defences that in AD 142 incorporated in the frontier works of the Antonine Wall, a chain of signal stations, camps and roads along a defensive line built of turf and stone that extended for 37 miles (see map).

The Antonine Wall functioned as an effective occupied frontier for only short periods of time, scarcely more than a decade on three separate occasions in the Roman centuries. By the end of the 2nd century all effective Roman control had ceased to the north of the Solway Firth: Hadrian's Wall, built between AD 123–128, marked the northern limit of the empire, and its impact on the countryside, within the British Isles.

The first towns

The establishment of towns was probably the most profound change wrought by the Roman occupation. There had been a few large settlements before and in places the Romans had built on earlier sites, as at Colchester. But the earlier Iron Age communities never had the urban character associated with Roman towns.

English county towns, the basis of regional life for so many centuries, reveal in many places a beginning as provincial centres in Roman Britain: Gloucester, Chester and Cirencester, for instance, betray their origins in their name (-cester originating in *castra*, meaning camp) but Lincoln and York as well as London were also Roman towns. But the Romans did not leave behind an unalterable blueprint for urban evolution; in most places the rectangular Roman street pattern did not survive to any extent.

The prehistoric flint mines of Grimes Graves in Norfolk: man's first industrial landscape

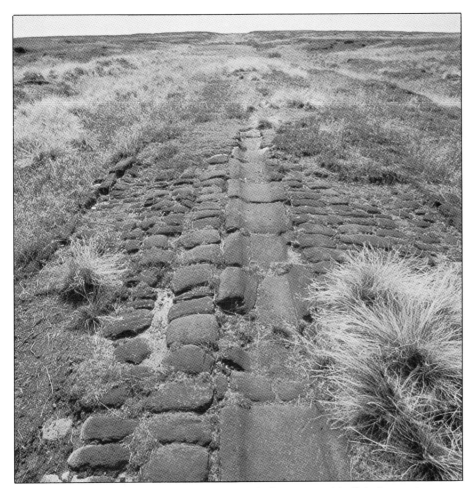

Roman road at Blackstone Edge in the Pennines: the best-preserved in Britain

Furthermore, some of the greatest Roman towns were to be extinguished either altogether at their original sites, as at Viroconium, Calleva and Verulamium which are short distances away from the modern village of Wroxeter, Silchester and St Albans respectively.

Many Roman settlements were military rather than civilian in nature. Within the confines of Dover Castle, above the famous white cliffs, is a unique survival of such a settlement: a Saxon church whose tower was originally built as a Roman lighthouse. It still stands 40ft (12m) high and is the sole surviving relic of the most important Roman naval base in England, *Portus Dubris*.

Dover was one of a line of ports that stretched from the Wash to the Solent, the so-called Forts of the Saxon Shore. Richborough (*Portus Rutupis*) was the main port of entry but Lympne (*Portus Lemanis*) and Dover were close rivals. In addition to commanding the sea routes across the Channel to Gaul, the forts were in some cases also ports with an important commercial role in the movement of minerals, grain, hides – and slaves.

Nine of the Roman forts still survive to some degree and in many cases their walls have remained remarkably intact, particularly at Portchester, the most westerly of the Roman Forts. Portchester is still on the coast unlike former ports and forts such as Pevensey, Richborough and Stutfall Castle at Lympne all of which are now some distance inland. Only Dover of the Kentish Roman forts and ports has remained immune to subsequent changes in the coastline.

The towns, whether military or civilian, were linked by an elaborate network of brilliantly-engineered roads (see map). At Blackstone Edge (above) on the Pennine Moors above Littleborough it is still possible to walk along a few yards of Roman road.

Only rarely does the original Roman pavement still exist – Blackpool Bridge in the Forest of Dean, Gloucestershire, is another site – but the routes chosen and laid down by the Romans have often survived. Sometimes they can be located only through the spade of an archaeologist or the observant eye of a local historian. But for many miles in many different parts of the country the routes are still used today. Even some of their names are as familiar as their characteristic straightness: Watling Street, Fosse Way and Stane Street.

Gold in the hills

The chief aim of the Roman conquest of Britain lay in the exploitation of the natural resources of these islands, above all its mineral resources of lead, gold, silver, iron, copper and tin. As one historian of the Roman period has written 'they came not to develop the country but to take from it what it already produced'. The legacy of Roman mining in the countryside of the 20th century is not easily recognised after so many centuries of later exploitation.

At Dolaucothi, in the gentle hills of south-west Wales, however, there are some remains of Roman mining that are unique in western Europe. Here gold occurs as a primary deposit in veins of quartz. Although the gold mines were worked as recently as the late 19th century, when new shafts were dug and engine houses and processing plant installed, the evidence of Roman operations is still to be seen. A seven-mile-long (11km) aqueduct, carefully engineered to take water from a narrow gorge in the River Cothi to tanks above the gold mine, can still be clearly traced. And some of the tunnels, too, in this deserted labyrinth are reminiscent in their form of Roman mines in the south of Spain with tool marks on the roof and walls suggesting that they were cut by hand.

Other areas likely to have been sites of Roman mining are the lead-rich hills around Matlock and the Forest of Dean, for centuries the most prolific source of iron ore in Britain. Roman mining in the Forest is well attested but the location of any particular working cannot be proved; among the likeliest places, however, is the Scowles, a wooded maze of

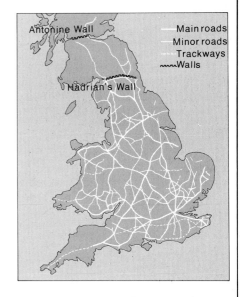

Roman roads covered the country far more extensively than is generally known

39

Hadrian's Wall in Northumberland: no monument to the 400 years of the Roman occupation of Britain is more enduring, no posting for the Roman

hillocks and deep rock-encircled, over-grown pits.

Villas and the middle classes

In the countryside of lowland England the effect of four centuries of Roman rule on the subsequent evolution of the land-scape is hard to define. The sites of 620 villas are known, but of these fewer than 100 could be described as luxurious country houses with the rooms, baths, heating systems and mosaics commonly associated with the term 'villa'.

Most villas were farm buildings, laid out on a rectangular Roman plan with no more than six rooms. It is believed that these were occupied by native Britons, a kind of rural middle class who were descendants of the builders of Iron Age forts and who had adopted the

habits of nearby Roman towns. The excavation of several villas has revealed the existence of an older Iron Age farm. Excavation has also shown how villas were rebuilt during the Roman years as their owners prospered.

In the parts of England most favoured by fertile soil, climate and topography there was therefore a continuity in farm-ing. The Roman villa and its estate represented essentially a modification of an older British farming system to the architectural fashions and market economy of the Mediterranean world. The North and South Downs, the Cotswolds and the area north of London are examples of areas where, although farming was intensified during the Roman centuries, it remained basically a

development of ancient systems.

Elsewhere there is evidence that im-perial estates were established where Roman experts pioneered the colonis-ation of fresh land for agriculture. Their most ambitious project was in the Fens where land was reclaimed early in the 2nd century AD. A canal called the Car Dyke was also cut from the edge of the Fens near Peterborough to the River Witham at Lincoln. The cargoes of corn destined for the huge garrison at York then passed by another Roman water-way, the Fossdyke, into the Trent before heading northwards via the rivers con-verging on the Humber.

Today, like the fields and farms of the imperial estates, the Car Dyke has all but vanished from the landscape. It appears

...gionnaires could possibly have seemed more bleak

The Dark Ages: the arrival of Saxons, Danes and Christianity

Almost 700 years separate the end of Roman government in the British Isles from the Norman invasion of 1066 – the Anglo-Saxon centuries or the Dark Ages as they are commonly known. The latter term reflects both the ignorance that once shrouded these centuries and the pagan years that followed the fall of Rome. But it is altogether too pejorative a description. By the time the Normans arrived these so-called Dark Ages had witnessed the founding of nearly every village which is on the map of England today and many of its county towns were flourishing. By then, too, Britain had been Christian for several centuries.

Political historians have established a degree of unity in this long span of time through the genealogies or family histories of the lines of Saxon kings, among whom the rulers of Wessex were to become supreme during the closing two centuries. But the epoch of the Anglo-Saxons has a lot to do with native Britons, peoples who were alien to the invaders and settlers from northern Europe who took over the south-east lowlands in the fifth century. Even the Romans had failed to incorporate the whole of Britain within their imperial territories so it was hardly surprising that the Saxons effectively occupied a much smaller part of the British Isles than their predecessors. A study of the scattering of the earliest Anglo-Saxon names across the English landscape suggests that the majority of their settlements early in the first half of the sixth century were to be found south-east of a line drawn from the Wash to the Solent.

There is no accurate means of telling the numbers of settlers who came to the British Isles from across the North Sea. Once it was believed that the great invasion swept all before it: that the British population of the lowlands fled to the west or was wiped out in the confusion of a savage military conquest. Now a somewhat different view is taken of these events. Archaeological research has shown recently that some Saxons were settled in Britain in the latter part of the 4th century – perhaps a generation and more *before* the Roman withdrawal.

Even more important in understanding the development of the landscape over the decades of transition from the Romans to the Saxons is the realisation that there was a continuity of British patterns of life into the middle years of the fifth century. Romano-British communities and pagan Anglo-Saxon settlers have been shown to be living side-by-side within the town walls of Canterbury, Dorchester-on-Thames and London long after the Roman troops had withdrawn to Europe.

And there is growing proof of a continuity of life in the countryside, too. For instance, a recently excavated villa at Shakenoak, in Oxfordshire, has shown that the farm was still inhabited, and presumably the estate was still productive, in the middle of the fifth century by people of a mixed Romano-British and Anglo-Saxon origin. In many places estates of the Roman centuries seem to have evolved into Anglo-Saxon manors. At Withington, in the Cotswolds, it has been argued that the present parish boundary and the lands of the medieval

on the ground as a scarcely perceptible hollow and embankment which wanders across lush pastures and meadows or else as a line drawn across the soils of freshly-ploughed land.

But knowledge of the countryside of Roman Britain is far from complete and never will be. Valuable evidence from villas, discovered in years gone by, has often been lost. New finds, especially in the past quarter century, have added greatly to our knowledge. Perhaps the most striking was the discovery in the 1960s of a Roman villa, till then unsuspected, at Fishbourne near Chichester. Nothing can compare with it elsewhere in Britain. Fishbourne, with its numerous mosaics has about 100 rooms, and has been described as a palace.

Offa's Dyke, photographed here near Clun in Shropshire, remains an impressive earthwork today 1200 years after it was erected as a Saxon boundary and barrier against the Welsh – see page 43

manor outline the extent and the limits of the much older Roman villa estate.

The Anglo-Saxon settlements of eastern and southern England and the emergence of a series of kingdoms from Northumbria to Wessex led to a sharp division of the British Isles into a Celtic west – a mostly upland Britain facing the Atlantic and focused upon the Irish Sea – and the lowlands of England facing the North Sea and the narrows of the Channel. Their development affected the landscape in different ways – as will be explained on the opposite page – but one common underlying factor was the movement towards political unity.

By the first half of the 10th century a new political order was emerging in the British Isles. Where 300 years before there had been 11 Saxon states, there was just Wessex as sole ruler of lowland England. The princedom of Gwynedd, based on its mountain stronghold of Snowdonia, was giving a sense of unity to Wales. Further north the medieval shape of Scotland was also emerging and in Ireland there were signs of lordships that were the beginnings of the four provinces of Ulster, Leinster, Munster and Connaught, with Meath on the Central Lowland.

The most striking consequence of this political unification in terms of the geography of Britain was the renewal of life in the towns. Yet urban ways had never been totally forgotten. There is now increasing evidence for the survival of communities through the early Saxon centuries in London, Canterbury, Bath and perhaps also in as remote a Roman town as Carlisle.

Greater impetus came, however, in the 9th and 10th centuries with the founding of *burhs*. By the time of Alfred the Great's death in 899, he had established 30 *burhs* which had all been fortified against attack from the Danes. All but one of these settlements – Buckingham – were south of the Thames, but by the first quarter of the 10th century defended towns were also established in the Midlands – at Warwick, Tamworth, Stafford and Bakewell to give but four examples. Recent archaeological research has also shown that streets and town centres were replanned during this time at Lewes and in the Wessex capital of Winchester. There was one other influence which encouraged the development of urban life at this time – the Danes, Scandinavians, Norsemen or, as they are most popularly if erroneously known, the Vikings.

The peaceful and linguistic legacy of the Viking conquest

The Vikings contributed far more to the development of the British Isles than the rape and plunder raids of popular legend. The last two centuries before the Norman conquest saw large-scale settlement in eastern England by Scandinavians. There were also substantial areas of Viking or Danish strength in the more exposed parts of Scotland, eastern Ireland, the Lake District and the Isle of Man (where a line of Norse kings reigned).

Scandinavian political power in England stretched east from a line running roughly between the estuaries of the Thames and the Dee – the so-called Danelaw. Wessex had regained control of virtually the whole of England by the middle of the 10th century, but the extent of Scandinavian influence is evident in the survival of many placenames. Among the most common of these are *by* (meaning a village), *thwaite* (a clearing) and *thorpe* (also village or a farmstead). See below for a glossary of some common place-names.

Norse influence had been particularly important in the development of urban life in many parts of the British Isles. Within the area of the Danelaw the new settlers developed existing Saxon towns into thriving *burhs* or boroughs that served as regional and trading centres. Recent excavations at York, for instance, have suggested that the city owes its importance almost as much to its revival under Norse influence as to its earlier Roman foundations. The success of these *burhs* led the kings of Wessex to develop their towns along similar defensive and commercial lines.

Around the coasts of Ireland the Vikings, having been fierce raiders early in the 9th century, began to exert a more positive influence. Some historians believe they introduced coinage to Ireland and they certainly founded the first towns in the trading ports of Dublin, Wexford, Waterford, Cork and Limerick. On the other side of the Irish sea Cardiff, Swansea and Chester (which had been almost desolate since Roman days) also owe much to the trade encouraged by Norse merchants. Far to the north Shetland, Orkney and the Hebrides were to remain part of the Scandinavian world for 400 years.

A glossary of some common placenames with Saxon or Norse origins

MODERN FORM	MEANING
Barrow-; Bar-; -berry; -burgh	Hill, mound, tumulus
Barton	Corn farm, outlying grange
Beck	Stream
Brock-; Brough-; -brook; -broke	Brook, stream
Brough-; -burgh; -bury; -borough	Fortified place
-bourne; -borne	Stream, spring
-by	Village, settlement, farm
Cleve-; Clif-; -cliff; -ley	Cliff, bank
Coate; Coton; -cot; -cote	Cottage
Deane; Den-; -dean; -den	Valley
Dun-; -den; -don; -ton	Down, hill
Ea-; E-; -ey; -eau	Stream, river, island
Frith	Woodland
Hale; Hal-; -all; -hall	Nook, narrow valley
-ham	Village, manor, homestead, meadow, enclosure
-hampton	Home farm
-hanger	Slope
-hay; -hey	Fence, enclosure
Had-; Hat-; Hed-; Heath-	Heath, heather
Holt-; -hurst	Wood
Lea-; -leigh; -ley; -low	Forest, wood, glade, clearing
Med-; -mede	Meadow
-mond; -mont	Mount, hill
-stead; -sted	Place, religious site
Stret-; Sturt-; Stred-; Strat-	Street
Thwaite-; -thwaite	Clearing or meadow
-ton; -tone	Enclosure, farmstead, village
Wick-; Wig-; wich; -wick	Dwelling, farm
-worth; -worthy	Enclosure

Landscapes of Anglo-Saxon England

The colonisation of lowland, south-eastern Britain by the Anglo-Saxons left its mark indelibly on the landscape. The newcomers from across the North Sea continued the attack upon the forests and established villages as the nuclei of their agricultural economies. Apart from some churches, or remnants of churches, Saxon buildings have long since vanished; they were too flimsy to forestall either decay or rebuilding in later centuries. But the great majority of villages on the map of England today were in existence by 1066.

The impact of the Saxon farmer and his English speaking descendants on the countryside is most evident in the abundance and distribution of place-names; see glossary of some common place-names on opposite page. It has long been accepted that many places whose names end in *ham* or *ing* belong to the earliest stages of the Anglo-Saxon settlement. The suffix *ham* is taken to mean anything from village to homestead or enclosure, and when *ing* occurs it is usually coupled with a personal name, one who perhaps acted as a tribal leader. For instance Hastings, it is believed, was founded by 'the followers of Haesta'. Sussex – which itself means the territory of the South Saxons – contains about 50 place-names ending with the suffix -*ing*.

Some places hark back to the earliest period of colonisation, before the conversion of the Anglo-Saxons to Christianity, in their commemoration of the pagan gods of northern Europe. Thus the Staffordshire Black Country remembers the god Woden at Wednesbury and Wednesfield. And in East Kent we find Woodnesborough meaning 'the *bury* or defended place of Woden'. There the church stands on a mound, slightly raised above the surrounding fields and lanes. Is this perhaps the last faint relic in the landscape of an Iron Age earthwork, a site that was taken over and dedicated to the worship of Woden by the earliest Anglo-Saxon settlers?

Place-names are also testimony to the agricultural activities of the Saxons. Their inroads into the forests are recorded for all time in such terms as *ley*, *hurst*, *holt*, *hey* and *field*. All are suffixes indicating clearings or places where log huts were raised and cattle pastured in the wild wood. And Chorley, a name that occurs in several parts of England, means 'the clearing of the peasants', suggesting long forgotten communal efforts in pushing back the frontiers of the

Skellig Michael: Dark Age monastic cells on a bleak island without worldly temptations

forests which covered the land.

The most impressive individual landmarks of the first four centuries of the Anglo-Saxon epoch are some huge linear earthworks of which Offa's Dyke, shown on the previous page near Clun in Shropshire, is the greatest.

Offa's Dyke is as magnificent in its conception as Hadrian's Wall, extending from the estuary of the Dee in the north to the mouth of the Wye – a distance of 120 miles (193km) which formed the western frontier of the kingdom of Mercia. It was raised in the reign of King Offa (757–795) and, unlike many lesser earthworks, remains an impressive feature of the landscape today.

To walk the length of the dyke, which now forms the basis for much of a long-distance footpath, is to discover insights into the landscape and society of the long-vanished society of Mercia. The strategic intentions of the earthwork are evident in the sections where the dyke strides across the slopes of westward-facing hills with long views into Wales. In Powys an Iron Age hill-fort, Burfa Camp, was incorporated in the line of the earthwork. A missing link in the line of the dyke in the plain of Hereford suggests that the dense primeval woodland that then existed there made the creation of a man-made frontier, with its raised banks and deep ditches, an unnecessary further protection.

Other Anglo-Saxon earthworks were less grand and today, except where they serve as parish boundaries or define the line of a footpath, they seem to be meaningless features in the landscape. Not so 1500 years ago when they marked boundaries of large estates as well as frontiers or defensive lines of kingdoms. Grim's Dyke in Cranborne Chase, Dorset, for instance, probably marked the boundary of a cattle ranch.

Landscapes of Celtic Britain

The influence of seven centuries of Dark Age history in the making of the landscapes of western and northern Britain seems remarkably slight. The early Christian church formed the most revolutionary element among peoples whose way of life, both socially and economically, essentially represented a continuation of the ways of the Iron Age.

St Patrick had converted most of Ireland to Christianity in the middle years of the fifth century and by the sixth century the gospel was also being spread in Scotland by the missionary activity of St Columba and St Moluag from their island monasteries on Iona and Lismore. Monasteries were the initial fulcrum of the church in Celtic Britain, whereas the later Christianity of Saxon England was organised territorially through bishops based on dioceses.

Most monasteries were centres of worship, learning and farming, but some monks sought special austerities and a few were hermits. Remains of normal monasteries, including churches, living quarters and Round Towers built to guard treasures against Norse raiders, survive in many places, for example Glendalough in Co Wicklow and Clonmacnoise beside the Shannon. Worldly temptations could be avoided in such places as Skellig Michael, a tiny rocky island 700ft (213m) high, in the Atlantic eight miles (13km) off the south-west coast of Ireland. The lack of any timber on the island meant that the monastery was built of stone and this, allied to its inaccessibility, has meant that small beehive-shaped cells and oratories still survive today.

Although people settled around monasteries, few villages developed. In this separate Celtic world of Wales, Scotland and Ireland farming was developing inside enclosures. In Ireland these were known as *raths*, if surrounded by earth banks, or *cashels*, if inside walls of stone; in all there is estimated to have been between 30,000 and 40,000 of these enclosures, each occupied by a farmer with perhaps 70 acres of land.

From the end of the 9th century the Church was absorbed into the Roman allegiance, centred as in England on dioceses with a bishop rather than on separate monasteries. But although archaeology has so far revealed little of the life of the monasteries, there can be no doubt that they had been the great centres of culture in Celtic Britain. In Ireland their cultural legacy is immense.

From top to bottom: the castles of Ludlow in Shropshire, Castle Rising in Norfolk and Harlech in Gwynedd. With the castles often came new towns. The streets of Ludlow still largely follow the grid-iron plan characteristic of Norman settlements established in the 12th century

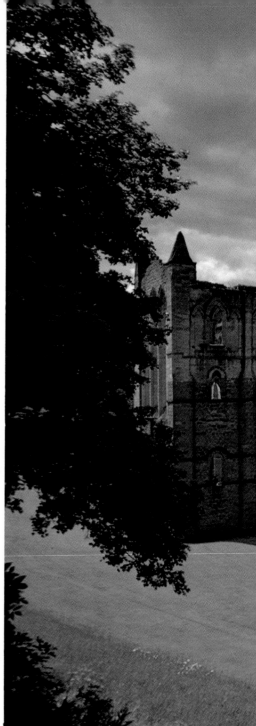

Cistercian monks sought isolation and bequeathed abbey

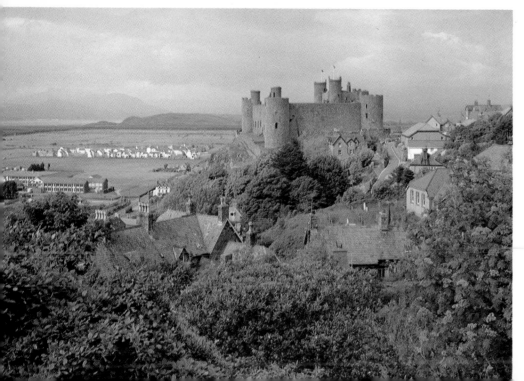

The Middle Ages: the citadels of conquest and the years of decline

The landscape of the Middle Ages can be detected without the assistance of either archaeology or aerial photography. It is evident in the 'fossilised' strips of open fields, in ruins of castles and monasteries, in the street plans of many market towns and cities, in the narrow winding lanes which join village to village and, above all, in the thousands of names of fields, farms and city streets.

Indeed the medieval centuries contributed so much to the visual wealth of England especially – in the shape of castles, monasteries, cathedrals and the domestic architecture of prosperous wool *to match the beauty of their surroundings. Above is Rievaulx Abbey, North Yorkshire, and below right, Melrose Abbey in the Scottish Borders*

towns – that this has become the prime tourist image of the British Isles. But it is a mistake to regard the entire period as a golden age of expansion. The two centuries up to 1300 were ones of growth, although this was most marked in England and southern and eastern England at that. The years that followed, however, witnessed a fall in population caused largely by the effects of climatic change, plague and wars, especially with the French and Scots. By 1485, and the founding of the Tudor dynasty in England, a slow recovery was under way.

But the story begins in the decades after 1066 with the building of castles to help the Normans control their newly-conquered lands.

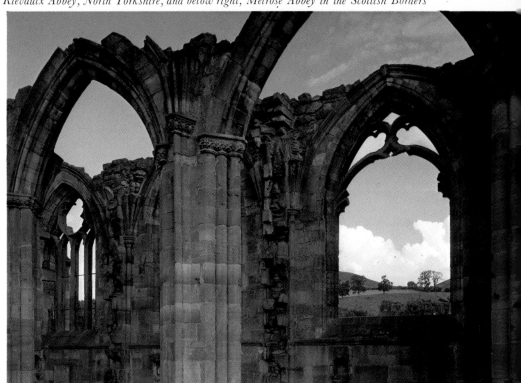

A great wave of castle-building followed the Norman Conquest during the reign of William I. Most of these were raised in the hearts of Saxon towns which already formed regional centres. The Domesday Book tells us that at Lincoln 166 houses were destroyed for the building of the castle while at Norwich 98 houses were pulled down in clearing the site for a huge earth motte, crowned by a forbidding stone keep.

Elsewhere the building of the castle preceded the creation of a town. The Domesday Book again records, for instance, the erection of a gigantic motte on the lip of the steep-sided Kensey valley in Cornwall; on the slopes beneath the castle the borough of Launceston was soon to come into being. The same process was repeated at many places in the Welsh Marches, an uneasy frontier zone ever open to raids from the west and border strife between the 100 and more territories of earls, barons and bishops that formed a mosaic of little states between the Bristol Channel and the Dee estuary. The building of Ludlow Castle along this frontier soon after 1085 was particularly remarkable since it also involved the creation of a planned town at the gates of the castle that retains its basic shape to this day.

The border territories where the claims of the English, Welsh and Scots were perpetually in conflict are inevitably rich in medieval castles and boroughs. North Wales has Conwy and Caernarfon castles, for instance, and in Northumberland the Normans established almost 20 'motte and bailey' castles. Some of these have faded into the countryside as no more than overgrown mounds and ditches but others, as at Alnwick and Warkworth for instance, were extended and elaborated throughout the medieval centuries to survive as some of the finest examples of the redundant technology of military architecture to be seen in Britain. Many Norman castles in Ireland were humble structures but most of the towns which developed around them had walls which in some places, including Dublin, can still be seen today.

The motte and bailey style of Norman castle

The 'ridge and furrow' of medieval farming remains visible near Southam in Warwickshire

Years of prosperity and growth

The population of England grew about threefold in the first two centuries after the Norman conquest: from about $1\frac{1}{2}$ million at the time of the Domesday Book in 1086 – an incomplete record since it did not cover all of England, let alone the rest of the British Isles – to around $4\frac{1}{2}$ million in 1300.

This growth was not evenly spread throughout the country. In the long settled tracts of southern and central England, where the opportunities for the expansion of farming at the expense of unreclaimed woodland were by then slight, the growth of population was negligible. Where wasteland, forest and fen were still available for colonisation, population grew rapidly.

In the south of Warwickshire, for instance, medieval records show some villages to have been the same size in 1279 as they had been in 1086. But to the north of the county beyond the River Avon in the densely-forested district of Arden the population grew dramatically as tiny clusters of farms and moated manor houses were planted in newly-cleared land. Remarkably high increases in population between 1086 and the early years of the 14th century have also been detected in the Fenland where the first extensive reclamation was carried out since Roman times. The number of tenants in Spalding, for instance, increased by $6\frac{1}{2}$ times over that period.

This age of expansion left its mark on both the countryside and the towns. In the country it was the heyday of open-field farming. This involved two, three and maybe more huge fields grouped around the nucleus of a village. Each field was then laid out in strips to be farmed by the individual farmers living in the village. The farmers ploughed up and down the strips with the plough throwing the soil towards the centre of the strip to form a ridge. Each strip was separated from its neighbour by a double furrow – hence the 'ridge and furrow' pattern that can still be seen not only through aerial photography but also on the ground, especially in winter when vegetation is bare.

The origins of this method of farming are obscure. It has traditionally been associated with the Saxons but some historians and geographers argue that it only came into being after the Norman conquest – perhaps as a consequence of the rising population and the need to work the land more intensively. There is, for instance, only one reference in the Domesday Book to strip farming – at Garsington in Oxfordshire – amid the endless statistics about plough-teams and ploughlands. What is certain is that this method of farming became much more widespread in the 12th and 13th centuries.

The wealth of these centuries is reflected in other changes. They saw the rebuilding of hundreds of parish churches as wooden Saxon churches were reconstructed in stone. However, an even more striking sign of the times was the founding of new towns and the granting of borough charters to already established settlements. By 1334 there were more than 200 boroughs in England alone. Some places which received charters were successful and continued down the centuries to form market towns or the great cities of the present day; others faltered in the economic decline of the later medieval centuries and not a few were failures from the beginning. In Lancashire, for instance, 23 boroughs were founded, but only four of them Lancaster, Liverpool, Preston and Wigan – could be described as towns at the end of the Middle Ages.

Some of Britain's most prosperous ports were founded during these two centuries of expansion; Boston, King's Lynn and Newcastle came into existence about 1100. Harwich, Liverpool and Portsmouth were founded about a century later and Kingston-upon-Hull was established about 1300.

The prosperous centuries of the early Middle Ages owe not a little to the numerous monastic foundations of the Plantagenet kings and private land-owners. In particular the coming of the new order of the Cistercians in the 12th century broke new ground over many acres of upland Britain, since it was an order that insisted upon isolated life in wild and lonely places. The Cistercian houses provide many of the finest ruins in Britain; among them are Rievaulx and Fountains Abbeys in Yorkshire, Tintern on the banks of the Wye and Melrose in the Borders. Their influence was more than architectural: they became vast landowners, invariably using their land for sheep rearing. Furness Abbey, for instance, owned thousands of acres above Eskdale and Borrowdale in the Lake District as well as the entire Furness peninsula between lakes Windermere and Coniston. The word 'grange' is a widespread reminder of monastic power since it originally meant an outlying monastic farm.

In Wales, Scotland and Ireland the pace of change was slower and the most remote parts remained unaffected by the patterns of development in the lowland areas of southern Britain. Nevertheless towns still grew up around Norman castles and churches with markets that became increasingly prosperous. Craftsmen were located mainly in the towns (most of which had a cornmill) but some, notably blacksmiths, were spread more widely through the countryside. A few even penetrated areas far from Norman influence, such as the Orkneys, where the 12th century cathedral at Kirkwall reflects the Norman skills of masons, glaziers and carpenters. At the same time continental masons were imported into Ireland to invigorate native customs and to produce at Cashel a church reflecting both prehistoric and medieval traditions.

Cashel was outside the area of the greatest Norman influence in Ireland. This was confined to the more fertile part of the country, mainly in the eastern part of the Central Lowland and in such valleys as the Nore, Suir and Barrow, all of which join to flow through Waterford Harbour. They made little impact west of the Shannon or in Ulster.

Norman political power also failed to encompass the greater part of Wales but the Welsh princes, the rulers of Gwynedd, encouraged the great Norman monastic orders to acquire property. For instance, towards the end of the 12th century, the Cistercians were endowed with Aberconwy, a place of high strategic importance which a century later was to be taken over by Edward I for the founding of the new town and castle of Conwy.

In the lowlands of Scotland, too, a strong centralised monarchy followed many Norman principles of organisation. Towns grew up around castles – such as Edinburgh in the 12th century – markets established to encourage trade, foreign monastic orders endowed with vast tracts of land which sometimes became centres of agricultural expansion. But the highlands and islands remained, largely immune from such changes and therefore continued to be dominated by clan rule.

☐ See page 24 for the making of the Norfolk Broads.

The Round Tower of Kilmacduagh, Co Galway, leans slightly out of the perpendicular. These towers are peculiar to Ireland and were used variously as hiding places and defences against Norse raiders. Here the tower stands next to cathedral ruins dating back to the 10th century

The years of deserted villages

The great divide in the Middle Ages came at the beginning of the 14th century. Population ceased to grow, indeed by the middle of the century, when the Black Death spreading from India wrought havoc all over Europe, there was a catastrophic decline of numbers in some parts of the country. As the plague raged between 1348 and 1350 it is estimated that between a third and a half of the population of the British Isles died, many of them in the towns.

The Black Death has been blamed for the economic stagnation, the abandonment of agricultural land, the desertion of hundreds of villages (see below) and the decline of population that is a characteristic of the 15th century. No doubt the Black Death and the succeeding epidemics of 1361, 1369 and 1374 were important factors in the economic and social changes of the late Middle Ages, but research has also shown that the long period of expansion and prosperity had come to a close a generation before the plague ever reached the British Isles.

Two severe periods of famine from 1315–1317 and again in 1321 seem to mark a turning point in the population history of medieval England. The onslaught of these famines which severely reduced the corn harvest, and consequently the stock of seed-corn for the next year, may well be explained by a deterioration in the climate of western Europe that set in at the beginning of the 14th century. It was a time of cool, sunless wet autumns when the corn failed to ripen. The Black Death came as the ultimate scourge among the troubles of those times. And, ironically, some villages were to die as a result of reviving prosperity rather than plague.

Ingarsby in east Leicestershire is one of more than 2000 deserted village sites in England alone. But it is unusual since it is known exactly when, and why, it became deserted. The year was 1469. The village had contained a dozen families according to a tax survey in 1377 but it became deserted overnight when it was bought and razed to the ground by Leicester Abbey.

The monks wanted the land as sheep pasture for the booming wool trade. Vast numbers of village desertions were caused by acquisitive landlords with interests in the wool trade that flourished from the second half of the 15th century.

The continued use of the Ingarsby site as pasture as opposed to arable land has meant that it is still possible to walk along the hollows of the former lanes between the grassy platforms where the farmsteads once stood. In the valley below, the earth dam which collected the waters of a brook in a large mill-pond can still be seen, as can the faint lines of 'ridge-and-furrow' field patterns encircling the old settlement.

It was once thought that the Black Death of 1348–50 had caused many village desertions but nowhere was this the sole factor. A great number of desertions occurred between 1450 and 1520 at a time when population in England was slowly rising once more and when the plague must have passed into the folklore of the nation. The motives for desertion in these latter decades were largely economic, determined above all by the movements in corn and wool prices.

The booming wool exports to Flanders and Italy and the rise of the cloth industry in Coventry, Norwich, the Cotswolds and the little towns of Suffolk brought about a rise in wool prices that ensured high profits to the landlord who could convert the open arable fields to pasture. The many village desertions in the counties of eastern England, therefore, are related to the location of the chief cloth-making centres, hence the scores of abandoned sites in Norfolk and south Warwickshire which offered not only good grazing land but also easy access to such wool-exporting ports as Boston and King's Lynn or the busy cloth town of Coventry.

The years of decline were most marked in Ireland, large areas of which retreated into fighting and traditional Celtic ways. The Celtic lifestyle was based on small self-sufficient hamlets without any of the commercial interdependence between town and country that had seen the birth of market towns in England. This was at its most deep-rooted in Ireland since it had initially survived for 1000 years without occupation by the Romans or their successors from the continent.

The Vikings had established the first towns – even the name Ireland has Norse origins – and the Anglo-Norman invasion of 1169 added more towns as well as the mixed farming methods of England to large areas of Ireland, particularly the south and east. But there were too few colonisers for the Anglo-Norman influence to withstand the difficulties of the 15th century. Even the towns with their castles fell into disrepair while outside the town walls Celtic influence reasserted itself as the widespread existence of Gaelic placenames still testifies.

The landscape revolution of the Tudor to Georgian years

The victory won by Henry Tudor on the open fields of the village of Bosworth in Leicestershire in 1485 saw the beginning of an era of unparalleled change in the landscape. Many of the features now regarded as integral elements in the 'traditional' countryside have their origins in the three centuries from 1485 that preceded the Industrial Revolution.

The fields were enclosed by hedgerows, country houses laid out in landscaped parkland, villages rebuilt in their local stone with sufficient solidity to survive to the present day. Industry, too, gathered momentum from small scale enterprises such as iron-smelting and glass-making in the Weald of Kent. Trade flourished and with it towns grew and communication routes improved – on land and water.

The impact of these changes was most marked in England and with good reason for these were centuries in which England emerged as a major political force in the world. And as English power came to dominate Wales, Scotland and, to a lesser degree, Ireland, so too did the fashions and practices of the English conquerors. Architectural styles and farming methods were thus implanted on vast tracts of the British Isles.

Quite when this English Revolution led into the Industrial Revolution is impossible to say. The 18th century saw the first stirrings of the Industrial Revolution in some parts of the British Isles while others, notably Ireland, were still adjusting to the agricultural changes of the previous two centuries. Improvements in road and water communications were also under way during these centuries, but their impact will be examined in the next section on the Industrial Revolution when their significance became most apparent.

But another revolution was slowly producing its own far-reaching transformation of the landscape. Piecemeal enclosure of the old open fields around the villages of England had been going on since the 14th century, particularly in the south-west and south-east of the country.

Improved techniques of animal husbandry offered wealthy landowners far more valuable returns than accrued from traditional farming. Many tenants of the open field therefore found themselves evicted and great hedged fields of pasture were created on their rich clay lands.

Field enclosures came later to upland areas like the Peak District (above) with drystone walls rather than hedgerows acting as boundaries

Kersey, Suffolk: the prosperity of the Tudor to Georgian years enabled quite humble cottages to be rebuilt in sturdy local materials

By the end of the 16th century only the shire counties of the English Midlands still had a high proportion of cultivated land farmed in unenclosed strips. And when the Parliamentary Commissioners set about completing the task of enclosures in the middle of the 18th century they found that in many areas it was only a mopping-up operation. The changeover to a landscape of hedged fields – to be so mourned when threatened with destruction in the 20th century – had been largely accomplished by private agreements.

Where the Commissioners did have a job to do, as in the Midlands and eastern England, they left behind a new countryside of large regular fields with straight hedges of hawthorn with perhaps the occasional ash or elm set within to give variety. New straight roads of specified width, and nowadays having wide grass verges, were another of the Commissioners' innovations. New farmhouses were also built and in many cases they were set within the new pattern of fields rather than standing next to the roadway as was characteristic of older dwellings.

The enclosure movement spread, albeit more slowly, to the less fertile uplands of Britain where local stone was often used to form field boundaries rather than specially-planted hedgerows. But the planting of hedgerows was not the only break with the 3000-year tradition of cutting down woodland for agricultural purposes. Many landowners planted new trees as copses during the 17th century, particularly after the poet John Evelyn had aroused concern among the intelligentsia about the wanton destruction of so much of the natural forests of Britain. Many of these copses were planted in the deer parks that surrounded country houses and which, as at Burghley, were sometimes destined to be landscaped by later generations of owners. Not all landowners planted trees for strictly selfless motives: many trees provided cover for foxes who were hunted enthusiastically by the new squires.

In Ireland trees were still being cut down. The 16th and 17th centuries were the years of the great 'plantation' movement with profound changes in the landscape. During these two centuries English and Scottish settlers made new towns, villages and farms. In Ulster, what had previously been a countryside ravaged by strife became prosperous, with domestic industry in the homes. In the remoter areas, especially the uplands, clusters of houses remained with

Glamis Castle in Tayside: rebuilt in the 17th century with the flavour of a French chateau

the land farmed in strips, but generally new fields were laid out, houses built, woods cleared and marshes or bogs drained. Hedgerows were grown in the lowlands though stone walls formed field boundaries in the mountains and in the west of Ireland from Donegal to Kerry. Some are of massive height to protect oats and potatoes from Atlantic gales. Traditionally the Protestants have had the largest and most fertile farms. Plantation thus had profound repercussions on the political history as well as the landscape of Ireland.

Country houses lose their defences

The stately homes of the 20th century tourist industry are often the country houses of the 16th century. The Tudor years saw the emergence of many such houses surrounded by private estates and many survive in largely unaltered form today. Rich people had always had their great private houses. Sometimes they were so rich and powerful that these were castles, but even lesser nobility had their manor houses.

But the country houses of the 16th and 17th centuries were a new phenomenon. They reflect more than the general prosperity of the age and more to, too, than the improvement in building skills; they are related directly to some of the key political acts of Tudor times. Henry VIII's onslaught on the Church and the dissolution of the monasteries released hundreds of thousands of acres. Much passed to the crown itself but the former monastic land also gave rise to a new breed of landed gentry, often royal favourites or those holding high offices of state. Burghley House near Stamford, for instance, was built by William Cecil, the

first Lord Burghley and Treasurer to Elizabeth I. It also reflects the Renaissance influence that had accompanied increased trade from Europe.

The Act of Union of 1536 which finally linked England and Wales had also encouraged the development of country houses. Greater political stability meant that new buildings could be less defensive in nature and more aesthetic in nature and appeal. Even former strongholds like Powis Castle, above the Severn near Welshpool, were transformed into comfortable country houses with formal gardens and a surrounding parkland.

Scotland and Ireland did not experience the same political stability and therefore lagged a century or more behind England in terms of country house building. Elizabethan Scotland still concerned itself with building fortified houses, only slightly more homely than the medieval castles. As late as 1680 Glamis in Tayside was rebuilt with an array of conical turrets and impressive massive stone walls. In the border centres like Jedburgh, even town houses had their architectural style influenced by the needs of defence. In Ireland it was much the same story with what were effectively 'castles' built by the powerful families who came in as planters and were given estates of several thousand acres; some, such as Kilkenny and Cahir in Co Tipperary, were already fortified centres of the Anglo-Norman period. As peaceful conditions developed the tradition of building fine country houses became stronger, with many outstanding examples dating from the Georgian years.

☐ *See also pages 80–85 about country houses.*

Reclaiming the Fens

The greatest single act of change in the 17th century as it affected the country-side was undoubtedly the reclamation of the Fens. For centuries this inherently rich area of fertile peaty and silty soils near the Wash had never realised its full potential. Despite Roman and other reclamation efforts, the area was still regularly flooded, particularly during winter months as rivers such as the Ouse, Granta, Nene, Welland and Witham overflowed their banks and spread out over vast areas of surrounding land.

The architect of the great reclamation was Cornelius Vermuyden, a Dutch-man. He first made his name as a drainage expert when he tackled the draining of Hatfield Chase near Doncaster. This work, important though it was, proved to be only an essential preliminary to the much greater task of draining the Great Level of the Fens. The problem, as Vermuyden saw it, was to get the water of the rivers draining into the peat 'bowl' away to the sea as quickly as possible. The Ouse, in particular, wandered seemingly without aim or purpose over vast tracts in a series of great meander loops. A shorter straightened course would give a more rapid run off and minimise the danger of flooding.

To achieve this a great artificial cut or canal known as the Bedford River was dug between Earith and Denver. It was 21 miles (34km) long and 70ft (21m) wide – a tremendous achievement to be accomplished only with the spade. The Civil War interrupted further work but in 1650 another period of draining began. This led to the cutting of a second artificial channel, now known as the New Bedford River. Water then had to be pumped from drains in the fields into these major drainage channels. This was done at first by windmills which became a characteristic feature of the Fenland scene. They were ultimately replaced by steam engines – the first of which appeared near Denver in 1820 – but one windmill has been restored and re-erected at Wicken Fen where some of the 'original' reed and sedge fen has been preserved in a nature reserve.

Reclamation has continued after Vermuyden's time so that large-scale flooding is now most unlikely. But some problems remain. Dust storms can occur during a dry spring and carry away the whole top surface of the soil while the peat itself is shrinking as the water level sinks due to drainage schemes.

An iron post from the Great Exhibition of 1851 was sunk into the peat of Holme Fen that year. Its top was then level with the surface at that time but now about 13ft (4m) is exposed. This wastage of the peat fen poses considerable problems, not least in the building of houses and roads on such an unstable foundation. In spite of this the Fens remain as an outstanding example of a man-made countryside where nature's endowment has been turned to advantage by the farmer. (Other areas of agricultural wealth, reclaimed at various times up to present times, include Holderness in east Yorkshire, the meres of south and west Lancashire, and the Somerset 'levels'.)

Harnessing the rivers

Such industry as existed during these centuries was on a small scale and dependent on local raw materials and the availability of water power. In the heavily-forested Weald of Kent and Sussex a rural iron industry flourished throughout the medieval period – its origins in fact go back to the Romans – with the ironmasters turning out a whole range of products from nails and horseshoes to firebacks and cannons. The industry really came alive in Tudor times when skilled workers from the continent brought in new techniques of smelting and casting. Using local iron ore and charcoal from the Wealden forests, furnaces and forges grew up at sites where it was possible to create a head of water by damming a narrow valley. It is these 'hammer' ponds of Kent, Sussex and Surrey which are the most obvious survivals in the countryside of the former industry, though the more observant and searching can still find pieces of bloomery iron around furnace sites like Lamberhurst and Ashburnham.

In upland Britain the power problem was solved by directly harnessing the swiftly flowing rivers. In 25 miles (40km) of the River Kent in the Lake District, for instance, there were no fewer than 90 watermills during the late 18th century. For a brief period at the turn of the 19th century this quiet corner of the Westmorland countryside had a more industrial society than the heart of the Midlands around Birmingham. Bobbins, textiles, paper and snuff mills, as well as the ubiquitous corn-grinding mill, were all using the ample power supplied by the Kent and its tributaries.

Only the advent of steam power and the coming of the railways with their cheap coal brought these essentially rural industries into decline.

Improving the uplands

The countryside of the British Isles on the eve of the industrial revolution in the 18th century was still intensely rural in character. Towns had grown, in England especially, but farming remained the main occupation. Many villages were simply collections of farms, perhaps looking out onto a central green where most of the social life was enacted. These smaller villages or hamlets are particularly associated with upland areas of Britain where agricultural advance in the Tudor and Georgian years was less dramatic.

The higher and wetter parts of Britain posed more intractable problems for agriculture. The soils were generally thinner and intensely leached by the heavy rain and rapid drainage over the steep slopes so that they did not readily respond to the efforts of the small band of 'improvers'. But despite these unfavourable and discouraging circumstances some attempts were made to reclaim even the upland wastes in the latter half of the 18th century. This has been explained by a variety of circumstances, including a favourable climatic period, expanding demand for farm produce, the growth of home spinning and weaving of wool, and an increasing population in all parts of the British Isles. Among the instances of upland development, large and small, were:

England. One of the last and perhaps the greatest attempts at landscape betterment was made on the heathery wastes of Exmoor well above the 1000ft (308m) contour. In 1818 John Knight, who had made his wealth as a Shropshire ironmaster, bought an estate of 15,000 acres centred on Simonsbath. In a generation he and his son Frederic brought about a complete transformation. The flat plateau tops were drained, ploughed and limed and then converted into fine pastures. A wall of stone 29 miles (47km) long was built to enclose the moorland property and 15 new farmhouses sprinkled over the vast area of his landholding. High earthbanks planted with hazel and shelter belts of beech and sycamore were all part of the scheme to tame part of Exmoor. How successful Knight was can be judged today by comparing the rich farmlands he created with the barren wastes of Dartmoor or Bodmin Moor at much the same height.

Wales. Thomas Johnes was the most notable pioneer with his country house, formal gardens and 'natural' landscaping of the Ystwyth valley inland from

Aberystwyth. More than four million trees were planted, mainly larch but also oak and beech in more sheltered places of a valley where the original wood cover had been destroyed by lead mining. Although some of the deciduous trees were quite foreign to the Welsh hillsides, the arboriculture was on the whole a success and Johnes' Hafod estate became 'one of the wonders of Wales' drawing visitors such as J.W. Turner who has left us with a painting of the now demolished house with its two long wings added by John Nash to the original design. Remnants of the estate survive today under the protection of the Forestry Commission.

Scotland. Sir John Sinclair adopted a slightly less eccentric approach to improving the wastes of his native Sutherland. The move from arable to pastoral farming was causing conflict between landlords and tenants as huge highland estates were increasingly turned into more profitable sheep runs. Sinclair, as a paternal landlord, tried to soften the blow by resettling his tenants in new coastal villages like Badbea and Sarclett near Wick where fishing could be combined with farming and craft industries. More successful, though, were his farm improvement schemes around the ancestral home of Thurso Castle and the 'new' village of Halkirk. Most landlords were not so benevolent and the great highland clearances caused great hardship as well as a complete transformation of vast areas of northern Scotland.

Ireland. Many landlords in upland areas planted fine estates (demesnes) with landscaped grounds, kept in order by numerous labourers housed in the villages. A few landlords, like Richard Edgeworth in Longford and Lord Altamont of Westport, tried to reclaim mountain land as well as bog and brought in new breeds of cattle to graze the improved pastures. But many landlords did little or nothing to improve the lot of their tenants; absentee landlords living off rents were regarded with particular odium. Generally the tenants had no security of tenure – the northern areas were more of an exception – and evictions were frequent. People without land became squatters on common land either on hillsides above the area generally farmed or on the edges of bogs. The overcrowding on the land became increasingly severe and with only a small proportion of the landless and jobless able to find work in the towns, emigration to Britain and America was increasing by the end of the 18th century.

The Industrial Revolution: Man leaves the land for the towns

There had been industry in the British Isles since prehistoric man first scoured the ground for flints. It had changed the landscape of areas like the Weald in Kent and Sussex where the iron industry had been so strong and around the Tyne where coal had long been mined or dug from open pits.

But the impact of these early industries on the overall landscape was small. Britain remained a predominantly agricultural country in the middle of the 18th century. Yet within 100 years a majority of the population lived in towns and depended on industry for their livelihood. Vast cities had grown, sometimes out of nothing, Vast mining enterprises littered and transformed the landscape with their residue.

The purpose of this book is neither to provide an economic history of the British Isles nor to dwell on the development of Britain's cities. The importance of the Industrial Revolution is treated here strictly in terms of its impact upon the countryside of the British Isles. This impact was considerable, not merely in the once unspoilt landscape that was devoured or disfigured by the new industries and towns but also in the vast tracts of the countryside apparently unaffected by industrialisation. Few areas, for instance, were immune to the influence of canals and railways. The legacy of the Industrial Revolution on the face of Britain is as varied as it is visible. Steam power transformed the British Isles, first by enabling large factories to be built – often alongside the rivers and canals initially used for trade – in the centre of towns and then through the railway age.

From the 1840s, when the railways covered almost the whole country, the growth of industry and towns was rapid, especially in coalfield areas. Older industrial areas, notably London with its growing port, Liverpool, Birmingham, Hull and central Scotland shared in this industrial growth. People left the land, particularly in upland Wales, Scotland and Ireland, to seek a new life in the towns so that only in Ireland was a majority of the population still dependent on agriculture at the close of the 19th century. Industry has continued to transform the landscape during the 20th century, but that is a story taken up in the final chapter of this book: The Future of the Countryside. It is a story that is far from being over.

Ironbridge: the first iron bridge in the world was erected in 1779 across the River Severn near Coalbrookdale: an area regarded as the birthplace of the Industrial Revolution

The birthplace of the revolution

If one area can claim to have been the birthplace of the Industrial Revolution, then it is the middle Severn valley around Coalbrookdale. Here, in a quiet corner of the Shropshire countryside, there was a fine river waterway available for transport, steep banks clothed with woodland ideal for making charcoal, deposits of iron and clay and accessible coal seams – all the ingredients to develop a whole group of industries.

It was a largely rural landscape in 1707 when Abraham Darby became ironmaster of a small blast furnace at Coalbrookdale in one of the steep-sided valleys running down to the Severn. It was here that Darby began experiments using coke to smelt the local iron ore. Since what there was of an iron 'industry' was gravely threatened by a shortage of charcoal, Darby's success ultimately revolutionised the manufacture of iron and steel and thus provided a firm foundation for widespread industrial growth. At first Darby used the local coal straight from the mine but when this did not answer his purpose he converted it into coke on a spot close to the furnace. Gradually the more readily available coke replaced charcoal in the manufacture of cast iron, though it was not until 1775 that charcoal ceased to be used in the forge where other forms of iron and steel were made.

Abraham Darby's family inherited his pioneering spirit: Abraham Darby II was to build the nearby Horsehay ironworks in 1755 and in 1779 Abraham Darby III built the first iron bridge in the world high across the Severn one mile (1.6km) downstream from Coalbrookedale. The bridge is no longer used for traffic but was an engineering masterpiece which served an important practical as well as symbolic purpose: it allowed raw materials and finished pro-ducts to pass freely across the Severn so that new industries like the tile works at Jackfield were set up on the other bank.

The area around Ironbridge remained important throughout the 19th century. It was, for instance, to Coalbrookedale that Richard Trevithick came in 1802 when building his steam engine. Isambard Kingdom Brunel also used iron rolled at the Horsehay works for his ship, the *Great Britain*. But the focus of the industrialisation shifted elsewhere leaving the Ironbridge area largely neglected and forgotten. Luckily, however, many remains of these birthpangs of the Industrial Revolution can now be seen under the aegis of the Ironbridge Gorge Trust.

The first factories and slums

Cromford in Derbyshire was to the textile industry what Coalbrookdale was to the iron industry. It was at Cromford that Richard Arkwright established his first textile mill in 1771 and began a social revolution that was to have far-reaching effects well beyond the Derwent Valley. It marked the beginning of a changeover from cotton industry to the factory system of production.

Previously such industry as existed had been mostly a small-scale affair. Even inventions like Hargreaves's spinning jenny in 1767 had initially aided home-based textile workers. And the dependence on water power had meant that industries were sited high up remote river valleys rather than in city centres or lowland plains; many of these are still visible, though generally in ruins, in Pennine valleys of Lancashire and Yorkshire.

Arkwright also relied on water power for his Cromford mill, but the sheer scale of the enterprise was revolutionary. More than 800 people were employed, many of them working at night. By then further mills had been built by Arkwright and others in the Peak District and Josiah Wedgwood had opened his first factory in the Potteries. The movement of people from the land to the factories was under way.

By the middle of the 19th century steam had replaced water power as the driving force of the industrial revolution and factory growth was swift. No longer were factories confined to the relatively remote banks of fast-flowing rivers. Now they could be built in the heart of cities, alongside the railways and canals that served their needs. And builders erected houses around these new factories whose quality was often epitomised in one 19th century word – slums.

In older towns open spaces were devoured by builders as populations grew rapidly. Birmingham, for instance, grew from 35,000 in 1760 to 73,000 in 1801 and 233,000 in 1851. Elsewhere in the industrial Midlands and North of England new cities were created out of tiny hamlets. A single farmhouse near the banks of the Tees in 1830 became the basis of Middlesbrough and a population of 50,000 just 50 years later. There were already signs by the mid-19th century that industrial towns were growing into one another, eventually to form 'conurbations'. A new landscape was being born.

It was least evident in Ireland which had hardly any coal and only a limited

Cottage industry: weavers' homes at High Ogden, near Rochdale, in Lancashire

industrial development. Without the stimulus of industry, except in Belfast after the 1850s and other Ulster cities, emigration to either Britain or America remained the only hope for people in much of famine-afflicted Ireland.

Mining ravages the landscape

Industry's voracious appetite for raw materials, especially metals, led to a determined exploitation of the potential mineral wealth of the country. As most of the ores were located in the older rocks of the British Isles, upland areas bore the brunt of much exploitation.

Quiet rural areas could be changed overnight following the discovery of a rich lode of copper, lead or tin and the lives of the local people altered completely. Unfortunately most mineral working, being a robber industry, brought only a short period of prosperity so that today many, if not all, the 19th century workings are abandoned. Although there has been considerable reclamation, especially since 1945, the legacy often remains in old buildings, mountains of waste, disused pit shafts, sheets of water known as 'flashes' caused by subsidence, and disintegrating workers' cottages.

These features are also typical of the landscape of coal mining, the longest-lasting and most extensive form of mineral extraction within Britain. But they can be found, too, outside the areas generally associated with coal mining and the Industrial Revolution.

Parys Mountain in Anglesey, for instance, is today a scene of great desolation with its multi-coloured waste tips, great open caverns, settling pits and ruined engine houses. And yet, in the latter half

of the 18th century, this was the site of the greatest copper mine in the world.

Cornwall, which still has some tin mines and china clay quarries, also has a rash of industrial remains, particularly the distinctive engine house and its adjacent chimney. Many dot the skyline of the rising ground between Redruth and Camborne where the mining for copper and tin was most intense. The famous coastal site of Botallack, not far from Land's End, is one particularly spectacular abandoned industrial site. But in Cornwall, as in the rest of Britain, much remains to be done to clear up the rape of the landscape which took place during the period of intense mining activity in the 19th century.

The Lady Isabella water wheel at Laxey in the Isle of Man is now a major feature of a 20th century industry – tourism. The 72ft (22m) wheel was built in 1854 to drain the rich but deep-seated lead mines of the Laxey Valley by using the waters draining off Snaefell. It was in use until the end of the First World War. It is the world's largest surviving water wheel

Transport: opening up Britain

Nearly 2000 years of transport can be seen in a 300-yard (270m) stretch of countryside three miles east of Daventry in the Midlands. The oldest of four lines of communication that run next to each other at this point is the A5 road which follows the line of the Roman Watling Street. Then, from the last 200 years, there are the Grand Union Canal, the main railway line between London and North-West England and, finally, the M1 motorway.

All forms of communication leave distinctive marks on the landscape. Whether these are regarded as 'good' or 'bad' tends to change with the passage of time. The architecture and earthworks associated with railways and canals were once regarded with the kind of horror modern conservationists often reserve for motorways. What is certain is that a radical improvement in transport was an essential element in the Industrial Revolution of the late 18th and early 19th centuries.

Until then rivers had formed the main arteries of communication for carrying bulky commodities – river ports such as Bewdley on the Severn and Totnes on the Dart still have long wharves and large warehouses as reminders of their former importance. Roads had been poor until the Turnpike Acts of the 17th and early 18th centuries. A road network did exist, however, and some routes dated back to prehistoric times, such as the Icknield Way across Southern England. There were also many drovers' trails for driving sheep and cattle from upland pastures to markets. These wide grassy paths can still be seen in many areas, especially in the northern Pennines, mid-Wales and Border country. Isolated pubs sometimes have their origins as drovers' inns.

The turnpikes improved road standards but left few reminders of their existence other than the occasional toll-house which can be seen alongside the road. But the better roads did increase travel during the Georgian years. This was the great coaching era and many fine country inns date from this period (see Chapter Three). It was not until the early 19th century that engineers like Macadam and Telford made great advances in improving the quality of the roads themselves. Telford, for instance, remodelled the old Watling Street route between London and Holyhead to provide a firm, well-drained surface and fewer sharp gradients. Telford's new road – now the modern A5 – crossed into Anglesey over the Menai suspension bridge. This bridge was completed in 1825, and thus coincided with the start of the railway era. It was only in the 20th century that the pioneering work of men like Telford and Macadam would assume major importance. And before railways had been born, another form of transport had achieved a far greater impact on the economic history and landscape of Britain – canals.

Artificial waterways had existed since Roman times, with their Car Dyke near Peterborough and Fossdyke between the Trent and Witham. But apart from the isolated 16th century exception of the canal between Exeter and the sea, they were phenomena of the late 18th and early 19th centuries when an intricate network of canals was dug across Britain.

History tends to credit James Brindley as the father of this canal movement following the construction of the Bridgewater canal to carry coal from mines at Worsley into Manchester. The first long-distance canal, however, was in Ireland and ran for $18\frac{1}{2}$ miles (30km) between the Upper Bann and Newry harbour. Building lasted from 1729 to 1742 and involved 14 locks to cope with changes of level.

Early canals tended to follow the contours but later, as engineering skills improved, they became much more direct plunging through hillsides in tunnels or across valleys in aqueducts. The distinctive features that canals brought to the landscape can nearly all be seen near the stretch of the Grand Union Canal referred to earlier: here there are wharves, locks, cuttings, tunnels, lock-keeper's cottages and canalside inns.

Elsewhere there are still great aqueducts (such as that built by Telford to take his Shropshire Union Canal across the Dee valley near Llangollen) and lifts (as at Anderton on the Trent and Mersey Canal). When the wharves and warehouses seem strangely large for tranquil spots, they are often remnants of the former importance of once major canal ports, as at Shardlow, at the junction of the Grand Trunk Canal and the Trent, and at Braunston, where the Grand Junction and Oxford canals met.

Cities and towns alike began to develop canal quarters with massive brick warehouses lining the bank of the waterway. One town, Stourport, was the sole creation of the canal age. It developed where the Staffordshire and Worcestershire Canal joined the Severn. A pair of dock basins was dug out in 1771 where craft could lie safely at anchor, away from the flood waters of the river. A new town quickly followed and its canal basins as well as the town itself, with its Georgian warehouses, inns and rows of terrace cottages, remain a worthy reminder of the past.

Some canals decayed as well as declined but many survived intact to find a new role today. Canals have become major leisure centres for boating, fishing and simply rambling along towpaths. They are often also important for wildlife and are particularly valuable in the high plateau area of the English Midlands which otherwise has few watery landscapes.

Railways have also become much loved, even as nature reserves along some disused lines. The shrunken railway network of today is not very different from the picture that had emerged by the middle of the last century. In their heyday railways fulfilled all the requirements of the Industrial Revolution, making it possible for heavy and bulky materials to be transported quickly from one part of the country to another. Among these materials were not only the fuels needed to fire the factories but also cheap building materials which greatly diminished the variety previously associated with vernacular architecture. The impact of railways on the landscape was also immense, of course. Vast cuttings were made – one at Tring, Hertfordshire, was $2\frac{1}{2}$ miles (4km) long and up to 60ft (18m) deep – and tunnels hewn across far wider areas of Britain than had ever been affected by canals. Ironically, Victorian railway architecture is now widely admired and cherished.

If railways did much to further the industrialisation of Britain, other than Ireland and northern Scotland, they also provided the means for town-dwellers to get out into the countryside and to the coast. Excursion trains quickly grew in popularity during the 19th century and accounted for the rapid growth in seaside resorts such as Brighton and Blackpool. Travellers with more rarified tastes could also use the railways to penetrate once remote parts of Wales and Scotland – railways reached Mallaig and Kyle of Lochalsh during the 1890s, for instance. Hotels sprang up in secluded parts to cater for a new class of tourist interested in 'country' pursuits like angling or hill walking that for previous generations had been often part of everyday life. For the first time the countryside was becoming the playground of urban man.

Chapter Three

Living in the Countryside

Gold Hill in Shaftesbury comes close to many people's image of the quintessential village street. Thatch and mellow brick cottages huddle together along a steeply-cobbled twisting street. Shaftesbury is more a market town than a village but the countryside is never far away. Gold Hill remains as much a monument to the prime of pre-industrial Britain as those green hills of Dorset. Yet beneath the apparent simplicity of country life, so alluring to modern urban man, is a depth of history which few cities can match. There is a complexity too which belies the picture postcard image of places such as Gold Hill. And there is continuing change as 20th century man shapes the landscape for his needs. From villages to market towns, cottages to country houses, churches to pubs, this chapter highlights country life – past and present

Villages: the alluring yet complex antiquity of country life

A dream village reeks more of nostalgia than the farmyard. The dream is potent but unreal. There is no quintessential village. There never has been. In many parts of the British Isles there are not even villages at all. The hamlet is the characteristic form of rural settlement for much of Britain; and in the hills and mountains even hamlets are secondary to a scattering of individual farmsteads.

Each settlement, whether village or hamlet, tells its own story. The clues are visible in position and shape, architecture and agriculture. Its very name can indicate age and original function. The longevity of settlement over much of the British Isles remains evident alongside 20th century phenomena as diverse as 'gentrification' and dereliction.

Where a hamlet ends and a village begins is as difficult to define as where a village ends and a town begins. It is not simply a question of size: what would now be classed as a hamlet in strictly population terms – fewer than 200 people – once would have been regarded as a village. A more satisfactory, and subtle, yardstick is that of the services and buildings which each community can support.

A church, school and craftsmen such as a blacksmith were an integral part of a village yet beyond the scope of a hamlet. A village was therefore largely self-supporting with only the weekly trip to the local market town required for trade. But if this traditional conception of a village is to be fulfilled today it requires a far greater population than it did 100 years ago, let alone before then.

With a population of 1000 people it might just be possible to maintain a single-form primary school but it would need 2500 people to ensure sufficient support for a doctor, shop, pub and bus services. Some villages may be luckier and, blessed by richness of either setting or inhabitants, be able to support adequate services on smaller numbers. But can less favoured villages grow much beyond 2500 people without losing their traditional character?

It is an academic question. The traditional character of villages has changed already and changed irreparably: they are no longer necessarily dependent on the land. There are villages now which live on tourism, villages which house mostly commuters or weekenders, even villages with 'light' industry. Yet apart

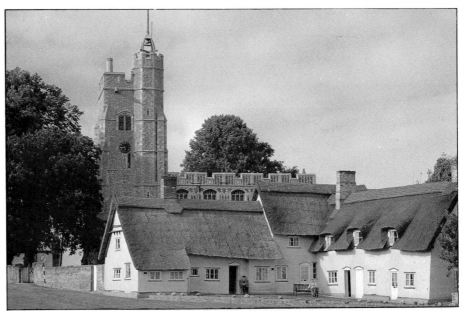

Village idyll: thatched cottages, Perpendicular church and green at Cavendish, Suffolk

Market town: the market-place (here with a fair) at the heart of Richmond, North Yorkshire

from the special case of fishing communities it was the land which not only gave life to all villages but also shaped the fundamental differences between types of rural communities.

Food, water, shelter and security have been the motivating forces of all communities ever since rudimentary advances in his primitive agriculture first enabled prehistoric man to settle in one place (hence 'settlement') for any length of time. And the form of agriculture he practised largely dictated the nature of the settlements in which man lived.

Quite how agriculture developed within the British Isles is far from fully understood and the subject of sometimes arcane dispute among academics. It used to be thought that arable or crop farming was predominant only in the lowlands of

southern and eastern Britain. But archaeological research and aerial photography over the last 30 years have demonstrated that quite extensive tracts of upland Scotland, Wales and the south-west peninsula of England were arable land in prehistoric times.

Geology, climate and the varying skills of the peoples who occupied different parts of the British Isles have all contributed to considerable agricultural diversity. Consequently this complexity – and, indeed, mystery – is reflected in the nature of rural settlements.

Two broad conclusions can be made, although each is subject to detailed qualifications and numerous exceptions:
1. Arable farming is more widespread in the lowland areas of the British Isles; pastoral farming is most common in the

Showpiece village: Lacock, Wiltshire, grew around the gates of an abbey, later a country house

ance of such factors as flat land, natural fertility and water supply. Thus what attracted the Romans to a particular site often attracted the Saxons and the Danes when they came to colonise the land in the centuries before the Norman Conquest. Professor W.G. Hoskins, author of *The Making of the English Landscape*, believes that many thriving villages still stand on sites first chosen by Bronze Age or Neolithic farmers.

These are most likely to be those on hill tops, sufficiently high above the forests for both protection and primitive agriculture. However it is now far from certain that Neolithic and Bronze Age settlements were confined to hills such as Salisbury Plain, the North and South Downs or the Cotswolds. Aerial photography in the past 20 years has revealed hundreds of lowland sites in the valley of the Warwickshire Avon, the Nene in Northamptonshire and the Trent.

Is it likely that prehistoric settlements existed only where they were later abandoned? The answer lies buried beneath the fabric of villages that have survived. Only unsuccessful settlements are generally traced archaeologically and even then the stone of Roman settlements is detected more readily than the wood and thatch of earlier communities.

Claims that some villages must have existed in the same place since prehistoric times are therefore plausible, but as yet unproven. It is the Domesday survey, a mammoth stock-taking of their newly-conquered lands completed by the Normans in 1086, that provides the first indisputable record of rural antiquity. But by then many, if not most, of the villages recorded in the Domesday book were already several hundred years old. Their names are the clues to their age and history.

Most place-names predate early documentary records of settlements, such as Domesday, and thus are often the only evidence available for reconstructing the ebb and flow of history across the landscape. Roman, Saxon, Celtic and Scandinavian names can all be identified within the British Isles, although few have escaped a degree of corruption as spellings and pronunciations have changed over the centuries.

This corruption means that names which are now identical may have had very different origins. Nevertheless scholars have established some general principles that have greatly increased understanding of the Dark Ages. The suffixes -*ley*, -*hurst* and *holt*, for instance, all indi-

upland areas of the North and West.
2. Villages are most characteristic of arable areas; hamlets and scatterings of individual farmsteads predominate in pastoral regions.

The reason for this difference is simple enough. Pastoral farming needs land more than it needs people and cannot support the larger concentrations of people found in the villages of predominantly arable areas. (Before mechanisation arable farming *required* relatively large numbers of people to pool their resources, especially at harvest time.)

Obviously geology and the fertility of the soil were important factors in determining these differences in agriculture and therefore settlement. Geography has also influenced the location of settlements, regardless of their size or form.

The defensive nature of hill forts was mentioned in the preceding chapter but settlements are also found at passes between hills, fords, bridging points and natural crossroads.

Another prerequisite for success was a natural source of water. The village pond or the well upon the green may now seem no more than a picturesque curiosity in places like Finchingfield, Essex, and Ashmore, Dorset, but they were once the very basis of the village's existence. Not even a community as powerful as Old Sarum, the precursor of modern Salisbury, could survive its lack of natural water.

Is it any wonder then that so many villages have such ancient antecedents? It is only the agricultural revolution of this century that has lessened the import-

Town and country: the Pennine mill town of Hebden Bridge, W. Yorkshire (above) and the fishing community of Robin Hood's Bay, N. Yorkshire (below)

Border country: the planned 18th century village of Blanchland, Northumberland (above) and the softer charms of Cardington, Shropshire (below)

cate the former existence of clearings in the woodland established by Saxon farmers as they pushed back the frontiers of the forests. A common Scandinavian equivalent in northern and eastern England is -*thwaite*, also meaning a clearing. Saxon and Scandinavian elements often take the form of prefixes and suffices – see glossary of some common place-names on page 42.

The Domesday picture was one of an overwhelmingly rural England – which is all it covered – with just one in ten of its $1\frac{1}{2}$ million population living in what could loosely be called towns. The village was the basis of English life and many, perhaps most, villages on the map of England today existed by the time of Domesday. There were exceptions, most notably in the northern counties more sketchily covered by the survey and those destined to be in the forefront of the Industrial Revolution.

There were also villages which would grow into market towns or great cities like Birmingham or Liverpool. And there were villages recorded in the Domesday survey which would die and that survive today only as names of individual farms, churches or at best hamlets. Some 2,000 sites of deserted villages have been identified in England alone (see page 48).

Coastal villages are often more recent than inland ones – it was only in the 15th century, for instance, that improved building techniques enabled large-scale construction of quays and jetties. Nevertheless, for England especially, the pattern of rural settlement was largely established 1000 years ago. And it is neither accident nor divine intervention that the church is invariably the oldest surviving building in a village: it was constructed with the best materials and attention which the villagers could muster. The 12th, 13th and 15th cen-

turies were particularly notable for church building.

More generally the higher the social scale, the better was the quality of building and therefore the older it is likely to be. But the prosperity of the Tudor years also enabled humbler dwellings such as farmhouses to be rebuilt in stone sturdy enough to survive to the present day.

This period of 'the great rebuilding' as W.G. Hoskins called it, when the vernacular regional styles of architecture were established, came later to northern Britain. But the English village at least, with its farmhouses, cottages and possibly school and almshouses, was still shaped more by the 200 years from about 1550 than any other period in its long history. Hoskins writes: 'Before that time life had been hard and comfortless, with little or no margin to spare beyond the necessities of living: what little there was went to the adornment and beautification of the parish church. After that time we witness the break-up of the village community, the degradation of most of the rural population and the flight into the towns.'

The 'degradation' of the rural population in Ireland was more a consequence of famine than the Industrial Revolution. But the development of Irish villages was always somewhat apart from that of the rest of the British Isles, even compared to Scotland with which it shares a Celtic tradition. This tradition saw agriculture and rural settlement based on large farmsteads or small hamlets. Irish villages therefore grew more slowly than their English counterparts and indeed it was the great English 'plantation' movement beginning in the 17th century that saw the first sustained growth of farming villages – often built close to the gates of a local landlord's estate or demesne.

In Scotland rural development was also somewhat different to that of England. The dominant theme in the 19th century was not so much the inroads of the industrial revolution (which were largely confined to the central lowlands) but the 'clearances' in the highlands. Sometimes people were shipped overseas – the island of Rhum, for instance, was totally deserted to make way for sheep farming and the population transported to the Canadian prairies. Sometimes they were settled on the coast in new fishing villages such as Golspie or Kyleakin.

Generally, however, it was the industrial revolution that shook the foundations of rural life. But the process of change has continued into the 20th century. More mechanisation means that fewer people are required to work on the farm. Fishing has also declined.

Villages must therefore find new roles if they are to survive. Some are favoured by their location, becoming either tourist attractions (such as Clovelly and Polperro in Cornwall, or Bourton-on-the-Water in Gloucestershire) or commuter bases around major conurbations (such as Hathersage in the Peak District near Sheffield and Hutton Rudby at the foot of the Cleveland Hills near Teesside). Even then a price can be paid for survival in terms of the so-called 'gentrification' style of modernisation which can destroy traditional rural character.

Smaller or less favoured communities can simply die, however. Because there is insufficient work on the land, young people start drifting to towns or larger villages. Because the population is falling, shops close, bus routes are abandoned and the population falls still further. A parish council can no longer be maintained and a more distant local authority decides it can no longer main-

The 17th century market hall at Ledbury, Herefordshire

The 18th century 'model village' of Milton Abbas, Dorset

tain the village school or health clinic.

The scenario is a familiar one; Scotland, for instance, lost its parish councils as long ago as 1929. And so public services such as schools and health clinics are channelled increasingly into 'villages' of 5,000 people or more where they are economically 'viable'. Almost inevitably such communities become increasingly urban in character. The consequences of designating villages for growth thus can be as profound for the chosen villages as those which are not chosen.

Yet it is facile to imagine that nostalgia can turn back clocks as well as minds. Most villages were made by man for an agricultural role that is no longer necessary. But as caring communities villages can still have a living role in impersonal 20th century Britain. Their size and traditions encourage a spirit of communal activity whether it be focussed upon the church or pub, women's institute meetings or cricket on the village green. Villages can continue to offer this timeless sense of community, as well as the physical ambience of the past, if only man fights to save what his forebears once struggled to create.

Market towns: trade supplants defence as the factor for success

It is only since the middle of the last century that a majority of the British people has lived in towns. Even today many towns are rooted more in the countryside than the industrial revolution. Market towns are as integral a part of the rural scene as villages, with their very names embedded in the language – not just the Market Harboroughs and Market Draytons but the Chipping Nortons and Chipping Sodburys, for 'chipping' comes from the Anglo-Saxon 'cheapen' meaning to buy.

Towns have not always had this function, however. Protection was a greater motivating force initially, as in the creation of many hill-top settlements and walled towns. It was the Romans who established towns on the face of England and in many cases the urban roots went sufficiently deep to survive Rome's decline. Although the Saxons were once regarded as primarily farmers, it is now known that urban life continued in towns such as Lincoln and Canterbury through the Saxon centuries. Even the Scandinavian *burhs* or boroughs established during the 9th century invariably had Saxon foundations; Derby, Nottingham and Stamford, for instance, were all active

The 16th century carved market cross at Chichester, West Sussex: the finest in Britain

towns before Danish settlers arrived.

Many *burhs*, whether Scandinavian or Saxon, retained a defensive or military character but increasingly they developed as administrative and trading centres. The Scandinavian influence was evident in fostering trade particularly around the Irish Sea, but the commercial spirit also surfaced in the Wessex kingdom of southern England where in the early 10th century Edward the Elder, son of Alfred the Great ordered that buying and selling should only take place in the presence of a town 'reeve' or elder representing the crown. It was only a short step to the selling of charters through which most market towns established themselves.

Barnstaple in Devon claims the oldest charter – dating back to 930 – but it was during the 300 years after the Norman Conquest that the trade in charters was most brisk. Kings, and occasionally monasteries and noblemen, raised money by selling rights of self-government to boroughs in the form of charters. Among the most important of these rights was the permission to hold a market, usually on a weekly basis. And the ability of a town to trade successfully, rather than as previously to defend itself, then determined prosperity and even survival.

Charters could not guarantee success. Devon, for instance, had 69 medieval boroughs in addition to Barnstaple. Many foundered, with only an unusually wide street, as at South Zeal, remaining to indicate former glory as a market-place. Towns could not prosper in defi-

ance of geography. Yet often what was good for trade were the same factors that had assured military success: a position controlling a pass or estuary, a bridging or fording point of a river, a natural geographical crossroads. Many market towns thus developed around military strongholds, such as castles, to serve their needs and to shelter under their protection; Arundel, Barnard Castle, Launceston and Ludlow are good examples of such towns. Sometimes it was a monastery or abbey around which a town developed as at Abingdon, Bury St. Edmunds and Evesham.

Most of Britain's cathedral cities are in fact also market towns, their religious and commercial activities long intertwined. Quite small towns, such as Helmsley in North Yorkshire, have a church overlooking the market-place. Church bells used to be rung to summon people to market as well as to pray and market crosses were built to invoke God's blessing upon the trade of a town. The finest remaining examples of such crosses are at Chichester and Malmesbury.

Precisely why market-places took different forms nobody really knows. A location along a main road, as at Marlborough in Wiltshire, makes it more likely that the market takes place in a greatly-widened thoroughfare rather than a separate square. Market towns on the coast are almost inevitably centred upon the harbour, although they need a hinterland to have grown beyond fishing villages. The nature of goods to be traded was another factor, livestock needing more room than farm produce. In practice a number of factors usually coalesced but whatever these were it was invariably the market-place which shaped the town.

The location of market-places at the heart of towns has made them vulnerable in the 20th century. Market squares have become parking lots, market crosses roundabouts; medieval market halls, where they have survived redevelopment schemes, shudder as juggernauts manoeuvre around them. Yet many market towns still provide buildings of great architectural distinction and their general prosperity remains based on their traditional role as a centre for trade. Often, too, the centre of the town's activity is the market-place itself. Livestock markets may be fewer but for one day a week at least 20th century wares are sold beneath the shadow of, say, a 17th century market hall in a 11th century market square.

The village pond: the teeming life above and below – the still waters

For many rural communities the village pond has often been as much a part of the local scene as the church, pub and green. In many cases, as the original source of water, it was the very basis of a village's existence. Sadly, not all villages have preserved their ponds. Over the years, their usefulness outlived, many have been condemned through neglect to become the last, weed-choked resting places for unwanted bedsteads and rusty bicycle frames. But in the past two decades the village pond has undergone a modest renaissance. In a number of villages, volunteers have cleared old ponds and restored to them the rich aquatic life that thrives in still waters.

Living within this enclosed order are not only the instantly visible creatures, like the familiar mallard, the drake easily recognisable with its glossy, bottle green head, but also the teeming denizens of the secret world beneath the surface.

Forming the foliage of this underwater jungle are various kinds of pondweed – Canadian pondweed, curled pondweed, grasswrack pondweed – and other aquatic plants such as waterwort, autumnal starwort and occasional rarities such as the holly-leaved naiad.

Outwardly still and serene, the pond seethes with life down below. Fierce carnivorous dragonfly nymphs, water scorpions and great diving beetles prowl the green depths in search of freshwater shrimps (actually relatives of the sandhopper) and tadpoles of the common frog. Ram's horn snails and great pond snails crawl among the submerged plant stems, browsing on algae with their rasping tongues, and are themselves preyed upon by the horse leech. Freshwater swan mussels rest on the bed of the pond.

The tadpoles hatch in May from the mass of jelly-like toad or frogs' spawn laid in early spring and, until they leave the pond in July as tiny, fully-formed toads or frogs, the tadpoles will share the water with another amphibian, the crested newt. This splendid jam-jar dinosaur with the polka-dotted orange belly can reach a length of 7in (18cm) or more, and is the largest of our three native newts. (The others are the smooth newt and the palmate newt.)

Not all fish can tolerate the torpid waters of a pond, but one that does is the diminutive three-spined stickleback. In spring the pugnacious male stickleback turns bright red and builds a nest in which the female lays her eggs. The male remains on guard at the nest until the fry are hatched.

The surface of the pond – the great divide separating the underwater life from that in the light and air above – is itself rapidly colonised by the flowers of yellow water-lily and water crowfoot, by floating carpets of duckweed made up of thousands of tiny individual plants, and insects such as the pond skater, a creature so light it can skim across the water without piercing the surface-film. The pond skater is a carnivorous bug, but it is

content with a diet of flies and other insects; whereas the water boatman, which lies on its back and rows with its hind legs, will also attack tadpoles and even small fish.

Village ponds are usually too small and too close to human habitation to make a suitable haunt for mammals, though the bank vole may build its grassy nest under the roots of a bankside tree. But a pond is ideal for water birds such as the coot and moorhen, which often become quite tame, and nest safely in the more inaccessible beds of reedmace – the plant with tall seed-heads like brown velvet sausages which most people call by their traditional country name of bulrushes.

Left: the surface tranquillity of the pond at Chiddingfold, Surrey

The coot and moorhen are easily identified: the coot by its bald white forehead; the moorhen by its sealing-wax beak and shrill, explosive 'prrk', uttered as it swims, head and tail jerking like a mechanical toy, among the water plants. Otherwise, both species have many characteristics in common; running fast on land, diving well, and flying low over the water trailing their feet behind them.

In late afternoon and early evening from May onwards, when mayflies are dancing over the water, the house martins which nest under the eaves of village buildings grace the pond with their acrobatic swooping flight and liquid silvery chatter. Britain's largest mayfly bears the scientific title of *Ephemera danica* – a lovely name for this ephemeral insect whose adult life lasts no more than three or four days. Anglers know it as green drake.

Mayflies and dragonflies all live through their larval stage under the water, when they are known as nymphs. But when the dragonfly nymph is fully grown it climbs from the water and clings to a reed stem while it sloughs off its larval skin. Some two hours later, its wings hardened and fully expanded, it takes to the air as a lustrous adult insect like the male emperor dragonfly in our illustration. The emperor belongs to the group of dragonflies known as hawkers. It has a wingspan of over 4in (10cm), may reach speeds of up to 30mph when pursuing insects or when alarmed, and can even fly backwards.

With its life cycle divided equally between the elements of air and water, the dragonfly is in many ways a symbol for the life of the village pond. And it is pleasing to think that these man-made

Key to illustration: 1 Emperor dragonfly 2 Green Drake Mayfly 3 House Martin 4 Coot 5 Moorhen 6 Reedmace 7 Bank Vole 8 Water Boatman 9 Pond Skater 10 Duck-weed 11 Water Crowfoot 12 Yellow Waterlily 13 Male Three-spined Stickleback 14 Female Stickleback and Nest 15 Smoth Newt 16 Crested Newt 17 Common Frog 18 Tadpole 19 Frog's spawn 20 Swan Mussel 21 Great Pond Snail 22 Ram's Horn Snail 23 Freshwater Shrimp 24 Dragonfly Nymph 25 Great Diving Beetle 26 Holly-leaved Naiad 27 Waterwort 28 Autumnal Starwort 29 Canadian Pondwood 30 Curled Pondwood 31 Grasswrack Pondweed 32 Mallard Duck and Drake 33 Water Scorpion 34 Horse Leech 35 Arrowhead.

habitats can harbour an insect whose ancestors were flying 300 million years before man had even set foot in Britain

Country churches: the embodiment of rural life and rural pride

Look at any village, and almost certainly it will be dominated by the parish church, the centrepiece, perhaps, of village green, manor house and pub. It is also almost certain to be the oldest building, however drastically it may have been rebuilt or 'restored' through the centuries. Only in the 20th century has its pivotal role been eroded.

Traditionally the church was the forum of the parish to which all came for secular as well as for religious purposes. Markets were held beside the church and dramas within it. As in Victorian times,

when elaborate town halls were built, so in earlier ages the church was the embodiment of community pride in addition to religious devotion. Thus churches can be far larger than necessary for the size of the parish, let alone the congregation. The great churches of Lavenham in Suffolk and Northleach or Chipping Campden in the Cotswolds were built and lavishly decorated from the profits of the wool trade, for instance.

Step inside a parish church and you immediately have an intimate view of a community's history. The feudal structure of the place is quickly assimilated; the aristocracy had comfortable private galleries or even private chapels, some-

times with their own fireplaces and entrance; the squirearchy sat in comfortable family pews but often erected vast monuments to lives that cannot all have been as charitable and holy as the inscriptions would suggest; and the humbler people who sat on plain wooden pews have mere tombstones to mark their personal tragedies and triumphs.

The word parish comes originally from the Romans, to whom it signified a large region or province. The earliest evidence of Christian worship in England is to be found in excavated Roman villas. But many churches were built on ancient pagan sites; circular churches or churchyards are particularly associated

Left: a church sale at All Saints, Biddenden, Kent – still very much the centre of a thriving village
Above: St James's of Chipping Campden, one of the most magnificent of the Gloucestershire 'wool churches' built from the profits of the medieval cloth trade
Below: St Peter and St Paul, Lavenham, Suffolk, set in one of the most unspoilt medieval towns in England, and also a 'wool church' of the 15th century

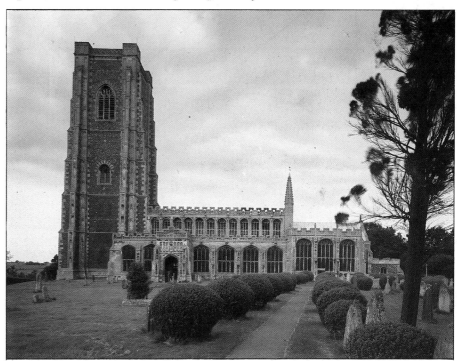

with pagan origins.

Christianity returned to England, after the departure of the Romans, from the Celtic North and West. The oldest post-Roman christian sites are known to be in Scotland, Wales, Ireland and the south-west peninsula of England, yet hardly any buildings survive from those times. The buildings simply were neither strong enough to withstand the elements for so long nor remote enough to escape attack.

The great majority of the parish churches of England were built after the Norman Conquest, but many had Saxon foundations. And from the earliest times the church, and more particularly the church porch, played a key role in the community: marriages and baptisms of course, but also trade between farmers, was carried on there. The churchyard was the site for fairs and dances; the church bells the signal to prayer or an alert in case of danger.

In the less prosperous uplands of Britain parishes tend to be large and churches simple – the rectangular building with the simple open belfry, for instance. Since settlement is often scattered the church, too, often stands by itself.

All parts of the British Isles have experienced religious turbulence which has left its mark on the countryside: the ruined monasteries of England; the Scottish churches abandoned after the Calvinist reformation (although burial grounds were often still used); the proliferation of churches of different faiths in Wales and Ireland.

Whatever the faith the church played an important cultural role in a community. The priest was for many centuries the most educated man in a village and many village schools were run by the clergy. The church building itself is also a living testament to the outstanding crafts of its villagers – masons, wood carvers and painters – who contributed to the richness and individuality of the most dominant building of the area.

Nine hundred years of church architecture. *The traditional country church is usually an amalgam of styles: Victorian stained glass, a Norman font, medieval carvings in the choirstalls and seventeenth-century monuments in the chapel. This is part of its charm. It is also a record through the centuries of craftsmanship, and a repository of the history of style*

Crenellated parapet with Crocketed Pinnacles.

Perpendicular tower pinnacled, and with its belfry windows and louvre-boards. Towers became indicators for the wealth of the region; Somerset has some of the most perfect examples.

Corbel often carved or moulded.

Limestone roofing slates.

North Aisle.

Nave main body of the church where the congregation sit.

Blind niche originally designed to hold a statue, many of which were destroyed in the Reformation.

Early English pew bench seat, often with beautifully carved bench-ends.

Clerestory dating mostly from the 15th century. A way of getting more light into the nave.

Hammer-beam roof most characteristic of East Anglian churches and most elaborate kind of roof. Hammer-beam projects into the church, often supporting vertical arches.

Jacobean pulpit octagonal, wooden. Stone pulpits are rare.

Choir often with most spectacular examples of medieval wood carving.

Rood screen so called because of the great rood or crucifix above it. It divides the nave from the choir and is mostly found in carved wood, some with painted panels.

Chancel arch disappeared at the end of the 14th century, replaced by rood screen.

Decorated window dating from the 13th century, and continuing into the first part of the 14th.

Brass usually found on floor or wall of church, marking spot where person buried. More brasses in England than in the whole of Europe.

Perpendicular window.

Norman door round arch, often lavishly decorated, sometimes with the characteristic zig-zag pattern.

Norman font usually square or circular and often with striking carving. Found at the west end of the church.

Porch usually on the south side of the church; important as a protection for the door, and as a place where many of the church services, such as baptism, were performed.

Chapel often constructed by rich landowning families for their private use.

Tie-beam roof large horizontal main beam in timber roof.

Reredos a backing for the altar in painted wood or stone. Underneath the east window and shaped to take the figures of the twelve apostles.

Georgian memorial at the end of the 17th century marble took over from alabaster and the style was classical.

Right: the round knapped flint towers of East Anglia are one of its most characteristic features. There are still some 119 surviving examples in Norfolk and 41 in Suffolk. This charming one at Fritton in Suffolk has the added attraction of a thatched roof. Below right: the exquisitely vaulted rood-screen in the church of St Andrew, Bramfield, Suffolk is one of the best of its kind in the county

Chancel part of the nave which contains the altar.

Buttress support on an outside wall.

Altar focal point of the church. Before the Reformation altars were built in stone, afterwards in wood.

Altar rail introduced after the Reformation to protect the altar when screens were disappearing. Usually in wood, sometimes wrought iron in the 17th and 18th century.

Far right: detail from the rood-screen of St Helen's, Ranworth, Norfolk. Medieval craftsmanship in all its original colour and richness, with painted figures of saints and the twelve apostles. Right: the monument to Mrs Arthur Coke by Nicholas Stone at Bramfield, Suffolk is a piece of superb Renaissance sculpture

Architectural gems of country churches

Late Norman carving: seen at its most magnificent, c. 1170, at St. Mary, Iffley, Oxfordshire. The rounded doorway arch, with several recessed arches, sports the typical Norman zig-zag pattern or chevron

Beakhead decoration: St. Peter, Tickencote, Leics., has the most splendid and massive chancel arch in England. Dating from 1160–70, it has the characteristically repetitive Norman beakhead decoration

Door knocker: 12th century bronze door knocker or sanctuary ring from St. Peter, Dormington, Herefordshire. It was originally used by those claiming the ancient rite of sanctuary within the church. The ring is held in the mouth of a demon head

Two roofs from the Perpendicular period: top: sumptuous 16th century fan-vaulting from St. Andrew, Cullompton, Devon. Below: the double hammerbeam angel roof of the nave of St. Wendreda, March, Cambridgeshire. A speciality of East Anglian churches, this one has nearly 200 angels

Corbel: there are some 80 corbels on this perfectly-preserved Norman church, St. Mary and St. David at Kilpeck, Herefordshire. The mournful-looking dog and child's view of a rabbit have strong Celtic influences, but look extraordinarily modern

Misericords: the tip-up seats, usually in the choir stalls of a church which are frequently decorated on the underside with satirical carvings. The wood carvers had great freedom of choice and subjects in this church, St Laurence in Ludlow, Shropshire, range from animals and birds to feminine headdress. Dating from the 15th century

Murals: they could often transform a nave or chancel of a church, and in the case of this church, St. Peter and St. Paul at Chaldon, Surrey, the whole west wall. The subject, 17ft long and 11ft high, is the Ladder of Salvation, c. 1200, and is the only remaining mural on this subject in England. The painting, in dark reds and yellow ochres, is divided horizontally by a band of cloud, being the dividing line between the souls who are saved and those who are struggling below in the torments and fires of hell

Monuments: an elaborate post-Reformation one is the Fettiplace tomb (top) at St. Mary, Swinbrook, Oxfordshire. There are two monuments, 1613 and 1686, commemorating the Fettiplace family in tiers of three. The earlier one shows the figures reclining in a rather rigid pose; in the later one they are lolling in a much more realistic manner. Above: the church of St. Peter and St. Paul in Lingfield, Surrey, contains the Cobham family tombs, exotic and medieval monuments dedicated to the founder and his family. The feet in this picture are those of the effigy of the first lord Cobham, one of the original Knights of the Garter

English Gothick: the original Norman church of St. John the Evangelist at Shobdon, Herefordshire was transformed in 1753 into a delightful white and gold stage-set piece after the style of Horace Walpole's 'Strawberry Hill Gothick'. Lord Bateman, lord of the manor and friend of Walpole, commissioned an unknown architect to direct this rococo change. The Bateman family pew is complete with fireplace and has its own separate entrance

Arts and Crafts church: St. Andrew, Roker Park, Co. Durham, c. 1906, architected by E. S. Prior, has carpets by William Morris, tapestry by Burne-Jones and choir stalls, pulpit and lectern by Ernest Gimson

Font: this magnificent stone font at St. Mary Magdalene, Eardisley, Herefordshire, belongs in style to a local school of carving, c. 1150. The subject is the Harrowing of Hell. The plaited motif above and interlacing pattern below are typically Norman designs

Bench-ends: St. Margaret, Cley-next-the-Sea, Norfolk. The tops of these ends are called poppy-heads, probably derived from *puppis* meaning figurehead. This fierce primitive little figure represents the ancient rite of the sacrifice of the Grass King

The Country Pub: from alehouses for the locals to inns for travellers

The country pub is an integral part of rural life, rivalling the church as a focus of village activity. In the more mobile and secular 20th century it is rarely difficult to detect which institution is prospering more. The church may have retained a greater hold over its rural congregations than those in the towns, but it is to the pubs that people drive on Sundays. You do not see country inns appealing for funds to repair roofs.

Yet it was not always so. Inns have had a chequered life in the 2000 years since alehouses were recorded in the British Isles. The Romans introduced wine (and also inn-signs) but ale was the indigenous drink for most of Britain, as it has remained through to the present-day preoccupation with 'real ale'. Usually ale was brewed and consumed at home but by medieval times every community had at least one alehouse where ale was brewed from malted barley.

This was usually just a cottage which advertised its presence by hanging an evergreen branch or 'bush' from a pole above the doorway. Every year the court leet of the manor appointed an 'ale-connor' to test quality. Alehouses or taverns on well-used tracks might cater for the traveller, providing a meal or a bed, but mainly they were simply for drinking and met only local needs.

Wealthy travellers would seek out the manor house where there would always be a traditional welcome. The poorer travellers were mainly pilgrims or traders. By the 12th and 13th centuries thousands of pilgrims were setting out every year for Canterbury, Walsingham, St. David's or Iona; some even under-took the arduous journey to Rome or Jerusalem. These pilgrims were helped by the monasteries whose 'Rule of Hospitality' laid down that all who asked should be given board and lodging. Simple hospices were provided, some of which still survive such as the *Pilgrim's Rest* outside Battle Abbey in Sussex and the 13th century *The Star* at Alfriston, Sussex. Monasteries also had their own brewhouses and made fine quality ales as well as some wine from home-grown grapes and mead from honey and water. In Ireland oats and malted barley were distilled to make usquebaugh which became a national drink.

The dissolution of the monasteries under Henry VIII meant that between 1536 and 1540 their hospices were also destroyed or acquired by noblemen. Alternative accommodation then had to be made for travellers and many new taverns and inns were built, sometimes on the site of the old hospice. *Ye Olde Bell* at Hurley in Berkshire is a good example. The *New Inn* at Gloucester is also on the site of an old hospice and is one of the few surviving examples of 16th century inn with a first-floor open gallery from which guests could watch performances by itinerant players in the courtyard below.

Elizabethan inns followed this pattern but the galleries, where they still exist, have now been enclosed to make draught-proof corridors – such galleries can still be traced in *The Bell* at Thetford, Norfolk, and *The White Horse* at Romsey, Hampshire. However, new building could not meet the increasing demand as people began to travel more. Many manor houses were therefore converted into inns, such as *The Oxenham Arms* at South Zeal in Devon and *The Lygon Arms* at Broadway in the Cotswolds (although in the 17th and 18th centuries the latter was known as *The Whyte Hart*).

Horse traffic greatly increased in the 17th century and posthouses were needed where horses could be changed. After 1663 when the first Turnpike Act was passed, roads rapidly improved and stage coaches brought new custom to the inns. *The Haycock* at Wansford, Cambridgeshire on the Great North Road (see overleaf) was built to meet this need with an extensive courtyard and stabling for 150 horses. At this time strong ale was still brewed but to this was added a heavy 'double beer' and 'small beer' which was so light that it became a family drink. Wines and cognac were imported, mainly from France, for wealthier customers. And the Scots had now started to distil whisky, the equivalent of the Irish usquebaugh, for local consumption.

The new roads also led to a further increase in trade, particularly the flourishing wool trade. Packhorses carried fleeces to the weavers and took cloth to the towns for sale. It is not surprising to find that Kendal, which was a collecting centre for wool from the fell sheep of the Lake District, has two old inns called *The Fleece* and *The Woolpack*. The *Black Swan* at Helmsley, North Yorkshire, and *The Swan* at Lavenham, Suffolk, (see overleaf) also have packhorse origins.

Inn building and conversion were given further impetus early in the 18th century with the establishment of a postal service throughout Great Britain. With mail coaches as well as private post-chaises now on the road the heyday of the coaching inn had begun.

Many Tudor taverns were accordingly enlarged, refurbished and given an imposing Georgian frontage; examples include *The Bear* at Devizes, Wiltshire, *The White Horse* at Dorking, Surrey, and *The Royal George* at Knutsford, Cheshire. Georgian inns became social centres as well as resting places for travellers. Local people came to the inn to collect their correspondence and leave letters for the mail coach. Some inns added assembly rooms for concerts and dances. Many magistrates courts were held in inns.

It was a period of heavy drinking. Porter appeared – a drink made from a blend of beer and ale much favoured in Ireland. Stout was brewed using roasted barley as an ingredient. Gin was made in vast quantities, though mainly in towns. A duty on French wines and cognac led

Santon Bridge: the simple tavern, as here in the Lake District, is the most typical of inns

The traditional male world of the old-style pub: for some the taste for real ale was a 1970s fashion, for others it never went away

to importations from Portugal and port became a national favourite. The duty on cognac, however, led the English to bring in whisky from Scotland.

The coaching inns were used by everybody, although coachmen and servants naturally had their own humbler quarters. Even royalty patronised inns. In 1835 Princess Alexandrina Victoria, with her mother the Duchess of Kent, dined and slept at *The Haycock* in Wansford on their way to York.

But by the time Victoria had come to the throne two years later the railway boom was well under way and beginning to entice custom away from the roads. New inns were built alongside railway stations but the old coaching inns were hard hit. Within a few years many had fallen into disrepair and closed. Even *The Haycock* surrendered its licence. However, some inns in tourist areas of northern England, Scotland and Ireland flourished. Their owners sent horse-drawn carriages to the nearest railway stations to collect patrons and their luggage, often for a stay of some days. The *Morritt Arms* at Greta Bridge in Teesdale, is a good example of such an inn.

The Industrial Revolution led to the rapid expansion of cities and some country inns were engulfed in urban development. Who would think that *The Curlers* in Byers Road, Glasgow had once been a country inn on the road through the Vale of Partick? It now caters for city dwellers, few of whom realise that in 1665 Charles II and his retinue played a curling match on a nearby pond and afterwards enjoyed the hospitality of the inn so much that the king issued a special Charter allowing it seven-day opening.

In the 1880s cycling became popular and many inns such as *The Anchor* at Ripley, Surrey put up the sign of the Cyclists Touring Club. Then followed the motor car and slowly the demand for roadside refreshment and accommodation grew once more. Old stables were converted into garages or pulled down to make room for car parks.

Between the wars old inns expanded and became 'hotels'; private houses were converted. In Ireland even some of the old castles were rebuilt or reconditioned. Kilkea Castle, the oldest in Ireland, is now a luxury hotel. So is Ashford Castle, on Lough Corrib. The Bishop's Palace at Holywood has become the *Culloden Hotel*. More typical of Ireland, and the more sparsely-populated lands of the North are simple alehouses or taverns, however. Many Irish bars are not even housed in special buildings, being attached to other shops such as grocers, drapers and, in at least one case, an undertaker's.

The great growth of car ownership in the last 30 years has had mixed effects. It has meant that people living several miles away can regard a pub as their 'local' and thus the increasing popularity of country inns has encouraged major brewing and hotel chains to extend their network into rural areas. Buildings have been preserved from decay, but not always with the best of taste. Individuality has also suffered, both in the variety of beers brewed and the loss of the owner-landlord of a 'free house' who could provide an atmosphere sometimes lacking if an inn is merely a link in a chain.

Despite all the changes, the tradition of the alehouse serving a local community continues. A few free houses remain where landlords retain the skills of keeping 'real' ale in the wood that were jeopardised by the moves to managers and keg beers. Major breweries are also increasingly sensitive to their customers' tastes. Roadhouses, motels and posthouses may be necessary for motorists in a hurry but it is the nostalgic, unhurried and apparently unchanging atmosphere of country inns that most people seek given the chance.

The Packhorse Inn: The Swan, Lavenham, Suffolk. *In Tudor times the inn was an important centre in every village, not only for travellers but for traders transporting goods. The woollen trade was by then well established and the making of cloth had been stimulated by Flemish weavers who had settled in a number of East Anglian villages. Lavenham in Suffolk was an important centre where the industry was carried on by rich merchants who exported cloth to Europe. They built fine houses, a Guildhall and a Wool Hall and as the trade expanded found the need for a centre where weavers from the villages of Lindsay and Kersey could bring their cloth. In the 17th century four old half-timbered houses were united for this purpose and provided with stables for packhorses. Thus the Swan Inn was born, later to become a coaching inn. Now it is part of a hotel chain and patronised mainly by tourists. These are often attracted to Suffolk partly by the oustanding medieval architecture of Lavenham of which The Swan itself is such a fine example*

The Coaching Inn: The Haycock, Wansford-in-England, Cambridge-shires. *During the 17th century traffic on the roads began to increase rapidly. Long distance coaches carrying passengers and mail had to change their horses at definite stages on the journey and the need for post-houses increased. To meet this demand alehouses or farms were sometimes rebuilt as inns. The Haycock at Wansford-in-England on the old Great North Road was built round existing courtyards where the old brewhouse is still to be seen. One yard had an open gallery (now enclosed to form a passage) of a kind often associated with Elizabethan taverns in towns. The coming of the railway reduced the volume of horse traffic and by 1887 the decline was complete with the inn becoming a farm. However, the advent of the motor car enabled the owner, Lord Fitz-william, to reopen as an inn again after a break of over 40 years despite a legal battle to secure a licence. Now it is by-passed by the modern A1*

Inn signs and their meaning

The idea of indicating a tavern or inn's existence by a sign outside its doors has been dated back to Roman times, but it only became at all widespread in the British Isles from the Middle Ages. Many derive from five broad categories.

Religion. Many inns date from medieval times and took their names from those given to abbey hospices. 'The Angel' honoured St Michael; 'The Salu-tation', the Annunciation of the Virgin Mary; 'The Anchor' was hope, described by St Paul as 'the anchor of the soul'; 'The Cross Keys', the emblem of St Peter. 'The Lamb and Flag' was the symbol of the Knights Templar pledged to protect pilgrims to the Holy Land. 'The Swan' was the emblem of innocence and 'The Seven Stars' represented the celestial crown. 'The George and Dragon', often shortened to 'The George', was a symbol of the Christian fight against evil. When a hospice was destroyed at the Dissolution and an inn was built on the site it was often called 'The New Inn'; such inns are usually about 400 years old.

Country life. The names of village inns often reflect farm life. 'The Plough' in England, 'Coulter's' in the Border country and 'Cornkist' in Scotland are symbols of cultivation, 'Sheaf and Sickle' of the harvest, and 'The Fleece' of sheep-shearing. 'The Maypole' is a symbol of the dance.

Crafts. Symbols of the craft guilds were used as inn signs. For instance, 'The Axe and Compass' (Carpenters), 'The Ram' (Clothworkers), 'The Three Tuns' (Vintners), 'The Boot' (Cobblers), 'The Masons Arms', 'The Weavers Arms' and 'The Smith's Arms'. Sometimes the alehouse or inn would also sell meat or bread. 'The Shoulder of Mutton' signi-fied the butcher, 'The Stone and Faggot' the baker.

Royalty. Many signs show respect for the monarchy. 'The Crown' is very common and royal badges often appear as 'The White Hart' (Richard II), 'The White Boar' (Richard III), 'The Blue Boar' (Henry VII). Also common are 'The Queen's Head', 'The King's Head' and 'The Feathers' (or 'Fleur-de-Lys'), badge of the Prince of Wales.

Sport. This has always been closely associated with British inns. 'The Bear' and 'The Bull' (bear-baiting and bull-baiting), 'The Bird in Hand' (falconry) plus some that speak for themselves – 'The Hare and Hounds', 'The Fox-hound' and 'The Cricketer's Arms'.

The country cottage: architectural riches amid the humblest dwellings

When the poets of the 18th century created their ideal of rustic simplicity they also focussed the attention of artists, landscape gardeners and architects on the visual merits of country cottages. For those who did not have to live in them they represented a dream of peace and honest toil: a pastoral picture of cows, milk maids and scented roses round the door. It made a pleasant contrast to squalor and tension in the growing cities.

The poets have moved on to other founts of inspiration, but to the ordinary city dweller a country cottage remains an ideal, often the ultimate ideal for retirement. It is interesting that cottages, however dilapidated, without drainage or mains water, with low beams to catch the heads of a taller generation, with rising damp, awkward stairs and several kinds of rot will often reach higher prices at auction than a new dwelling complying with every byelaw. The old cottagers happily leave for a new dry council house, while the new owners eagerly prepare to spend a small fortune to make the old place habitable.

In carrying out the improvements they should remember Oscar Wilde's words 'Innocence is like a peach, touch it and the bloom is gone'. For alone among domestic designs, cottages are unpretentious direct expressions of the builder's art. Often the builder was the owner, with help from his neighbours, but even if built by farmers or landowners the same precepts were followed.

Local knowledge dictated the best places to build: cottages are usually on sites that have been used and tested many times before. The healthiness of the area, the quality of the soil, the micro-climate, protection from high winds or flooding and convenient supplies of fuel and water all had to be considered. A good view was not important unless livestock had to be watched. Since work was so much harder in the past, time was valuable so cottages were built simply and durably.

Today one should marvel that it was possible to build low-cost houses in the 15th century that would not only be standing 500 years later but be a much sought-after home for people with a completely different life style. There were simpler dwellings, similar to wigwams, for the very poor but examples of these have not survived – many early 'cottages' are in fact the former homes of small farmers. Although fuel was more plentiful in the past, it still took valuable time to gather so heat insulation was an important factor in cottage design. The traditional mud and thatch cottage with its small windows has a much better standard of heat insulation than a contemporary house.

Cottages built before 1800 had to use local materials; transporting heavy materials along roads which were poor at best would have been too expensive. In early times there was a plentiful supply of wood, cheap and easy to use but as it became scarcer local stone began to be used or brick where this was not available. Fire was always a hazard, especially with thatched roofs, so the increasing affluence of the 16th and 17th centuries would probably have led to the increased use of stone and brick in any case. The use of local materials led to the development of local vernaculars and the regional designs so much admired today.

The hard granites of Cornwall, the north of Wales and Ireland, Cumbria and Scotland cannot be carved easily like the limestones from Wiltshire and Oxfordshire. It was fortunate for Britain that the stone areas lie in the parts that get the worst weather – the western half. In the south-east, which has little or no stone, it was possible to develop light timber frame buildings (the timber often imported from Scandinavia) covered with plaster rendering which could then be moulded into decorative forms, called pargetting. Technology was another factor in determining local variations, usually following the broad ethnic divisions of the country. Before the 19th century the population was much more static than it is today. The railways blurred regional differences by transporting building materials as well as people more easily around the country.

The traditional cottage, built as the home for an unlettered man and his family represents his feelings for home as a simple, well-proportioned space, fitting the surrounding landscape: a warm, often dark interior in contrast to the dazzling light of the fields on a hot summers day or the blasting winds of the winter. The cottage garden, much admired and copied since William Robinson and Gertrude Jekyll wrote about it at the end of the 19th century is a functional extension of the cottage way of life.

The cottage orné, designed by architects and landscape gardeners during the eighteenth and nineteenth centuries, took the most decorative forms of the traditional cottage and put them together with up-to-date methods of construction. But designed on the drawing board, not in the field, they often miss the vital quality of simplicity.

Later, Voysey and Lutyens among others were much impressed by the cottage styles and used them as an inspiration for their own domestic designs. Their influence was huge and dictated the design of the semi-detached style that formed the basis of the inter-war period suburban development in Britain that was something unique in Europe. Today, the teaching of Le Corbusier and other leaders of the modern movement have made homeliness an uncomfortable word for architects to use and so the cottage style has little influence on them. But the popularity of the cottage ideal remains unabated.

Intricate pargetting – plasterwork mouldings – at Much Wenlock, Shropshire

Cob cottages in Minehead, Somerset, with walls made from loam, chopped straw and gravel protected by rendering. Cheap, warm and up to 300 years old, they could be built easily by their owner

Carefully restored thatched limestone cottage in Milton, Wiltshire, dating from the 17th century. The chimney stacks are in brick as they would be too difficult to make in stone. The porch is added

17th century limestone cottage near Banbury, Oxfordshire. Originally single storied, it now has upper windows with a later brick chimney and porch: a lesson in how to change without destroying

Rendered 'clay bat' cottages in Melbourn, Cambridgeshire, made from thin blocks of yellow clay and straw cast in moulds, air dried and used like lightweight concrete blocks. Early 18th century

A terrace of 17th century cottages at King's Lynn, Norfolk, built with Snettisham sandstone under a local pantile roof. There are six different dates of window: the surviving original has lead lights

Late 18th century stone cottages in Heskett Newmarket, Cumbria, painted in the manner traditional to the area. Two of the original horizontally sliding windows, first made in Yorkshire, remain

Box-frame timber cottages in Blackstone, Sussex, of a type widely built from the 14th to 17th centuries. The steeply pitched roof reveals it was once thatched. Originally the windows were leaded

These late 18th century weatherboarded timber frame cottages in Mitcham, Surrey, are of a type once common in the villages that now form South London – the originals for the US 'colonial-style'

19th century stone cabin in Murroogh, Co Clare, Eire. The small windows face away from the sea and are primarily for ventilation. Light is provided by opening the door, originally just a straw mat

A terrace of 17th century fishermen's cottages at Porlock Bay, Somerset, built from boulders collected on the beach, here in the foreground. Its fat, rounded shape follows the landscape

18th century brick and flint cottage in Peppard, Oxfordshire, with its traditional cottage garden. The windows are painted in the old way with the opening sections in white and the outer frames in colour

A 20th century return to simplicity: pleasantly coloured corrugated iron roof with black weatherboarding for a cottage by Orford Castle in Suffolk. The factory-made windows show today's need for light

Change in the countryside: new life for redundant rural buildings

As rural industries have withered, many village buildings have become redundant: mills, maltings, oasts, barns, not to mention once essential service buildings such as schools, churches and railway stations. Must these buildings simply be demolished or left to rot, or can a new use be found for them?

In many cases it can. They are often eminently suitable, once local planners make the mental adjustment, for conversion into offices, museums, craft centres and, perhaps most frequently of all, housing. Over the past decade or so much of the threatened fabric of British villages has been rescued as the conservation movement gathered momentum. Conversion of old buildings to new uses has been most common in southern England, where the demand for housing is greatest. But it is spreading throughout the British Isles, especially to Scotland where there is still a wealth of mills, barns and crofts.

The thousands of old buildings that have been converted mostly owe their continued life not to government finance, but to the enthusiasm and hard cash of private individuals. Two bodies, however, merit commendation. The Civic Trust has encouraged the conservation movement in general and sensitive restoration in particular, notably through its stewardship of European Architectural Heritage Year in 1975; and the Landmark Trust has 'rescued' some startlingly diverse and historic buildings such as castles, a railway station, martello tower, mills, a fort, medieval halls and, in Cornwall, even an entire hamlet.

For individuals restoration offers the possibility of living in unusual and often architecturally distinguished dwellings; for rural communities the buildings at least have been saved from decay or death. But conversion to alternative uses can compound the problems of village life. A maltings that has been turned into flats (as at Beccles, Suffolk) or a textile mill that is now an antiques gallery (as at Malmesbury, Wiltshire) is less likely than ever to revert to its original and essential role – providing employment.

A few attempts are being made to redress the balance: in Exmoor, for instance, there is a scheme called the Small Industries Group which aims to encourage one or two-man businesses to set up in derelict rural buildings. But such schemes are few and tentative, so the conundrum remains: how to save old buildings without damaging even further village life? Here, very briefly, are some of the main types of redundant buildings – other than cottages – now being given a new lease of life.

Barns

Increased mechanisation and farm mergers have made many storage buildings such as barns superfluous. Indeed, whole farms have sometimes been converted as at Wytham, Oxfordshire, for housing or Culzean, Ayrshire, for a country park headquarters. Barns are especially suited to conversion, despite problems of insulation and drainage. An 18th century barn and listed building near Seaford, Sussex, is also being used as an 'interpretive centre' for a country park. Many have been converted into private housing where the main aesthetic problem is where to put the windows necessary for human (as opposed to animal) habitation without destroying their character. For King's Barn, at East Hendred, Berkshire, a Grade II listed building, the problem was solved by keeping windows small and high under the eaves on the street side with larger windows on the garden side to let in more light.

Oast houses

Oast houses, once used for roasting hops, are thick on the ground in Kent and Sussex and scattered more thinly elsewhere. Most date from Victorian times and many have been converted into striking homes. But sadly many conversions have paid scant regard to the unique shape and working heritage of oasts. As with barns, roofs and windows pose the greatest difficulties; tall and narrow windows are generally the most aesthetically successful, dormer windows the most disastrous.

Mills and maltings

Three types of mill have attracted conversion: 19th century textile mills, which are common in Lancashire and Yorkshire; earlier watermills that had been used for grinding corn; and, perhaps most romantic of all, windmills. Maltings, which are characteristic of East Anglia, have also come in for their share of conversion – as with the now famous concert hall at Snape founded by Benjamin Britten for the Aldeburgh Festival in Suffolk.

Textile mills are invariably too large for conversion into a single home and most have been turned into warehouses, offices or flats – or a combination of both. A few have found new life as museums or art galleries, however. A museum is also housed in a National Trust owned watermill at Burwash, Sussex, and another Trust watermill is the City Mill in the heart of Winchester, which is also probably the most unusual youth hostel in the country.

The charm of watermills is their location on rivers or streams; their snag is often the lack of surrounding land. But several successful conversions have been made into houses as well as museums: that of Castle Mill, at Dorking in Surrey, won an Architectural Heritage Year award for a restoration accomplished, as the photograph shows, in a manner which respected its 19th century origins.

Preston Watermill, near Dunbar: working museum for the National Trust for Scotland

Castle Mill, near Dorking: 19th century watermill restored to be 20th century home

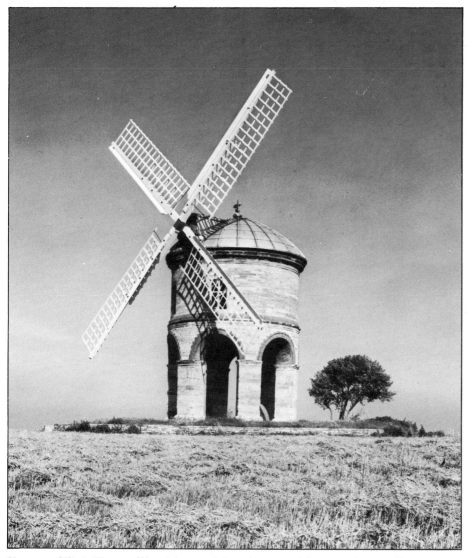

Chesterton Windmill, near Warwick: a stylish 17th century folly as much as a mill

The restoration and conversion of the extraordinary 17th century Chesterton windmill in Warwickshire won an 'exceptional merit' Heritage Year award. The celebrated Jack and Jill windmills on the South Downs near Clayton, north of Brighton, are also now used as homes while that at Heage, Derbyshire, has become a working museum of the millwright's craft.

Schools

Most village schools that become redundant are Victorian, like the former school and meeting hall in Westbourne, near Emsworth, Sussex – a conversion which shows that a building can be adapted quite dramatically for its new function without destroying its character. School closures, as rural populations shrink, have brought many old school buildings onto the market, although none are probably older than the 1556 grammar school restored by the Landmark Trust at Kirby Hill, near Richmond, North Yorkshire. Schools were generally soundly-built and the internal space of classrooms and staff quarters often lends itself readily to conversion into village meeting halls, old people's day centres or private homes as at Westbourne.

Churches

Among other uses, churches and chapels have been converted into arts centres, bookshops, old people's day centres, concert halls, theatres, shops and museums as well as houses over the last 20 years. Acquiring a church for conversion can be a complicated process, however, since plans have to be approved by ecclesiastical authorities in addition to local government planners. Other problems commonly associated with churches are lack of drainage, electricity and insulation. Noncomformist churches tend to be sold with fewer reservations than Anglican ones, and some have even become factories.

Stations

Many railway stations were closed during the 1960s as a result of the decision to close uneconomical railway branch line services. Several stations have since been converted into private houses, usually as at Alton (a Landmark conversion) where the line is also closed but occasionally on lines where expresses still thunder past the bedroom windows. Larger stations that were closed in towns were generally redeveloped for their site value but where disused lines have been turned into paths or bridleways some former stations serve as information, refreshment or picnic areas.

Country houses: shaping society in addition to the rural landscapes

In her novel *Night and Day* Virginia Woolf makes Ralph Denham comment with approval on the Lincolnshire countryside: 'Real country. No gentleman's seats.' This attitude may seem curious today when the cult of the country house is at its height. But it does underline the fact that the relationship of country houses to the countryside is more complex than that of farmhouses or cottages. The latter were built for people who earned their living by working the land. The essential common factor of the people who lived in country houses was not that they farmed the land, but that they owned it.

Most country houses had a home farm intended to supply fresh food to the house rather than to make a profit. A proportion of country-house owners (varying very much from century to century) went in for farming or forestry on a bigger scale, in order to make money. But the main basis of country houses was always rent – rent from tenant farms or house property, supplemented in recent centuries by income from shares and mineral royalties. Oddly enough it is in the past few decades, since changes in the law have made tenanted farms a doubtful asset, that large numbers of country-house owners have become working farmers on a very big scale.

The object of acquiring a country property was not just to enable its owners to live a comfortable life off their rents.

Owning land was the only reliable and lasting way of getting into the ruling class. For many centuries the country was effectively ruled by, or through, its landowners. In early days their tenants, servants, and retainers fought for them; later on they voted for them. The important posts at court or in the government or in local administration were handed out by the Crown in return for their support. The landowning classes did everything they could to keep outsiders out – unless they joined the club by buying land themselves. The system only began to break down in the 19th century. It was then that the Industrial Revolution gradually began to shift power and money from the country to the towns.

So country houses were power bases as well as pleasure bases and family homes; they were more than homes, they were 'seats'. They were the outward and visible sign of a complex power structure based on property, service, protection, contacts, entertainment, tradition, and the mystique and affection which grow round anything that lasts many generations. A structure of this kind took time to build up, and its value was much more than a cash one. This was the main reason why landowning families held on to their houses from generation to generation.

The fact that they were a ruling class largely supported on unearned income meant that, unlike farmers in their farms or cottagers in their cottages, they were not tied to the country, and they were not tied to one kind of activity. Most country

houses of any size were linked to a town house – in London, in the case of the richer families, and in York, Exeter, Norwich or wherever the county or local centre happened to be, in the case of the smaller ones. Both pleasure and power attracted country-house owners to the town – sometimes for very long periods. They went to London to attend Parliament or the court, to fill jobs in the government or to go to parties and

Today Longleat is committed to the stately home business. In the 17th century (top right) it attracted visitors who were unaware of such future delights as safari parks, garden centres and charabancs

gamble at Crockford's and White's. They went to Bath or Buxton or Baden-Baden to recover from London. They travelled round England and many of them roamed round the world as well. In the Middle Ages they went on pilgrimages or crusades; in the 18th century they did the grand tour, and sent back crates of marbles and pictures; in the 19th century they went big-game hunting and brought back elephant trunks to make umbrella stands and rhinoceros heads to decorate their front halls. Even when they stayed in the country they followed their own bent. Some hunted and shot; some built temples, others built churches; some developed coal mines; some bred race horses or prize pigs. Mr Fox Talbot, in Wiltshire, pioneered photography; General Pitt Rivers in Dorset dug up prehistoric sites; the Duke of Bridgewater built canals; the Earl of Rosse built the world's biggest telescope on his front lawn.

As a result nearly all country houses had two aspects – a country aspect and an exotic aspect. On the one hand they were linked to their farms, woods and villages and the people who lived in them – and in a less immediate way to the whole neighbourhood. On the other hand they were linked to the outside world – and were often the main means

Holkham Hall, Norfolk: an 18th century Palladian-style mansion designed by William Kent

by which the local countryside kept in touch with what was going on in this wider world.

Most country houses were periodically shut up, sometimes for a few months, sometimes for years at a time. When the families came back to them, they brought every kind of novelty to astonish the neighbourhood – from a Negro page to a visiting Prime Minister, or a statue by Canova to a De Dion-Bouton, complete with French chauffeur. The first Palladian porticos, and the parks that went with them, must have seemed extraordinarily exotic to the locals; they certainly did not 'grow out of the countryside' but were sophisticated importations from Italy. But they grew *into* the countryside; their classical detail and clumps and belts of trees were copied in a modest way by lesser gentry, farmers and rectors, until what had been last century's novelty began to seem part of country life.

The more one knows about the background to country houses, the more one can look through their physical structure to the different varieties of family pride and ambition, hospitality, political calculation, private enjoyment, dynastic alliances, travel, fashion, class solidarity, individual taste, sense of responsibility and good stewardship which lie behind them. Any country house with a long history can be dissected into layers, like an archaeological dig. This kind of archaeology is social as well as architectural; country houses were built or adapted to fit a way of life.

The age of ceremony

Most people have some sort of picture of what life was like in country houses in their great days. Dinner is served at tables glittering with glass and silver, by silent footmen who melt imperceptibly into darkness beyond the candlelight. The squire walks home across the park in the evening light, his gun under his arm, his dogs behind him, and a brace of woodcock slung over his shoulder. Guests chat and lounge in the library, or play croquet on the lawn. Pretty maids in print aprons rustle up and down the backstairs. An apple-cheeked housekeeper sits amid her preserves, dealing out cakes and candies to the young ladies. The people in these vignettes are likely to be wearing 18th or 19th-century dress.

Everyone knows that country-house life in earlier centuries was somewhat different – but perhaps they don't realise how very different, and in what ways. For instance, not only were there no print aprons; there was no housekeeper and almost no maids. Medieval and Elizabethan households were almost exclusively male. In the 1520s the household of the Earl of Northumberland contained 166 men and nine women – his wife, his daughter, and five waiting-women and two nurses to look after them. Food was cooked, clothes repaired and the house kept clean (in so far as it was kept clean) entirely by men. This was standard practice; it was only in the 18th century that women servants began to approach the number of men servants

in country houses, and only in the 19th century that they exceeded them.

The social reality which lay behind this was that early households were not all that far removed from a military garrison – even when they were not actually inside a castle. The power and status of a family were still ultimately based on the number of people who would fight for it. There were arms and armour hanging in the hall, and more in the armoury – at hand to turn the household into a fighting force. It was organised like an army, with the servants graded into the equivalent of officers, NCOs, and other ranks. The officer element in a big household were all gentlemen, often related to their employer. The household was constantly on parade. The colour and ceremony were different from that of a modern army, but there was an extraordinary amount of it. It all centred round the head of the household, who was treated as though he was an amalgamation of a high priest and a field-marshal. If he was sufficiently grand he ate seated beneath a canopy, and only talked to his social equals. A gentleman without a title would feel deeply honoured to be asked to sit at the same table as an earl, and would only speak to him if the earl spoke first. But usually he would eat at a separate table, and often in a separate room.

The popular picture of a medieval or Elizabethan great hall, filled with long tables of wassailing and carousing figures, bears only an approximate relation to reality. A rigid sense of hierarchy permeated every aspect of life. By the end of the Middle Ages the high table in big houses had been moved out of the hall into a room one storey above it, known as the great chamber. Serving dinner to the high table, whether in hall or great chamber, was a protracted ritual. It involved both the ceremonial preparations of the table and the bringing in of each course by a platoon of servants in livery, preceded by a household officer and accompanied by a fanfare of trumpets.

In smaller houses this kind of ceremonial was confined to great feasts, but in big houses it went on all the year round. The object of having large num-

Top right: billiard rooms became standard features of country houses from the 19th century. This one is at Newnham Park in Herts. Near right: the formality of the Great Hall at Blenheim Palace. Far right: the Hall as sitting room at Kinloch Castle, Isle of Rhum

To entertain Edward VII at a house party was the summit of social ambition. Here he sits by his host, the Duke of Marlborough, at Blenheim Palace

bers of servants and retainers constantly on view was partly to induce a spirit of *esprit de corps*, partly to bolster the image of the head of the household, and partly to display the number and spirit of his supporters to visitors.

In the later 16th and 17th centuries households gradually ceased to have a fighting function. The officer-and-gentlemen element disappeared and servants began to develop into the inconspicuous background figures of later centuries. But life in country houses was extremely formal. It was widely believed that a social hierarchy was not only useful but also divinely ordained and approved. A great man knew how and when to unbend, but even so, distinctions of rank were underlined by an elaborate system of ceremony and etiquette – and by the architecture and arrangement of the houses in which the action took place.

This arrangement was based on the apartment system. Every guest or member of the family had his or her own 'apartment' which varied from one room to five or six – like a grand hotel suite. An important visitor would expect a good apartment and be extremely disgruntled if he did not get it. Formal calls were paid from apartment to apartment, almost as though from house to house. A visit to a grand apartment was regulated according to the social rank of the visitor and the importance of his business. The higher he rated, the further into it he penetrated. The first room or rooms of an important person's apartment were used for his *levée*, at which he presented himself

each morning to receive petitions or compliments, while his valet finished off his *toilette*. More privileged visitors would penetrate into his bedroom. Bedrooms were used for receiving calls as well as for sleeping in, and on certain occasions beds assumed an important ceremonial function – christening, for instance, normally took place in the bedroom, with a splendidly-dressed mother ensconced in a magnificently apparalled bed. Beyond the bedroom was a little room known as the closet or cabinet. To be allowed into a great man's closet was the greatest distinction of all.

The age of the house party

A fascinating account exists of how the King of Spain was entertained at Petworth in 1703 by its owner, the Duke of Somerset. The endless ceremony, the formal visits from apartment to apartment of the various people involved, the minute attention paid to who was received in what room and even to what grade of chair they were asked to sit in, gives a vivid picture of country-house life at its most formal.

A hundred years or so later numerous descriptions survive of life at Petworth under the Duke's descendant, the Earl of Egremont. the contrast is quite extraordinary. Formality had vanished entirely. As one guest put it: 'Everyone is left to take care of themselves, with all that opulence and generosity can place at their disposal entirely within their reach.' Guests were given the freedom of the great house, and the park and countryside around it; the library, the sculp-

ture gallery, horses, guns and carriages were at their disposal. They often did not see their host except at breakfast and dinner; and one guest was treated exactly like another, regardless of rank.

The two hosts were admittedly extreme examples of their period. The Duke of Somerset was famous for pride and stiffness; he is said to have cut his daughter out of his will for daring to sit down in his presence. Lord Egremont was equally renowned for his hatred of any kind of ceremony; he could scarcely bring himself even to say 'Good morning'.

But the change did correspond to a general change. By the early 19th century a new pattern of country-house life had been established. With variations, it survived into this century; to a certain extent it still survives, however much eroded and altered by modern conditions. Country houses had become like little republics on the ancient Greek model – assemblies of more or less equal citizens, living a life of cultured elegance and ease made possible by a substratum of servants. Anyone admitted to the republic was admitted to all its amenities and treated like an equal – as in a small officers' mess, where the youngest subaltern calls the colonel by his Christian name.

The political and social reality which lay behind this was that the old model of the universe as a series of stratified and divinely ordained hierarchies, with kinds at the top of them, had collapsed in favour of government based on the ownership of property. England was ruled by her property owners, whose forum was the House of Commons – an organisation which only began to be democratic, in the modern sense, at the end of the 19th century.

It was the 'upper 10,000' who effectively ran the country. But they ran it as a result of constant bargaining and negotiation within the group. A big property-owner inevitably carried a great deal of weight, but he had only become really effective if he carried sufficient smaller property owners with him. Conscious of their independence and importance, the lesser gentry refused to be patronised, or to enter great households as superior servants as in earlier days. The house-parties which filled 18th and 19th-century country houses, and the balls, garden-parties and dinners at which they entertained the neighbours were partly just a pleasant way of passing the time. But they were also a useful way of striking up alliances and extending influence.

Of course, property owners had the good sense to realise that they had to look after their property – and the people who lived on it. The social and political side of country-house life shouldn't make one forget the other side – the running of the estates, the interest in farming and forestry, the care taken of retired servants, the visits made to the old and sick in the villages, the contact with local farmers on the hunting or cricket field. The relationship was a highly paternalistic one; but it was a real one.

Nonetheless, it was the needs of house-parties, friends and family that largely dictated the arrangement of country houses. It was true that most of them had a capacious hall, regularly used to give dinners or dances for the tenantry or the servants. But even these tended to fill up, in the intervals, with sofas, writing tables and games.

The pattern of social life produced a country-house pattern which also lasted, with modifications, right through the 19th century into the 20th. It was radically different from the earlier pattern. Apartments vanished. A bedroom, with a small dressing room next door for the husband, was the most that any except a royal couple could expect. Bedrooms on the ground floor, and grand reception rooms on the first floor – both regular features of earlier centuries – disappeared almost entirely. Instead, the ground floor was filled by a series of big living rooms designed for the recreation of large house parties – a morning room for the ladies, a smoking room for the gentlemen, a hall as a communal sitting room for both sexes, a billiard room, a library, a dining room, a drawing room in which to assemble before and after dinner, a dining room and sometimes a music room and breakfast-room. These were all normally on the ground floor, so that they could have a comfortable relationship with the garden, by means of low sills, French windows and conservatories. The garden tended to become a series of outdoor living rooms, used for afternoon tea, croquet, and tennis. Lawns and turf replaced formal parterres and avenues. Servants, far from being on display, were kept as invisible as possible; dinner was conveyed from the kitchen to the dining room by backstairs and back passages, instead of being carried in a grand procession up the main staircase.

This kind of arrangement tended to produce a particular kind of house – rambling and irregular, with a long servants' wing discreetly tacked on to one side of the main block, where the gentry lived. New country houses assumed this shape automatically. Older houses were adapted to a greater or lesser degree.

Minley Manor, Hampshire: to cater for house parties a huge kitchen presided over by a chef was an essential feature of Victorian country houses

Chapter Four
Wildlife in the Countryside

One of the greatest glories of the British countryside is the wealth of wildlife
to be found in every corner of the landscape, from the windswept summits of the Highlands
and Islands to the soft, low-lying watermeadows of the southern counties.
There are so many wild plants and creatures that it is impossible to include them all
in a single chapter. Instead, the following pages are intended more as a celebration
of a wild heritage and a guide to the most important wildlife habitats.

In purely global terms the wildlife of the British Isles represents only a fraction of life on earth as a whole. There is, for instance, nothing to match the richness of the Brazilian rain forests, or the spectacle of the African savannah with its elephants, great carnivores and immense herds of plains game.

But then the wildlife of the British Isles is also infinitely less hostile. There are no dangerous wild animals; only one poisonous snake (none in Ireland), a couple of fish with poisonous spines, and a few deadly berries and fungi. Our jungles – marsh, moor, meadow and forest – are gentle ones compared with most other countries. This is what makes them so beautiful. This, and the fact that everything is on a much smaller, more intimate level, often enclosed within a habitat no bigger than a hedgerow or a village pond.

Nevertheless, the British Isles possess many wild plants and creatures of exceptional splendour. Among the mammals; red deer, wild cat, otter and grey seal. Among the birds, some of the world's most magnificent raptors; peregrine, osprey, red kite, golden eagle. The coasts are the stronghold of internationally important seabird colonies; the estuaries are major wintering grounds for huge populations of wildfowl and wading birds. The rivers are the home of the Atlantic salmon, king of fishes. The countryside is host to a year-long pageant of wild flowers; snowdrops, bluebells, foxgloves, orchids; and rare butterflies such as the swallowtail and purple emperor which are every bit as gorgeous as their tropical counterparts.

Furthermore, there is a great tradition of love and respect for wildlife in the British Isles, which manifests itself both in the form of protective legislation and in the abundance of nature reserves and organisations such as the Royal Society for the Protection of Birds, all of them

Close-ups in the wild. Above: Flourish of foxgloves, common flowers of the mid-summer countryside. Right: Face of the fox, a born survivor, still thriving in most parts of the British Isles despite a history of persecution

dedicated to the concept of nature conservation. This national passion for wildlife is essential in a countryside as small and heavily cultivated as that of the British Isles, and holds out the greatest hope for its survival.

Britain's share of the world's wildlife is also quite modest in terms of actual species. Countless plants and animals were lost in the Ice Age. Then, after a brief post-glacial period of recolonisation, the British Isles were marooned as the sea finally severed us from the wildlife of the European continent. As a result, most of the plants and animals are descendants of the species which existed when the British ark was finally set adrift.

Since then, of course, some animals like the wolf have been deliberately exterminated, and many other plants and wild creatures introduced, either deliberately, like the rabbit and the

walnut tree, or by accident, as in the case of the muntjac and Chinese water deer, alien species which escaped from captivity and are now well-established in the wild.

Another factor limiting the numbers of wildlife species is Britain's temperate climate, with its frosty autumn and winter seasons. To survive, wild life must be frostproof, or able to migrate like the swallow. Also, this time of short days and cold nights creates a season when plants cease to grow and life is dormant. This inevitably reduces the amount of food available, which in turn reduces the number and variety of creatures which the British Isles can support.

Even so, the array of wild plants and animals to be found in these small islands is quite astonishing. There are 70 different mammals, including seven kinds of deer and 14 kinds of bats; 38 freshwater fishes; six reptiles; eight different frogs, toads and newts; over 200 breeding birds and at least as many more which appear every year. There are more than 2000 wild flowers, 150 wild grasses, 600 mosses, at least 10,000 kinds of fungi and scores of trees (though only about 35 are regarded as true natives). And there are the insects; at least 20,000 in all, including some 250 different bees, nearly 50 ant species, 27 dragonflies, nearly 70 butterflies and over 2000 kinds of moths. Add the rich living world of the seashore and the overall picture is truly impressive.

Note: some of the illustrations in this chapter show wild plants, insects and other creatures which in real life would not necessarily appear together at the same time of year. For instance, spring and summer flowers are shown in bloom, irrespective of their proper seasons. But without this measure of artistic licence, it would not be possible to do justice to the immense variety and richness of the habitats portrayed.

The world's longest wildlife refuge

Key to illustration: 1 Oak 2 Scalloped Oak Moth Caterpillar 3 Honey-suckle 4 Wasp 5 Peacock Butterfly 6 Dog Rose 7 Chaffinches

8 Kestrel 9 Garden Spider 10 Cow Parsley 11 Ladybird 12 Flesh Fly 13 Hazel 14 Holly 15 Hawthorn 16 Hedge-brown Butterfly 17 Hedgehog 18 Whitethroat and Young 19 Hoverfly 20 Peacock Butterfly 21 Harts Tongue Fern 22 Ivy 23 Adder 24 Garlic Mustard 25 Cuckoo Pint

26 *Bramble Flowers* 27 *Wall Pennywort* 28 *Bluebell* 29 *Stoat*
30 *Six-spot Burnet* 31 *Rabbit* 32 *Common Vole* 33 *Dragonfly* 34 *Rushes*
35 *Water Mint* 36 *Great Diving Beetle* 37 *Common Frog* 38 *Banded*
Snail 39 *Wood Mouse* 40 *Primrose* 41 *Early Purple Orchid*

42 *Bumble Bee* 43 *Common Vetch* 44 *Germander Speedwell*
45 *Wolf Spider* 46 *Dog Violet* 47 *Dandelion. Text begins overleaf*

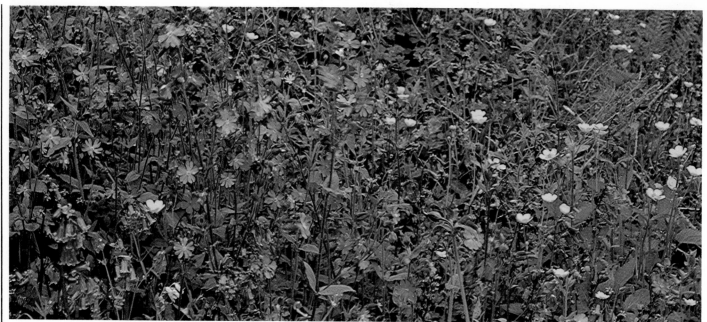

Hedgebank pageantry: bluebells, buttercups and red campion are three common wildflowers to be seen in hedgerows in May

Life of the hedgerow

The beauty of the British countryside owes much to its patchwork landscape of criss-cross hedgerows. The pattern was largely complete by the 18th century, though many hedges are much older than 200 years. Always they were planted for sound practical reasons: to mark boundaries, to contain footloose stock, to enclose. At any one time they were a windshield for crops, a shelter for animals and a handy timber-yard for the farmer. But in time they became something more. Every hedgerow is, in effect, a miniature wood, teased out in a thin green line. What has been created un-intentionally is an unofficial nature re-serve 600,000 miles (966,000km) long: a self-renewing lifeline for countless species of wild plants and animals.

The oldest hedges are often richest in wildlife terms. A rough yardstick used to estimate the age of a hedgerow is to count the number of different shrub species – hazel, hawthorn, elder, spindle, and so on – growing in each 30-yard (27.5m) length, allowing a hundred years for each species.

In reality you will not see at any one moment as much as we show within the few square yards or metres in our draw-ing. But you might if you watched long enough. There lies the first lesson: a plant or animal is playing a part in a chain of events, which you could not guess from a single sighting of it. Everything you see is part of a bigger, dynamic picture.

Let us take one simple example: the cow parsley at the hedge foot. This common umbellifer has many close rela-tives. Each one flowers in a different span of summer; each supplies food to different generations of flies and other insects.

The world of the hedge itself is divided into numerous micro-habitats, like chinese boxes, one within the other, all offering a niche to different species. A damp ditch for the frog at the base of the hedge; hawthorn for the chaffinch to nest in on top. No space is left unoccupied. Even the cracks between the stones of the wall on which this hedge is based provide a roothold for plants such as the wall pennywort and harts tongue fern.

One yard or metre of hedge may be very different to the next. Similarly, the sunny side offers a very different habitat to the shady side. The cuckoo pint grows on shady banks; the basking adder seeks the sun. Soil also plays a part in determ-ining what grows. Lowland clays grow rich meadow grasses, clover and butter-cups. Chalky soil has fescue grasses, orchids and other attractive flowering plants. And the constant fall of hedge debris – twigs, bark and leaf litter – create a rich humus for flowers like the bluebell and primrose.

Like all habitats, the hedgerow is a savage jungle in which life is a story of eating and being eaten. Plants obtain their food energy from non-living sources such as sunshine and salts in the soil. Some animals like voles and rabbits, eat plants, or parts of them. Other animals like the stoat eat the plant-eaters. But plants come first. Without them there would be no animals.

The cross-linking of each animal's food requirements builds up into a com-plicated food chain. On the bramble, the spider catches the fly, but is eaten by the foraging whitethroat, which in turn may fall victim to a marauding sparrowhawk.

The bramble is a stage upon which another strand in this complex plot is revealed. The wasp, the fly and the peacock butterfly all feed on blackberry. The wasps arrive first, cutting the fruit's firm skin with its strong jaws. When the skin is broken, flies are able to suck up the pulpy juices. But the butterfly has to wait until the juice is fermented and thin before it can feed through its delicate mouth tube.

Nothing is constant in the countryside, and hedgerows are no exception. At one time, during the 1950s and 1960s, Britain was losing on average about 4500 miles (7242km) of hedgerows every year. Even so, it has been estimated that today nearly half-a-million acres (202,300 hec-tares) of hedges remain, forming a total area twice the size of all our national nature reserves put together. End to end, it must add up to the longest wildlife refuge in the world.

But the hedgerow scene demonstrates its fragility. Yard for yard and metre for metre, it is a small and vulnerable world. If it were grubbed out, or regularly shorn with a heavy duty cutter, or accidentally sprayed with pesticide, how much of its wildlife would survive?

The alternative is a countryside of fences. But is that sound economics? Fences support no life, offer no shelter, grow no timber and need replacing every few years. But a hedge, cut-and-laid every five or ten years, lightly clipped every winter, may live – with all its wealth of wildlife intact – for the next 800 years.

The vanishing meadow

More than half of the entire land surface of the British Isles lies under grass. Much of it is permanent pasture, but naturalists are concerned by the speed at which old meadowland is disappearing. In many parts of dairyland Britain the traditional summer image of cows wallowing up to their udders in buttercups is fast becoming a childhood dream. Every old meadow that survives is a reservoir of wild flowers and grasses. A good site can hold a hundred or more different plant species, together with innumerable insects, birds and small mammals.

In the bad, old, inefficient days the grass was allowed to grow in its own sweet way, enriched by nothing more revolutionary than the cow-pat. It was a way of farming which made for harmony and tolerance between man and the land. But in the hard economic world of modern agri-business there is no room for the flowers of yesteryear. Increasingly the old turf is being ploughed under, primed with chemicals and re-seeded.

So meadows once bright with ox-eye daisies now sway with monotonous maxi-crops of cultivated grass or Italian rye. Not that you would notice the difference at first glance. But a closer inspection reveals a world of difference. Unlike a modern ley – a short-term sward which may consist of a single species of cultivated grass – an old meadow is a bewildering mixture of natural grasses and wild flowers.

The British Isles contain more than 150 species of wild grasses, and many can be found growing in our old meadows. Among them: crested dog's tail, meadow brome, the coarse cocksfoot with its distinctively clustered seedheads, the soft and hairy Yorkshire fog, and the common cat's-tail, also known as timothy grass, after Timothy Hanson, who introduced the species to the USA in the 18th century.

Grasses are generally pollinated by the wind, and by June most of our native species are at their best, their ripening spikes and nodding panicles adding rich glints of tawny, pink and purple to the fields. One exception which flowers earlier, in mid-April, is the sweet vernal grass. Locked in its plumes of spikelets is a secret smell of summer – an essential oil called coumarin that gives the meadows their fragrance.

Permanent pasture is frequently found on heavy soils or in low-lying, badly-drained spots too wet to plough. And here, especially in the wetter west of England, you are likely to find tussocks of the common soft rush growing among the pitted hoof-marks of grazing cattle.

Rushes are water-loving relatives of the grasses, with nearly 30 species growing wild in the British Isles. In former times their soft pithy core was soaked in kitchen fat and used to make rush-lights. Often growing in the company of rushes in the softer corners is the marsh horsetail, a primitive plant with a curious hollow jointed stem. Its ancestors were the giant horsetails which flourished when the coal measures were laid down 280–345 million years ago.

To be a real meadow sleuth you need to know the floral clues that reveal the presence of ancient pasture: cowslip, meadowsweet and yellow rattle are three of them. They are all flowers whose presence indicates undisturbed grassland. If you should also manage to track down uncommon plants such as the green-winged orchid and dyer's green-weed, then you know you have stumbled on a genuine antique plot. Other, more commonly encountered meadowland plants include the meadow buttercup, knapweed, ox-eye daisy, dandelion, bugle, red clover, creeping thistle, ribwort plantain, and the rusty spikes of the common sorrel, whose arrow-head leaves have a pleasant vinegary taste when chewed.

One of the prettiest meadow flowers of spring and early summer is the cuckoo flower, or lady's smock. It favours wet meadows and its delicate pale mauve flowers are an irresistible attraction for the orange-tip butterfly which is on the wing at that time of year. In midsummer clouds of butterflies start up at every step in the waist-high grasses; common blue, small copper, and most common of all our grassland butterflies, the meadow brown.

You may also disturb two common day-flying moths in the long grass: the weakly fluttering cinnabar, whose conspicuous black-and-yellow striped caterpillars feed on ragwort, and the fast, whirring silver Y moth, a migrant from southern Europe.

In summer the meadow teems with other insects. From July onwards there is the rasping song of common green grasshoppers (*Omocestus viridulus*), and in August the daddy long legs or crane-fly emerges. This gangly creature belongs to the family of two-winged flies, the diptera, and its larvae are the destructive leather-jackets which devour the roots of the meadow grasses.

Also on the wing is the common bumble bee (*Bombus terrestris*), largest of Britain's 16 bumble bee species, laden with pollen on its way back to its nest among tufts of meadow grass. At dusk the drowsy hum of the bees is echoed by the metallic blue-black dor beetle, droning through the warm summer air. The larvae of the dor beetle grow fat on the dung of the cow-pats which cover their earthen chambers. The sexton beetle (*Necrophorus humator*) has an even more unsavoury appetite. It is a carrion eater, feeding and laying its eggs on the bodies of dead animals. (In our illustration on the following pages, the corpse is a dead field mouse.

The open meadows provide little cover for mammals, but small rodents, such as the short-tailed vole, tunnel among the grasses on which they feed. In the so-called 'vole years' their numbers can mushroom to plague proportions – a time of plenty for predators such as owls, stoats and foxes. That other common meadow mammal, the mole, spends almost all its life underground, only revealing its presence by the mole-hills pushed up as a result of tunnelling in search of the earthworms which are its favourite food.

The abundant insect life of the meadows makes the grasslands a rich source of food for birds. In spring and summer swallows skim the grass-heads, snapping up dipterous flies and other winged insects, while the lapwing, a typical bird of green pastures, both upland and lowland, runs and pauses to peck up a wireworm. And in autumn, when the swallows have gone, flocks of goldfinches descend on the thistle heads to hunt for seeds.

Sometimes you may flush a covey of common partridge. Though essentially ground birds, they are fast fliers, alternately whirring and gliding on downcurved pinions. The call of the partridge is a curious rusty creak, but the true voice of the meadow belongs to the elusive corn-crake. The sound is similar to that made if you rub your thumb along the teeth of a comb. But alas, it is seldom heard nowadays except in Ireland and among the Scottish Highlands and islands. Like the old meadow itself, the rasp of the corncrake is fast becoming a part of yesterday's countryside.

Living world of the meadow

Key to illustration: 1 Bramble 2 Ragwort
3 Goldfinches 4 Creeping Thistle 5 Cinnabar
Moth 6 Cinnabar Caterpillars 7 Cowslip

8 Bugle 9 Dor Beetle 10 Mole 11 Dandelion
12 Sexton Beetle 13 Field Mouse 14 Ribwort
Plantain 15 Yellow Rattle 16 Corncrake
17 Orange Tip 18 Ladybird 19 Cuckoo

Flower 20 Common Green Grasshopper
21 Crane-fly 22 Common Blue 23 Red Fescue
24 Common Sorrel 25 Common Bumble Bee
26 Black Knapweed 27 Small Copper

28 Crested Dog's Tail 29 Meadow
Sweet 30 Marsh Horsetail 31 Soft Rush
32 Green-winged Orchid 33 Lapwing
34 Meadow Foxtail 35 Cocksfoot

36 Common Quaking Grass 37 Ox-eye Daisy
38 Dyer's Greenweed 39 Short-tailed Vole
40 Red Clover 41 Meadow Buttercup
42 Silver Y Moth 43 Common Partridges

44 Annual Meadow Grass 45 Yorkshire Fog
46 Meadow Brown 47 Timothy Grass
48 Common Rye Grass 49 Sweet Vernal Grass
50 Meadow Brome 51 Swallows

Fruit of the earth

From earliest childhood, fungi often exert a mysterious fascination. In part it originates from the pleasures of mushrooming, from folklore, fairy rings and nursery illustrations. But there is also something faintly sinister about them. Their pallid flesh and flaccid gills, earthy smells and strange other-worldly shapes arouse feelings of apprehension that cannot be entirely explained away by the knowledge that some species of fungi are poisonous.

In fact, of the 10,000 or so fungi which grow in the British Isles, no more than a score or so are dangerously poisonous, and of these only two or three, notably the death cap and destroying angel, are lethal. On the other hand there are at least 100 edible species in addition to the common field mushroom. Unfortunately many of them can be easily confused with similar species which are either inedible or positively poisonous. So the golden rule is: *never* eat a fungus unless it can be positively identified as edible.

All fungi, whether mushrooms, toadstools or puffballs, are non-flowering plants without chlorophyll. Unable to absorb carbon dioxide from the air and manufacture their own carbohydrates in the normal way, they must obtain their nourishment from other plants, either parasitically from living organic matter, or more usually, from newly decaying plant litter.

Fungi prosper therefore in habitats rich in humus, such as old-established woods and pastures, forming · woolly webs of thread-like cells in the rotting underworld of manured meadows and forest floors. Then, when the mysterious alchemy of warmth and dampness create the right conditions, the fruiting bodies we commonly know as mushrooms and toadstools push up through the turf or leaf-mould and unfold their parasol caps to release their reproductive spores.

Fungi are divided into two main groups. The first group, the *Ascomycetes*, produce their spores inside sacs; these include the morels, truffles and cup fungi. The second group, the *Basidiomycetes*, contains the more familiar puffballs, bracket fungi, mushrooms and toadstools which produce their spores on the outside of radiating gills, or, in the case of the boletus family, in tubes which appear as sponge-like pores on the underside of the cap.

Cep Edible.

Sickener Poisonous.

Earthy Inocybe Poisonous.

Destroying Angel Deadly Poisonous.

Fly Agaric Poisonous.

Field Mushroom Edible.

Shaggy Ink Cap Edible (but not with alcohol).

Oyster Mushroom Edible.

Woolly Milk Cap Poisonous.

Stinkhorn
Inedible.

Yellow-
Staining
Mushroom
Poisonous.

Panther Cap
Extremely
poisonous.

vit
le.

Chanterelle
Edible.

Death Cap
Deadly
Poisonous.

Beef-steak Fungus Edible.

Common
Puffball
Edible.

Parasol
Mushroom
Edible.

Devil's
Boletus
Poisonous.

Life on the down

Chalk and limestone both give rise to very distinctive scenery. But just as landscapes reflect the composition of the rocks beneath, nature, too, has had to adapt to cope with the well-drained slopes and thin, calcium-rich soils of the chalk downs and limestone hills. More than that, it has had to learn to live with the cultivating hand of man and the nibbling teeth of sheep and rabbits. That process began over 5000 years ago when the first Neolithic farmers started to clear the wildwood from the southern chalklands. The resulting close-knit turf with its skylarks and butterflies and lime-loving flowers, is the oldest man-made habitat in the British Isles.

English chalklands are recognised by their curving skylines and plunging scarps, their combes, dry valleys and beechwood slopes. The Chilterns are chalk hills, and so are the Wolds of Lincolnshire, but the classic chalklands are the downs, the long green hills that rise in Kent and reach deep into Hardy's Wessex.

In Hardy's time a century ago the downs rose in huge grassy swells. Flocks of sheep shone like constellations of stars on their green flanks, keeping the turf in constant trim. In spring and summer every fold and combe was strewn with the wild flowers of the high chalk; harebells, bee orchids, carline thistles. Chalk-hill blue butterflies scattered at every step and skylarks sang over the burial mounds of the long-dead chieftains whose flocks were the first to graze these hills.

But modern farming technology and the pressing need to grow more food brought about a downland revolution. Arable farming has largely replaced the old sheep walks so that today, stripped of their thin green rug, vast acres of chalk down lie bare all winter long until the barley hides their flinty bones. The new landscape is not without a beauty of its own. But nothing can match the rich wildlife of the ancient pasture. And although much of it has gone under the plough, enough of the original living carpet remains to delight nature lovers each year with its chalkland flowers and summer butterflies.

One of the most prominent features of the downland turf is created by one of its smallest inhabitants. Long before the Romans came, *Lasius flavus* was busily colonising the downs. *Lasius flavus* is the scientific name for the yellow field ant whose hillocks strew the slopes like grassy scatter-cushions. Each dome conceals a complex underground citadel honeycombed with passages and chambers. One colony may contain as many as 30,000 ants, and the hills they raise may last for decades – even centuries.

Among the downland flowers found among the anthills is the horseshoe vetch, foodplant of the chalkhill blue caterpillar. Its sweet secretions are sought by the ants who cluster round to lick its

body. In return, the ants protect the caterpillar from parasitic insects. The chalkhill blue is found south-east of a line from the Severn to the Wash, and the adult butterfly is on the wing in July and August. Other downland butterflies to be seen in summer are the marbled white, dark green fritillary and silver-spotted skipper. All three species are attracted to flowering thistles. Often they share the same flower head with the six-spot burnet, a common and lethargic day-flying moth.

Less conspicuous than the moths and

butterflies but no less a part of the downland scene are the purseweb spider, which bushwacks its insect victims from a silken trap spun in the ground, innumerable grasshoppers, including the rufous grasshopper, the bombardier beetle (so-called because of its ability to squirt a burning liquid from its rear), and an edible, chalk-loving gastropod, the Roman snail.

Larger forms of life are less common, though the brown hare is a typical mammal of the open downs. You can tell a hare from a rabbit by its larger size and

Key to illustration: 1 Kestrel 2 Hawthorn scrub 3 Skylark 4 Beechwood 5 Wheatear 6 Hawthorn 7 Chalkhill Blue 8 Chalkhill Blue Caterpillar 9 Horseshoe Vetch 10 Yellow Field Ant 11 Purseweb Spider 12 Bee Orchid 13 Marjoram 14 Meadow Oat Grass 15 Salad Burnet 16 Bombardier Beetle 17 Wild Thyme 18 Roman Snail 19 Rufous Grasshopper 20 Meadow Pipit 21 Sheep's Fescue 22 Marbled White 23 Common Centaury 24 Narrow-leaved Meadow Grass 25 Bird's Foot Trefoil 26 Dark Green Fritillary 27 Round-headed Rampion 28 Six-spot Burnet 29 Carline Thistle 30 Silver-spotted Skipper 31 Harebell 32 Yew 33 Common Quaking Grass 34 Brown Hare

Beauty of the Burren.
Flowers in a Limestone Landscape

Unlike the gentleness of the chalk downs, limestone country has a harder edge to it, pushing through the skin of turf to form grey cliffs and crags, or spreading in fissured pavements and barrenlands known as *karst*. Such a place is the Barony of Burren, a lunar limestone plateau filling 100 square miles of County Clare, in the west of Ireland.

The Burren – its name means 'great rock' – is a miraculous botanical cross-roads, a giant natural rock garden in which alpine, arctic and Mediterranean flowers and rock plants thrive happily side by side, sustained by the same, soft cloudscapes of the Atlantic Ocean which beats against Clare's western ramparts, the colossal Cliffs of Moher. For the botanist, the living treasures of the Burren are one of the glories of Ireland.

Key to illustration:)1 Pyramidal Orchid 2 Shrubby Cinquefoil 3 Maidenhair Fern 4 Mountain Avens 5 Biting Stonecrop or Wall Pepper 6 Spring Gentian 7 Hoary Rockrose 8 Bloody Cranesbill 9 Royal Fern 10 Dark Red Helleborine

longer, black-tipped ears. Hares feed on the sweet downland grasses; sheep's fescue and totter grass, or common quaking grass, with its beautiful panicles that shake in the slightest breeze.

Without the constant attention of grazing animals the downs would soon revert to a tangle of hawthorn scrub, and eventually to woods of beech and yew. Fortunately there are still generous sweeps of open turf where the typical downland flowers harebell, round headed rampion, salad burnet, common centaury and bird's foot trefoil – still

bloom. But the most beautiful of all the chalkland plants are the orchids. They include the bee orchid, so-called because its velvety flowers look remarkably like bumble bees. The likeness is no accident. Orchids rely on insects for pollination. A male bee, mistaking the flower for a female, alights on it and attempts to mate. And in doing so is anointed with pollen. Yet if orchids are among the most marvellous sights of the downs, the most evocative smell is surely the tang of herbs crushed underfoot on a hot summer's day: wild thyme and marjoram.

River banks and running waters

All living things are dependent on water. It is the land's lifeblood. And the streams and rivers are its veins and arteries. Wherever water flows – from the tumbling peat-stained upland burns to the slow spread of the widening estuaries – wildlife burgeons. Even the biggest river begins as no more than a trickle, sometimes along spring lines, sometimes in the clefts and hollows of the hills.

In their infancy, upland streams are lusty and fast-flowing, leaping over rocky ledges in their haste to reach the valleys below. As yet the current is too fast to offer a safe anchorage for flowering plants. But the dipper and grey wagtail bob on the midstream boulders, snapping up mayflies and other insects.

The clean, well-oxygenated waters suit pollution-prone fish such as the stone loach, and also the brown trout which flit like shadows through the rocky pools. To protect itself against these and other predators, the caddis fly larva builds a tubular shell of sand grains and bits of dead vegetation.

By the time the stream has reached the lowlands it has merged with other minor tributaries, growing in volume until it becomes a fully-fledged river. Here, salmon lie in the deep holding pools, bound for the spawning redds upstream, and the banks are lined with water-loving alder trees, though the elusive otter prefers to make its holt in the subterranean root-caverns of a riverside ash. Otters feed mostly on eels and other fish, but they will also take freshwater crayfish where they occur in chalk and limestone streams. These small crustaceans grow up to 4in (10cm) long and are mainly nocturnal, hiding beneath stones by day.

Much easier to see are the shoals of hungry minnow darting about in search of midge larvae. The minnow in turn is eaten by many predators, from the pike in the reeds to the kingfisher on its overhanging perch. The kingfisher may be Britain's most colourful bird, but it lays its eggs in a tunnel in the bank on a midden of stinking fish bones.

In May and June the chalk streams of southern England turn white, not with chalk but the flowering tresses of an aquatic buttercup: the lovely water crowfoot. Flitting above the surface on wings of gauze is a beautiful aquatic insect: the banded demoiselle, *Agrion Splendens*. Damsel flies and demoiselles are related to dragonflies, but unlike the dragonfly, they close their wings like butterflies when they settle.

As the year progresses the waterside vegetation becomes increasingly lush. Spires of purple loosestrife line the banks. The air is pungent with the smell of water mint. Ripening panicles of lofty reed grass rustle in the breeze. And the butterbur, having flowered in early spring, now covers the sides of the stream with giant heart-shaped leaves, like a kind of coarse wild rhubarb. Elsewhere the great willowherb flourishes, food-plant of the elephant hawk-moth caterpillar, which feeds at night on the soft hairy leaves. (The moth itself is on the wing in June.)

Farther downstream the widening waters flow still more slowly, meandering through flood plains where willows grow. The graceful foliage of the white willow is eaten by the fierce-looking but harmless puss-moth caterpillar, and the bark may harbour an elegant green musk beetle with long antennae and a distinctive musky smell.

Here the river is opaque with silt and suspended algae. There is less oxygen, and red-finned roach take the place of trout. The grey heron stalks through the shallows, spearing eels with its dagger bill. And soon after sunset, Daubenton's bat – also known as the water bat – may be seen hawking for gnats above the surface of the water.

A series of holes in a grassy bank may reveal the presence of the water vole. Often mistakenly called the water rat, it is the largest British vole, measuring about 1ft (30.5cm) from blunt, twitching nose to thin hairy tail. Water voles are extremely short-sighted and seldom stray more than a few feet from the river. They are completely vegetarian, nibbling the grass around the entrance to their burrows to form close-cropped patches known as water vole 'lawns'. Like the smaller, black and white water shrew, water voles are expert swimmers. With both species, air bubbles are trapped in their dense fur when they dive underwater, giving them a fish-like quicksilver sheen.

In its final stages, the river spreads in ever-widening coils until, far out in the salt-smelling world of sand bars, salt marsh and tidal mudflats, its brackish waters merge and finally become one with the sea.

☐ *See Chapter Six for seashore and estuary wildlife.*

Key to illustration: 1 Dipper 2 Grey Wagtail 3 Brown Trout 4 Mayfly 5 Alder 6 Otter 7 Ash 8 Banded Agrion Demoiselle 9 Reed Grass 10 Musk Beetle 11 White Willow

12 Kingfisher 13 Puss Moth Caterpillar
14 Grey Heron 15 Butterbur 16 Daubenton's
Bat 17 Water Vole 18 Great Willowherb
19 Elephant Hawk-moth Caterpillar

20 Elephant Hawk-moth 21 Purple Loosestrife
22 Water Mint 23 Water Crowfoot
24 Minnow 25 Water Shrew 26 Roach
27 Pike 28 Damsel Fly (Pyrrhosoma nymphula)

29 Salmon 30 Freshwater Crayfish
31 Stone Loach 32 Caddis Fly Larva

Freshwater fishes

The freshwater fishes of the British Isles are few in species. Fewer than 40 kinds are found here – a legacy of the Ice Age which literally froze the life out of most British lakes and rivers. But many of the individual species found today occur in large numbers – to the delight of anglers everywhere.

BULLHEAD
Small (3–4″) fish also known as miller's thumb because of its broad, flattened head. Hides under stones.

STONE LOACH
Streams that suit the stone loach are swift, clear, shallow, stony, and above all, clean. Maximum length: about 5″.

TENCH
Essentially a fish of still waters and weed beds, where it feeds on bottom-living insects, pond snails and water plants. Once called the 'doctor fish' because its slime-coated body was reputed to have curative properties that could heal sick or wounded fish

THREE-SPINED STICKLEBACK
The jam-jar tiddler of juvenile anglers. Common everywhere except in mountain districts, swarming in shoals in ponds and streams. Average size: 2½–3″.

CHUB
Solidly built, blunt-headed river fish which can grow to between 8–10lbs or more. Widely distributed south of the Firth of Forth but absent from Ireland.

MINNOW
A fish of clear streams, common in Britain but more local in Ireland. Breeding males have a red belly. Maximum size about 4″

EEL
Common all over the British Isles, even in polluted waters. Eels are believed to spawn in the Sargasso Sea. From there, the tiny leaf-like hatchlings drift to Britain on the currents, become finger-long elvers and wriggle up the rivers to mature. A full-grown female may measure 36″, a male seldom more than 20″.

BRONZE BREAM
Widespread in sluggish lowland waters throughout much of Britain and Ireland. A bottom-feeder living on worms, molluscs and insect larvae. Bronze colour identifies it from the smaller silver bream of

RIVER LAMPREY
The river lamprey, or lampern, belongs to the primitive class of jawless fishes. The adults live in the sea and are entirely parasitic, preying on other fish, to which they attach themselves with their rasping sucker mouths. But they return to breed in the Severn and other rivers, where they are quite common though seldom seen. Average length: about 15–20″.

GRAYLING
Game fish related to salmon and trout but easily identified by its sail-like dorsal fin. Thrives best in fast-flowing streams with plenty of water and a stony bottom.

RUFFE
The ruffe, or pope, is a small member of the perch family, 6–7″ long. Found only in eastern England.

RUDD
A fish of weedy lakes, small ponds and sluggish rivers. Grows to a length of 14–18″. Easily confused with roach, but the rudd has redder fins and its dorsal fin is set farther back.

GUDGEON
Small (6–8″) relative of the carp. Absent from Scotland but widespread elsewhere in rivers with sand or gravel bottom.

PERCH
Common all over the British Isles except the far north. (A 5lb fish is not uncommon)

CARP
Deep-bodied descendant of the fish bred in medieval monastic stew-ponds. Common and long-living, carp thrive best in still, weed-tangled waters, feeding mainly on water plants and occasionally weighing in at up to 40lbs.

DACE
Slender, dashing fish, smallish (about 10″) and silvery. Favours swift clear waters, where it is often seen shoaling close to the surface. Common in England, absent in Scotland.

ROACH
One of our commonest freshwater fishes, living in shoals in slow-moving lowland rivers, lakes and ponds. Seldom exceeds top weight of about 3lbs.

– the two pairs of sensitive feelers attached to its upper lip. Can exceed 3ft in length.

TWAITE SHAD
Uncommon member of the herring family. A plankton-feeder which only enters fresh water when it runs up the rivers – notably the Severn and Shannon – to spawn in the spring. Will grow up to 24" but is smaller than its scarcer relative, the allis shad.

TORGOCH OR WELSH CHAR
Another fish related to the salmon. 'The torgoch – its Welsh name means 'red-belly' is found only in the lakes of Snowdonia.

PIKE
Fierce freshwater predator which can attain a length of 36" and weigh 30lbs or more. The torpedo body and backward set of the fins are designed for the sudden lunge at startled prey – fish, water voles, ducklings and moorhens. The gaping duck-billed jaws are armoured with sharp backward-curving teeth to make sure there is no escape.

BROWN TROUT
Found all over Britain in clean rivers and lakes, from rushing Highland burns to the classic Hampshire chalk streams. A length of 18" is a good size, but trout twice as big have been taken.

SEA TROUT
Migratory trout which can grow to the size of a small salmon. Fresh run fish returning from the sea to spawn are a magnificent new-minted silver. In Wales and Ireland sea trout are known as sewin.

BLEAK
Active small surface-feeder found in many English rivers but absent from Scotland and Ireland. Feeds mainly on insects, often leaping for them like a trout. Maximum length: about 6".

SALMON
The king of game fish. Breeds in freshwater but spends much of its life at sea. Spawning takes place from November to February, the female laying her eggs in 'redds' – hollows dug in clean gravel. The fry hatch in early spring. After one year they are called parr. After four years they become smolts and migrate to the sea.
Some return after little more than a year. These are called grilse.
But the big fish may be away for four years, feeding and growing to a length of up to 5ft before running up the rivers to spawn. Big males acquire a hooked jaw, or kype. After spawning, the adults are called kelts. Many die, but some, the so-called mended kelts, reach the sea and return to spawn again.

Wildlife of the wetlands

Marsh, broad and fen are three of the most evocative words in the English language for any naturalist. They conjure up visions of flat horizons and huge skies filled with swirling flocks of wildfowl. A low-profile paradise of dykes and reed beds, alive in summer with the harsh chatter of reed and sedge warblers, and heady with the mingling of marshy smells; mud, reeds and water mint.

A thousand years ago that description would have fitted large tracts of lowland Britain. However today the half-drowned landscapes in which Alfred the Great and Hereward the Wake found refuge have been largely reclaimed. But in parts of Somerset and the Norfolk Broads, and in the nature reserves of Minsmere, Wicken and Woodwalton, a few precious pockets of the old Saxon fens survive. These relic wetlands are exceptionally rich in wildlife, and in many cases are the last stronghold of species found nowhere else in the British Isles.

Foremost among these is the largest British butterfly, the swallowtail, pride of the Norfolk Broads. Late May and June is the best time to see this beautiful insect. The caterpillar feeds mainly on milk parsley. Another rare butterfly, the large copper, is found only at Woodwalton Fen in Huntingdonshire, where it was introduced from the Netherlands in 1927 after the native British breed had been hunted to extinction.

The summer sun brings out numerous dragonflies; big hawker dragonflies with a 4in (10cm) wingspan, and broad-bodied darter dragonflies (so-called because of their darting flight) such as *Libellula depressa*. Sitting watchfully on a floating leaf or rushing over the surface of the dykes in pursuit of insect prey is the raft spider, the biggest British spider. The female of the species has a body measuring 0.75in (1.9cm) long. Beneath the surface lives the water spider, unique among spiders in its sub-aqua lifestyle. It makes its home underwater by spinning a silken bathysphere and filling it with air bubbles, which it traps on the surface with its body hairs.

The banks of dykes are a good place to look for the grass snake, a non-poisonous reptile which loves to bask in the sun. Frogs form a large part of the grass snake's diet, but the marsh frog could prove too much of a mouthful since the female can grow to about 5in (12.7cm) long. This is the largest British frog, but is not a native, having been introduced from Europe in 1935, and it is found only in Romney Marsh.

Another wetland alien is the coypu, a Latin-American rodent the size of a cat. Brought to Britain in the 1930s for fur (nutria) farming, some coypu escaped and quickly established themselves in the Norfolk Broads where their destructive burrowing undermines the river banks.

Among the many interesting fenland plants are the marsh fern and rare marsh pea. Everywhere, vegetation fights for light and space. Lilies and pondweeds carpet the sluggish waterways, pierced in May and June by pink and white spikes of bogbean. The burnished gold flowers of the marsh marigold, or kingcup, are followed by a succession of other flowers; early marsh orchid, marsh helleborine and yellow iris.

But the most characteristic feature of the fens are the near-impenetrable reed-jungles; the vast beds of tasselled common reed (*Phragmites*) and fen sedge (*Cladium*) which provide a perfect refuge for the marshland birds. So dense are the reeds that the bittern is heard more often than seen; its strange, booming cry carries more than a mile. Equally elusive is the water rail, a furtive relative of the corncrake that squeals like a stuck pig as it runs through the reeds.

Many birds build their nests in the reeds. The great crested grebe, easily recognised by its slim, upright neck posture and prominent ear tufts, moors its floating nest of weeds to the edge of the reed beds. The bearded tit is altogether more secretive. It nests at the base of the tall *Phragmites* reeds; while the reed warbler weaves its nest among the stems.

Reed warblers are frequently chosen as the unwilling hosts of the cuckoo, whose parasitic nesting habits are as well-known as its springtime voice. It deposits its eggs in other birds' nests, leaving the young to be raised by the luckless foster-parents. In flight the

Key to illustration: 1 Marsh Harrier 2 Cuckoo 3 Bearded Tit 4 Reed Warbler and Nest 5 Sedge Warbler 6 Fen Sedge 7 Bogbean 8 Raft Spider 9 Coypu 10 Marsh Frog 11 Grass Snake 12 Marsh Marigold 13 Marsh Helleborine 14 Early Marsh Orchid 15 Marsh Pea 16 Swallowtail Caterpillar 17 Milk Parsley 18 Swallowtail 19 Marsh Fern 20 Large Copper 21 Water Rail 22 Great Crested Grebe 23 Bittern 24 Yellow Iris 25 Common Reed (Phragmites) 26 Libellula depressa Dragonfly

cuckoo bears a fleeting resemblance to the kestrel, but there is no mistaking the marsh harrier as it quarters the fens on buoyant, leisurely flapping wings, looking for frogs and small mammals. Unlike the cuckoo, the marsh harrier is a true fenland bird, though its numbers are few. It is now possibly the rarest daylight-hunting bird of prey breeding in the British Isles.

The lowland heath

Heathland occurs on the sands and gravels of southern England. From Breckland to the Lizard, around the Hampshire and London basins, wherever the soil was too poor to bring into cultivation, the open commons glow with the rich colours of heather, gorse and bracken. Heaths are, in effect, lowland moors. And, like the moors, they support their own distinctive wild plants and creatures.

Centuries ago the heaths were covered by woodland. The woods were cleared long ago, but the acid sandy soils were of little value except as rough grazing. Even today, without constant grazing by all kinds of animals – cattle, deer, wild ponies – and the regular devastation caused by accidental fires, the open heaths would eventually revert to woodland. As it is, considerable areas of heathland have been colonised by trees, notably Scots pine and birch (*Betula pubescens*), which thrive on sandy soils.

But the dominant plant species are the head-high bracken, the golden flowering gorse (also known as furze and whin), and above all, the pink and purple heaths and heathers; wiry, shallow-rooted plants, well suited to their impoverished environment. There are five different species in Britain, including the bell heather of the drier heaths, and the cross-leaved heath of the boggier areas. The Cornish heath is a more local species, being found only on the Lizard peninsula in south Cornwall. The Dorset heath (*Erica ciliaris*) also grows in Cornwall but its main strongholds are the Purbeck heaths.

Numerous grasses also grow on the heaths, including the common bent and wavy hair grass. Here on dull summer days the small heath butterfly rests with wings closed among the grass stems. But when the sun shines it takes to the wing, together with that other typical heathland butterfly, the silver-studded blue. The grayling, on the other hand, is a butterfly which likes to settle on paths and bare patches where its subtle stony colours blend perfectly with its background.

Ants, bees, wasps and beetles are all numerous. Keep an eye open on sandy paths for the irridescent green tiger beetle. You may also disturb a devil's coach horse, a fierce black beetle which

runs with its tail arched over its head, scorpion fashion. Moths are also plentiful, in particular the fox moth, which flies in June, and the clouded buff. The fox moth caterpillar feeds on bell heather and is $2\frac{1}{2}$in (6.3cm) long when fully grown in autumn.

The presence of the pinewoods allows the hobby to breed on southern heaths. This beautiful sickle-winged falcon – like a miniature peregrine – usually chooses an old carrion crow's nest for its eyrie.

On hot days, above the murmur of

bees and the crack of gorse pods bursting in the sun, you may hear a sound like two pebbles being tapped together. The source is a small, rufous-chested bird perching in a very upright position on fence posts or gorse bushes: the stonechat. At first glance the resident stonechat is easily confused with its close relative, the whinchat, a summer migrant. But the males may be quickly identified; the stonechat by its all-black hood; the whinchat by its bold white eyestripe. Other birds of the lowland heath are the linnet and the woodlark. And the rarest heathland bird? Undoubtedly, the Dartford warbler, now, alas, confined to a few pairs in the hinterland of Poole harbour, Dorset.

The Dorset heaths are also the stronghold of Britain's two rarest reptiles: the sand lizard and the harmless, 18in (46cm) long smooth snake. They share their native refuge with the common lizard and Britain's only poisonous snake, the adder. (For illustration, see p89.)

Like so many wildlife habitats, heathland is in rapid decline. Some areas have been reclaimed for agriculture; others planted with conifers or swallowed up by urban sprawl. Those areas that remain are desperately vulnerable to fire in dry summers. One carelessly tossed-away cigarette end can cause irreparable damage, immolating rare creatures such as the sand lizard and smooth snake, together with fledgling birds and other small creatures unable to escape from such a holocaust.

Key to illustration: 1 Woodlark 2 Bracken 3 Wavy Hair Grass 4 Clouded Buff 5 Sand Lizard 6 Common Lizard 7 Rabbit 8 Stonechat 9 Gorse 10 and 11 Silver-studded Blue 12 Cornish Heath 13 Fox Moth 14 Fox Moth Caterpillar 15 Ground Tiger Beetle 16 Grayling 17 Cross-leaved Heath 18 Devil's Coach Horse 19 Smooth Snake 20 Dorset Heath 21 Heath Potter Wasp 22 Whinchat 23 Small Heath Butterfly 24 Common Dodder 25 Heather 26 Dartford Warbler 27 Common Bent Grass 28 Linnets 29 Hobby 30 Silver Birch 31 Scots Pine

SCOTCH ARGUS

HEDGE BROWN OR GATEKEEPER

1 LARGE HEATH

3 COMMON BLUE

3 SMALL BLUE

F RINGLET

1 MOUNTAIN RINGLET

1 SMALL HEATH

3 ADONIS BLUE

3 SILVER-STUDDED BLUE

3 CHALKHILL BLUE

1 MEADOW BROWN

1 SPECKLED WOOD

3 LARGE BLUE

3 BROWN HAIRSTREAK

3 BROWN ARGUS

3 HOLLY BLUE

3 WHITE-LETTERED HAIRSTREAK

1 MARBLED WHITE

1 WALL

5 DUKE OF BURGUNDY FRITILLARY

3 LONG-TAILED BLUE

4 MONARCH OR MILKWEED

3 BLACK HAIRSTREAK

1 GRAYLING

3 GREEN HAIRSTREAK

3 PURPLE HAIRSTREAK

2 CLOUDED YELLOW

3 SMALL COPPER

3 LARGE COPPER

2 SMALL WHITE

2 WOOD WHITE

2 LARGE WHITE

2 ORANGE TIP

2 GREEN-VEINED WHITE

2 BRIMSTONE

Butterflies of the British Isles

KEY M–MALE F–FEMALE U–UNDERWING

FAMILIES 1–SATYRIDAE (BROWNS) 2–PIERIDAE (WHITES AND YELLOWS) 3–LYCAENIDAE (BLUE

6 RED ADMIRAL

6 COMMA

6 PAINTED LADY

6 SMALL TORTOISESHELL

6 PURPLE EMPEROR

6 WHITE ADMIRAL

6 DARK GREEN FRITILLARY

6 SILVER-WASHED FRITILLARY

6 SMALL PEARL BORDERED FRITILLARY

6 LARGE TORTOISESHELL

6 PEACOCK

6 CAMBERWELL BEAUTY

6 PEARL BORDERED FRITILLARY

6 GLANVILLE FRITILLARY

6 HEATH FRITILLARY

6 HIGH BROWN FRITILLARY

6 QUEEN OF SPAIN FRITILLARY

6 MARSH FRITILLARY

8 SWALLOWTAIL

7 GRIZZLED SKIPPER

7 ESSEX SKIPPER

7 LARGE SKIPPER

7 CHEQUERED SKIPPER

7 SILVER SPOTTED SKIPPER

7 LULWORTH SKIPPER

7 DINGY SKIPPER

7 SMALL SKIPPER

3 GREEN HAIR-STREAK

CM

Butterflies: insects of beauty

Butterflies are the most beautiful of all insects – creatures of the sun, with names as gorgeous as their wings, such as purple emperor, red admiral and Camberwell beauty. About 70 different kinds of butterflies can be seen in the British Isles, and most of them are shown here.

British butterflies are divided into eight families, each with a scientific Latin name. The *Satyridae*, or browns, and the moth-like *Hesperidae*, or skippers are essentially grassland species. The *Lycaenidae* include the irridescent blues and coppers of downs and meadows, and the woodland-loving hairstreaks. The *Pieridae* include not only the familiar and destructive cabbage whites, but also the beautiful clouded yellow and delicate wood white. The largest family, the *Nymphalidae*, covers the fritillaries (a distinctive tribe of tawny-gold butterflies with black freckles and silver-splashed undersides), the purple emperor, the admirals (red and white), peacock and painted lady. The three remaining families are each represented in Britain by a single species: the *Papilionidae* by the swallowtail; the *Danaidae* by the monarch, or milkweed; and the *Riodinidae* by the Duke of Burgundy fritillary.

The brimstone – both the sulphur yellow male and its pale greenish mate – are usually the first butterflies to appear. Brimstones winter in Britain and emerge after hibernation during the first warm days of February or early March. Other species quickly follow, including the very common small tortoiseshell, and in May no country lane would be complete without an orange-tip flitting among the cow-parsley (though only the males flaunt those candescent wing-tips).

In high summer the downs and meadows are alive with blues, browns, skippers and small coppers. During good butterfly years, migrant species such as the painted lady and clouded yellow swarm in from the Mediterranean. Other species are confined to specific localities. The swallowtail, the largest native butterfly, occurs only in Wicken Fen and the Norfolk Broads. Sometimes rare vagrants turn up; a monarch from America, a Camberwell beauty from Scandinavia. These you are unlikely to see. But some of our loveliest butterflies – peacocks and red admirals – will grace any garden where buddleia, valerian and Michaelmas daisies grow.

The butterfly is the end process of a life of metamorphosis which begins with an egg, hatches to become a caterpillar, pupates as a chrysalis, and finally emerges as the imago – the adult insect. Most butterflies of the British Isles spend only two or three weeks in the chrysalis stage, though there are exceptions. The green hairstreak, for instance, hibernates right through the winter as a chrysalis.

The food plants of caterpillars vary from one species to another; buckthorn for the brimstone, garlic mustard for the orange tip, succulent oak buds for the purple hairstreak, dog violet for the pearl-bordered fritillary and stinging nettles for the peacock, small tortoiseshell and red admiral. Nettle eaters like the peacock form conspicuous colonies, festooning their host plant with gossamer marquees. Each cobweb purse contains a wriggling mass of black and bristly caterpillars, progeny of the gorgeous adults that will hatch in mid-July.

Butterflies themselves are attracted by sight and smell to the nectar of flowers, especially mauve flowers such as thistles and buddleia, while species such as the hedge brown and the white admiral are drawn irresistibly to bramble flowers. Some also feed on honeydew, sap, rotting fruit, and even – in the case of the purple emperor – on the putrefying juices of a dead animal. Butterflies can taste with their feet. As they light on a flower and detect its sweetness, the watchspring tongue uncoils to probe for nectar.

The colours of butterflies have a twofold purpose. They help the males to recognise the females (in some species colouration is strikingly different between the sexes), and they provide protection from predators. When a comma closes its ragged wings it looks exactly like a dead leaf – a perfect camouflage to avoid being eaten by birds. The bright 'eye' markings on the wings of many butterflies serve a similar protective purpose. They deflect attention away from the vital parts, often enabling the butterfly to escape with nothing worse than a tattered wing.

Today, inevitably, butterflies are fewer. Insecticides, climatic changes and loss of habitat have all taken their toll. The large blue, numbered in thousands only two decades ago, was pronounced 'probably extinct' only last year. The Queen of Spain fritillary has not been seen for over three decades. But county naturalists' trusts and the British Butterfly Conservation Society, aided by a growing general awareness of the need for conservation in all its forms, are fighting hard to make sure that the most important butterfly haunts survive.

Twilight world of hungry hunters

When evening comes, the woods and fields awaken as nature's night watch takes over, and a host of creatures seldom seen by day creep out under cover of darkness, to eat – and be eaten.

With the fading of the light, the sun's warmth evaporates. The air grows cooler, distilling itself as dew in the open meadows as the moisture level rises. With the chill onset of evening, many day-flowering plants close their petals to protect their delicate stamens. But some, like the night-flowering catchfly, remain closed by day and only unfurl at dusk to release a fragrant scent and attract the night-flying insects which pollinate them.

The most spectacular of the night-flying insects are the moths. More than 2000 species occur in the British Isles, ranging from the hordes of tiny micro-moths to the large and handsome hawk-moths with their fat furry bodies.

Most moths rest during the day, relying on disguise to escape detection. In the case of the lappet moth, its wings are the exact colour of withered bramble leaves. But when day is done, they whir through the dusk, hunting for favoured flowering food-plants such as honeysuckle, whose sweet odour they locate with their incredibly sensitive feathered antennae. Moths themselves emit scents to attract mating partners, and from June onwards the male ghost moth can be seen hovering over long grassy meadows as it attempts to entice a smoky gold female.

The twilight wealth of flying insects – midges, moths, dancing gnats – attracts larger winged creatures. In midsummer the swift flies late into the evening, screaming and racing over village rooftops. And in June and July, as the insect build-up reaches its peak, bats give birth to their young to coincide with this time of plenty. The commonest bat is also the smallest: the tiny, mouselike pipistrelle, or flittermouse. A pair of them scarcely weigh more than one ounce (28gm). At the other end of the scale is the noctule bat, with a 15in (38cm) wingspan.

The needle-thin cries of bats are so high-pitched that many people are unable to hear them, but there is no problem in hearing the nightingale, which arrives in late spring and sings by day and night until the young hatch in June.

The woodcock, its plumage patterned like dead oak leaves, is also hard to see, being mainly nocturnal in its feeding habits. But during the breeding season the male performs a curious display flight known as 'roding', in which it flits slowly down woodland rides at dusk, emitting a low croaking call.

On open heaths the midsummer dusk vibrates to the strange churring song of the male nightjar, a moth-eating migrant with a gaping mouth evolved for catching its prey on the wing. But not all the night noises are made by birds. In late summer, especially in southern coastal counties, the hedgebanks ring to the stridulations of the great green grasshopper. This is Britain's biggest grasshopper, with a length of over 2in (5cm).

The humid conditions of the advancing night favour creatures such as slugs and snails, which would lose moisture in the heat of the day. One of the prettiest of these gastropods is the white-lipped banded snail. But pretty is not the adjective most people would use to describe the great grey slug, which grows up to 8in (20cm) long and mates upside down on a 'cord of communal slime.

Slugs and snails are eaten by the voracious larvae of the glow-worm, which is not a worm but a beetle. Damp meadows are a favourite habitat, and on warm evenings in July you may see the

bright greenish-yellow pinpoints of light which are the females shining in the grass. Damp nights also bring out the earthworm from its burrow. A single acre of meadowland may hold three million earthworms. As they search for leaves the worms are themselves sought by many creatures, and are devoured in large numbers by the shy nocturnal badger. This powerful, short-legged woodland dweller sleeps by day deep within the underground chambers of its sett, but emerges after dark to patrol its miles of well-trodden territorial paths.

Sometimes a fox will take over a disused badger sett to raise a family, and on warm summer evenings the vixen and cubs can sometimes be seen playing at the entrance to the earth.

If you hear a sharp, dog-like bark, it is more likely to be the alarm signal of a roe deer, another largely nocturnal mammal which lies up by day and emerges at dusk to browse at the edge of woods and clearings. The bark of a deer may be unfamiliar, but there is no mistaking the soft, quavering hoot of the tawny owl. This mournful cry, and its sharp 'ki-wik' – uttered as it flies on silent, rounded wings is the sound of a true night hunter.

Even more eerie than the voice of the tawny owl is the screech of the barn owl, which prefers to hunt in more open

country, ghosting over the meadows like a huge, pale moth. Not quite so well-known are the yowling and yelping cries of the little owl, though the bird is now widespread in England and Wales, having successfully established itself since it was first introduced into the British Isles during the 19th century. Another British owl, the long-eared owl, is a bird of the conifer forests, and is much more nocturnal. The so-called 'ears' are simply feathered tufts whose sole purpose is for courtship display. The true ear orifices, as with all owls, lie hidden behind the facial disc.

When dusk has deepened into dead of night there is a lull in the activity of creatures such as owls and bats. But in the grey, misty hour towards first light there is another brief flurry of hunting and feeding before the dawn chorus announces the return of the day shift and the prying eyes of man.

Birds of winter

In winter the woods fall silent, the fields lie dormant. Few birds sing. The battalions of summer migrants – warblers, swallows, cuckoos and turtle doves – have long since fled to sunnier haunts. Without them, the land seems strangely empty. But migration is a two-way traffic, and winter brings some exciting visitors to these shores. For bird-watchers, this is one of the most rewarding times of the year, especially around the coasts and estuaries of the British Isles where wintering wildfowl and waders gather in enormous numbers.

On the Dee estuary, for example, large mixed flocks of waders congregate, with perhaps as many as 40,000 dunlin, 40,000 knot and 20,000 oystercatchers. Large flocks of Greenland white-fronted geese winter on the marshes around Wexford harbour in Ireland, amongst other places, and in winter Essex becomes host to half the world population of dark-bellied Brent geese, which fly in from Siberia.

One of the commonest winter visitors is the fieldfare, a handsome, slate-headed Scandinavian thrush with a harsh chuckling cry. With the first real cold snap of the year they are joined by flocks of redwings, and they are often seen feeding together, either in open fields or stripping hawthorn berries from the hedgerows. The waxwing, a much scarcer visitor with a prominent chestnut crest, prefers rowan berries, but will also happily plunder rose hips, pyracantha and cotoneaster berries from gardens.

The brambling, a Scandinavian relative of the chaffinch, frequently appears in large numbers when beech mast is plentiful. Its plumage blends well with the winter beechwoods. The snow bunting nests in the Scottish mountains, but flocks move south in winter and may be seen feeding on seeds in coastal areas.

The great grey shrike is a loner, a bold pied bird with the hooked beak of a predator and a habit of impaling its victims – mice and small birds – on thorns or even barbed wire. Among the true birds of prey to be seen in winter are the rough-legged buzzard, whose plumage is paler than the resident common buzzard, and the short-eared owl, a daylight hunter with a moth-like flight and a taste for voles. The magnificent snowy owl is a true bird of the arctic, and seldom seen in Britain outside Orkney and Shetland, where it now breeds on Fetlar.

Like the snowy owl, the dumpy grey and white knot is a bird of the high arctic, but in winter these diminutive waders form compact flocks of up to 10,000 birds, and head south. In mid-winter there may be a quarter of a million of these arctic refugees feeding around our coasts. More solitary, much less common is the green sandpiper, an inland wader which prefers the cover of ponds, streams and riverbanks. When flushed, it zigzags skywards with a startled fluting cry.

On estuaries, reservoirs and other inland waters, huge flocks of wintering wildfowl gather. Some – mallard, teal, tufted duck – are permanent residents. But many are migrants escaping from harsher northern latitudes. Rafts of pintail bob on the waters. They use their elegant tails to balance as they up-end to feed. Flights of wigeon come whirling out of the sky, the drakes uttering their whistled exclamations of surprise. And on northern and eastern coasts broad chevrons of pink-footed geese fly in from their mudflat roosts to feed among the stubble. The jangling music of flighting pink-feet is one of the most thrilling sounds of the British countryside; the shrill nasal 'ang-ank' of the male easily distinguished from the yelp of the female, which is exactly one octave lower.

Another sound guaranteed to lift the hairs on the nape of a bird-watcher's neck is the melancholy bugling of wild winter swans – the whooper swan from Iceland and Lapland; Bewick's swan from arctic Russia. In the field they are hard to tell apart. Both species have buttercup bills with black tips, but the whooper is the bigger bird, with an $8\frac{1}{2}$ft (2.6m) wingspan. One of the best places in Britain to see Bewick's swans is the Wildfowl Trust's headquarters at Slimbridge, Gloucestershire.

Not all winter birds are true migrants. Some, like the lapwing, remain all year, but flock together in winter and move south during hard weather, where they become a familiar sight as they forage for worms in the fields and ploughlands. Other residents undergo a complete change of plumage to see the winter through. The most striking example is the ptarmigan, which loses its mottled summer coat and turns white to merge with the snows of the Highland summits. Survival is the name of the game, and a white ptarmigan in a winter landscape is more likely to evade the watchful eyes of hunting eagles.

Fieldfare: The grey rump and head are useful identifying features

Green Sandpiper: In flight this freshwater wader has a very black-and-white appearance, and a bold white rump

Ptarmigan: Highland resident that turns white in winter to hide from golden eagles

Wigeon: The drake (shown here) has bold white wing-flashes in flight

Redwing: Hawthorn
berries are a favourite food
but they also feed in open fields

Waxwing: Exotic visitor from
Scandinavia with a taste
for garden berries

Great Grey Shrike:
Fierce fence-post
sentinel. Its victims
are impaled
on thorns

Brambling: Northern finch,
sometimes mistaken for the common
resident Chaffinch

Snow Bunting:
In flight its beautiful black
and white markings
are unmistakable

Snowy Owl: The remote
Shetland isle of Fetlar is
the only British breeding
site of this splendid
arctic bird

Short-eared Owl:
Daylight hunter of saltmarsh
coasts and open countryside

Rough-legged Buzzard:
Paler than the resident
Common Buzzard, this
rare but regular visitor
arrives in October

Bewick's Swan and (right)
Whooper Swan: Confusingly
similar, but smaller Bewick
usually swims with tail end
well above water

Pink-footed Goose:
Upward of 50,000 birds
winter in the British Isles

Lapwing:
Also known
as the Green Plover

Pintail: Long pointed tail
identifies the drake (shown here in
full winter plumage)

Knot: Migrates as far
south as West Africa, but
the British Isles are
its main winter stronghold

Great
Spotted
Woodpecker

Nuthatch

Sparrowhawk

Green
Woodpecker

Jay

Grey
Squirrel

Nut Weevil

Cockchafer
Beetle

Oak
Bark
Beetle

Purple
Hairstreak

Caterpillar

Marble
Galls

Oak
Apple
Gall

Andricus
kollari

Biorrhiza
pallida

Young Leaves
and Blossom

Common Oak Leaf and Acorn

Tree
Creeper

BlueBell

Early Purple
Orchid

Woodruff

Wood
Sorrel

Mistletoe

Lichens

Wood Anemone

Primrose

Weasel

Polecat

Bracket
Fungus

Ivy

Teeming tenants of the oak

The richest of all our greenwood habitats in wildlife terms is the oakwood: a nature reserve in its own right. Every oak is host to (see left) plants, insects, birds and animals from the oak bush crickets which browse on its crown to the roe and fallow deer which walk in its shade. Compare, for instance, the wealth of insect life in an oak (284 different kinds) with that of alien species such as the horse chestnut (five) or the plane tree (only one). There are bugs that feed on oak flowers, beetles that eat the bark, and caterpillars like those of the purple hairstreak butterfly that eat the young leaves.

The insects attract birds: tree-creeper, nuthatch, pied flycatcher, wood warbler. The great spotted woodpecker nests in holes drilled into the hollow heart of rotten branches. Acorns provide food for the jay and grey squirrel, and the abundance of wildlife attracts fierce predators such as the weasel, the sparrowhawk and the rare polecat.

Galls are caused by parasites. Most conspicuous are the hard marble galls and oak apples, caused by the larvae of the gall wasp. Galls are made by the tortured tissue of the host tree, not by the insects. In the light shade and rich loam of the oakwood floor many wild flowers thrive. Among them are bluebell, primrose and wood anemone.

As the tree grows older it may be invaded by ivy and rarely, by mistletoe, and in wetter, western districts, by mosses, lichens and ferns. As it approaches the end of its 250-year lifespan, the crown grows stag-headed. Death is hastened by fungi which invade the wood and feed on its cells, causing rot and decay.

How the woods were made

The British Isles are among the least wooded countries in Europe. The collective woodland canopy scarcely covers 15 per cent of the land. In the past 40 years, more than half our mixed native woodland has become open field or conifer plantations. It is an old story. Man has been hacking away at the greenwood since the Stone Age. In the process, our use and abuse of trees, both native and alien, has helped – perhaps more than any other single factor – to shape the countryside we live in today. When the Ice Age was ending Britain was a treeless tundra still joined to the Continent. As the climate improved, the time was ripe for arboreal invasion. Dwarf birch, juniper, willow and Scots pine formed the advance guard. Then, following still warmer weather, came oak, hazel, ash and elm. These trees gradually became the dominant species, usurping all others except in the far north where the Great Wood of Caledon clung to its fathomless forests of pine, forming the untamed wildwood which still covered most of Britain right up until Saxon times. In the wildwood the lime tree also flourished, especially in the east, and alder in the wetter places.

From the Stone Age onwards, man's impact upon the wildwood grew with every passing century. Even in those primitive times it has been estimated that three men with stone axes could fell 600 square yards of forest in four hours.

By the Norman Conquest the boundless no-man's land of the old wildwood was already a folk memory. Even the composition of the ancient broad-leaved canopy was changing. The Romans had introduced walnuts and sweet chestnuts. Many other species, including the ubiquitous sycamore and horse chestnut – the conker tree beloved by generations of schoolboys – would become established by the 16th century.

But by then even the traditional method of woodland management known as coppicing was in decline. A thousand years ago woods were crucial to the economy. They provided logs to burn, timber to build, and shelter for the deer whose venison filled many a royal paunch. So early Britons learned to live with their woods, not clear-felling them as if they were cornfields, as some modern foresters do, but using them wisely as a renewable resource.

In this they were assisted by the remarkable ability of most British broad-leaved trees to regenerate themselves by sending up vigorous new shoots from the stump or stool, after they have been cut down. Thus coppicing evolved, where favoured hardwoods – hazel, ash, hornbeam – were cut on rotation to provide a regular crop of staves and poles from the same parent stool.

A coppice needed to be well protected, otherwise deer and cattle would eagerly browse the tender young shoots. So an alternative cropping method known as pollarding developed. Pollards are a kind of up-in-the-air coppice, where the trees are cut above the reach of browsing animals, leaving a stump between six and 15ft (2–4.5m) high, called a bolling.

Willows were pollarded in the same way (and still are in Somerset) to produce slender withies for basket-weaving. But the best examples of ancient pollards are to be found in places like Burnham Beeches, in Buckinghamshire, and in the relic scraps of the medieval royal forests, such as the New Forest in Hampshire and Hatfield Forest in Essex.

Cathedral columns of an English beechwood: few plants grow in its dense shade

Pedunculate Oak
Quercus robur
Massive, long-lived
tree of the clay vales.
So-called because its acorns
sprout from *peduncles* (stalks)

Holm Oak
Quercus ilex
Also known as ilex or
live oak. An alien evergreen
from southern Europe

English Elm
Ulmus procera
Towering hedgerow
colossus. Now, alas,
fast-disappearing due
to Dutch Elm disease

Ash
Fraxinus excelsior
A lover of limestone
country. Distinctive
sooty buds and bunches
of winged seeds (ash 'keys')

Beech
Fagus sylvaticus
Beautiful smooth
silver-grey bark; dense canopy
beneath which little grows.
Autumn leaves a glowing
golden brown

Hornbeam
Carpinus betulus
Superficially similar
to the beech.
Essex, Middlesex
and Hertfordshire
are its strongholds,
where many fine
old pollards survive

Alder
Alnus glutinosa
A tree of riverbanks
and fens. Unique
among our broad-
leaved trees – it is the
only one to bear cones

Crack Willow
Salix fragilis
So-called because
its twigs are easily
snapped off. Can reach
70–100ft (21–30m)

Sallow
Salix caprea
Also known as
goat willow and
pussy willow. The
first willow to flower,
with yellow (male) and silver
(female) catkins

Silver Birch
Betula pendula
Weeping branches
identify it from the
common birch (*Betula
pubescens*). At its
best in the Scottish
Highlands. In autumn the
leaves are purest gold

Walnut
Juglans regia
Famed for its
nuts – ripe by October
– and the handsome
grain of its wood

Small-leaved Lime
Tilia cordata
The honey-dew fragrance of its
sweet-smelling flowers is one
of the delights of an English
summer

Among the coppices, some trees, especially oaks, were left and allowed to
reach maturity before being felled.
These, the standards or maidens (un-
touched trees) were grown for their
timber. The medieval woodman made a
clear distinction between wood and
timber. Wood was anything from brush-

wood and firewood to the poles obtained
by coppicing. Timber was a term reserved
for the heavy stuff.

After the Middle Ages, and after the
kings had relinquished many of their
hunting forests, the woods were plun-
dered by charcoal-burners to fuel the
furnaces of the iron-masters. They

shrank before the onslaught of expanding agriculture. The great oaks were laid
low to build Tudor towns and Georgian
battle fleets. Railways and the age of
cheap coal undercut the firewood trade.
Two world wars, the felling of timber to
pay death duties, the grubbing out of
hedgerows – and the ravages of Dutch

Sycamore
Acer pseudoplatanus
Hardy, grow-anywhere
alien introduced to
Scotland 400 years ago.
Spreads by means of its
whirling winged 'keys'

Grey Poplar
Populus canescens
Grows to height of
80–90ft (24–27m). Attractive
red catkins; leaves
with downy grey undersides

Black Poplar
Populus nigra
Rare, craggy 100-ft (30m)
giant. Grows fast,
loves damp. Not found
north of Trent

Field Maple
Acer campestre
Smallish tree
about 25ft (8m) high
Small leaves a
rich yellow-gold in
autumn

Hazel
Corylus avellana
Mostly seen as
hedge or coppice but will
form small tree if left.
Dusty yellow 'lamb's-tail'
catkins at winter's end;
sweet edible nuts
in autumn

Horse Chestnut
Aesculus
hippocastanum
Pride of parks and
avenues. Sticky buds,
huge waxy candle
flowers, shiny conkers

Sweet Chestnut
Castanea vulgaris
Can outlive the oak.
Massive trunk with fissured,
spiralling bark. Edible nuts
encased in prickly green
hedgehog shucks

Holly
Ilex aquifolium
Small evergreen
with glossy prickly
leaves and clustered
scarlet berries

Mature
tree

Mature
cone

Young
tree

Scots Pine
Pinus sylvestris
Scotland is its native
stronghold, but grows
just as happily in Hampshire's
New Forest

Young
cone

Larch
Larix decidua
Attractive conifer
which sheds its
needles in winter, replacing them
with delicate spring greenery

Mountain Ash
Sorbus aucuparia
Propagated by
birds – especially
the thrush family – which
strip the scarlet berries

Yew
Taxus baccata
The sombre
evergreen of country churchyards.
Grows to a great age

Elm disease have all conspired to reduce
our woodland heritage to a shadow of its
ancient glory.

Yet enough trees remain in our man-
made landscape of field and hedgerow to
create the illusion of wooded countryside, enclosing, shading, walling in
with cliffs of leaves. The wildwood is
gone for ever, to be replaced by something no less precious: a scattered mosaic
of clumps and copses, beech hangers and
pagan groves of yew, pocket woodlands
and thin green lines of waterside willows.
And sometimes, the welcoming depths of
a true forest – a Savernake or a Wyre –
preserved with all its living elements.

□ Of the trees shown here, all but one
(the black poplar) are common, and all
but six (holm oak, walnut, larch, sycamore, horse chestnut and sweet chestnut) are true natives. Our guide shows
leaves, fruit, and appearance in summer
and winter. These clues will help you to
recognise different species.

The primeval pinewood

Even to Sassenach eyes, the Scots pine is a familiar sight. It thrives all over England, from wildest Lakeland to genteel Bournemouth. But only in the Scottish Highlands can it be seen in its true glory, growing as nature intended in majestic stands among the lochs and glens, where it provides both food and shelter for the wildlife of northern Britain.

In the shadow of the Cairngorms at Rothiemurchus, at Beinn Eighe on the west coast, in the Black Wood of Rannoch, Glen Affric and a few other places, are the last relics of the Great Wood of Caledon, the primeval northern pine forest. The Great Wood once covered more than three million acres. Wolves and wild boar roamed there, sharing the trackless deeps with brown bear, lynx and elk. Outlaws found refuge in its glens and hollows. For centuries the pines grew undisturbed. Far to the south, the Romans came and went. The Saxons carved out petty earldoms.

Then came the Vikings, and the war on the Great Wood began. In the west they fired the forests and felled the tall trees to carve as dragon prows for their longships. The wildlife of the forest began to go, too, as their stronghold diminished. The bears were gone by the tenth century; the last wolf was killed in Inverness-shire in 1743.

Further inroads were made by the impoverished clan chiefs who, forced to pay homage to Hanoverian overlords, sold off their timber to English ironmasters. Two world wars and the Forestry Commission in its bad old backwoods heyday finally brought the Great Wood to its knees, reducing it to railway sleepers and telegraph poles. Today the remaining 20,000 acres (8093 hectares) are mere remnants, with no more than about 4000 acres (1619 hectares) of true closed forest in which it is still possible to catch the illusion of a long-vanished Caledon.

The relic trees support forms of wildlife seldom seen outside the Highlands. The pine is host both to the fish-eating osprey, which builds its massive eyrie in the topmost clefts of the spreading crown, and to the crested tits which excavate their nests in the rotting stumps. Pine seeds provide food for the crossbill and the red squirrel. The squirrels in turn are hunted by the rare pine marten, the fierce tree weasel whose chief stronghold is in Beinn Eighe National Nature Reserve.

The fresh green shoots are eaten by the caterpillars of the pine beauty moth, and also by the capercaillie, the giant grouse of the Caledonian forest. During the 'lek' – the season of courtship and display – the woods echo to the popping and wheezing cries of the aggressive males as they perform their extraordinary antics, strutting and leaping with swollen necks and fully-fanned tails. The capercaillie was exterminated in Scotland during the 18th century but was reintroduced successfully from Sweden in 1837.

When the pine needles fall they are gathered up by the wood ant, the largest British ant, to form a mound sometimes several feet high covering the main subterranean nesting chambers and galleries. Here, too, on the forest floor, you may find two wild orchids seldom seen elsewhere: creeping lady's tresses and the coralroot orchid.

Unfortunately, man's tampering with

the works has broken down the Scottish pine forest's system of natural regeneration. When squirrels and crossbills scatter the pine seeds there are no longer any boars, bears or elk to root in the undergrowth and open up the soil to aid germination. Worse, any seeds that do actually reach the seedling stage are speedily chewed up by the red deer.

The final blow could be the fickle British climate. Over the last few centuries the weather has been getting warmer and wetter. That process may now have been reversed but the damage has been done. As a result the forest floors

Left: Monarchs of the glens. Native Scots pines provide a rich habitat for Highland wildlife

are suffering a creeping invasion of spongy, soaking sphagnum moss, piling up in thick cushions among the trees. Tear up two handfuls and you can wring a cup of water from it. And that, to the Scots pine, is disaster. The accumulated wetness is steadily loosening the clenched roots until in the winter gales, even the strongest tree will lurch from its socket like a rotten molar.

Fortunately there is now a greater awareness of the pine's plight. The Nature Conservancy Council is involved in schemes to save the forest. Some areas have been declared national nature reserves or sites of special scientific interest, although that is no cast-iron guarantee against the forester's axe. The Govern-

ment has finally recognised the landscape value of Scots pine on its native ground and has greatly improved the grant available to private foresters who plant native pine. As for the Forestry Commission, it no longer regards the Scots pine simply as a cash crop. Its Glen Affric forest, for instance, is now managed as a Caledonian pine reserve.

Its value is twofold. Firstly, there is the beauty of the forest. The way the trees grow wide apart, almost in glades, in a way that lets in the light and creates magical depths of space and serenity. There is the way they grow in company with the beautiful weeping Highland birch (*Betula pendula*), and still retain a rich wildlife. And there is the beauty of

Key to illustration: *1 Scots Pine 2 Pine Beauty Moth 3 Pine Beauty Caterpillar 4 Crossbill 5 Coralroot Orchid 6 Creeping Lady's Tresses 7 Sphagnum Moss 8 Chickweed Wintergreen 9 Wood Ant Nest 10 Capercaillie 11 Heather 12 Hairy Wood Rush 13 Red Squirrel 14 Wood Ant 15 Crested Tit 16 Pine Marten 17 Osprey 18 Red Throated Diver*

the individual tree itself; the flaky fissured bark, all silvery-grey and flaming salmon-pink; the blue-green canopy; the gnarled and craggy shape. Like the oak, it has a courageous quality that suits its wild surroundings. It is the Scots pine, not the red deer, that is the real monarch of the glen.

The last wilderness

The mountains and moorlands of the British Isles form our last great wilderness. Barren, desolate and at first glance empty, they support a spectacular variety of wild plants and creatures. Many of the rarest flowers and the most magnificent birds and animals find sanctuary in the fastness of these remote and beautiful rainswept uplands.

Moorland occurs on the uplands of the north and west of the British Isles where the old, hard rocks rise up and the moist Atlantic airstream creates a constantly waterlogged habitat which encourages the formation of peat and bogland. It takes a special breed of plants to cope with the harsh climate and thin soils.

Most characteristic of all moorland plants is heather, a close-knit evergreen undershrub with tough woody stems covering immense tracts of peaty uplands. There are five different species but the commonest is *Calluna vulgaris*, the true heather or ling. Its clustered spikes of tiny flowers are rich in nectar, and from July to September they transform the burnt cork hues of the drier moors with a glorious blaze of summer purple. From May to late July the flowers of the heath spotted-orchid are fairly widespread on the moors. One of the most interesting plants to look for on these acid peatlands is fir clubmoss, which is neither a fir nor a true moss, but a primitive, 6in (15cm) high relative of the ferns.

Heather is a valuable food plant for many creatures, including the caterpillars of the emperor moth, which feed on the leaves from June to August. When fully grown they are about 2in (5cm) long, and pupate in a spun silk cocoon. The adult male moths can be seen whirring over the heather on sunny days in April and May; the females have the same bold eye-spots but are a ghostly grey and fly by night.

On grouse moors large swathes of heather are regularly burned to encourage the growth of succulent new shoots for the red grouse. The guttural chuckling go-beck, go-beck of grouse is one of the most evocative sounds of the high moors. The heather feeds the grouse; the grouse, in turn, is eaten by the golden eagle, Britain's largest bird of prey. Something like 200 pairs of eagles breed in Scotland, nesting on remote crags or in old Scots pines. The eyrie is a huge pile of sticks sometimes measuring

Barren world of the Highland summits above Loch Inchad, near Rhiconich, Sutherland

Key to illustration: 1 Heather 2 Heath Spotted orchid 3 Fir Clubmoss 4 and 5 Emperor Moth and Caterpillar 6 Red Grouse 7 Golden Eagle 8 Merlin 9 Meadow Pipit 10 Bilberry 11 Bilberry Bumble Bee 12 Cotton Grass 13 Sphagnum Moss 14 Bog Asphodel 15 Round-leaved Sundew 16 Greenshank 17 Curlew 18 Sheep's Fescue 19 Mat-grass 20 Mountain Ringlet 21 Red Deer 22 Wild Cat 23 Mountain Hare 24 Ptarmigan 25 Moss Campion 26 Starry Saxifrage

Where the peat thins out at around 2000ft (610m) the herbage becomes sweeter and more alpine in character, with grasses such as sheep's fescue and mat-grass, food plant of the mountain ringlet caterpillar. The mountain ringlet is Britain's only alpine butterfly, a glacial relic, found locally in Scotland above 1500ft (457m). The adult insect is on the wing during July and August, flying close to the ground on sunny days.

In summer the red deer move to the high corries to escape the irritation of biting flies. The red deer is Britain's largest living wild land mammal. A full-grown Highland stag can weigh over 200lbs (91kg) and stand 4ft (1.2m) high at the shoulder. The stags shed their antlers at the end of winter. By late August their new antlers are complete and clean of velvet. September and October is the time of the rut, when the stags roar and wallow and round up their harems of hinds. Outside the rut, the females and immature males live in separate herds from the mature stags. The calves are born in May and June.

Among the crags and summits of the mountains the wild cat finds refuge from persecution, making its lair among the boulders and slopes of shattered rock. Record length for this fierce predator with the flat head and ringed bottle-brush tail is 3ft 9in (1.14m). Its prey includes the mountain hare, the only true mountain mammal in Britain. In winter its thick coat turns white except for the black tips of its ears.

Another mountain resident which turns white in winter is the ptarmigan, seen here in summer plumage. It lives in the harsh world of the high tops, where the snow lies among the rocks for maybe eight months or more. Yet even here, spring and summer bring a delicate beauty to the wet rock ledges. Moss campion and starry saxifrage are among the hardy wild flowers which evolution has shaped for survival in the climate of Britain's highest mountains.

10ft (3m) across. Immature eagles retain distinctive white patches on wings and tail until they are five years old. Sharing the eagle's domain but at the opposite end of the scale is the diminutive merlin, the smallest falcon in Britain, scarcely bigger than a blackbird, but a fast, dashing flier with a taste for meadow-pipits. Look for merlins perched on fence posts or telegraph poles along lonely moorland roads.

Where the peat becomes deeper and wetter, and along the upper limits of the heather moors, bilberry often becomes the dominant ground cover. From April to June its flowers provide nectar for the bilberry bumble-bee. The sweet, edible berries appear from July onwards. Another familiar sight on wet moorland is cotton-grass, its seed heads adorned with cotton wool tufts in May and June.

In the hollows and on the wettest hillsides the spongy ground is carpeted with blanket bog. Here a different range of plants grow, cushions of sphagnum moss in varying colours from green to red, the beautiful bog asphodel which blooms in August, and a living fly-trap, the round-leaved sundew. Sundews supplement the poor nutrient levels they receive from the blanket bog by catching insects with their sticky red leaves. When an insect becomes trapped, the leaf folds up and digests its prey.

Birds which feed in the soft peat of the blanket bog include the greenshank, a rare Highland wader, and the curlew, a more common wader with a gull-like flight and the most beautiful call of all moorland birds, as it cries its own name with a mournful, broken liquid whistle. The greenshank's long bill is slightly upturned; that of the curlew curves downwards; but both are adapted for probing in soft mud in search of worms, grubs and small snails.

Chapter Five
Working in the Countryside

The countryside is a place of work and country life is often hard and rigorous.
Yet for many the satisfactions of working in it are deeply felt.
Shepherding high above Loch Katrine in Scotland demands special qualities of
man, dog and sheep. This shepherd's flock of Scottish Blackfaces is bred
to survive the meagre grazing and heavy weather of the hills. Even so
without his care and stamina, many would die. For such a man shepherding
is a way of life rather than just a form of employment. The
uncompromising economics of hill farming underline this. This chapter explores
his world and that of other farms and farming, presents detailed
and personal profiles of rural craftsmen, recalls the working countryside of
yesterday and identifies what there is left of it still to see

It is easy to overlook the countryside as a gigantic food factory in which harsh practicalities take priority over pretty views. In the last 50 years farming in the British Isles has created its own 20th century Agricultural Revolution. This has transformed it into a highly efficient, highly mechanised science-based industry, worth over £7,000 million a year in receipts; an industry in which more and more crops and livestock are being produced with less land and labour. In the process it has altered the appearance of wide areas of the countryside as dramatically as did the great enclosure movements of earlier centuries.

A drive through the countryside in 1930 would have revealed a farming landscape hardly changed for a century. Heavy horses – Shires, Clydesdales, Suffolk Punches and Percherons – over a million of them, worked the land pulling only slightly modified versions of the implements invented by the farm improvers of the 18th and 19th centuries.

The few primitive tractors in use had made little impact and men still sweated behind horse and plough, breaking the earth in a patchwork of small, thick-hedged fields. Rattling horse-drawn harrows crumbled the soil into a tilth fit for seed; and drills, which seemed all spring, sprocket, cog and wheel, metered seed into the soil down vibrating coiled-spring tubes.

Farmworkers scythed the edges of the fields, cutting a swathe through the grass and corn to make access for the mowing machine and reaper. There was a lot of grass, permanent pasture for the cattle, and mostly it contained species of grasses which had altered little since the pastoral farming of early man.

Cereals were grown from tall-strawed strains which the farmer's grandfather had sown. At least harvesting them was easier than haymaking. The reaper-binder, which both cut the corn and tied the sheaves, was a miracle of the 1880s for which farmers still gave thanks, although plenty of manual effort was required to stand the sheaves into stooks to dry before being carted to the stackyard to await the thresher in the autumn.

Large as a country bus and hauled by a hissing traction engine, its arrival brought a temporary interruption to rural tranquillity. The laboured beating of its engine, the whirr of the driving belts, the tinny percussion of the grain sieves and the cries of the men made it a time of great animation and prodigious thirst.

Amidst clouds of chaff and smoke the grain was flailed from the wheat ears, cleaned, graded and bagged. A mound of chaff grew beneath the belly of the machine; pummelled straw was cast out behind to be re-stacked for use as animal bedding and feed.

This was a climax to a year in a system of farming which was largely self-sufficient. In 1930 farmers grew both crops and kept livestock. Wheat, potatoes and some of the pea crop were sold but most of the other produce was consumed on the farm. The horses ate much of the oats and hay. The remainder, and a lot of barley, was eaten by the cows, which, with beef cattle and sheep, fed on swedes, turnips and kale too. Barley straw, chopped fine, provided bulk in the cattle's diet; bedding too. Straw, when mixed with dung and trodden down,

Power and productivity on the farm

Horse and ploughman 1930

Output: horse and man could plough one acre (0.4 hectares) a day

Numbers: a 350 acre (142 hectares) mixed farm had six horses and four horsemen. Work on arable land kept them busy most of the year

Cost: £50 to £60 for a heavy working horse, £25 for a set of harness and from £9 to £12 for a plough

Ploughman: worked longer hours. Implements had to be man-handled at end of each furrow. After work horses had to be watered, groomed, fed and bedded down

Food: a daily diet of 16lbs of oats and 16lbs of hay (7.25kg) and 10lbs (4.5kg) of roots or greens

This shows the changes on a 350 acre (142 hectares) mixed farm in the last 50 years. Yesterday's farm occupies the half of the illustration to the left, the modern farm the half to the right. The major alterations, discussed in more detail in the main text, are in the size of the fields, larger with fewer hedges; the crops in them, more pasture then, more ploughed land now plus new crops like maize; and in the machinery working them which has taken the place of horses and a greater number of men.

Haystacks have given way to silos, milk churns to mobile tankers, animals and poultry in the fields to animals and poultry indoors. The harvest scene has changed enormously and helicopters were hardly heard of – let alone used to spray potatoes with fungicides.

The farm used to employ four stockmen, four horsemen and a shepherd; today a family runs it with two workers. It then cost £1,000 to equip the farm with machinery, including the horses; at 1980 prices the machinery – tractors, combine, ploughs, harrows, rollers, mower, forage harvester, muck spreader and so on – would come to well over £80,000. To run the machinery the farm uses 6,000 gallons (27,274 litres) of diesel a year and just over 140 tons of fertiliser for the fields instead of 64 tons.

Some of the 1930 fields used to grow hay and oats to support the farm's working horses. Now they grow hay and barley to feed livestock for meat and milk production.

Today the farm's dairy herd consists of 80 Friesians yielding over 60,000 gallons (272,700 litres) of milk a year which have replaced yesterday's 20 lower yielding Dairy Shorthorns. The arable land produces 500 tons of crops against just over 80 tons 50 years ago. In 1930 good agricultural land cost £20 an acre. Today it averages over £1,300 an acre.

Tractor and driver 1980

Output: modern 90hp tractor and driver can plough an average of 25 acres a day, more if necessary

Numbers: on a 350 acre mixed farm one 90hp and two 65hp tractors. One driver

Cost: 65hp £8,000, 90hp £11,000, 180hp £26,000 and the newest 400hp tractor £40,000

Driver: a skilled mechanic whose tractor has air-conditioning, all-weather, tinted glass cab and radio-cassette player. After day's work he switches off ignition and goes home

Fuel: a 90hp tractor working with a 3-furrow plough uses 3 gallons (13.6 litres) of diesel per hour

provided the main enrichment for the land.

By-products of the farm dairy – skimmed milk, buttermilk, whey – went to the pigs together with waste from crops and kitchen. Chickens were fed on tail corn (grains too small to sell) and what they scratched from the farmyard.

There was a great variety of animals: more breeds of dairy cows, beef cattle, sheep and pigs than there were counties. Farms in the wetter southern and western counties, where grass grew best, tended to specialise in dairying and cattle raising with sheep on the hills.

Ploughing featured less and less the farther west one travelled. The 1930s were characterised by steadily decreasing acreages under the plough throughout the whole of the British Isles. The emphasis was on permanent grass and livestock.

Hill farmers in the mountain areas and the Pennine, Dartmoor, Exmoor, Antrim and Wicklow uplands were heavily dependent on sheep. Lambs and older ewes from Herdwick, Cheviot, Blackface and other mountain breeds were sold to farmers in the lowlands for fattening or breeding. This produced healthy cross bred lowland flocks with the vigour of mountain sheep and the meat and wool growing ability of lowland ones.

Similarly hill cattle, Welsh Blacks, Galloways and long-haired West Highland breeds, sometimes crossed with beef Shorthorns, provided store cattle to be sold to lowland farmers for fattening.

The pace and the power of the horse, and the endurance of human muscle, determined the progress of work in the fields. Wooden waggons with wheels

Traditional farmscape near Nymphsfield, in the Cotswolds. The old farmhouse and its out-buildings, made of the beautiful local Cotswold stone, blend perfectly with the surrounding fields

This livestock farming, requiring fewer men, aggravated the problems of rural unemployment and by 1930 the British Government was moving towards a pro-gramme of State aid for farmers. Throughout the Thirties it was expressed in the form of subsidies for wheat, barley and oats and meat. There were import quotas on foreign food and central mar-keting boards were established to control sales of milk, bacon, hops and potatoes at guaranteed prices.

Government policy even put new crops into the fields. Before World War One sugar had been entirely imported but by the early 1930s substantial sub-sidies encouraged farmers to go in for sugar beet. The new home industry soon supplied a quarter of the country's sugar needs.

All these measures gave agriculture a slight lift but even so the drift from the land continued, and 1930 was half-way point in a twenty-year inter-wars period which saw many thousands of labourers leaving the countryside. At the end of World War One there were one million farmers, their families and workers on the land in Great Britain. By the end of World War Two their numbers had shrunk to 889,000. Today there are just over 500,000.

The year 1930, then, was marked by much rural hardship and deprivation but save for macadamised roads, grow-ing numbers of National Grid electricity pylons and the city-dwellers out for a drive in their square-backed saloon the rural landscape still retained much that had enchanted painters like Constable a hundred or so years earlier.

Today many features of that land-scape have vanished. Milk churns no longer await collection by the roadside; instead milk is pumped direct from the cow, through filters, to a stainless steel holding tank where it is chilled and stored until the tanker lorry comes. Cot-tage-loaf haystacks, thatched to keep out the rain, have been replaced with great blocks of machine-handled bales pro-tected by black polythene sheeting. Fields are larger, hedgerows fewer, so that huge costly machines can be easily and profitably used. The power of the tractor has increased, in cases up to 300hp, as the labour force on the land has fallen. A heavy horse and a man working a field is a rarity (see p 136) and great hedgeless tracts where there is not a cow to be seen are commonplace in the eastern half of the country.

But in other areas modernisation of

six ft (1.8m) in diameter lurched through the farm loaded with dung. Hay and wheat were hauled home on large, flat carts, sometimes elaborately decorated.

Most farm buildings were made of local materials used in characteristic regional styles. Only the curved and arched corrugated iron roofs of the big open sided Dutch barns struck a mass produced note.

Farms were smaller than today's: 63 acres (25.5 hectares) for the average sized holding then against an average of 120 acres (48.5 hectares) now. And 75% of the farmers in the United Kingdom were tenants in contrast to the 60% who now own their farms. In Ireland by this time thousands of tenant farmers had – with the active assistance of the State

through the Irish Land Commission – disabused themselves of landlords and were establishing themselves as peasant proprietors, setting a pattern of small, dispersed but compact family farms which persists over much of the country today. Nearly 70% of all holdings are less than 50 acres (20 hectares).

The economic climate of 1930 had much to do with the look of the farming landscape. In World War One the Government encouraged the ploughing of grassland to grow more cereals and won the co-operation of farmers by giv-ing them guaranteed prices. But after the war agriculture slumped, the price of wheat halved, farmers were no longer bolstered by government aid, so they returned the ploughed land to pasture.

farming has been at a slower pace. In Ireland many farmers still take their milk to the creameries in churns, and herds of cows being driven to the milking byres are a common sight on the roads.

The changes in farming have thrown up new silhouettes on the skyline. It is puzzling to know what Constable would have made of the silver, cylindrical, space-age silos which stand in the old stackyards; or the long factory-farm sheds with their rows of roof-top air vents; or the huge, slowly revolving, cantilevered spray-irrigation systems in the fields.

The animals, often unseen, have changed. So, too, have the crops (see pp 129–135) and the greater use of fertilisers, insecticides and herbicides and the application of new scientific discoveries in animal and plant genetics have transformed farming.

Detailed understanding of how hereditary characteristics are transmitted from parents to offspring, and the way in which these can be controlled and exploited, has led to the introduction of new, disease-resistant, high-yield varieties of crops and improved breeds of animals.

Artificial insemination, introduced in the 1940s, has enabled the advances in animal breeding to be widely adopted. It means one outstanding bull can father calves in cows anywhere, 600 a year instead of the 60 he used to serve naturally on a few score farms within reach. Nowadays 80% of all dairy cows are inseminated artificially.

A further development is ovum transplant. Eggs shed by a high performance cow during ovulation (most of which are normally wasted) can be collected, fertilised artificially and the resulting embryos stored in deep freeze until planted in the womb of a foster cow who bears the calf in the normal way. Thus quite ordinary cows are able to bear outstanding calves.

Dairy herds are now dominated by one breed, the tall, black-and-white British Friesian which has eclipsed other well known breeds (see p 132) because it is a high milk yielder and its male calves make good beef, even better when the cows are crossed with beef breeds such as the stocky brown, white-faced Hereford. In beef farming success depends on the daily rate at which cattle increase in weight in relation to the amount of food they consume. This is why high meat yielding foreign breeds and their crosses can now be seen in the fields (see p 132).

Harvest, ancient and modern. Above: Machine-handled bales await collection in the wide fields of East Anglia. Top: Barley stooked in the old manner on a Scottish croft

The only pigs seen outdoors are likely to be pregnant sows whose owners feel that added exercise makes them fitter for motherhood. Most breeding sows, like their fattening piglets, are kept indoors all their lives. They are very different animals to the pigs which snuffled and grubbed in the mud patches of the past (see p 135); modern hybrids which have little resemblance to their individual parents but are uniform in looks and performance and, in any given batch, are all ready for market at the same time.

Most poultry are also hybrids, producing a predictable number of eggs or weight of meat when automatically fed on a uniform diet in battery house or broiler shed.

Precision feeding of animals, the daily ration to give a predicted weight increase, is pointless if the performance of the animals is very variable. To avoid this breeders use computers to make thousands of calculations in a technique known as progeny testing. Before a bull's semen is used to artificially inseminate cows on a large scale, farmers will want to know that the calves will prosper uniformly. Computer analysis of statistics from accumulated experimental inseminations enables breeders to give this assurance.

On some advanced dairy farms cows wear plastic necklaces which house radio transponders. These emit radio signals with different frequencies for individual cows. The cow's identifying signal, linked to a computer, enables her output to be recorded while she is being milked. And, as she lowers her head to the feeding trough, the signals also tell the computer whether she is getting the right amount of food to support her output.

Scientific measurement in the cowshed also extends to piggeries. Electronic sensors measure the thickness of the lean and fat on the animal's back and the pig farmer is able to tell precisely whether it is ready for butcher or bacon factory.

The great expansion of the area devoted to cereal crops, especially wheat and barley (the latter is now the single most important crop grown) has been at the cost of ploughing several millions of acres of permanent grass since World War Two. Areas such as the Chalk downlands and parts of Exmoor have increasingly come under the plough. In recent years this huge new cereal acreage, much of it is in eastern England, has been associated with new, improved strains which are much more compact than they used to be: larger heads carrying more and bigger grains are borne on shorter, tougher stems which are better for supporting heavy crops without collapsing in bad weather.

Such cereals have been created in the laboratory by 'engineering' the genetic materials in the sex cells of the plants. The increased yields resulting from this are startling. In 1930 16cwt per acre (2008 kilos per hectare) was thought good for winter wheat. One of today's improved strains can yield up to 5 tons (5.08 tonnes) per acre on good land in a good season.

Genetic engineering of this sort has also led to leafier cabbages which store better, vastly improved potato crops and more productive grass. It has also brought new strains of crops which previously did not do well in the British Isles. Maize is an example (see p 129).

The need for the continuing application of fertilisers and pesticides throughout the growing season has made its own impact on the fields. Rows are left unsown at specified intervals so that tractors can get through easily and apply nutrients and pesticides with greater precision. The tractor-wide stripes across the fields are called 'tramlines'.

Hills farms have been the least obviously touched by the farming revolution. This is not surprising since the flavour of the past is always more persistent where it is hardest to make the profits to finance change. Both the terrain and the nature of the farming make it difficult to use machines to replace

men. But better longer-lasting sheep dips have helped the shepherd keep his flock free from parasites and some hill farms have managed to finance buildings in which sheep can shelter a few weeks before lambing which greatly reduces losses. And the occasional patch of emerald green on the hillside signifies at least one farmer who has found money to drain, lime and re-seed his pasture.

At first sight dairy and cattle farms have changed little; fields are still small for easy control of grazing, walls and hedges still provide shelter in bad weather, and their main crop is still grass. The grass may look the same as it did in the 1930s, but it isn't. The old grass sward had a dozen or more of grasses and other plants in it. The new pastures which have been sown have no more than four – and they are much more productive.

There is rye-grass which begins to grow earlier in the year, takes longer to reach the less digestible flowering stage and yields more hay or silage per acre. The clovers in the new mixtures are as pretty as the wild ones of old but are more robust and erect, with bigger leaves like solar panels trapping more of the sunlight.

Haymaking is wholly mechanised. Instead of being carted loose the hay is compressed by machine into bound bales, rectangular blocks of 30 to 40lbs (13.6 to 18kg) in weight. The large rolls seen in the fields – they weigh more than half-a-ton (508kg) – are mostly straw bales. Grass for silage is mown and left for several hours to wilt. Then it is gathered by a forage harvester, a spectacular machine which chops it into tiny pieces and blows it in a plume into an accompanying trailer.

The chopping helps it lose even more moisture and pack tightly into the silo. Tight packing excludes air and allows the right type of bacteria to develop. These produce the acid conditions which suspend further activity and preserve the grass green until required as winter feed. Grass has its highest food value when young so it is cut for silage several times a season. This gives more, higher quality fodder than if cropped for hay.

Some farmers believe that allowing animals to trample grass they are grazing is wasteful. So they keep them in covered yards using a mower and forage harvester to cut and carry the fresh grass to them daily. This is known as 'zero-grazing'.

Tractor mounted scrapers, lifting buckets and mechanical muck-spreaders

make returning the dung to the fields much less of a burden than when it was horse-and-carted. Some yards have perforated floors through which the dung is trodden into a channel below. This is wide enough to allow the passage of a tractor-mounted scraper.

Liquid dung, or slurry, may be pumped into large storage lagoons where it is allowed to drain free of most of its surplus water so it can be spread as a solid. Sometimes it is pumped to the fields and spread, under pressure, as a coarse spray.

So the hand-forking of dung, a simple but back-breaking job, is another chore which has disappeared from the country scene. Some, no doubt, regret this and all the other changes on the farm. But those who work the farm may well feel that the new landscapes are better, less demanding than the old.

Yet, however the farming landscape looks and whatever the changes, the job of the farmer remains *fundamentally* the same. Soil is prepared; crops sown, harvested and sold; or fed to animals to be converted into meat, wool, hides, eggs and dairy produce. The farmer captures the sun's energy and uses it together with gasses in the atmosphere, minerals in the soil and moisture in the air to produce food.

Science and technology take him only so far. His success or failure is still very much determined by the weather and that indefinable quality, an amalgam of wisdom, wile and expertise, which marks the good farmer from the bad.

Hill farms. Their mainstay are sheep, supported by cattle. Land use varies with altitude and time of the year. The unfenced, open high country may be grazed with other farmers, each having a quota of grazing animals. Better pasture on the lower slopes may be walled or fenced off. This is privately owned and was originally reclaimed from rough pasture and improved. The best land is on the valley floor. This is the 'inland' or 'inby' where grass is rotated with roots and other crops to provide winter feed. Spring lambs born here are moved up the hill in late spring after they have been earmarked and the male lambs castrated. Later the flock is brought down to be sheared, then returned to the hills until late autumn. It is then brought pro-

Right: Pennine hill farm. The best land lies nearest the farm on the valley floor. The open moors above are fit only for rough grazing and may be covered in snow for much of the winter

Making 'hay' the modern way. Forage harvester gathering grass for silage in rural Warwickshire

gressively down the hillside to winter in the lower fields. Lambs and old ewes are sold in late summer to lowland farmers for fattening and breeding. Most hill cattle are cross-bred. Calves stay with their mothers on the hills for the summer and are sold to fatteners in the autumn.

Dairy farms. Modern dairy farms are sophisticated, highly mechanised factories for converting grass into milk. The average yield for a cow is 1000 gallons (4545 litres) a year. In summer the cow giving three gallons (13.6 litres) a day gets her daily food requirements by eating 167lbs (75 kilos) of fresh grass. On this she gives nearly 4% butter-fat milk and will be gaining weight. The lactation period, the time she gives milk after calving, is about 300 days. She produces a calf a year for five or six years. Most farmers have their cows calving in the autumn to take advantage of higher winter milk prices. In summer the cows are kept out in the fields; in winter they stay in a large covered shed where they can move freely. But each cow has a cubicle of its own where it can lie and chew the cud. Machine milking, twice a day, is a slick mechanical operation. Up to 20 or more cows can be milked simultaneously in a herring-bone milking parlour. This takes eight to 10 minutes.

Arable farms. The big specialist arable farms of eastern England which tend to specialise in barley, wheat, potatoes and sugar beet range in size from 400 to 1000 acres (162 to 405 hectares). They contrast sharply with the smaller farms of 50 years ago which produced comparatively small amounts of a wide variety of crops. Factors which favour large scale arable farming in the east are drier conditions which enables grain to ripen more easily, soils heavy enough to give cereals a good root base and light enough to allow reasonable drainage, and level land which facilitates minimum use of labour and maximum use of machines: up to 50 tractors and half-a-dozen combines on some farms. Some are operated with virtually no labour, all the work being put out to specialist contractors. Barley is the biggest single crop grown for animal feed and the higher quality varieties for malting. Crop rotation is less important now because pesticides and herbicides are efficient at cleaning the land and synthetic fertilisers boost the soil without having to rest it.

Fruit farms. Apples, pears and plums are the main orchard fruits grown. The character of the orchard, however, has changed. The tall trees of the past have been replaced with small, compact bushy trees which are easy to prune, spray and pick. Good orchard land is expensive, five times as much as arable land, so it must be intensively cultivated to get maximum yields of high quality fruit. Trees are planted close together in rows and the alleys between them are just wide enough for a tractor. Special narrow-width tractors have been designed so that even less land is taken up by the alleys. This type of orchard should produce six tons of apples an acre compared with three to four tons for orchards with larger, wider spaced trees. Pruning takes place from November to February. Spraying to control grass, weeds and pests and to apply foliar feeds and hormones to regulate fruit set and growth takes place up to a dozen times a season. Some picking takes place from tractor-drawn platforms instead of ladders. Early Worcesters and late picked Cox are still favourites. Newer varieties like Crispin and Spartan store well. In soft fruits the emphasis is on strawberries, raspberries and black and red currants. Many of these farms have gone over to Pick-Your-Own. This cuts out costly labour.

Market gardening. The deep-freeze has had a marked influence on the character of this. The traditional small-holding of a few acres has not the output to keep the freezer plants and canneries busy, so in areas like Norfolk and the Fens there has been a significant increase

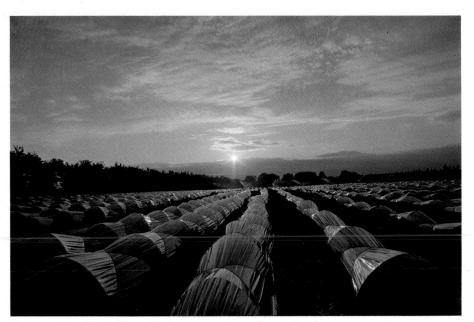

Frostproof farming in Kent. Cloches protect the market gardener's tender young crops

Colourful crop of oilseed rape. Its oil goes into margarine and other uses in the food industry

in the growing of peas, beans and sprouts on a field scale. This requires investment in expensive machinery like pea-viners. But in traditional smallholding areas like the Vale of Evesham the produce is grown for direct supply to the big urban markets of the Midlands. Much is sold direct to motorists from roadside stalls. Here holdings vary from a few acres up to 50 (20 hectares). Many are fragmented and scattered, creating practical diffi-culties which do not arise on the Fenland farms. Growing lettuces, broccoli, cauli-flowers and, under glass, tomatoes and cucumbers requires very intensive farm-ing with a high investment in glass-houses, irrigation systems and fertilisers. The market gardener's most important asset is the soil itself which has to be kept in good heart. Over years of intensive working a market gardener sometimes virtually creates a new, improved soil. But in the early days 'gardens' tended to be located on light, easy to work soils which warmed up early. Nearness to large cities was also important but with rapid transport this is less so now. As with soft fruit, Pick-Your-Own is a developing trend.

Crofting and cottage farming. These are forms of subsistence farming found in the Highlands and Islands of Scotland and on the Atlantic coast of Ireland from west Cork northwards to Donegal. Scot-land has seven designated crofting coun-ties – Argyll, Inverness, Ross and Cromarty, Sutherland, Caithness, Ork-ney Islands and Shetland Islands. The living from this type of farming is mea-gre. Landholdings are small, often frag-mented with some rough grazing held in

common. Crops are mainly confined to oats and potatoes for use on the farm. Sheep are the important livestock of the croft; cattle stand above sheep on the Irish cottage farm. Both are usually supplemented by other activities: fishing, tourism, home spinning and weaving. They are characterised by little capital, little machinery, rugged environment, windy and wet climate and the remote-ness and isolation which make tradi-tional farming methods extremely diffi-cult to maintain. Various forms of Government aid – grants, loans etc – have been forthcoming both in Scotland and Ireland for this type of farming.

New crops in the fields

New and unfamiliar crops have been appearing in farm fields in recent years.

This is because plant breeders have been able to produce versions of crops like maize suited to British conditions and climate. Thousands of acres of this 'green giant' are grown annually, especially in the south. Mostly it is used for animal fodder; all the plant including the cob.

Fields of flaring yellow oilseed rape are becoming a much more obvious feature. This is grown to provide vegetable oil for the food industry. Much of it goes to the making of margarine.

In areas like Norfolk fields are being cropped with Chinese cabbage to meet a growing demand for a leaf vegetable which is dual purpose, eaten as salad or cooked as a green.

The next generation of new field crops are already on their way: lupins for high protein animal feed and enriching the soil; sunflowers for animal feed and oil; and Navy beans for the baked bean food canners who have had to rely until now on the United States for the crop.

The arrival of new, tall grass forage crops could have a dramatic impact on the farming landscape. One of these grasses is a cross between sorghum and Sudan grass and has been specially bred to give high yields of animal feed in the climatic conditions of southern Britain. The grass can grow to 7ft (2m) although ideally cattle would graze it when it was 3ft 6in to 5ft (1m to 1.5m) high. Its other advantages are that it yields in late summer when other grasses are at their weakest and after its first few weeks it is a very rapidly growing crop. The breeders who produced it believe it unlikely that any other summer forage crop currently grown in Britain can equal it for yield.

Subsistence farming. Cottage farmstead in the limestone landscape of the Burren, Co Clare

Anatomy of the barn

Crown post frame with vertical crown post

Cruck built: the oldest style

Post and truss: typical of 17th and 18th centuries

Porch: later a lean to with modern roof

Dovecote: young pigeons used to provide rich food

Matched slates brought from Wales

Owl hole for barn owl resident rat killer

Stone tile roof: the courses narrow toward the ridge

Thatched roof with half hipped ends

Tiles: look also for the curved pantiles

Perching hole: trap door for topping up pile of sheaves

Threshold leading to central threshing floor

Stone barn from the Cotswolds

Split oak pales the oldest surviving technique

Weather boarding: common in southern England

Brick barn: the bonding (arrangement) of bricks is English bond

Plinth base of brick or stone

Ventilation slits let fresh air in, keep strong winds out

The barn, as old and historic as the farmhouse itself, is a casualty of modern farming methods with no real function left for it. Some fine barns are literally falling to pieces because they are too costly to restore and it is cheaper to replace them with a modern building. Yet old barns reveal much about the working countryside of yesterday.

A barn is not a cowshed, a stable, a carthouse, a hayhouse, a granary or another of the innumerable buildings seen on farms. A barn is a barn, a special building, built in a certain way for a certain use.

The word 'barn' itself comes from Old English for barley store. Barley was the favourite grain of the Saxons, and probably they had barns, although the first written record of a barn is from some years after the Norman Conquest.

In those early centuries, farming was growing grain and grazing cattle. The building for grain became the barn; the cattle quarters became the yard, and together with the living hut, they set the style of the farmstead of today.

Barns were work places, not just store huts. The corn was cut by hand, bound into sheaves which were propped up to dry in the sun. They were then taken into the barn to be piled deep on one side of it. The central space of the barn, stretching between the facing pairs of doorways, was the threshing floor. Threshing was a winter job; the summer-cut sheaves were

pulled on to the threshing floor and beaten with flails. The spent straw was then piled into the other side of the barn, for the cattle. The chaff was winnowed from the grain with the help of the breeze whistling through the wide central doorways. And the grain was usually stored in 'cornholes' next to the straw before being taken to the granary.

Barns remained essentially simple in plan for centuries, utility buildings, built of utility materials and from what was cheapest or closest to hand. Skills, or the lack of them, and local custom were handed down without question. The result was that the style of barns varied from parish to parish.

The illustration shows just a handful of types. The cruck style of construction is probably the oldest; today, examples are still found and they are commonest in the West and North. The crucks took the weight of the roof directly. But big trees were needed if the barn was to be of any size. The frame construction overcame this problem to some extent. The gaps between the timbers were traditionally filled with split oak pales, or weatherboards could be tacked up. Occasionally the wall was infilled with brick or stone.

Some of the ancient features which have been copied into more recent building are intriguing. Many stone barns have a pattern of ventilation slits on the end walls, allowing air to reach the stored straw and grain. But often these

'loopholes' are the same as the arrow slits of castles, wider inside than out. The design aerodynamically allows fresh air to seep through the slit while blocking sharp gusts of wind. Another advantage is that more light enters the barn.

By the beginning of the 19th century the threshing machine was replacing the old-fashioned flails. The first threshers were wooden contraptions powered by a horse walking round in a circle. Some northern areas have round sheds (called gin gangs) built alongside the barn, for the plodding horse.

At first, the steam engines were stationary, maybe thumping away on the floor of the barn. But later they became giant monsters, like road rollers, taking power out to the fields. The corn was threshed in the open, and the barn lost its use as a work place, becoming a storage place only. It meant the end of building new barns to old patterns. It also meant the beginning of the decline of existing barns. Large roofs were expensive to maintain, and British farming was in the doldrums – the result of imports of cheap foreign corn. Many barns were converted into cowsheds and other uses.

Unexpectedly, the farmyard barn was given a new lease of life this century. The new combine harvesters thresh the corn in the fields but bring the grain back wet. It had to be dried and the old, under-used barn was an obvious place in which to put the grain drier.

Above: Farm cathedral. A fine example of a long tithe barn's timbered interior at Frindsbury, Kent. Below: Built to last. A well-preserved tithe barn with a magnificent tiled roof at Lenham, Kent. The tithes, a tenth of the farm produce of a parish given to support the clergy, were stored in such barns

Strangers on the pastures

A quiet revolution is taking place on the cattle pastures of the British Isles. In an effort to bring lean meat to beef production – and in the process improved profits for the farmer – unfamiliar breeds of cattle from the Continent, such as the Charolais from Burgundy and the Simmental from Switzerland, are being introduced.

As a result British herds are having the biggest injection of foreign blood in their history. This is why the appearance of beef cattle in the fields is very different to what it used to be.

Thus the traditional Sunday joint of beef is coming to owe more and more to these 'exotics', which is what farmers call the European breeds, than to native beef breeds alone.

Critics of the latter argue that while hardy and capable of thriving on poor pastures provided under extensive ranching systems abroad, they were not converting grass into meat at home as well as the 'exotics'. This was because home breeders, with an eye on the export market and the show ring, were producing animals which were too small and grew too slowly to make beef profitable.

Argentina, for example, was the biggest export market for Herefords, and her cattle raisers became the target for British breeders who knew the Argentinians favoured a smaller, more compact strain of Hereford than the animal which grazed the Herefordshire pastures at the turn of the century.

But the smaller animals and their crossbred calves matured earlier and at lower weights than their forebears. Attempts to feed them to greater weights led to accumulations of fat which butchers could not sell to housewives. The Hereford cows, or female crosses, produced less milk than their ancestors and since the mothers were less provident the calves' diet had to be supplemented with expensive concentrate feeds.

It was to overcome these defects that the first Charolais bulls were imported in 1961. The first results were dramatic: their crosses with Friesian cows grew faster than Hereford-Friesian crosses, were more efficient at converting food and the carcases had much less fat.

It takes a long time to judge whether the results will be sustained. Charolais and Simmental bulls now provide over 20% of all artificial inseminations in Britain but Hereford bulls are still the leaders at over 60%.

The success of the Charolais has prompted the introduction of other breeds. The Limousin, bred for survival in the hills of France's Massif Central, produces good lean beef from rough grazing. The Blonde d'Aquitaine capable of enormous growth, four lbs (1.8 kilos) or more a day, and the Maine Anjou, also capable of putting more size and a faster rate of growth into British crossbred beef, are both from France.

The robust Simmentals are natives of the Simme Valley in Switzerland's Bernese Oberland and quickly produce quantities of quality meat from grass and straw. The Chiananas are the largest and fastest growing cattle in Europe, frequently measuring up to 6ft 6in (2m) at the shoulder. They come from Italy.

The crosses resulting from putting these animals to British breeds clearly benefit from the characteristics fostered by Continental breeders in their animals. For instance, cattle there have long been used as draught animals for ploughing. When the farmer feeds his oxen he wants the food converted into lean muscle not layers of fat. For draught work he also wants large animals with massive loins and hindquarters – and these are the areas where the best cuts of meat are.

Continental breeds also tend to be dual purpose providing both milk and meat and this means they are good mothers with plenty of milk for their calves.

A characteristic of British beef production is that the bulk of it comes from the dairy herds: about 60% from calves born to dairy cows – and 80% of these cows are British Friesians. The calves are either pure Friesian or result from the cows being crossed with pure beef breeds.

In the dairy herds the pre-eminence of the Friesian is unchallengeable. For years the old favourite, the Dairy Shorthorn, has been losing popularity to the Friesian because its milk supply is lower, its calves are slower growing and its produces carcases which are over-fat.

By 1955 the Friesian accounted for just over 30% of the United Kingdom dairy herd. Now it stands at over 80%. In the Republic of Ireland the breed accounts for 68% of all dairy cows.

Beef cattle

Sussex. Has a reputation for thriving on poor pasture. Now a rare sight

South Devon. The largest British breed with bulls reaching 1 to 1.5 tons

Lincoln Red. Lincolnshire version of the Shorthorn. Numbers have dwindled

Galloway. These animals are tough enough to winter on the Galloway coast

Hereford. The most popular British beef breed, now spread all over the world

West Highland. A tough picturesque descendant of the original wild Scottish cattle

Beef Shorthorn. In the 1930s the commonest breed in Britain

Welsh Black. Thrives in conditions many other breeds would find intolerable

Blonde d'Aquitaine. This heavyweight aristocrat from across the Channel is the most scientifically selected of all French breeds

Dairy cattle

Charolais. A native of the Charolais region of Burgundy. Introduced to Britain in 1961

Kerry. A small black breed indigenous to southern and western Ireland

British Friesian. Predominant breed in British Isles. First introduced from Holland

Jersey. Smallest and perhaps prettiest of the dairy breeds. It produces very rich milk

Aberdeen Angus. No other breed has its capacity to provide highest quality beef

Dairy Shorthorn. In Ireland still the most popular breed after the Friesian

Ayrshire. The only mainland native breed of pure dairy cattle to originate in the UK

Guernsey. A small animal, although slightly larger than the Jersey

Best of British sheep

The British Isles are the most important sheep farming area in Western Europe. This position is rooted in a long tradition of sheep raising which goes back to the Middle Ages. Then the emphasis was on wool which was exported to the Continent and made up into cloth. Later with the growing urban population of the Industrial Revolution the emphasis was switched to sheep for meat.

Today wool is still a major source of income for many farmers but the production of fat lambs for the table is increasingly important. Selective breeding and improved feeding now produce sheep which are larger and carry more meat than the animals of 200 years ago.

The main breeds are shown here, although there are many others which are often confined to a particular locality. The mountain breeds which are hardy, produce good mutton and wool are the most numerous, especially in those areas where sheep dominate the farming scene: the highlands and moorlands of Scotland, Wales, Ireland, the Pennines and the Lake District. Lowland areas such as Romney Marsh and the Downs are celebrated for their sheep. So are the lowland areas west of the Shannon where farmers combine sheep with cattle rearing. But the general trend has been for sheep to give way to the plough and more profitable types of lowland farming.

Lowland sheep

South Down. Smaller than many lowland sheep but produces the best carcase quality of any breed. It also produces high quality wool. Used in crossing with other breeds to improve their meat production

Border Leicester. The rams of this breed are much used to cross with Cheviot or Black Face mountain ewes to produce the ubiquitous Half-Bred and Mule (or Greyface) ewes. These are crossed with other lowland breed rams to provide lamb and wool

Dorset Horn. Unlike other British sheep this has flesh coloured lips. Its wool is fine and very white. Both sexes carry prominent, highly curled horns. It will breed earlier than other breeds sometimes producing lambs in October. This makes it valuable in cross breeding for fat lambs for the early market

Hampshire Down. This developed as the ideal breed for grazing the chalk downlands of southern England. It tolerates being confined to arable field feeding areas. Its crossbred lambs grow well and put on meat quickly

Suffolk. Originated in East Anglia but is now seen in many other areas of the British Isles. It is also much used in cross breeding for meat production. It is prolific and popular

Romney Marsh. This is a heavy animal which produces high quality wool. It is the dominant breed in the densely sheep-stocked area of Kent, the name of which it bears

Hill sheep

Clun Forest. A hardy, thrifty breed used on mixed farms for consuming crops on arable land in winter. Both sexes are hornless. Common in the Midlands and Southern England

Kerry Hill. Originally from Kerry Hill, Montgomeryshire, this is a large breed popular in the Welsh borders. Its white face is broken by black markings on the muzzle. Neither sex has horns

Mountain sheep

Welsh Mountain. Small with a characteristic narrow shouldered, long necked appearance. The rams have strong horns; ewes are hornless. Kept for meat

Scottish Blackface. Small, shaggy with both ewes and rams carrying small horns. Thrives well on high heather moors of Scotland and north of England. But now widespread, being reared mainly for meat

Cheviot. Strongest mountain rival of the Blackface. Hornless in both sexes. Tends to do best on coarse grass rather than heather. Has spread to Wales and even Exmoor. A good lamb producer

Herdwick. Predominant breed in the Lake District. It has the coarse, shaggy fleece of the Blackface but some of the rams are hornless. Lambs' face colour is black, later turning grey and white in old age. Kept for wool

Swaledale. Slightly larger than the Blackface but carries less wool at its fore end. It has a dark grey face with a mealy coloured nose. Hill farmers sell its lambs for lowland fattening

Pigs with a purpose

The changing face – and form – of the British pig is one of the least evident aspects of a changing countryside. Fifty years ago the leading breeds of pigs (illustrated here) could all be seen in the fields. Now pigs are rarely found out of doors. Instead they spend most of their lives in clinical (compared to the old farmyard sty) factory pig units.

The danger of rearing livestock intensively is fast-spreading disease. So buildings are made from modern, easy to disinfect materials – plastic and weatherproofed compressed board on prestressed concrete or steel frames. Since infant mortality is one of the main scourges of the pig farmer some breeding stock are surgically removed from the mother's womb prior to birth and kept under hygienic conditions all their lives.

Some of the breeds which were once so popular occupy a much less important place in the pig herds now. Moreover they are losing their individual breed identity. Yet more pigs are being raised than ever. The United Kingdom herd has nearly trebled to 6.5 million since 1930. The Irish herd has remained much as it was at just over one million.

Today's most popular pig is a hybrid with all the good points of other breeds bred into him (see illustration). The Large White and Landrace have been dominant in these breeding programmes.

Large White. High reputation as a producer of quality bacon. Boars have been used in cross breeding programmes throughout the world

Landrace. Introduced from Scandinavia in 1949. Celebrated for the length of its back, providing a longer, leaner carcase for bacon production, and large litters

Welsh. Hardy pig which is excellent for grazing outdoors. Also a good bacon pig much used in breeding programmes

British Saddleback. Takes its name from the prominent white 'saddle' across its black back. Another good grazer. Renowned for its mothering qualities

Breeds better. Produces larger, stronger, faster growing litters

Good mother. Docile and easily managed

High quality meat. Little superfluous fat

Strong body ensuring longer life and lots of litters

Free from most endemic pig diseases

Efficient converter

The Super-pig. In recent years breeders have been attempting to combine the best qualities of all the formerly common breeds. Already 50% of the pig herd consists of these modern hybrids and the drive for a superior pig, aided by computer controlled breeding programmes, continues. All hybrids show what is known as 'hybrid vigour', an explosion of energy and performance capability which is released when pure strains of animal, or plant, are closely inbred for a number of generations – and are then crossed with other similarly inbred strains, A good example of the modern factory-produced pig is the Cotswold Hybrid which has Large White, Landrace, Welsh and British Saddleback in it.

Middle White. Smaller than the Large White. Too fat for bacon but widely used for crossing to produce good pork

Berkshire. One of the first to be improved by scientific breeding in the 19th century. It was raised for its high quality pork but is now rare

Large Black. One of the oldest breeds, favoured in the South West and East Anglia. Often used in crosses with Large White for bacon production

Rural craftsmen: Blacksmith

There is always admiration for those who create with their hands and a set of tools which seem as old as time. Yet few of us have other than the most perfunctory notion of the tried and tested expertise which is the skilled countryman's inheritance. Rural crafts and skills have always been part of the enduring continuum of country life but unhappily some are now long past their heyday. Others show surprising signs of life.

There are a few old time blacksmiths left, but not many. Mostly their forges are cold and silent. Twice a week, maybe, they coax a little life into the embers. Smokeless stuff fuels their fire these days, and it is mild steel they heat in it, for they can't get iron any more.

Only occasionally does a diehard farmer turn up with a broken plough or harrow; or a trawler skipper need a bit of new tackle; or a coal merchant want a new floor-plate for the cab of his lorry. Few of the jobs fall readily into the old workaday mould. Decorative stuff is now his mainstay.

By 'decorative' the true smith does not

mean the lacy, light-weight wrought-iron gates of suburban gardens with their shallow scrolls and fishtails. These are cheap frills and look it: thin strips of metal 'cold-forged' (ie bent) to shape and spot-welded together. They have felt only the blacksmith's scorn, never the blush of his fire.

To see what a pair of proper, craftsman-forged gates looks like, take a trip to the municipal cemetery. Or Royal palace. Or the Falls Church National Memorial Park in Virginia. Its five pairs of particularly imposing gates all came from small blacksmith's shops in Devon.

One of these same five Devon smithies – it has been in business in Dartmouth since early in the 19th century – has also turned out railing scrolls and finials for London's Natural History Museum, and repaired cannon for the Tower of London, which is a far cry from the days when the local gas board regularly employed them as surgeons to fractured street lamps.

Door-knockers, fire-baskets and a whiff of nostalgia are, you might suppose, all that remains of the old days. Wrong,

Above: Old-fashioned horse-power on the farm.
Right: Blacksmith in the heat of his forge

for three generations of the same family, the youngest aged but 11, are still rippling their biceps over the self-same forge.

Great-grandfather, the firm's founder who stares down yellowly from his dessicated photograph on the office wall, would recognise the pride in a job done permanently, and the gentle precision with which big men apply their enormous strength to tasks of small detail. An exquisite music stand, suffering no loss of strength or vitality through the delicacy of its design, permits a quiet satisfaction in its creator, but nothing more. They like to innovate and invent, and give their imaginations a bit of an airing. But so did great-grandfather. What kind of craftsman would he have been if he didn't?

A blacksmith does not so much mend things as recreate them. A broken bell-clapper from a church tower, demanding great particularity in weight, length and strength, is welded in the fire until only the brightness of the metal betrays the repair. You would search for ever to find the weak spot: there isn't one. In another corner, a weather-vane is shaping up for a local bank; and next to it, a horse-head paper-knife for official presentation to a visiting dignitary at an agricultural show. From a gate-hinge to a gazebo: if you want it in metal, the blacksmith will make it. Plain or ornamental; everlasting or simply strong. But whatever it is, there is no way you will outlast it. Smithing is not like other trades, where a good job ensures a good customer. Here a job well done is a job never seen again.

Except, of course, in the matter of farriery. A good shoeing smith can not do much to prolong the life of a horse-shoe, though he can do a great deal to prolong the useful life of the horse. He is the archetypal rural craftsman, clothed in shiny hide apron, with rivulets of sweat carving pearly channels across his smoke-blackened skin. A bit of a character who might hobble and throw a kicking gypsy pony and shoe it upside down.

Give or take a bit of tail, there are 247 bones in a horse. Thirty-six of these are in the lower legs and depend for their trouble-free service on the skill of the farrier. The nine bones of each lower leg are powered, hinged and held together by a mass of tendons, ligaments, muscles and blood vessels, culminating in the horny outgrowth of the hoof itself. Simple it is not, and it can be cast into lame and limping disorder by any small disparity in a shoe. Nature can and does permit itself the luxury of a minor discrepancy here and there. Not so the smith. Not only must he avoid inexactitudes of his own; he must also compensate for nature's.

Few pairs of hooves are the same; yet the horse's comfort depends upon his heels riding at a uniform height and on each foot being level all round. It is a balance which can be achieved only by carefully cleaning and trimming each hoof, and by bespoke shoeing. Each shoe begins as a straight bar, gripped in the pincers and brought to white heat in the fire. The hammering at the anvil may look frantic, but it is merely rapid – and necessarily so. Mild steel cools quickly. The blows seem wild and impossibly massive for an operation which depends for its success on meticulous accuracy. But there is culture in the brawn. The farrier will check and recheck the fit, heat and reheat the shoe, until it is as personal as a fingerprint. It will roughly fit a great many horses; precisely fit only this one.

The final test, after the shoe has been burnt on with its alarming (to visitors) billows of sour acrid smoke, is the nailing, during which the unskilled operator (there are a few) has his greatest opportunity to cripple the horse. And himself, for that matter. Few animals are docile enough to suffer a puncture of living tissue without dealing out a retributive kick or two.

There is no telling where you might encounter a shoeing forge these days. On the M5 perhaps, or in a city high street. Most modern farriers have unshackled themselves from their Vulcan's caves and switched to portable, gas-fired forges mounted in the backs of Land Rovers or light vans. No shiny hide apron; no smoke-blackened skin; no drama. The horse stays where it is and the smith comes, like a hired servant, to the door.

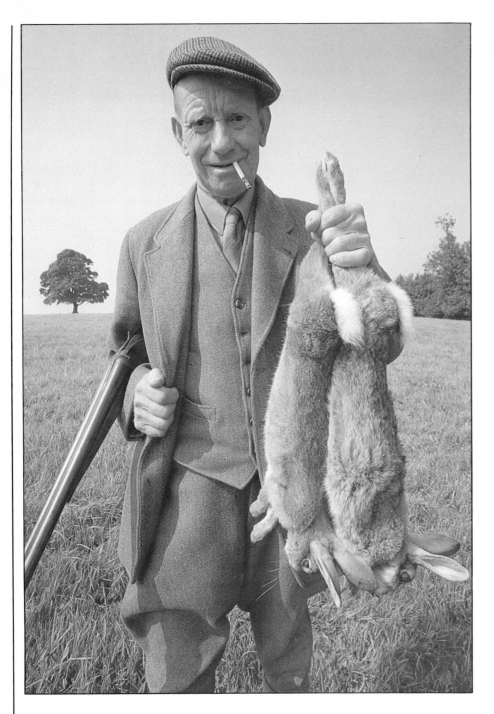

The gamekeeper's year

A man in a green tweed hat is wading through a turbulent sea of maize. Wind whips the leaf-tips into brisk little ripples, and there is a forceful undercurrent – a gathering wash of sound that swells uphill, ahead of the man. And then the first wave breaks cover. The pheasants have been driven along the ground as far as their nervous dispositions will withstand. As they emerge from the maize they are confronted on the skyline by a rank of men and boys with flags. Up they go, standing on their tails with their bellies to the breeze, then wheeling away to ride the wind home. Straight over the man in the green tweed hat; straight across the line of guns.

For the guests with their fingers on the triggers, the day's sport is served on a plate. The birds come fast and hard, scrambling higher and higher into the sky as the danger declares itself. Tested to the limits, men and their gun-barrels grow hot with the effort.

For the head gamekeeper, the man in the green tweed hat, it is a confrontation that has taken a year's work to contrive. Nothing has been left to chance.

The gamekeeper is an expert at bending nature to his purpose. He does not want tame birds: there is no sporting challenge in a turkey shoot. But he does want wild ones whose instincts he can harness and whose behaviour he can predict. To such an end, there is no easy means.

First, the land must be right. Game birds need cover, to breed and to roost. Woods are handy – particularly if they are in the middle of the estate. On the boundary they are a mixed blessing: too many birds are liable to emerge on the wrong side. If there is not enough cover within the estate, then the gamekeeper must provide more. An island of kale, forlorn in an ocean of cereal fields, is a good indicator of a keeper at work. The kale provides both shelter and food for the birds, and its position will have been carefully plotted. The keeper's aim is to produce a good sporting flight, and his calculations will have been mapped out on paper, taking account of contours, existing boundaries and prevailing wind. He will have tried to *think* like a pheasant. How far would he run when flushed out? Where would he take to the air? In which direction would he turn in flight? If he is right, and his theory works in practice, then the cover becomes permanent. He will plant a thicket of bushy shrubs – lonicera, for instance – often with an adjacent 'garden' of kale or maize.

So here is another clue for the observer. Any patch of apparently uncleared scrub in the middle of well-kept farmland usually means game cover.

The keeper's year begins as soon as the last cartridge has been expended at season's end. He traps the surviving hen birds in coops (not all of them: just as many as he needs to produce eggs for next season), hobbles their wings with leather brails and releases them into laying pens. This is his investment for the future, and he treats it appropriately. Lavish feeds of wheat give way to a controlled diet of breeder's pellets and grit at around the beginning of March, and laying begins in early April. It is a period of anxiety, ceaseless hard work and unyielding routine. Four times a day until late June he goes to the pens and lifts off the glossy, grey-green eggs – up to 15 per bird. The eggs are bathed in a harmless disinfectant and placed in an incubator room at 60°F (16°C). Every day they must be turned to ensure that there is no settlement in the yolks.

At the same time each week – say 8am on Friday – the week's entire collection is moved into an incubator cabinet where it will be kept at a steady 100°F (38°C). After precisely three weeks, at the same time on Friday morning, the eggs are moved to a hatcher – still at the same temperature – within which the young birds will emerge after another three or four days. For three or four days more, the poults will gather strength in a warm room; then they will be carried to heated brooders in the wood, where they will slowly be introduced to the idea of freedom. Gradually they are released into larger and larger enclosures until, after six weeks, they are ready to move into a release pen.

Throughout the year – not only in the breeding season – a bloody battle wages. A pheasant's egg is a popular delicacy among nature's scavenging classes, and chicks and mature birds are ready meat for a whole catalogue of predators. Most persistent egg-stealer is the stoat. Whenever one of these razor-toothed bandits is seen, the gamekeeper must be resolved to kill.

A single stoat, loose in a laying pen, will clean up every egg it can find, and will keep on coming back for more. The risk simply cannot be taken. Next time the stoat passes, he will find a neat avenue of upright sticks leading into a fresh dry tunnel with a comfortable earth-strewn floor. The tunnel is a six-inch(15cm) drainpipe. Concealed in the earth is a humane trap from whose jaws, once triggered, there is no escape. Here perish not only stoats but the occasional weasel and a multitude of rats.

One invader the gamekeeper cannot skin – though he might like to – is the poacher. Game-stealing these days is carried out on almost an industrial scale, with commercial vehicles driving long distances to pick up loads worth hundreds of pounds on the London market. There are a number of simple electronic aids which can help a gamekeeper police his wood; but the main weapon in his armoury is still the same – vigilance. He is never off duty; seldom takes time off to visit a pub. It does not do, he says, for people to know where he is.

His dedication is total. His pheasants and his partridges – particularly his partridges, which are under great pressure from intensive farming techniques – are his treasure. He knows they will be shot; but nothing gives him more pleasure than the sight of a good strong bird beating the guns.

And nothing arouses his anger more than their theft. He will track down poachers with ruthless energy – even if the offenders are local men from neighbouring villages. It does not make him the most popular man in the rural working community. But then he never thought it would.

Logistics of a Suffolk shoot

The 1500 acre Suffolk estate shown in the illustration supports 17 organised shoots a year, including duck-flights. One gamekeeper works here with two guns (one shotgun; one rifle), five dogs, a dozen broody hens and a boy. The guns are for vermin. The dogs are for fetching and carrying. The broody hens are for hatching a few extra pheasants' eggs. The boy is for licking into shape.

The gamekeeper's equipment ranges from the money-gulping sophistication of the sporting catalogues (heated incubators, hatchers and brooders) to the age-old simplicity of the wire snare. Among the statistics of his trade, the one most difficult to calculate is his own working week. Nature never stands still; neither does the gamekeeper. In a good year he will successfully hatch 2,000 pheasants' eggs; 300 partridge; 50 mallard. These will cost him numberless hours of effort, and $21\frac{1}{2}$ tons of special feed for nesting mothers and chicks.

To protect the nests he will set 130 humane sprung traps in which he will expect to catch at least 1,500 head of vermin every year. In 15 years working the same estate, he has seen 29,000 assorted pests fall victim to trap, snare, gas and gun.

On a typical shooting day there will be nine guns. In the 1978/79 season, the total bag was: 461 cock pheasant and 373 hens; 3 young grey partridge and 19 old; 53 young French partridge and 104 old; 19 hares; 4 rabbits; 27 pigeons; 75 mallard; 8 teal; 8 gadwall; 46 moorhen; 1 jay; 2 Eastern collared doves; 1 coypu; 5 tufted duck; 2 woodcock; 11 pochard; 2 coot; 1 guinea fowl. That was not a good season: 500 head down on the year before. The pheasant season opens at the beginning of October and ends at the beginning of February; the partridge season is from the beginning of September to the beginning of February.

| Flagmen | Beaters | Guns | Stops | A New wood under 15 years. B Game strips (maize, kale). C Grassy areas and lonicera. D Established wood. E Poplars. |

The arrows show the expected direction of flight on each drive during a typical day's pheasant shooting on a Suffolk estate. Under the direction of the head gamekeeper, the birds are walked up through the cover by beaters. Flagmen prevent birds running out of the flank of the drive; other men and boys, called stops, are positioned to prevent their escape at the far end

Thorn hedge and dry-stone wall

Barbed wire was to the hedge-layer what the pneumatic tyre was to the wheel-wright. Not quite the death-knell, but near enough. Anyone that remains is an anachronism to be remarked upon.

A few of the hedges that made up the 'typically English' enclosed field system were planted for shelter alone. Many were to keep in the livestock; others to make arable farming compact and efficient. None were provided for the ex-clusive benefit of wildlife. They were, in short, a convenience for the farmer. And it is a new sort of convenience that has persuaded him to grub so many of them up. Of those that remain, almost none are trimmed by hand. It is far too slow; far too expensive. But the mechanical flails are not a complete answer, even in a purely practical, non-conservationist sense. Over a long period, the top-chopping encourages the lower growth to thin out so that the hedge ceases to be stockproof. And when that happens the farmer has only two choices. He can put up a fence; or he can employ a hedge-layer to repair the damage.

Most stockproof hedges are hawthorn. And, although there are (or were) distinct regional variations in style, they all began in much the same way. Four-year-old thorn saplings were planted four inches apart along the line of the in-tended hedge: almost 16,000 to the mile. For their first few years they were kept weeded and trimmed, and often pro-tected from the livestock by wattle hurdles or post-and-rail fencing. It was when they reached a height of seven feet (2m) or so that the hedge-layer demon-strated the nub of his craft.

He was always an individualist: a solitary worker whose bulky outfit (this was winter work) was completed by fingerless gloves of hard yellow horse-leather, and thick leather knee-protec-tors. Using a combination of billhook and long-handled slasher (whose precise patterns varied from region to region) he would cut away the rough, tangled

Hedges (top) are considered too slow and too costly to cut by hand nowadays. But wherever they remain, as in the hilly pastures of Somerset (centre), they help to perpetuate the typical chequered pattern of the English countryside. In the north and west of the British Isles, hedges give way to dry-stone walls (left), seen here at Ullswater, in the English Lake District, where there is an abundance of fieldstone. It is the very dryness of such walls which helps them with-stand the worst of wind and frost

Jigsaw puzzle in stone. For a dry-stone wall to last, the pieces must be fitted with a craftsman's finely-judged precision

growth, taking care to leave a good number of strong upright stems. Always he cut *upwards*, with the grain, to leave a smooth clean cut. Ragged ends looked untidy, encouraged fungus growth and were the mark of a sloppy craftsman.

Some of the uprights were half-severed from the rootstock, with downward strokes of the billhook just above ground level. Others were simply topped at the intended level of the hedge. Then the hedger laid down the half-severed stems, called plashers or sears, and wove them into the uprights. Kept alive by their union with the roots, the plashers quickly threw out a thick infill of thorny branches. If the upright stems were too young and flimsy to bear the pressure, wooden stakes were driven into the ground to hold the plashers in place.

'Hedger' is not a universal term for such a craftsman. In Cornwall, a 'hedge'

is a stone-faced earth bank; while in Ireland a Cornish hedge is a 'ditch' – a word that also serves for a dry-stone wall. To add to the confusion, a dry-stone wall in Scotland is a 'dyke', a word which almost everywhere else means a ditch. It is not only etymologically that dry-stone walls have their regional peculiarities. Like hedges, they submit to local styles of construction and profile. But, also like hedges, there is a broad uniformity of method.

Dry-stone walls are basically a phenomenon of northern and western uplands of Britain, and parts of Ireland as well, where the poor growth-potential of hedging plants is balanced by an abundance of available fieldstone. Having collected his granite, or Cotswold stone, the waller (or dyker) begins by removing turf and topsoil along the line of the wall to provide a solid footing. The wall itself

rises in two converging 'skins', each tapering inwards at the rate of around one horizontal inch per vertical foot. The real hand-and-eye skill of the expert is in the selection and placing of each stone. The novice holds a rock in his hand, turns it and tries it in a variety of positions before he succeeds. The expert does it with the speed of a child who has learned a jigsaw by heart, pinning each stone with smaller ones to hold it firm and always making sure that each block is resting on two beneath, like brickwork. He spends his material economically, often splitting a stone with precisely-calculated hammer blows to make it do double duty.

But he is going the way of the hedger. To see a waller at work today is unusual. When the old boundaries begin to crumble, it's not craftsmanship that fills the gaps. It's barbed wire.

Thatching: one of the oldest crafts

Thatch belongs with green hills and valleys, nestling villages and church towers, and the art of it is probably the most ancient building craft in Britain.

In Norfolk, for good reason, there is much thatch and quite a lot of it is on the churches. The thatched naves of these flint-napped, field-corner cathedrals are a peculiarity of the region: a natural marriage of the two most abundant local materials.

Here is thatch in its warmest maturity. Here, too, is thatch in its earliest infancy. The native reed in the fens and marshes of Broadland is *Phragmites communis*: Norfolk reed, the finest in the world. If you imagine that this abundance of the thatcher's favourite material is a happy accident, you are half right. Happy it certainly is. Accidental it is not, save in the combination of natural conditions that enable it to thrive. Those feathery, nodding acres – the home of bittern, reed bunting and otter – which make up some of East Anglia's richest natural habitats, are all farmed. If they were not, they could not exist. Uncut and undrained, they would degenerate to a useless, impenetrable tangle of alder thicket.

The new year on the reed-marsh begins in early spring when the harvest is finished. Among the stubble of the old reed can be seen the first fleshy tips of the new growth, each no bigger than the nail of a little finger. When the cutting is finished, they get a generous soaking. The sluices are opened and the dykes flood across the fen in a single unbroken sheet. At the second high tide, the sluices are closed and the water locked in for a full two weeks before it is allowed to drain off again.

By July, the shoots will have raced away to make a solid green jungle, six feet (1.8m) tall. They will die and dry through autumn and winter, ready for harvesting the following spring.

The trouble is that demand for thatching reed, given the gentrification of the country cottage, now easily outstrips supply and the modern thatcher can ill afford to be choosy. Even the old-timer has learned to accept a proportion of old reed mixed in with the new – a compromise he would once have rejected out of hand.

In the drier eastern counties – given good maintenance and occasional repairs to the ridge – a reed roof will give good service for up to 80 years. Norfolk reed and Norfolk thatching skills are universally in demand: commissions for North Walsham men have come from as far away as the United States of America.

But – although no son of Norfolk will easily admit it – there is another thatching material: what in the West of England they call wheat reed. What in Norfolk they call, with the barest suspicion of a curl in the lip, straw.

However, not any old wheat yields a thatching reed. The modern, jug-eared varieties stand barely 18in ($\frac{1}{2}$m) tall. In terms of grain yield they have all the over-compensating vigour of the diminutive. For the thatcher, they are useless. He needs an old-fashioned variety, with stems a full three feet (1m) long. Not many farmers grow it and it is money rather than a sentimental attachment to the past that prompts those who do.

They get two cash crops in the space of one: thatching reed *and* grain.

Cutting and preparing the wheat is more of a performance than harvesting water reed. Most Norfolk marshmen these days use mechanical cutters and haul the reed from the fen on sleds behind load-spreading Snowcat-type tractors, which have solved the problem of driving heavy vehicles across the spongy peat. (In the old days the reed was all cut by hand and brought off the marsh by boat. A bristling lighter, loaded down like a floating haystack, was as slow as it was picturesque.) But the wheat-reed harvest is still firmly rooted in the pre-combine age. Cutting is by old-fashioned binder, and the grain is separated from the ear in an old-fashioned threshing machine, with a mechanical comber attached to keep the stems straight and unbroken. Such a machine requires eight men to operate it.

Wheat reed is sold to the thatcher in 14lb (6 kilo) bundles. After hand-combing to remove dead leaves and other debris, Norfolk reed is sold in 'standard bunches', each 24in (609mm) in circumference, measured one foot (304mm) above the butt-end. Six of these make one 'fathom'.

How do you tell a *Phragmites communis* roof from a wheat-reed roof? It is not easy for the layman, but largely a matter of habitat. On the steeply-pitched roofs of East Anglia, it will almost certainly be Norfolk reed; on the softer, more rounded roofs of the south and west of England, there is a better chance that it will be wheat. Before they are fixed to the roof, of course, the two materials are easy to distinguish. At six feet (1.8m) long, the average Norfolk reed is double the average wheat reed; and absolutely any townie can tell an empty wheat ear (which is left attached) from a *Phragmites* feather. In the far soggier West, the longevity of thatch is much reduced: 30 years would be considered not bad.

With both kinds of reed, the thatching method is essentially the same hard physical work. The reed is scratchy and sharp, damaging to clothing and flesh alike. Leather pads give a measure of protection to the knees, but hands and elbows have a hard time of it. The roof grows from the bottom upwards, with the first bundles laid cut ends downwards, projecting well out from the wall to form the eaves. Working upwards towards the ridge, each bundle overlaps the one below it to make a weatherproof seal.

Thatch in its warmest maturity – on the roof of a cottage – is the product of the oldest of crafts

New thatch for an old roof. Thatchers are in great demand. Each leaves his own distinctive mark

The spread of forests

It is a peculiarity of the English (as opposed to Scots and Americans who know better) to regard a forest as exclusively a thing of oak and ash, and a forester as a bulky tartan shirt with an axe. Industrialised conifer plantations are scoffed at as if the trees were in some way less real, less worthy of a place in the landscape. 'Outdoor pit-prop factories' is the way one acid-tipped critic described the Forestry Commission's woodlands.

In a sense that is exactly what they are: an astonishingly high proportion of the timber does still go to the pits. But they are much more besides. Take Thetford, on the sandy wastes of Breckland, on the Norfolk–Suffolk border: 80 square miles (20,720 hectares) of it, the largest lowland forest in England. Gone is the straight-line planter's geometry. Gone are the Keep Out notices. In their place are an energetic concern for environmental propriety, and an open-armed welcome to the public that is almost embarrassing in its effusiveness. There are picnic sites, camping and caravan grounds, nature trails and waymarked footpaths, all adding up to a pine-scented playground which attracts visitors in their thousands.

A great forest is like a great sea. Sense of time and direction are under siege from the sheer scale of it. Eighty square miles of trees growing 550 tonnes of new green wood a day is more than most English imaginations can take.

It all begins in a particularly unlikely way, in a particularly dog-eared potting shed. Here for a few days in March, and again in April, nimble fingers drop locally-collected seeds into biodegradable growing-containers. Immediately, the statistics gnaw at the edges of credibility. One man can sow 10,000 tree seeds a day; and the germination rate is nudging 100 per cent. What this means in terms of tree production can be better understood in the plastic cold-tunnels where the trays of seedlings are raised. A thick green carpet of infant trees translates in the imagination into mile after mile of unbroken leaf canopy: 140,000 trees in a single tunnel. Toughened by strictly-controlled temperature and watering, they will be ready to plant out in the forest within six months of sowing. Not long ago, before the growing-container came along, a seedling would need two or three years' growth before its roots would tolerate transplantation to the growing site.

The thatch is pinned to the battens with horizontal hazel rods, usually called sways, and with twisted split-hazel pegs, usually called spars. For each 'square' of thatch (10ft × 10ft, the thatcher's standard unit of measurement), there are 300 spars. For all the thatcher's materials and tools, local names abound. To a Norfolk man, for instance, a spar is a broche. And to a Devonian, hazel is nuthalse.

Devon men use more blades for trimming their roofs than the Norfolk thatchers, but both use a legget to tap up and tighten the ends of the reed beneath the sways. There are individual variations on this, but it is typically a piece of elm plank on a short, angled handle, generously packed with horse-shoe nails. Pressed down by the sways, the packed reed is bent slightly upwards so that, in the finished roof, it is only the cut ends that are visible.

At the ridge, the joint between the two pitches is made watertight by a layer of pliable sedge or straw, extending a foot or two down each flank and clipped into varying patterns of scallops or chevrons, individually designed to suit each thatcher's personal taste. It is the way he adds his private signature to the landscape.

All Thetford's new planting is on sites that have already produced their first crop. The methods are modern. There are no axes here (when the foresters needed one for an historical pageant, a special emissary had to be sent to the ironmongers!), but no forest worker need feel unmanned by the loss. His virility is handed back to him in the shape of a pulverising machine, armed with a catch-all assembly of whirling blades to smash the last relics of the original timber. It chews its way across the glade behind an armour-plated tractor. (It is not left-over army landmines that exercise the anxiety: it is left-over pine-stumps, against which ordinary tractor bodywork offers no defence.)

The planting process itself is an almost surreal conjunction of ancient and modern. Behind the same armour-plated tractor lurches an enclosed orange planting machine whose tapering, backward-facing jaws give it the aspect of a praying mantis. At the front, a steel cutter slices open a planting furrow. At the back, a pair of angled wheels neatly earths it over again. It looks relentless, thoroughly automatic. But in the mantis's deeper recesses, suspended in mid-technology, is a man in a knitted woolly hat, manually placing the seedlings into the furrow, one every two metres. At no greater cost to himself than mild lumbago and a grain or two of compost beneath his fingernails, this man can plant a forest of 7,000 pine trees a day.

On the meagre soil of Breckland it is a Mediterranean immigrant, the Corsican pine, that adjusts most readily to the conditions. Superior yield and faster maturity (50 years) have underwritten

telegraph pole stage) will be well under way. It is not difficult to calculate the age of a growing Corsican or Scots pine. The branches climb the stem in easily discernible levels: for each level, count one year. A mature tree grows to more than 145ft (44m) with a trunk diameter of up to 5ft (1.5m).

In the nicest sense, pine trees are arboreal pigs: cut up and used, with hardly any waste. No remnant is too small, or too awkwardly shaped, to be ground up for chipboard or woodwool. Felling is by chainsaw, de-limbing is done by machines on the spot; and radio-controlled Commission vehicles are used to direct customers' lorries immediately to the felling site. Only 40 per cent of the output would satisfy the mind's eye impression of 'timber' – large logs for sawing into planks. A full 20 per cent still goes for pit props; 20 per cent makes pulpwood, principally for motor car lining panels; eight per cent makes chipboard; six per cent makes woodwool for packing and insulation. Then there is ground bark for gardener's soil-improver (or for horse-bedding: Newmarket is only a gallop away); and even charcoal. A private charcoal burner leases a pitch in the forest and turns out five tons a week. Which is an awful lot of barbecues.

Aesthetic objections to the 'unnatural' appearance of the plantations are being appeased by a mixed border of native hardwoods softening the outlines of the forest's edge. Among the forest wildlife perhaps the most significant new species is the naturalist. Human noses might once have been turned up at the man-made habitat, but the deer and red squirrels have had no such purist qualms.

All this calls for a lot of people. Thetford Forest employs 300: a head forester, 30 qualified foresters and specialist teams to handle every task from motor repairs to campsite management. But if you are a visitor remember that the foresters already have all the pests they need: pine shoot moth; pine shoot beetle; black pine beetle; pine weevil and conifer heart rot fungus. With modern pesticides and virulent fungi they can now hope to keep all these at bay. Against only two threats do they lack defence: freak gales (many acres were flattened in early 1976), and the idiot with the match.

Growing forests for the future

Thetford is the largest, man-made lowland forest in the British Isles. It is also the largest production forest, producing more timber than other forests which are bigger in area. The New Forest and the Forest of Dean make up the trio of big forests in the south of England.

Most of the major forests, established in mountainous or other open country, are designated as forest parks. These are open to the public for recreation although their prime purpose is growing timber commercially. They are the Snowdonia Forest Park in Wales and the Galloway, Queen Elizabeth, Argyll, Glen More forest parks in Scotland. The Border Forest Park, most of which is in England, is the largest man-made forest in Europe. Forest parks in both the Republic of Ireland and Northern Ireland – there are well over a dozen – are less extensive than those in Britain.

About 50 per cent of all productive woodland in Britain (4.2 million acres, 1.7 million hectares) is owned or managed by the Forestry Commission. The remainder is privately owned. British forests employ over 20,000 people and nine per cent of the land is devoted to forestry in the UK compared to 78 per cent to agriculture.

Above left: Forester David Hudson hauls logs by horse in a Northumbrian forest. Right: Wild wood anemones bloom in a man-made habitat. Encouraged by forest staff there is now rich plant and wildlife in the forests

its challenge to the more traditional Scots pine (65–70 years). It takes three or four years for a young Corsican to reach Christmas-tree size; after that it will make about 19 to 20in (0.5m) of new growth a year. The leaf canopy closes overhead after 20–25 years, by which time a programme of thinning (this is the

Chapter Six
The Sea and the Countryside

Nature's great divides are places of high drama and compelling interest. None more so than the margins of the British Isles where two worlds meet as here at Durdle Door, Dorset; where the towering cliffs of upland coasts and the crumbling clays of lowland ones display their strengths and expose their weaknesses to encircling seas. This chapter tells the story of the making – and unmaking – of the sea coasts and looks at the rich mix of shore life at the water's edge

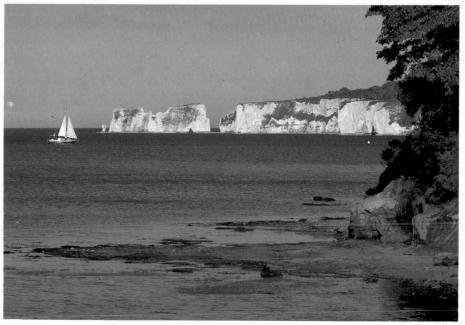

Most people have some idea of the shape of the British Isles. The classic atlas 'picture' of these islands surrounded by sea, lying off the north-west coast of Europe, is an image etched upon the mind from early schooldays.

Their configuration is all the more distinct precisely because they are islands outlined against the traditional atlas-blue of the sea. It is the sea which sharpens our perception of the coastline's shape. And it is the same restless sea, with its waves, tides, currents and winds, which helps give the coastline shape.

In places the sea is bent upon destruction, cutting back the cliffs, wearing down the rocks, sometimes at a frightening, relentless pace when the loss of land is measured in yards from one week to the next. At other places where the rocks are

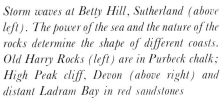

Storm waves at Betty Hill, Sutherland (above left). The power of the sea and the nature of the rocks determine the shape of different coasts. Old Harry Rocks (left) are in Purbeck chalk; High Peak cliff, Devon (above right) and distant Ladram Bay in red sandstones

hard and unyielding the process is slow, almost imperceptible, and a man will scarcely notice any change in his lifetime.

Yet, just as the sea destroys, so it builds, taking the detritus of its destruction and depositing it elsewhere, throwing up sand bars and shingle spits, and creating the tidal marsh from which reclaimed farmland comes.

The shore of the English Channel between Poole Harbour and Studland Bay is a cameo of the British coast – and an exhibit in the battle between these

two processes. From the dunes to the south of Poole Harbour, first look across Studland Bay to Foreland Point and Old Harry Rocks. Here the waves are cutting an ornamental edging to the coast, scalloping out the chalk cliffs.

Now turn and look in the opposite direction towards the sheltered creeks, mudbanks and salt marsh of Poole Harbour. Here the sea is returning what it is taking farther along the coast – as well as re-working silt carried down by rivers – to make the marshes grow. So, within a few square miles, two different views encapsulate the character and variety of the British coast.

The coastal variety is not solely the work of the sea. The land's abrupt and often awesome confrontation with the ocean is made with all manner of rocks,

and it is these which give different coasts such distinctive form, colour and texture.

The reefs and skerries of the Hebrides are a world away from the sea-sculpted red Devonian rocks seen from the train between Dawlish and Teignmouth. Just as is the Cornish granite which built the seamed and weathered headlands of Bosigran and Treen Cliff from the glittering mudflats and coarse grasses of the Essex marshes.

From Delabole to Bude black, knife-blade reefs of killas – the Cornish word for slate – tear at the incoming surf. On the other side of England a soft line of sand dunes at Horsey on the Norfolk coast holds back a sea intent on invading the Norfolk Broads.

In west Dorset foundering cliffs of gault clay, greensand, marl and lias

The Seven Sisters. Here the South Downs end – in magnificent chalk cliffs. The 'sisters' are truncated spurs at the cliff face

sometimes slip to the shore making strange, boggy 'weares' or undercliffs where wild orchids grow. Far to the north sea-lochs run deep into the coast of Scotland bringing salt water to what seems almost the heart of the land.

All this gives the British Isles coastal scenery second to none, a fretwork of bay and headland, sea stack and island, cliff and sand dune, shingle beach and marsh.

Sea cliffs

Sea cliffs provide some of the most spectacular scenery in the British Isles. The highest cliffs are found where the relentless Atlantic rollers have cut deeply into the seaward slopes of the western mountains, mountains already sharpened and steepened by former ice sheets.

On these exposed, windward coasts, open to the maximum fetch of the waves (the distance they are blown across the sea), wave energy is at its greatest. The sea battering Land's End, or any other great headland, in the fury of a gale is testimony to the prodigious force of the waves. Then, even the greatest of cliffs – and the British Isles are endowed with some of the most formidable in Europe – shudder from the assault.

Croaghaun cliff at 2192ft (668m), on Achill Island, Co Mayo, is western

Europe's highest. Ireland has three other high cliffs: Slieve League 1972ft (600m), Co Donegal; Sauce Creek 1400ft (426m) on Mt Brandon, Co Kerry; and Knockmore 1520ft (459m) on Clare Island, Co Mayo. In Scotland only the isolated island of St Kilda has anything of comparable stature in Conachair 1379ft (420m). Exmoor's Countisbury Hill at 990ft (302m) holds the record for southern Britain. Golden Cap 619ft (188m), near Seatown in Dorset, is the highest cliff on England's south coast.

It has been suggested that since most of these examples are not vertical they are not true sea cliffs; that the sea is responsible only for the relatively small active cliffs at the foot of the slopes. Vertical cliffs more than 1000ft (305m) in height are rare, but when they do occur they are an awesome sight, especially when viewed from below. One example is St John's Head, Hoy, which towers to 1140ft (347m) above the Orkney ferry boat as it creeps across the waters of the Pentland Firth.

Such steepness depends on a pattern of well-developed vertical joint-planes (cracks formed along planes of weakness) in the rock. Continuous weathering by wind and rain along these cracks causes

loosened blocks to fall directly into deep water instead of mantling and protecting the cliff foot from further wave erosion.

Other high vertical cliffs are those of Clo Mor 921ft (281m) near Cape Wrath; Dunvegan Head 1025ft (312m) and Waterstein Head 966ft (294m) on Skye; the Cliffs of Moher 668ft (203m) in County Clare; and Beachy Head 534ft (160m) in Sussex.

Beachy Head and the other chalk cliffs of southern England are remarkably vertical because the fallen masses of chalk are quickly destroyed by the waves, thus exposing the cliff foot to renewed undercutting.

Flamborough Head and The Needles, two of the most striking chalk coastal features in the British Isles, are very different in character. Flamborough Head, honeycombed with caves, is the northernmost nose at the end of the great chalk escarpment which runs from Devon to Yorkshire. Not far from the other end of the escarpment lie The Needles; more precisely they are part of a ridge of chalk which runs east-west across the Isle of Wight, and once continued to the Dorset mainland.

From the cliff above The Needles it is possible on a clear day to see how they

Sea cliffs and caves near Wick in the north of Scotland. Caves like these sometimes coalesce to form natural rock arches

fall in line with the chalk cliffs of Foreland Point and Old Harry Rocks across the water in the Isle of Purbeck. The Needles and Old Harry are remnants of the marine-eroded ridge. And, just as the sea detached The Needles from the Isle of Wight, so it detached the Isle of Wight – but over a much longer period – from the mainland (see illustration p. 153).

The chalk here and in Dorset has been up-ended by the folding and thrusting which occurred in the great earth movements which built the Alps. Indeed The Needles owe their resistance to the hardness imparted by these movements.

The hardest chalk is in the south face of the Needle nearest the shore. A slight broadening of this hard belt of chalk accounts for the increase in the size of the stacks seawards.

At Flamborough the chalk, unlike that of the south coast, lies in nearly horizontal beds which produce an impressive range of almost vertical cliffs. The headland itself is covered with thick boulder clay and the erosion of this above, and the chalk below, gives it a character not found elsewhere in chalk cliffs.

The different rates and magnitudes of cliff erosion depend not only on the hardness and the jointing pattern of the rocks but also on any structural weaknesses such as faults. Where these occur, or where relatively weak rock layers alternate with more resistant layers, waves will etch out a complex mosaic of caves, arches, stacks and geos. A marine cleft, or geo, may commence life as a sea cave, perhaps with a spectacular blowhole at the inner end, like the Kettle Spout in North Uist, but roof collapse and a coalescence of geos will produce a variety of arches and stacks along the fretted shore-line (illustration next page).

All these features are displayed on one of the finest limestone coasts in the British Isles, the Stack Rocks area of the Pembrokeshire Coast National Park, near Flimston.

Here flat-topped, near-vertical cliffs of Carboniferous limestone are under constant attack from the sea, which has cut into the coast to produce the striking promontories of St Govan's Head and Stackpole Head. The plateau behind the cliffs was planed flat by the sea at a time when the sea level was higher.

This area has a wealth of stacks, arches, cauldrons and blow-holes, the result of marine erosion working on a mass of limestone already rich in caves, swallow-holes, faults and other lines of weakness in the rocks.

An outstanding feature is the Green Bridge of Wales, an arch formed of massive limestones. This was created when caves on opposite sides of a headland were cut back farther and farther by the sea until they coalesced. Nearby the twin Stack Rocks, pinnacles of limestone thick with colonies of sea birds, rise from shallow water close inshore. They are the remains of an old headland destroyed by the sea.

To the east of these is the Devil's Cauldron, a peninsula riddled with caves and passages formed by the sea eating away at lines of weakness in the rocks. The Cauldron itself is the result of a number of blow-hole caves coalescing and then collapsing.

Continuing erosion by the sea over a long period will transform this peninsula into a series of stacks and arches which are likely to be even more spectacular than the Green Bridge of Wales and the Stack Rocks.

Some of the most famous sea caves are found in the basalt lavas of the small Scottish island of Staffa where Fingal's Cave has basalt columns similar to those of the Giant's Causeway in Northern

At Fingal's Cave on the island of Staffa marked differences can be seen in the structure of the rocks. These differences tell the story of a mass of molten lava and the different rates at which it cooled as it was pushed up from within the Earth millions of years ago.

The very top layer of rock is a structureless, slaggy crust which now forms the roof of the cave. This cooled rapidly from above where it was losing most heat.

The middle section also cooled from above.

As the molten rock began to solidify it contracted to form a hexagonal pattern rather like cracks that form in mud as it dries. These cracks followed the solidification down through the molten rock, still cooling from above, but at a slower and more uniform rate. This led to the formation of the narrow columns of basalt.

The lavas at the base of the cliffs are massive, regularly spaced columns forming the 'causeway' into the cave. These cooled from below.

Ireland. How these columnar lavas are formed is clearly illustrated above. There are more of these to be seen in the cliffs of western Mull. There the lavas must have flowed into a forest, for trees have been found preserved in them.

Smoo Cave – from the Norse *smuga* meaning cleft – near Durness on the north coast of Scotland has the added attraction of a subterranean waterfall at the back of its limestone chamber. It has been created partly by the underground river which runs through it and partly by marine erosion. It is easy to imagine the sea-filled gorge outside the cave entrance once roofed by a layer of limestone, long since collapsed.

Examples of partly collapsed caves can be seen at the Bullers of Buchan, north of Aberdeen, and at the narrower Hunts-

man's Leap near Tenby. Some of the more spectacular coastal arches in Scotland are the Brig o' Trams at Wick, the Devil's Bridge at Scrabster in Caithness and the Bow Fiddle at Portknockie, Banff.

Farther south the Green Bridge of Wales, already mentioned, Durdle Door and Stair Hole in Dorset are well known tourist attractions.

Of the sea stacks, Orkney's Old Man of Hoy is the best known; St Kilda's gigantic stacks are the highest, with Stac Lee 544ft (166m) and Stac an Armin 627ft (207m); and the Needles and Old Harry on England's south coast among the most photographed.

The Devon and Cornish coast between Hartland Point and Boscastle has magnificent cliffs which are being cut by the sea

in such a way that it is possible to get excellent sectional views of a wide variety of rock patterns.

The folding and faulting has produced almost museum models of sharp anticlines (upfolds), synclines (downfolds), vertical strata, small faults and other interesting features.

This stretch also has some of the finest coastal waterfalls in England. Streams drain the land for only a few miles from the coast and in their short length they have carved deep wooded valleys which end with the streams falling over the cliffs. Normally the streams would cut down into the rock so that their mouths were at sea level. But here the coast, under attack from the waves, is being worn away more quickly than the streams can cut down. Thus their valleys are left 'hanging' with the water dropping over the cliffs.

Litter Water, nine miles (14km) south of Hartland Quay, ends in a sheer fall of over 70ft (21.3m). In other places the streams cascade over more irregular cliffs, especially where layers of rock of different hardness have caused 'steps' in the descent.

Islands

Most people are fascinated by islands, none more so than the inhabitants of the British Isles who have no fewer than 1040 dotting the seas which surround them. Among these, differences in geology, topography, soils, vegetation and climate have created islands of contrasting shape, colour and land use. But whether the land use best suited to an island is still being achieved depends largely on its remoteness or accessibility.

Some islands are so remote that they are rarely visited. Rockall, about 200 miles (320km) to the west of North Uist, is the most extreme case. This island is no more than a 70ft (21m) pinnacle of granite washed over by the storm waves. It rises from a submarine platform of volcanic rocks.

The cutting of a cliff coast. 1 Waves attack softer, less resistant rocks and 2 structural weaknesses such as faults, etching out geos or clefts. Blowholes form. 3 Caves begin to form on the fault line and a marine arch is produced by two caves coalescing. 4 Stacks remain as arches collapse

Some tiny specks such as Shetland's Muckle Flugga, the northernmost British landfall, Cornwall's Bishop's Rock and Ireland's Fastnet are occupied only by lightkeepers. Fair Isle, midway between Orkney and Shetland, is the most isolated inhabited island.

The rocky, windswept expanses of the Scottish Hebrides and Ireland's western isles support traditional fishing-crofting communities which are only now being touched by tourism. On these peat-covered, treeless margins of the 'Celtic Fringe' the magnificent scenery, booming surf and unforgettable sunsets are but one side of the coin; the islanders' precarious livelihoods are reflected in declining populations.

St Kilda, some 60 miles (96km) west of the Outer Hebrides, is renowned not only for its cliffs and stacks – homes of the world's largest colony of gannets – but also for the primitive life style of its former inhabitants, the last of whom were evacuated to the mainland in 1930 because of the harshness of life there.

Ireland's Blasket Isles, once a thriving community in the 'next parish to America', are now virtually deserted.

The neighbouring Skellig Rocks, seven miles offshore across the turbulent seas of St Finan's Bay, are even more remote. Their grey, splintery outlines rise out of the Atlantic to produce a series of fantastic spires and pinnacles.

They have long been abandoned but are famous as one of the strongholds of British Christianity during the Dark Ages, inhabited by a handful of Celtic monks. Perched on ledges in the cliffs are a number of drystone buildings which are a legacy of this remarkable monastic settlement.

The other well-known monastic islands of Lindisfarne (Northumberland), Caldey (Dyfed) and Iona (Scotland) have fared somewhat better, bolstered by recently developed tourism.

The Welsh isles of Skomer, Skokholm, Grassholm and Ramsey, once the haunts of Vikings, are now more celebrated for cliff scenery, seals and bird life than sporadic attempts to re-settle them.

In the Bristol Channel the inhabitants of Lundy's granite isle have maintained a successful farming community. Farther up-channel the conspicuous shapes of Flat Holm and Steep Holme are built of white Carboniferous limestone, the bedding planes of which – these are the surfaces which separate one layer of rock from another – provide ledges for countless seabirds.

How the Isle of Wight became an island. It was separated from the mainland when the sea broke through the chalk ridge which once connected the two. The lower broken line marks the old cliff line of chalk. The sea breached it after marine erosion caused the coast to retreat from its former position farther out in the English Channel. The Needles and Old Harry Rocks are remnants of the ridge.

Limestone islands are often uninhabited because of water supply problems. This makes the Aran Isles of Ireland's Galway Bay all the more remarkable because of their thriving population in a limestone 'desert'.

Nearly every field has been made by the islanders artificially. Owing to a lack of soil on the bare limestone they have, over the centuries, carried thousands of tons of sand and seaweed from the low-lying north-eastern shores and piled it on the limestone 'pavements' near the village.

To preserve their new soil the joints in the limestone were first filled with rubble and the small plots surrounded with drystone walls, as protection against the wind. The islands are criss-crossed with miles of these walls within which cattle are grazed and potatoes grown.

The sea cliffs of Aran are constantly being eroded and undercut by Atlantic waves and consequently the horizontal layers of limestone often overhang the ocean. These have been used as fishing stances from time immemorial.

The islanders of Clew Bay, Co Mayo, are better blessed – geologically speaking! They gather rich hay harvests from their emerald green archipelago, for their islands are the well-watered remnants of boulder clay drumlins which were drowned by the sea.

The carefully manicured fields of the Scillonian islanders sit on the partially drowned tors of a granite massif which was reputedly inundated and isolated from Land's End when the intervening land of Lyonesse was submerged by a rise in sea level after the glaciers had melted.

The Isle of Man also was once part of the mainland. Submarine contours indicate that a broad ridge of less than 20 fathoms depth (120ft, 36.5m) joins the island to the English mainland.

Generally there is no simple and complete answer to the question: how are islands formed? In the previous section it has been shown how the sea, by cutting away softer rocks and attacking lines of weakness in them, can separate one land mass from another.

Sometimes, as a river cuts its valley down to sea level, a rise in sea level drowns the low lying land and leaves the higher parts as islands. This, plus continuous erosion by the sea, is how the Isle of Wight was cut off from the mainland. At one time its chalk ridge and those of Dorset were continuous and the Frome river valley extended along the present Solent and Spithead (illustration above).

How Anglesey, the lowest area in North Wales, came to be a plateau which rises to less than 300ft (91m) above sea level, is not so certain. One theory is that it is a platform which was shaped by waves when the sea advanced over the area, slicing across hard and soft rocks alike, flattening their structures. Across the Menai Straits, in a coastal strip several miles wide, plateau levels of a few hundred feet above sea level persist – and they are more comparable with Anglesey than the mainland about them.

An alternative theory is that Anglesey represents a land surface from which a former cover of New Red Sandstone has been stripped, just as the Torridonian sandstones are being stripped off the Lewisian gneiss in Scotland.

The 15 mile (24km) long channel of the Menai Straits which separates Anglesey from the mainland looks much like an enlarged river valley. It is probable that this was once cut by glacial meltwater. Later, like so many Cornish valleys, it was drowned by the post-glacial rise in sea level.

Straits

The Straits of Dover are one of the most celebrated stretches of sea round the British Isles: a narrow piece of water, 18 to 25 miles (29km to 40km) wide separating Britain from France.

This, however, was not always so. The affinity of the geological structures of Kent and Sussex with those of northern France suggests that a land link once existed. This was 250,000 years ago. How, then, was the connection with the Continent broken? How were the straits formed? In short, how did the British Isles become the British Isles. There are two theories.

A chalk dome, the remnants of which can be seen in the long ridges of the North and South Downs, formed the original isthmus, with rivers flowing on one side to the North Sea and on the other to the Channel, which then reached only to Beachy Head. Even when the crest of the chalk dome had been breached, to reveal the underlying Wealden rocks, the rivers maintained their courses across the ridges, just as the Medway cuts through the North Downs and the Cuckmere through the South Downs today.

While this was happening the sea was also cutting into the isthmus on both its flanks. This slow process of erosion was assisted by the gradually rising sea level which led to the isthmus being breached. This may have occurred more than once – the isthmus being reconnected and breached again.

The other, but less likely explanation is that during the Ice Age a huge glacial lake was impounded behind the land-bridge. As the ice sheets covering the North Sea melted the level of the lake rose until it overflowed the lowest part of the chalk ridge, perhaps cutting a gorge which was later widened by erosion. Following this the rising sea level would have submerged the remaining part of the ridge.

Again, since sea level fluctuated with the advance and retreat of the ice sheets it is likely that the straits alternated between land and water several times. If the Ice Age were to return it is possible that the straits might become land once again. At their deepest they are no more than 300ft (91m).

Estuaries and bays

The beauty of the coastline does not depend solely on cliffs and islands. They provide the *fortissimo* passages in the coastal symphony but the waters of the Dart, Helford River with its woods fall-

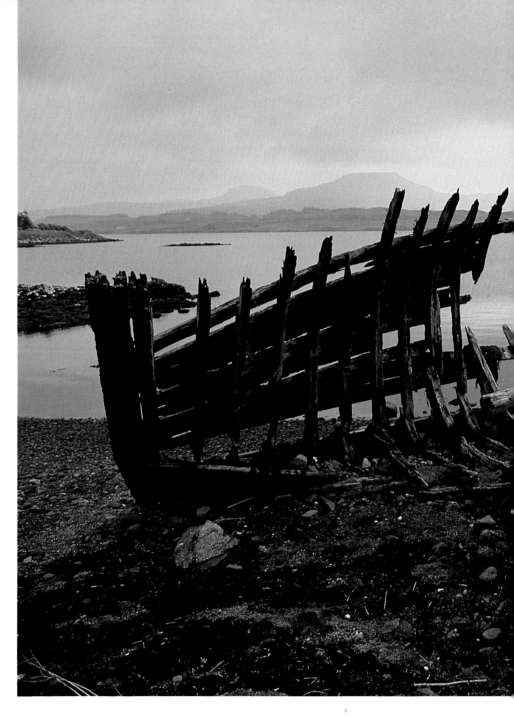

ing to the water's edge and the serene countryside of Constable's Suffolk drifting down to the Stour and Deben represent gentler *pianissimo* moods.

These three estuaries have in common the manner of their origin. They are former river valleys which were drowned by the rise in sea level of about 100ft (30.5m) which accompanied the melting of the ice sheets 10–20,000 years ago. When this happened in upland areas the mountainous divides were transformed into headlands like the Iveragh Peninsula in south-west Ireland. Simple, funnel-like bays like Bantry and Kenmare River contrast with the more tortuous drowned river channels in nearby Kinsale and Cobh. Here the coastal configuration closely resembles south-west Britain, an area in which tidal waters have burrowed deeply into flat, rocky plateaux.

The picturesque, tree-lined shores of Milford Haven in South Wales are echoed by Cornwall's Helford River, with its famous Frenchman's Creek, and by the submerged estuaries of the Fal and Fowey. Whether in Ireland or Cornwall they are all typical coastal features known as rias. Plymouth Sound, possibly England's best known ria, is the estuary of the Tamar. It can be seen to great effect from Brunel's famous Saltash railway bridge or the Tamar suspension bridge. The smaller, sheltered estuaries of the Yealm, the Dart and Salcombe are nearby. One of the finest views of the Salcombe estuary is from the National Trust gardens at Sharpitor.

Fjords, also the result of a submerged coastline, are valleys which have been greatly over-deepened by glaciers. They are typical of the coasts of North West Scotland and Donegal. They are most weight caused considerable downsags in the Earth's crust. The localised coastal uplift which raised the beaches represents the slow recoil of the Earth's crust when relieved of this weight.

In the softer clays of lowland England the drowned estuaries are not cliff-bound but are stitched around with a maze of winding, shallow creeks, mud-flats and broad tracts of tidal marsh.

With some notable exceptions (see page 160) these are coasts of deposition where off-shore bars, sand spits and forelands help straighten out the many indentations caused by the submergence of the coast.

Thus, the marshy backwaters of Poole, Portsmouth and Chichester are almost closed off from the Channel but are kept open by tidal scour. Similar coastal scenery occurs round the Isle of Sheppey and the Medway in north Kent and in the great Essex marshlands of the Crouch, Blackwater and Colne. Farther north are the broad, drowned estuaries of Suffolk's Deben, Orwell and Stour.

Since waves attack any chink in the coastal armour, most of the largest bays in the British Isles are carved in rocks of relatively poor resistance. Belfast Lough, Solway Firth and Morecambe Bay occupy submerged basins of New Red Sandstone cradled between older, harder rocks. The Welsh bays of St

Celtic seascapes. The bones of a long-abandoned boat (left) near Dunvegan, Isle of Skye. Across the turbulent waters of St Finan's Bay, Co Kerry (below) lies the rock of Skellig Michael and its ancient monastic site

deeply cut where the glacier was constricted in its journey down valley. But near the valley mouth, where the glacier spreads out, downward erosion decreases. The deepening is not so marked and a rocky threshold bar occurs at the mouth of the valley. Sometimes this is amplified by a terminal moraine left by the glacier. This is why a fjord shallows at its mouth, unlike a ria which is at its deepest at its mouth. The characteristics of these two coastal features and the differences between them are shown in the illustration overleaf.

To complicate matters the rise in sea level which made the rias and fjords has been exceeded in places by an uplift of the land itself. This has created the so-called emergent coastlines of Ulster and Western Scotland which are seen in the raised beaches of those areas. Here the ice sheets were at their thickest and their

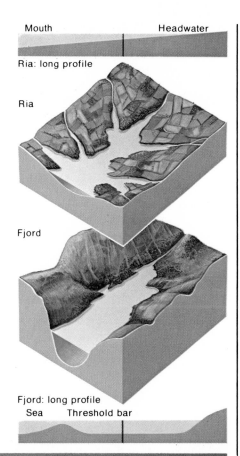

A ria is formed when a river valley is drowned by a rise in sea level (above and top right). The Salcombe estuary shown here is a ria. Its deepest point, as the profile of its slope from source to sea shows, is at its mouth. A fjord also results from a drowned coastline but its valley was previously over-deepened by glaciers. Its shallowest point, as the lower profile shows, is at its mouth

Mouth Headwater

Ria: long profile

Ria

Fjord

Fjord: long profile
Sea Threshold bar

The way a coastline is shaped when waves attack the cliffs depends on how resistant its rocks are. On the Dorset coast softer rocks adjacent to harder ones are being cut away more rapidly. This process has produced notable features such as Worbarrow Bay and (above) Lulworth Cove. At these places the sea has breached the Purbeck and Portland limestones and is cutting out the softer clays and sandstones

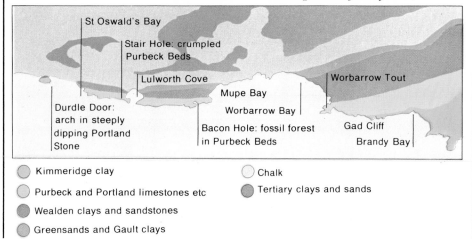

St Oswald's Bay

Stair Hole: crumpled Purbeck Beds

Lulworth Cove

Worbarrow Tout

Mupe Bay

Durdle Door: arch in steeply dipping Portland Stone

Worbarrow Bay

Bacon Hole: fossil forest in Purbeck Beds

Gad Cliff

Brandy Bay

- Kimmeridge clay
- Purbeck and Portland limestones etc
- Wealden clays and sandstones
- Greensands and Gault clays
- Chalk
- Tertiary clays and sands

Brides, Carmarthen and Swansea were eroded largely in Carboniferous rocks. On a smaller scale the detailed differential etching of hard and soft rocks is well shown by Lulworth Cove and Worbarrow Bay in Dorset (illustration below) and by many of the North Devon coves between Lynmouth and Croyde.

Orkney's Scapa Flow and Shetland's deep-water voes, or inlets, are neither drowned estuaries nor simple bays. They are thought to have been formed in part by the post-glacial drowning of depressions formed by Earth movements.

Beaches and dunes

Camas Sgiotaig, a remote northern bay on the Hebridean Isle of Eigg, is the site of a rare and curious phenomenon. Here the sands of the beach 'sing' when walked upon. The Gaelic name means Bay of the Musical Sand.

In fact the song is not particularly musical but more of a squeaking note. Scientists have shown that the sound is something to do with (although no one knows exactly what) the uniform size and rounded form of the local sand grains which come from the weathering of a calcareous sandstone.

Other beaches have sands which do the same. Near Banff on Scotland's north-east coast the singing white sands come from the tough local quartzite and those at Porth Oer in the Lleyn Peninsula, Wales, are derived from similar rocks.

Not all beaches have sands, let alone singing or whistling ones. Whether a beach is sandy, pebbly or muddy depends partly on the character of the local bedrock.

If sandstones, or sand from glacial meltwaters predominate, then sandy beaches usually occur. Where chalk is exposed, flinty shingle beaches are common. Where rocks rich in clay are being eroded, or where muddy rivers debouch into estuaries, mudbanks abound. Sometimes beaches yield pebbles of great beauty (see page 171).

On the beach at Port na Churaich, the spot where St Columba landed on Iona more than 1400 years ago, it is possible to find beautiful Iona pebbles. These come from a submarine extension of Iona marble which the sea has eroded. This attractive green and white rock a white metamorphosed limestone streaked by a green variety of serpentine – occurs in narrow veins among the Pre-Cambrian rocks of the seashore at the south end of the island.

It does not follow that a beach will be

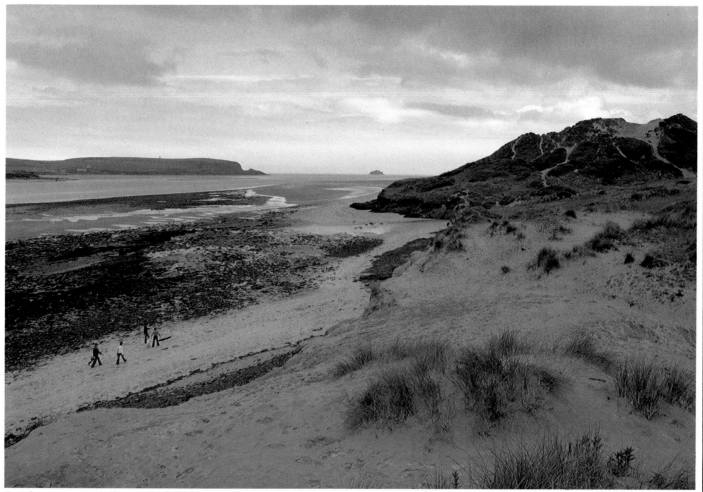

Camel estuary, north Cornwall. Within a small compass this has every sort of coastline feature – cliffs, bays, dunes, mudflats and marshes

Maldon, Essex. A small, picturesque port at the head of the Blackwater estuary much concerned with sailing barges and the making of sea salt

made up of one type of material whether it be fine sand or pebbles. It is common to find within a single bay a beach which grades from the coarsest shingle through intermediate sands to the finest muds. This is because waves and currents are constantly sorting these different sized materials.

Not all beaches, whatever the publicity brochures claim, possess golden sands. Most are shades of yellow, red or brown but they can also range from purest white to dramatic black.

At Arisaig, south of the River Morar, the road passes through some of the most magnificent coastal scenery in Scotland. Here a narrow outcrop of psammite, a mica-spangled quartzite rock, has weathered into the glittering silvery sands which adorn a multitude of tiny bays. Yet at Glenbrittle on the Isle of Skye the beach sand is black, derived from the gabbro rock of the Cuillins. At Duntulm, Skye, where olivine minerals are common, the sands are dull green.

Many of the dazzling white beaches of Ireland's Connemara or the Hebridean 'machair' strands (illustration below) are due to the presence of myriads of broken shells.

A few localities boast coral beaches. At Claigan in northern Skye tiny pieces of attractive pinkish material have apparently been broken off growths which flourish just offshore in a few fathoms of water. But this Hebridean coral, like that in Connemara and at Tanera Beg in the Summer Isles near Ullapool, is the product not of coral polyps but of a seaweed called *Lithothamnion calcareum* which abstracts carbonate of lime from sea water.

Sand dunes occur on exposed coast-

Lack of harbours forces fishing boats to launch from the beach. These are at Hastings

lines where prevailing winds blow copious quantities of sand from the foreshore at low tide. Most large dune areas in the British Isles are found, therefore, on westerly coasts. Unspoiled stretches can be seen at Braunton Burrows, North Devon, and Perranporth, Cornwall. Wales has Harlech, Pendine and Swansea Bay. In north-west England there are the dunes of the Duddon estuary. Western Scotland boasts the Uists and Tiree while Dingle Bay and Donegal have Ireland's best examples.

Occasionally, the mobility of sand dunes has led to the burial of coastal settlements: 'lost' villages and churches occur at Kenfig Burrows, South Wales; St Piran, Cornwall; Forvie and Rattray, Aberdeenshire; and, most famous of all, at Skara Brae, Orkney, where an entire Stone Age village has been excavated.

Spits

Chesil Beach is a long, unbroken ridge of shingle which extends for over 15 miles (25km) on England's south coast from Bridport to the Isle of Portland. For eight miles south-east of Abbotsbury it is separated from the mainland by the tidal waters of a lagoon called the Fleet which is fed by the sea through a breach in a smaller, subsidiary bank of shingle running between Portland and Weymouth.

Chesil Beach is made up largely of rounded pebbles of flint. There are also some of quartzite and, at the Portland end, some local limestone pebbles. What is so extraordinary about the beach and its pebbles is the way in which they are systematically graded throughout its length. They increase in size from north-west to south-east, being about the size of a large pea near Bridport to fist-size and larger at Portland.

Experiments have shown that brick fragments thrown down on the beach move to the part of it where there are pebbles of similar size. Even more curious is the claim that the pebbles below water increase in size in the opposite direction!

It is this process of grading which makes Chesil Beach unique in the British Isles – and possibly in the world. Predictably this, and the sheer accumulation of material making the beach, has caused much controversy and speculation among geologists.

Various theories have been advanced as to how it was formed but it seems likely that it owes its origin to longshore drift (illustration opposite) which in this case cut off an existing body of water, leaving it as a lagoon. Another explanation is

Machair | Rough grazing | Bare rock

Beach | Dunes | Shell sand | Shell sand over peat | Peat over boulder clay | Peat stripped off boulder clay

W | | | | | | E

Sea level

Lewisian Gneiss

The 'machair' is an unusual coastal landscape found in Scotland's Western Isles which has its origins in wind-blown sand.

The low, flat stretches of true machair lie to the landward of the beaches and dunes. It is a mixture of glacial sands and numerous marine organisms which have improved formerly barren tracts of land and made them capable of growing good crops.

Today, after hundreds of years of agricultural use the machair is a mature surface which has dark, rich, stoneless loams. It depends for its stability on nit-

rogen fixing plants. The key to its formation is the stabilizing of coastal dunes by marram grass. A later stage is the development of a dune pasture.

It is a vital ingredient in the economic and cultural life, and on an island like Uist it demonstrates how physical processes which shape the land surface, the growth of vegetation and land-use are interwoven into a delicately balanced system.

On these areas village settlement was arranged in strips, at right angles to the coast, so that each crofter had a share of each of the different soils.

that it was constructed by some form of off-shore bar being driven towards the land to form a bayhead bar, a shingle or sand bar which, as it names suggests, cuts off a bay. Those in Ireland west of Carnsore Point, Wexford, are similar but less impressive examples.

Off-shore bars are low, sandy, pebbly islands formed either by material combed down the beach by the back-wash of waves or more likely by material drifted by currents along the shore and deposited at the line where incoming waves first break. Off-shore bars can be seen at Culbin on the south shore of the Moray Firth, in the island of North Uist and at Scolt Head, Norfolk. Similar to Chesil Beach are Slapton Sands, Devon, and Loe Bar, Cornwall.

These different types of bars are classic features of what geologists call a constructive coastline. This is one being built up by marine deposition which produces smooth curving beaches of sand and shingle. The character of a constructive coastline, whether it consists of bars, spits or forelands (these will be explained below) depends on the nature of the original coastline, upon the energy of the constructive waves and tidal currents and on a continuing supply of sediment.

Where longshore drifting of material crosses river mouths it is unlikely that the estuary will be blocked because of continuing river action and tidal scour. Nevertheless, shingle spits have deflected rivers varying distances from their former mouths and away from the direction of dominant wave approach.

In East Anglia the rivers Alde and Butley have been deflected southwards by the pebbly extension of Orfordness. The Alde flows behind this for about nine miles parallel to the sea (see illustration). Yarmouth, Blakeney Point and Spurn Head (see page 162) are other well known East Coast spits. So are those on the south coast at Hurst Castle and Calshot in the Solent, the Sandbanks peninsula at the mouth of Poole Harbour, Dawlish Warren and Braunton Burrows in Devonshire and, in the same county, the splendid pebble ridge of Westward Ho!

Occasionally an extending spit will join an existing island to the shore creating a tombolo. By linking Portland Island to the mainland Chesil Beach created Britain's largest and best known tombolo, but on a smaller scale there are numerous examples in the Isles of Scilly, Orkney and Shetland including the picturesque St Ninian's Isle. In Ireland there are large tombolos at Rossguill,

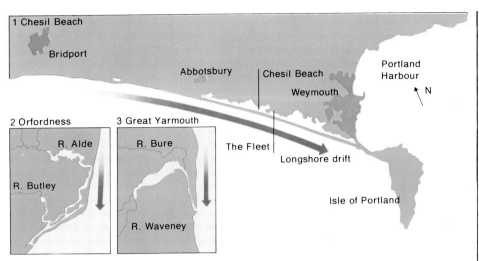

How spits are formed. 1 At Chesil Beach the longshore drift of material has cut off an existing body of water leaving it as a lagoon. 2 The spit at Orfordness has deflected rivers southwards so they flow parallel with the sea. 3 Much the same has happened, but on a smaller scale, at Great Yarmouth

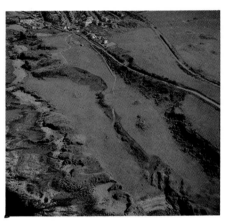

Raised beaches, Dunure, Ayrshire. Signs that sea level was once higher

Donegal, and at Castlegregory, Kerry.

At certain places on the coast waves approach from more than one direction and because of this, complex shingle forelands accumulate. Here shingle spits coalesce and cut off the former coastline completely from the sea, leaving the intervening space to be converted into marsh. The best example of this is Dungeness in Kent with its abandoned shoreline and Romney Marsh behind (see page 163).

In post-glacial times during periods of higher sea level waves and currents fashioned other forelands which remain today as raised beach features. Selsey Bill, Sussex, is an example of one of these 'fossil' forelands. So is Magilligan Point, Co Londonderry. On the Moray Firth there are a pair of matching raised beaches at Chanonry Point. At Ardersier a whole suite of raised beaches occurs.

The extensive raised beaches of Northern Ireland and Scotland contain many other cases of old shorelines of deposition which are now high and dry above the waves.

Wind-blown waves play a powerful part in shaping the coast. As a wave approaches the shore its lower part is slowed by friction with the sea-bed. Its upper part continues moving but since it is unsupported from below it develops into a breaker which topples over and sends a mass of water foaming up the beach. This is called the swash. Its return is the backwash. The first pushes pebbles and sand towards the land, the latter carries them back towards the sea. Constructive waves 1 have a powerful swash and little backwash. Destructive waves 2 have a

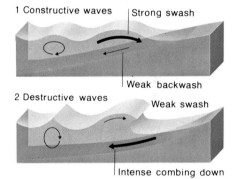

strong backwash which combs down the beach material. In calm conditions only limited amounts of beach material are moved; in storms quite the opposite. If the prevailing wind drives the waves ashore obliquely, then sands and pebbles are also pushed up the beach obliquely. The backwash then returns them straight down the beach. This continual zig-zag move-

ment which transports material lengthwise along the coast is known as longshore drift. Groynes help arrest it and build up a beach.

Left: The progress of the Severn Bore showing the time it takes to reach successive points up-river. Centre: Corrievreckan Whirlpool on Scotland's west coast is at its fiercest when the flood tide flows north through the Sound of Jura and then west into the strait between the island. Right: The Portland Tidal Eddy in the English Channel has built up a huge bank of shell fragments called the Shambles

Tides

The periodical rise and fall of large masses of water is a remarkable phenomenon of the coast. The tides can make as much as 40ft (12m) difference to the depth of water in places although the average tidal range in the British Isles is about 15ft (4.5m).

Most places get two low and two high tides every 24 hours. There are exceptions to this pattern: Southampton gets a double high tide, that is four high tides a day.

This is partly due to the existence of two entrances to the Solent. The tide of the Channel gives it its first high water by way of the West Solent, its second by way of Spithead two hours later. This unusual tidal regime has favoured the development of Southampton as a port.

The usual interval between the tides is 12hrs 25mins, roughly half the time the moon takes to circle the earth. The gravitational pull of moon, sun and earth combine to produce the tidal pattern; the tidal rise and fall is related to the relative positions of the moon and sun, with the tide reaching a maximum height a day or so after a new or full moon.

This is called a *spring* tide (nothing to do with the season) which rises higher and falls lower than usual. The minimum tides with small range are called *neap* tides. Both occur at intervals of about a fortnight.

About the time of the spring and autumn equinoxes in March and September, when the length of day is equal to night, the spring tides are generally the highest and lowest of the year.

A rising tide is known as a flood tide, a falling one an ebb tide. Slack water occurs between ebb and flood when the tide is almost at a standstill.

The configuration of an estuary or river mouth can turn a rising tide into a tidal wave called a bore. The Severn Bore is a wall of water 3ft to 9ft (0.9m to 2.7m) high which moves upstream during the period of spring tides.

The bore is most striking during the equinoxes. As the incoming tidal water is driven into the constricting estuary it rises in a high, abrupt front which overrides the slower river flow. It can pass from Sharpness to Gloucester at a rate which increases from $5\frac{1}{2}$ to 13 mph (8.8 to 20.9kph). It is best seen at Stonebench (see map) on the eastern bank of the river, three miles (4.8km) downstream from Gloucester.

There are places where the tide forms whirlpools. Corrievreckan Whirlpool on the west coast of Scotland is a 9-knot tidal race which produces a swirling pool of water of intense ferocity.

It is caused by rock pinnacles below water and develops most strongly when the flood tide sets north through the Sound of Jura (see map) and then drives west into the strait separating the northern tip of the island of Jura from neighbouring Scarba.

With a westerly wind blowing the roar of the whirlpool can be heard on the mainland coast five miles away at Craignish – and it can be seen from the hill above this point.

The Portland Tidal Eddy is another great circulating mass of water but larger than Corrievreckan. It develops in the English Channel in the lee of Portland Bill as the flood tide makes progress eastwards (see map). Within the slack water of the 'eye' a great bank of broken shell fragments, the Shambles, has been built up over the centuries. Although the Shambles is not visible from the shore it produces disturbed water and rips under certain conditions of wind and tide.

Coastal erosion

An unceasing battle between land and sea is being waged on the coasts of the British Isles. In places the sea is winning, eating into the land with dramatic results. Elsewhere the land is gaining from the sea.

The Holderness coast of Yorkshire is suffering the worst coastal erosion in Europe, possibly in the world, and now lies nearly a quarter-mile (402m) back from where it was 200 years ago. Farther south, off the Suffolk coast, the once thriving port of Dunwich is no more than a scattering of masonry on the sea-bed. Yet, in other places the valuable process of coastal accretion has resulted in the reclamation of substantial tracts of land, especially on the estuaries of the Humber and the Ribble, and around the shores of the Wash. A rough stocktaking suggests that the British Isles gain as much from the sea as they lose to it.

This is small consolation to owners of cliff-top properties on the Yorkshire and East Anglian coasts who have watched them destroyed by the North Sea's onslaught. Here it has been devouring land throughout recorded history. In the days of Julius Caesar the Holderness coast was, according to some estimates, two miles (3.2km) farther east than it is now. Such loss of land, however, would not be attributable to erosion alone. In those days the sea level was lower but after 1200 it rose again drowning the low lying land.

In recent times the parish church at Mappleton, south of Hornsea, has increasingly come under threat. In 1786 the church was 633yds (579m) from the sea; in 1835, 554yds (506.5m), and in 1912, 418yds (382m). In January 1979 it was only 170yds (155m) from the nearest point of the cliff top, and the sea is still advancing. In 1978 the owner of a shop and cafe at Skipsea reported losing 64ft (19.5m) of land to the sea in four years.

The stretch of coast between Bridlington and Spurn Head boasts more villages swallowed by the sea than anywhere else in Europe. About thirty have vanished from the map (see p. 162). Auburn, south of Bridlington, was the last to be lost. All that remains of the name is Auburn Farm which once had the village to the east of it. The farm itself has lost 17 acres (6 hectares) to the sea in the last 40 years.

Some experts see continued erosion producing catastrophic results. Towns such as Hornsea and Withernsea are protected by sea walls but as the coast between them is gnawed away they are

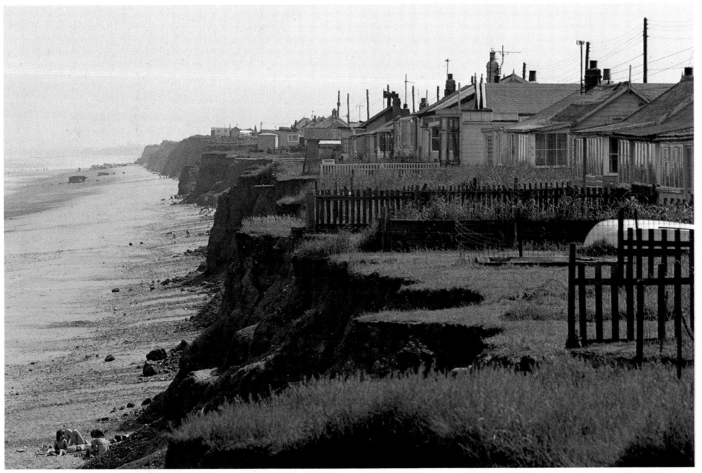

The crumbling coast of Holderness. At Skipsea cliff-top chalets are losing their gardens to the sea. Before long waves will destroy the chalets too

Derelict barn slipping into the sea at Waxholm and the end of the road at Tunstall. Both are on the vulnerable Holderness coast

Collapsing cliffs near Dunwich, Suffolk, and beach defences at West Runton, Norfolk. Groynes protecting one beach may starve another of sand   161

The lost villages of Yorkshire's Holderness coast. Each black dot represents a settlement claimed by the sea. Over 30 have vanished between Bridlington and Spurn Head

Town plan of Dunwich, Suffolk, in 1589. The broken lines show past coastlines and how much of the once-thriving town has been lost to the North Sea over nearly 400 years

gradually becoming 'capes'. If the sea were allowed to break through into the inland drainage system of Holderness they could become isolated at the end of peninsulas.

The sand and shingle spit of Spurn Head is the most vulnerable part of this coast. It used to lose land to the sea at a rate of a metre a year but this is now increasing. Although groynes have helped hold the spit, the cutting back of the coast farther north means that it too is forced to retreat. A north-westerly gale combined with abnormally high spring tides could wash the southern end of the point away.

There are two views as to what has happened and is happening to the spit. One is that over the centuries the spit has shown periods of growth and retreat with several changes in its position. The cycle of change is thought to take place over a

The changing face of Spurn Head. In a little over 100 years the shape of this famous East Coast spit has altered dramatically. In 1852 it consisted of a chain of islets. By 1959 it was a continuous unbroken coastal feature, as it is today. Without man-made sea defences it would become a string of small islands again

period of about 300 years. Its present position has been held for 150 years.

An alternative view is that the present continuous feature is artificially maintained. If it were left to natural forces it would break down into a string of islets as it was in the first half of the last century.

Should the sea breach the spit, creating a tidal channel between it and the estuary, a new Spurn Head would appear, extending west of the present one, which would disappear.

Why is this coast so fragile? Holderness is a gift of the Ice Age which the sea is taking back. The coast consists of soft boulder clay deposited at the foot of the old line of chalk sea cliffs along the edge of the Wolds. If erosion worsens there is a possibility of Holderness disappearing and the sea washing against its former cliffs once more. This would take thousands of years and assumes no emergency coastal defence measures.

Obviously the soft cliffs of sand and clay which occur along much of England's east coast are particularly susceptible to erosion during winter storms. Steep-fronted waves breaking along the shoreline can, within a few hours, lower a beach by as much as 10ft (3.5m). Then the waves are able to launch a frontal assault on the cliffs.

This happened at Torcross in Devon in January 1979 when property was severely damaged by the sea. An earlier storm lowered the beach level which left little protection from the January storm.

Dunwich provides an exceptional record of coastal retreat over several centuries. Founded in the 7th century it became an important medieval town

and seat of a bishopric. Then it suffered almost total destruction by the sea. In Norman times its lands were already being eaten away and in 1326 a great storm caused severe flooding and destruction. A detailed town plan of 1589 shows how much of the town remained even then (see map) but the sea was paring back the cliffs at a rapid rate. By 1677 it had reached the market place and the inhabitants sold the market cross. Twenty-five years later the Town Hall was destroyed and the sea was washing at the doors of St Peter's Church. Between 1589 and 1753 a broad strip, 1000 feet (304m) wide, on the outer edge of the town was lost. The remains of All Saints, last of old Dunwich's churches, finally fell down the cliff in 1919.

Erosion has continued to the present day (although at a slightly slower rate) leaving only a vestige of town and port.

At Hallsands, South Devon, man himself has contributed to coastal erosion. Until 1897 this was a fishing hamlet of 16 cottages tucked beneath the cliffs and apparently safe behind a broad beach of shingle. Then a contractor was given permission to remove shingle from close inshore for construction work.

But he removed 500,000 tons from the beach itself which was lowered by about 12ft. Soon the cottages were under direct attack from the waves. The final blow came in 1917 when a severe storm from the east virtually destroyed the hamlet.

In the constant battle between land and sea the outcome is not always on the debit side. Today there are thousands of acres of valuable farmland which were once beneath the sea. The process of regaining it is often started by the sea itself and then completed by man.

In sheltered situations mud brought in by the tides accumulates to a great thickness. When the sea is excluded by throwing a bank round the area the land can be reclaimed. On the Norfolk shore of the Wash 8000 acres (3239 hectares) have been gained since Roman times and in the South Holland area of Lincolnshire 37,000 acres (14,980 hectares).

Reclamation has also taken place at the mouth of the River Parrett in Somerset, round Southampton Water and Poole Harbour, and in Morecambe Bay. In the last 100 years *Spartina townsendii*, a species of salt marsh grass with the ability to hold and bind silts and muds, has been an important aid in gaining land.

An outstanding example of the sea itself making land is provided by Romney Marsh. Here, long before there was

Romney Marsh today. Rich lowland sheep country which had its beginnings in sandbanks similar to the Goodwin Sands

any marsh, the sea threw up a barrier of sandbanks and from that point in pre-historic times the evolution of the present day Romney Marsh can be traced.

This, and the development of the Dungeness promontory, has taken place over thousands of years. The rise of sea level following the melting of the ice sheets led to the formation of a shallow bay enclosed by a low line of cliffs. This persisted for much of pre-historic time.

Elongated sandbanks which formed offshore were very much like the Goodwin Sands of today. When the Romans landed and over-ran Kent these 'island' sandbanks, surrounded by accumulating marsh, formed the only suitable areas for settlement.

The area between these dry points and the old cliff line was damp and marshy. From about the 6th century the sea level began to drop and this marshy area became better drained and more suitable for settlement.

But in the 13th century violent storms and a period of rising sea level posed a serious threat. Only the building of Dymchurch Wall and the drainage schemes of Dutch experts prevented the marsh from returning to the sea.

The cost of fighting the sea is high. Sea-walls, which last 30–40 years, cost about £1.5 million a mile to build. Revetments, lines of boulders or large stones piled at weak points, are cheaper but have a shorter life. And a well-built groyne costs about £50,000.

Groynes which successfully prevent a beach from being stripped away rely on the longshore drift (see page 159) of sand and shingle. Most of the sand comes from

The four stages in the making of Romney Marsh from prehistoric times to the present day

cliffs which are being eroded; but if the cliffs are being protected successfully by sea defences the beaches down-coast are starved of sand.

Then the groynes cease to do their work effectively and what was a stable beach starts to be eroded. This can be seen at Clacton, Essex, where the beach is disappearing because its supply of sand has been reduced by sea defence work and dredging farther north.

It might, however, be restored by 'beach feeding'. Some engineers believe money spent on such schemes is better used than on building groynes and sea-walls. They argue that a good beach is the best defence against the sea.

Beach feeding involves either pumping sand ashore or dumping it on the beach by lorry and letting longshore drift transport it to where it is needed elsewhere. The technique is quite common in the United States and Holland and has been tried successfully at Portobello, near Edinburgh, and at Bournemouth and Teignmouth. Not only does it help protect coast and property. Popular seaside resorts which depend for part of their prosperity on their sands may see it as a way of protecting their prime asset.

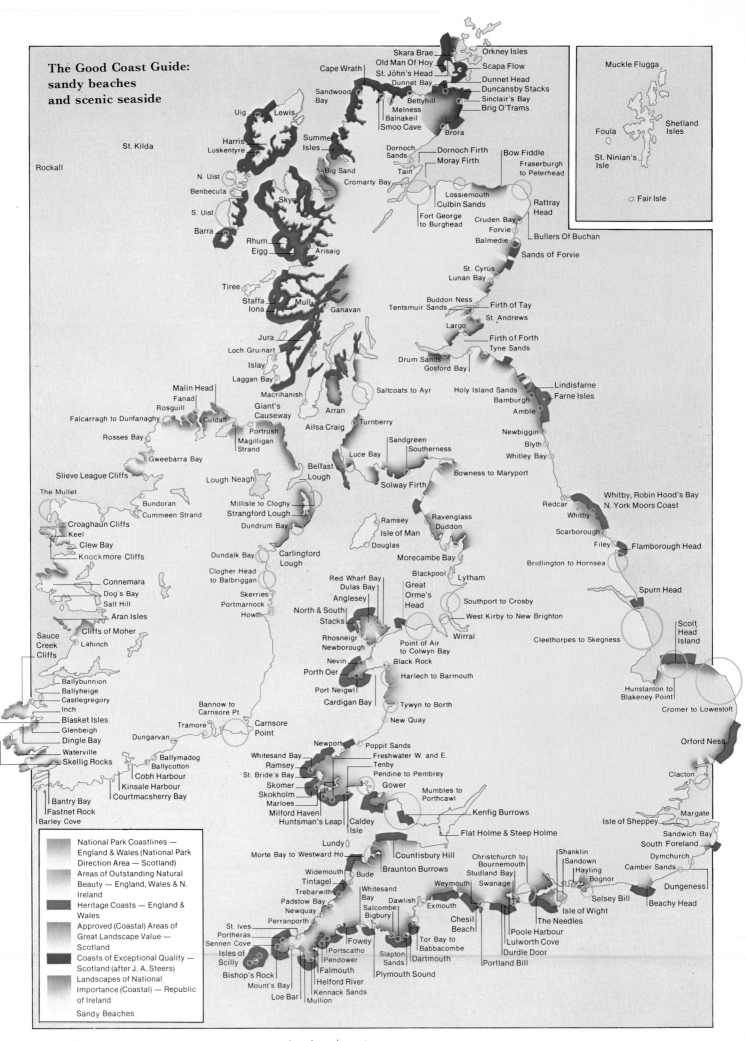

The Good Coast Guide:
sandy beaches and scenic seaside

Major coastal features mentioned in this chapter are plotted on the map

Map labels (Scotland & Northern Isles):

Muckle Flugga · Foula · Shetland Isles · St. Ninian's Isle · Fair Isle

Orkney Isles · Skara Brae · Old Man Of Hoy · St. John's Head · Scapa Flow · Dunnet Bay · Dunnet Head · Duncansby Stacks · Sinclair's Bay · Brig O'Trams · Cape Wrath · Sandwood Bay · Bettyhill · Melness · Balnakeil · Smoo Cave · Brora

Uig · Lewis · Harris · Luskentyre · Summer Isles · Big Sand · Dornoch Sands · Dornoch Firth · Moray Firth · Tain · Cromarty Bay · Bow Fiddle · Fraserburgh to Peterhead

N. Uist · Benbecula · Skye · S. Uist · Barra · Rhum · Eigg · Arisaig · Lossiemouth · Culbin Sands · Fort George to Burghead · Cruden Bay · Forvie · Balmedie · Bullers Of Buchan · Sands of Forvie · Rattray Head

Tiree · Staffa · Iona · Mull · Ganavan · St. Cyrus · Lunan Bay · Buddon Ness · Firth of Tay · Jura · Loch Gruinart · Islay · Laggan Bay · Tentsmuir Sands · St. Andrews · Largo · Firth of Forth · Tyne Sands · Drum Sands · Gosford Bay

Malin Head · Fanad · Rosguill · Falcarragh to Dunfanaghy · Culdaff · Macrihanish · Giant's Causeway · Arran · Turnberry · Saltcoats to Ayr · Holy Island Sands · Lindisfarne · Farne Isles · Bamburgh · Amble · Newbiggin · Blyth · Whitley Bay

Rosses Bay · Gweebarra Bay · Portrush · Magilligan Strand · Ailsa Craig · Sandgreen · Southerness · Luce Bay · Bowness to Maryport

Slieve League Cliffs · The Mullet · Bundoran · Cummeen Strand · Belfast Lough · Lough Neagh · Millisle to Cloghy · Strangford Lough · Solway Firth · Ramsey · Isle of Man · Douglas · Ravenglass · Duddon · Whitby, Robin Hood's Bay · N. York Moors Coast · Redcar · Whitby · Scarborough · Filey · Flamborough Head

Croaghaun Cliffs · Keel · Clew Bay · Knockmore Cliffs · Dundalk Bay · Carlingford Lough · Morecambe Bay · Bridlington to Hornsea

Connemara · Dog's Bay · Salt Hill · Aran Isles · Cliffs of Moher · Lahinch · Clogher Head to Balbriggan · Skerries · Portmarnock · Howth · Dundrum Bay · Blackpool · Lytham · Great Orme's Head · Southport to Crosby · Spurn Head

Sauce Creek Cliffs · Ballybunnion · Ballyheige · Castlegregory · Inch · Blasket Isles · Glenbeigh · Dingle Bay · Waterville · Skellig Rocks · Red Wharf Bay · Dulas Bay · Anglesey · North & South Stacks · Rhosneigr · Newborough · Nevin · Porth Oer · Port Neigwl · Cardigan Bay · Point of Air to Colwyn Bay · Black Rock · Harlech to Barmouth · Tywyn to Borth · West Kirby to New Brighton · Wirral · Cleethorpes to Skegness · Scolt Head Island · Hunstanton to Blakeney Point · Cromer to Lowestoft

Bannow to Carnsore Pt. · Carnsore Point · Tramore · New Quay · Orford Ness · Dungarvan · Newport · Poppit Sands · Whitesand Bay · Ramsey · Freshwater W. and E. · Tenby · Pendine to Pembrey · St. Bride's Bay · Skomer · Gower · Mumbles to Porthcawl · Clacton · Ballymadog · Ballycotton · Cobh Harbour · Kinsale Harbour · Courtmacsherry Bay · Skokholm · Marloes · Milford Haven · Huntsman's Leap · Caldey Isle · Kenfig Burrows · Isle of Sheppey · Margate · Bantry Bay · Fastnet Rock · Barley Cove · Lundy · Flat Holme & Steep Holme · Sandwich Bay · South Foreland · Morte Bay to Westward Ho · Countisbury Hill · Christchurch to Bournemouth · Shanklin · Sandown · Hayling · Bognor · Dymchurch · Widemouth · Bude · Braunton Burrows · Studland Bay · Swanage · Camber Sands · Tintagel · Whitesand Bay · Weymouth · Selsey Bill · Beachy Head · Trebarwith · Padstow Bay · Dawlish · Chesil Beach · Isle of Wight · Dungeness · Newquay · Salcombe · Bigbury · Exmouth · Poole Harbour · The Needles · Perranporth · Fowey · Tor Bay to Babbacombe · Lulworth Cove · St. Ives · Portscatho · Slapton Sands · Dartmouth · Durdle Door · Portheras · Pendower · Sennen Cove · Plymouth Sound · Portland Bill · Isles of Scilly · Falmouth · Bishop's Rock · Helford River · Mount's Bay · Kennack Sands · Loe Bar · Mullion

Legend

- National Park Coastlines — England & Wales (National Park Direction Area — Scotland)
- Areas of Outstanding Natural Beauty — England, Wales & N. Ireland
- Heritage Coasts — England & Wales
- Approved (Coastal) Areas of Great Landscape Value — Scotland
- Coasts of Exceptional Quality — Scotland (after J. A. Steers)
- Landscapes of National Importance (Coastal) — Republic of Ireland
- Sandy Beaches

Rockall · St. Kilda

The living world of the sea coast: its marvels and its mysteries

In the beginning the sea was life. Scientists believe that plants and animals of the land, ourselves included, originated in its salty, life-supporting waters. In the story of evolution the margin of sea and land was a great barrier which had to be crossed. It was a crossing which lasted millions of years. Yet much of the marvel of that great evolutionary progress, which took the creatures of the sea and made them into creatures of the land, is still to be seen upon the shore.

Changing conditions imposed by tidal regimes, the seasons and the terrain require of the plants and animals that live there a degree of adaptability and development near to miraculous. And, for all the hazards of pollution and development by man, it still provides a home for a wide variety of them.

It is not the easiest of environments, although parts of it are more felicitous to life than others. The problems of its inhabitants are those of coping with extremes: the alternate wetting and drying out of the shore with the flooding and ebbing of the tides; the mixing of salt water with fresh in river mouth and estuary; the violent turbulence and pounding of the waves one moment, the switch to a profound calm the next.

Yet, for all its harshness, it is beneficient, supplying the essential ingredients of life — light, water, oxygen and minerals. They are provided within the context of a remarkable tidal rhythm to which the pulse of seashore life is tuned.

Life at the top of the beach, where tides rarely reach, is moistened by spray. Life at the very bottom of the beach thrives in a world which is nearly always covered by salt water. And between the first, which marine biologists identify as the splash zone, and the latter which is the lower shore, other zones of life grade one into another. Each of these zones provides a different habitat to which seashore creatures and plants have adapted.

The variety of life also depends on whether the shore is one of rock, sand, shingle, mud or marsh. On rock beaches the signs of life are much more obvious, with animals and plants clinging to the rock surfaces; on sandy beaches, where animals burrow below the surface, less so. In the following pages some classic seashore habitats — cliffs, sand, shingle and saltmarsh, and rock pools — are described, and their mysteries and inhabitants revealed.

Seabirds soar at cliffs by making use of 1 eddies produced by off-shore winds and 2 up-draughts created by on-shore winds

The sea cliffs: precarious refuge for determined colonists

Sea cliffs are among the last true relics of wild Britain. Lashed by gales, battered by waves, the bare, steep cliffs present an inhospitable and barren face to man. But their narrow ledges and breezy tops provide a precious foothold for wild flowers and a near impregnable refuge where seabirds can find space to form colonies and breed.

For, among all the birds of the British Isles, it is the seabirds who most prefer living in colonies. Many of them return to the same cliff nesting site year after year. Some of the sites are enormous. St Kilda in the Outer Hebrides, famous for its fulmars and gannets, has colonies with tens of thousands of nests. The most crowded are usually those of gannets and guillemots. The reasons for living in colonies are related to various factors. The abundance of fish as a food supply and the security of living in large groups in a safe site are the most important.

One of the sights of the sea cliffs are the birds soaring about them. As the wind from the sea hits the cliffs, gulls and other birds ride the updraughts which are produced. If the wind is blowing in the opposite direction, from the land, it spills over the edge of the cliff and then curls upwards in eddies which the birds use to gain height (see illustration).

By harnessing the roller-coaster power of these invisible air currents, the cliff dwellers — gulls, kittiwakes, fulmars, ravens — are able to conserve precious energy.

A past master of the soaring technique is the herring gull. Of all the sounds of the sea cliffs, none is more evocative than its wailing cry as it glides about its business. The red spot on the beak stimulates the chick to beg for food. Its rapacious relative, the great black-backed gull has a deeper cry and is the largest of the native gulls, with a 65in (1.6m) wingspan.

The kittiwake which cries its own name, is a successful cliff ledge colonist. It cements its seaweed nest to the rock with guano. The guillemot and razorbill belong to the auk family, cliff-dwellers which spend much time swimming and diving for fish, and are therefore particularly vulnerable to oil spills. The puffin is another auk. It nests in clifftop burrows and is easily identified by its multi-coloured parrot bill.

The cormorant and its smaller, bottle-green cousin, the shag, prey on fish which they chase underwater. Afterwards, they perch on rocks to dry their outstretched wings. The gull-like bird boomeranging around the cliffs on stiff, straight wings is a fulmar. The curious tubular nostrils are an ornithological mystery; their function is still obscure.

Farther out to sea, the big snowy white bird with black wing-tips soaring and skimming the troughs and crests of the waves is the gannet, an ocean wanderer and spectacular crash-diver that breeds in large offshore colonies on rock stacks, from Scotland to the Skelligs.

Around the coasts of Wales and Ireland the chough may be recognised by its curved red bill. Impossible to confuse them or their shrill whistling with the

White sea campion on flower-covered cliff

Key to illustration: *1 Red Valerian*   *4 Puffins 5 Guillemot 6 Peregrine Falcon*   *9 Rock Dove 10 Herring Gull*

166   *2 Humming-bird Hawkmoth 3 Fulmar*   *7 Cream-spot Tiger moth 8 Golden Samphire*   *11 Kittiwakes 12 Herring Gull 13 Clouded*

Yellow 14 Clover 15 Kittiwake 16 Raven
17 Black-backed Gull 18 Cormorant 19 Sea

Pinks 20 Gannet 21 Gannet 22 Basking
Shark 23 Atlantic Seals 24 Slender Thistle

25 Painted Lady 26 Chough 27 Razorbill
28 Sea-Campion 29 Oak Eggar Caterpillar

guttural croaking of the raven, a bird of the rocky western coasts where it can often be seen twirling and tumbling in the up-draughts. Here, too, the peregrine breeds in remote eyries, dashing out to stoop at a luckless rock dove, ancestor of our town pigeons.

Other cliff-top fliers are the painted lady and clouded yellow. These butterflies are summer migrants from across the Channel. Thistles attract the former, clover the latter.

In June they are joined by another migrant, the day-flying hummingbird hawkmoth, seen here buzzing around red valerian. The cream-spot tiger is more nocturnal, and most commonly found in the southwest, where you may also see the finger-sized full-grown caterpillar of the oak eggar crawling over the cliffside turf in midsummer.

In summer the cliffs are bright with cushions of thrift or sea pink, together with sea campion, a flower which may have lived in Britain since *before* the Ice Age, and the fleshy-leaved golden samphire. Lichens add a deeper splash of yolk yellow to the rocks. Our illustration shows the common *Xanthoria parientina*. Like all lichens, it is a good indicator of clean air.

On the rocks below, the grey or Atlantic seal rests between fishing forays. An adult bull seal can reach a length of 12ft (3.6m). The basking shark is even bigger, but is harmless and feeds on plankton. In Atlantic waters basking sharks often cruise close inshore during warm weather.

Sand, shingle and saltmarsh: wildlife at the tide's edge

On low lying coasts the cliffs give way to shingle bars, sand dunes and salt marsh – three very different wildlife habitats, each with its own characteristic flora and fauna, and sometimes problems.

The pounding of the waves on a shingle beach can, as we have seen, strip it of several feet of material. Even in calmer conditions wave action constantly grinds the pebbles and sand grains against each other, crushing and destroying anything living. Anyone who has paddled on such a beach knows how painful it can be as each wave, charged with pebbles and shingle, swirls round the feet. A shingle beach is virtually a desert. Yet plants do survive.

One of the most spectacular flowers of a shingle coast is the frosty blue sea holly. The beautiful yellow horned poppy, with

long curved pods like curlews' bills, grows here too.

A familiar bird of the shingle ridges is the ringed plover with its harlequin head and liquid cry. The nest is a mere scrape among the stones, in which eggs and chicks are perfectly camouflaged.

Another bird which breeds on shingle spits is the little tern, smallest of the terns or 'sea swallows'. All terns have forked tails but the little tern may be identified by its yellow legs and black-tipped yellow bill as it hovers in search of sand eels or whitebait.

Sand dunes, where the spray is salt, the sun hot, the wind strong and the sand always on the move, often drifting in huge quantities, make a difficult environment. The plants which survive most successfully are those which sprout easily, send runners through the sand, can cope with drought and struggle back to the surface if they are buried.

The most distinctive is marram grass. Invaluable in the fight against erosion, its long, tough 20ft (6m) roots bind the shifting sands. Among the prettier plants is the sea bindweed with its pink and white striped flowers. Growing along the drift line on the seaward side of the dunes, look for the succulent leaves and pale lilac flowers of sea rocket.

On the Lancashire coast near Southport, freshwater pools, or dune-slacks, appear among the sandhills, providing a breeding ground for one of Britain's rarest wild creatures, the endangered natterjack toad.

The richest of all coastal habitats are the estuaries, a magical mingling of mudflats, salt marsh and coiling tidal creeks which are usually sheltered from the ferocity of the sea. They are alive with the wild cries and flickering wings of wading birds like the redshank. The mudbanks harbour enormous populations of lugworm, ragworm, crustaceans and molluscs. The handsome shelduck, a common sight on many estuaries, feeds mainly on molluscs. It nests in old rabbit burrows.

In summer the saltings are bright with marsh flowers; sea aster and purple swathes of sea lavender. Here, too, grows the succulent marsh samphire, a great East Anglian delicacy which can be

Key to illustration: 1 Yellow Horned Poppy 2 Ringed Plover 3 Little Tern 4 Sea Rocket 5 Sea Holly 6 Marram Grass 7 Shelduck 8 Sea Aster 9 Redshank 10 Sea Lavender 11 Marsh Samphire 12 Spartina 13 Natterjack Toad 14 Sea Bindweed

boiled and served with melted butter.

The carpet of the sea marsh is composed of tough grasses that thrive on the salty inter-tidal mudflats. Among them, spartina, which binds the mud to form continuous stretches of turf, helps raise the level of the marsh.

The rock pool: round-the-clock struggle for survival

The rock pool is a mysterious world: a complex habitat of vibrant colour and varied life-forms evolved for survival in the transitory no man's land between the tides.

Every rock pool is an ocean in microcosm. But whereas the ocean provides a relatively constant habitat, the rock pool is exposed to a daily cycle of extremes dictated by the tides, and the life that thrives within it has had to adapt to the perils and hardships of an inter-tidal existence – or perish.

An obvious hazard is the sheer weight and force of the crashing waves. To withstand them, the limpet clings fast to its rock with proverbial tenacity. But there are many other problems which marine life has to overcome before the rock pool can be colonised.

Hot sunny days cause rock pools to evaporate and become saltier; rainy days dilute the sea water. At night the water temperature in a rock pool may fall below that of the sea by several degrees. On a sunny summer's day it may become much warmer than the sea only to be rapidly cooled by the returning tide. (In winter, when the wind is colder than the sea, the effect is reversed and the incoming tide can actually warm the pool.)

The smaller or shallower the pool, and the farther it lies from low water level, the greater the extremes of temperature and salinity are likely to be. Indeed, some pools – those that lie in the so-called 'splash zone' above the high water mark – are replenished only by spray or by the waves of exceptionally high tides or rough seas. Their brackish waters are more hostile and lack the rich variety of life to be found in the true marine pools which are filled by the tide every day.

Photosynthesis – that miraculous alchemy which enables plants to harness the energy of sunlight with the aid of chlorophyll and manufacture food from carbon dioxide and water – also exerts a powerful influence on rock pool life.

By day the seaweeds are busily taking in carbon dioxide and liberating precious oxygen into the water. After dark, when photosynthesis ceases, the process is reversed, and all rock pool life – plants as well as animals – relies on the dissolved oxygen and releases carbon dioxide in exchange. In the open sea the effect is minimal, but in the miniature crowded world of the rock pool the build-up of carbon dioxide causes the water to become increasingly acid as the night goes on. These changes could render the rock pool uninhabitable, had not life adapted to withstand such extremes.

It is a tight-knit world, in which surprising relationships sometimes develop. The hermit crab and its anemone

are a well-known example; a symbiotic association between two different species for their mutual benefit. The anemone attaches itself to the discarded whelk shell in which the soft-bodied hermit crab has taken up residence, and its sting-armed tentacles provide additional protection for its host. In return the crab transports the anemone around the pool, providing it with more feeding opportunities.

Unless you approach a rock pool cautiously, you will miss half of what is there. Animals like the tube worm retract instantly at the slightest shadow; shrimps and small fish like the shanny, rock goby and (harmless) sea scorpion dart away.

The most rewarding pools to explore are those which provide plenty of cover – stones, crannies and clumps of seaweed – where animals can find refuge from the hungry prowlers of the tidelines.

Oystercatchers stab with bright orange bills at bivalve molluscs such as the glossy clusters of blue-black mussels. Turnstones use their slightly upturned bills to pry under stones – hence their name – in search of small crustaceans.

So camouflage plays an important part in the lives of the rock pool inhabitants who seek to avoid detection. Prawns and shrimps are hard to see because they are translucent. The chameleon shrimp, a small relative of the common shrimp or prawn, goes one step further and disguises itself by changing the size of its colour spots to merge with a red or green background. But it is a slow job, taking about a week to change.

The dog whelk changes colour with its diet. It is a flesh-eater, preying on barnacles and mussels (which cannot move away) or limpets (which can). The predatory whelk bores through their shells with its rasping tongue and sucks out the succulent innards. White or yellowish dog whelk shells mean a diet of barnacles; brown or mauve mean mussels.

Not all the animals move. Many sit tight and wait for the food to come to them. Sponges are primitive animals living in colonies, sifting the water which passes through their communal pores. Sea anemones, those exquisite flowers of the rock pool, are in fact animals, who wait for their prey with gently waving tentacles. A shrimp or small fish touching the tentacle is first dazed by the anemone's sting; other tentacles close round it, and stuff the living food into a central maw. The common beadlet anemone has a blue spot at the base of each tentacle, which marks a battery of stinging cells. The beadlet anemone retracts to a blob of jelly when struck or when the tide leaves it exposed. The larger dahlia anemone does the same, but is disguised to look like rock by the warts on its body.

Much of the pool life emerges at night, and just like the African plains, there are hunters and browsers. Among the latter are the limpets, which move around when the tide is in, grazing the rocks bare of algae.

Many animals cannot see red light so if you want to extend your exploration, go down to the beach with a red torch. But whether you investigate by night or day, remember that pool life, like any wild life, is finely in balance. If you disturb stones in your quest, replace them as they were, because animals which live on the bottom side of the stone cannot survive on the top. Such is the exact fit of rock pool life.

Pebbles. The sea coasts of the British Isles have an enormous variety of pebbles. The following selection describes some of the most distinctive and commonly found types.

1 Flint. The pebbles vary in shape from highly irregular to spherical. Being so hard they may have a high degree of polish. Flint pebbles can be picked up almost anywhere on the coast from Humberside to South Devon.

2 Quartzite. The pebbles are grey, yellow or liver-coloured. Hard, smooth and rounded discs, rollers and spheres occur by the million in the famous Budleigh Salterton bank in south Devon. Also Scottish, Yorkshire, Hampshire, Devon, Wirral and Lancashire coasts.

3 Granite. The rocks range widely in colour and texture. All are largely composed of the hard minerals quartz and feldspar. Their pink or yellow colours are due to tiny amounts of iron oxides; the dark specks are mica or tourmaline. The coast of east and south-west Scotland, north-west and north-east Ireland and south Cornwall have large granite pebble populations.

4 Jasper. These pebbles, distinctive and rare, occur in areas where the dominant materials are granite and basalt ores. Silica, in the form known as chalcedony, is the principal constituent of jasper. The blood-red colour is produced by submicroscopic iron oxide particles.

5 Limestone. This is so variable in composition and physical character that it is difficult to generalise. The pebbles can be any colour, soft or hard, full of calcite crystals or fossils. Some, such as marble, can be polished until they have a mirror-like quality. At the other extreme is the limestone pebble which has been bored by tiny organisms, penetrating the outer centimetre or so, until it resembles a sponge. How it happens is still uncertain, for every surface of the pebble seems to be covered uniformly. They are common along many coastlines.

6 Porphyry. This pebble is a trachyte in composition. This means it is made up of the minerals feldspar and amphiboles with their crystals characteristically set in a finer-grained homogenous matrix which gives the porphyritic texture. The white pieces are feldspar crystals, the much smaller greenish specks are crystals of amphiboles. Porphyries are hard volcanic or igneous rocks. They are very attractive and can be dressed or polished for building and ornamental purposes. The pebbles are found along the Cornish coast and, more easily, along the coasts of western Scotland, Northern Ireland, and south-east Ireland.

7 Milky Quartz. Quartz is the most indestructible and one of the most widespread of all common rock-forming materials. It occurs in virtually every kind of sedimentary and crystalline rock. Flint, chert, jasper, chalcedony, agate, smoky quartz, rose quartz, milky quartz are all varieties. Pebbles are common on the Celtic coastlines – south-west England, Wales, Scotland and Ireland. They are also abundant in glacial deposits along the northern and eastern coasts.

Chapter Seven
Leisure in the Countryside

It is only in the last 100 years that the countryside has become a playground for urban man.
Before that it was simply where most people lived and worked. Now it is being
used for recreations as diverse as the landscape itself. For some, like these ramblers in the
Peak District, it is the rugged slopes of upland Britain that beckon. Others take to the
hills on horseback or to climb precipitous rock crags. Then there are the gentler pursuits
of angling, boating or merely enjoying a picnic and a simple drive or stroll through
pleasant countryside. Even in these crowded islands it is possible to leave the bustle of city
life far behind, especially if you know how to use a map. How to enhance your
enjoyment of such diverse activities in the countryside is the theme of this chapter

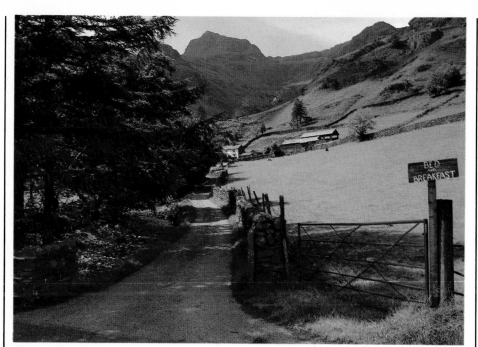

Bed and Breakfast: a welcome sign for travellers found from farms to bungalows

Rambling: exploring 120,000 miles of public right of way

Rambling in the British Isles is more than a holiday and satisfying form of exercise. It is a close and natural contact with the land which provides a more intimate insight into the mysteries of the countryside and enables you to enjoy sights, sounds and scents denied to road or rail travellers. Moorland, coastal or pastoral scenes lie within easy reach of virtually every town or city and are often accessible only on foot.

Footpaths exist in Britain in greater number than anywhere in the world. But despite their supposed legal protection they are all too often overgrown, obstructed, vandalised or even ploughed up. The illustration shows ramblers their rights, the slight protection given to wild animals and plants – and what abuses walkers might find. The greatest hope for saving footpaths as public rights of way undoubtedly lies in the popularity of rambling itself.

Since 1935 the Ramblers Association has campaigned to secure legislation for the protection of natural beauty, the establishment of national parks, the preservation of footpaths and the right to walk on mountains, moors and shores. The result is a network of well over 120,000 miles (192,000km) of footpaths and bridleways where the public has the legal right to walk. There are also great tracts of common and access land which offer unrestricted walking and many nature or forest trails offering scenic routes through beautiful woodland

Nor is rambling limited to summer. Properly clothed and equipped, you can walk throughout the year. Only when you take to the hills is it vital to follow the rules. They are detailed overleaf, but the most important is never to allow enthusiasm to overtake ability and experience.

Where to walk

Any common or heath where the going is rough underfoot offers a good introduction to rambling. Failing that, try short evening strolls across the local parks. Aim to work up to five-mile (8km) Saturday afternoon hikes and then on to a 10-miler (16km) for which you should allow a day. Weekend and holiday rambling requires careful planning, even when following one of the waymarked long-distance footpaths (see overleaf).

You always need a map and guidebook. The 1:50,000 Ordnance Survey sheet of your chosen region will show the possibilities; a guidebook of the area will show specific details of different walks. Guidebooks range from the excellent long-distance footpath series published for the Countryside Commission by HMSO to the multi-paged looseleafed AA-Readers Digest compendium of short walks called *No Through Road*. National Park authorities often publish their own 'walk sheets' and these, along with many other publications, are sold widely in the area concerned.

When you have chosen your route, make a route card detailing each leg of a day's trip, with 10–15 miles (16–24km) across country being good going at first. A rough rule of thumb calculation is that

1 Birds eggs
It is generally illegal to take or destroy the eggs of wild birds, exceptions sometimes being made for edible eggs of gulls, for example. Birds themselves may not be shot or harmed by members of the public or even, in the case of rare birds of prey, to be photographed at the nest in case this causes any disturbance

2 Rare plants, and those not so rare
It is now totally illegal to damage or even pick our 21 rarest flowers (see Ch. 10), except for 'good farming' or licensed research. It is also illegal to dig up any wild plant without the permission of the landowner or occupier, mushrooms and their like excepted

3 Rare animals
It is illegal to kill, injure or capture (or attempt to) smooth snakes, sand lizards, natterjack toads, large blue butterfly, otter and two rare species of bats

4 Is it a footpath?
The definitive maps showing footpaths and bridle paths can be consulted in District and County Council offices; also some libraries. These maps show up-to-date changes. (However, Ordnance

13

Survey maps are a good guide.)

5 Signposting

Footpaths should be marked with a sign (County Council's job) where they leave a metalled road. Many councils have not done their job. Some volunteer organisations have always waymarked their local paths across country

6 Piles of litter

Litterers can be fined if caught (and prosecuted). In view of the deterioration caused by litter and rubbish, not many people can have doubts about reporting offenders – to District Council (or to police if there is urgency or danger resulting)

7 Up on the hills

Can you wander where you like? Generally walkers are tolerated, but only sometimes are there legal rights of access to some commons, or rights gained by agreements between councils and landowners

8 Path disappears

Walk on, in single file. If you edge round the field to protect the crop, you can be sued for trespass. Farmer should notify the County Council at least seven days before ploughing and make good the path

after; but few bother, and fewer councils take any notice if they don't

9 Other traffic

You can take a pet (within reason, no horses or elephants) on a footpath, but farmers can shoot uncontrolled dogs worrying animals. Horses are allowed on bridle paths, and cycles, but they have to put up with pedestrian-oriented surface. Cars and motorbikes can be driven on footpaths only with permission of landowner; otherwise they are limited to within 15 yards of the road (and landowner can still order those cars off)

10 Whose path?

Who owns the path? The surface 'belongs' to the County Council (which is the Highway Authority), but the soil under the surface belongs to the owner of the neighbouring land, and the landowner enjoys some rights, and obligations

11 Gates and stiles

In bad repair? The owner of the land must maintain them in good order, but can claim a quarter of the cost from County Council. It can do the work, and charge him with cost, if he fails to keep them in good repair

12 Bulls

Only a few counties allow bulls to be pastured in fields crossed by footpaths. If you are attacked, remember that they have difficulty in stopping or turning on a down slope; but there is no magic formula to get you away safely. You can try suing the farmer if you are hurt, but with no guarantee of success if bull is pastured legally. If illegal (if a by-law is disregarded) inform local police

13 Paths churned up, overgrown

Maintenance of surface is the job of County, District or (sometimes) local Parish Council. They can request landowner to trim back overhanging branches

14 Barbed wire, bungalows

And other obstructions; the landowner cannot close a path, so report any obstructions to the County Council. If you are a bona fide traveller, not just a troublemaker, you can lawfully continue on your way but causing as little damage as possible. You can bring a private prosecution alleging obstruction

15 Misleading notices

Report them to the highways department of the local council

you will walk at 2½mph (4kph) plus an extra half hour for every 700ft (210m) climbed. But this does not account for rests, extra weight carried, companions who prove unfit or delays caused by mist, wind and bad weather. High, remote and exposed ground can be risky at any time of year. At 500ft (150m) a mild valley breeze becomes an icy gale. Temperatures drop fast, rain becomes heavier. Always let experience govern ambition, always respect the elements.

How to walk

This is not the daft question it might seem. Nor is there a simple answer. Walking footpaths is different from walking city streets, walking off the beaten track altogether very different again. Long grass, loose stones, concealed holes, tree roots, heather clumps, matted bracken, greasy boulders and scree slopes require a knack which only comes with practice. And nowhere is this difference shown more than in ascending slopes where the urban walker tends to spring off the toes trying to lift the knees too high – a style ensuring strain.

Two general tips are always to begin slowly and allow your system to warm-up; and to know that it will warm-up very quickly so only wear waterproof clothing when it is either raining or bitterly cold. Too many walkers wear far too much clothing and become 'heat exhausted' without knowing why.

When to walk

Sunstroke (when your body temperature gets too high) and hypothermia (the opposite effect) are hazards to be avoided by leaving off or putting on layers of clothing as you travel. Such a system of 'climate control' mean it is possible to walk in any weather the whole year through – although winter rambling needs extra safeguards (see page 217). Climate control, however, does depend on carrying a full issue of bad weather clothing in your rucksack in the first place – an important safety precaution.

Where to stay

Lists of farms offering bed and breakfast can be obtained from National Park information centres, public libraries in walking areas and from the Ramblers Association. Youth hostels are a popular alternative. And while the by-laws of popular tourist regions require campers to tent together on official sites, there is still scope for anyone prepared to walk some way from the road and agricultural land on to upland slopes. In more remote areas you can pitch camp wherever a farmer gives permission.

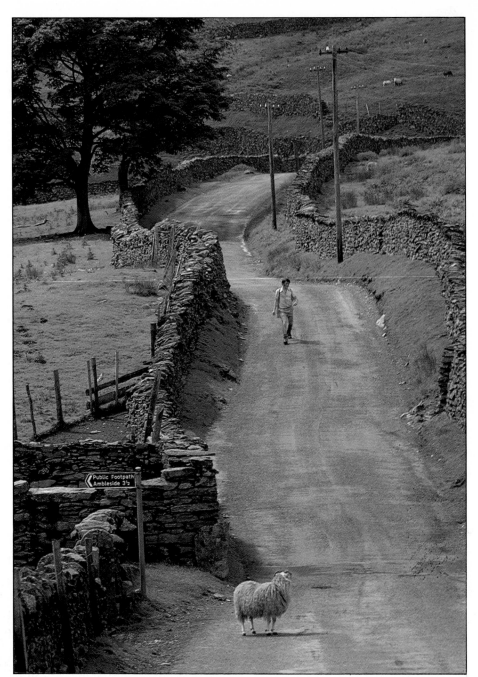

A quiet lane lined by high drystone walls in the heart of the Lake District. Here walking can range from well-worn lakeside paths to the high open fells for which a compass is often essential

Backpacking

Backpackers, unlike ramblers, carry everything they need to survive at least a long weekend in the wilds. Properly kitted-out, and with enough food, drink and the right protective clothing, they can safely penetrate the most remote and wintery regions. Solitude is what they seek. And where better to find it than in darkest winter when the wild places are empty and brittle with ice? For many backpackers the season begins in October, just as the majority of Britain's fair weather walkers are starting their hibernation. The rewards in return for careful and prudent planning, and a little fortitude, can be spectacular.

Kit is carried by pack frame or anatomic-shaped rucksack with light flexible internal frame, a padded waist belt giving vital additional support from the pelvis. Tents are nylon and double-skinned which greatly reduces the condensation inside and from which rainwater is easily shaken – their weight down to as little as 3–4lbs (1½–2kg). Sleeping bags filled with man-made fibre like Fibrefill 2 and P3 are more efficient than duck down when wet. Synthetic fibres can be wrung out and still work. Insulation from ground chill is provided by close-cell foam mats which are light and non-absorbent. Meths storm cookers are becoming increasingly popular since the heat goes into the pan instead of dissipating into the wind.

The long-distance paths

Eight long-distance paths have been established across some of the most beautiful countryside of England and Wales. Their routes are shown on the map on page 251 of the Days Out section of this book. They can be followed in their entirety or in shorter stretches – several one-day walks along long-distance paths are included in the 1000 Days Out section.

Ramblers' groups have developed other long-distance routes, such as the Cotswolds Way and Cambrian Way. But the 'official' paths run by the Countryside Commission are:

Pennine Way: 250 miles (402km). The first of the long-distance paths and still the one regarded as the greatest challenge. It runs through three national parks. A high-level route along the backbone of England this is rugged walking that, more than any other long-distance path, requires close attention to weather and equipment.

Pembrokeshire Coast Path: 167 miles (269km). This runs along the entire coastline of Pembroke (now a part of Dyfed county), mostly on clifftops, and offers some of the finest scenery in Wales. The route is also rich in bird and plant life. Only the more industrial section around Milford Haven is outside the Pembrokeshire Coast National Park, although even here there are fine opportunities for bird watching.

South West Peninsula Coast Path: 515 miles (825km). Really a combination of five separate coastal paths stretching from Somerset to Dorset via Land's End. Its length inevitably means a great variety of scenery. It also means that it is more likely to be used in relatively short stretches by holidaymakers than by ramblers trying to complete it all at one time.

Offa's Dyke Path: 168 miles (271km). This mostly follows the remarkable 8th century earthwork described earlier in this book (page 43). The scenery varies from the wooded river valleys such as the Wye and Dee to the heathland of the Black Mountains with views into the heart of Wales. The dyke is only a remnant of its former size but still impressive for much of its length.

Cleveland Way: 93 miles (150km). This has two distinct parts – a coastal section along some of the most dramatic sea cliffs of the east coast and an inland section looping over and around the magnificent Cleveland Hills. It is signposted Coast Path and Moors Path respectively and the latter can be difficult going, especi-

TWELVE RULES FOR SAFE RAMBLING

DO check the weather forecast first. Leave word where you are going and when you expect to be back. Keep to your planned route if possible. Let your route suffer rather than yourself and turn back when conditions worsen. Let those expecting you know when you are back. Phone those expecting you (or the police) if you end up at some other point away from the original destination to avoid search parties setting out. Do follow the rambler's code (below).

DON'T be over-ambitious in your routes. Ignore the risks of crossing swollen streams (detour instead, even if it adds miles to your route). Travel alone in hills. Split your group instead of keeping together. Walk in groups of less than four or more than six on mountains and moors (too many is risky in case of accident and difficult to keep together in bad weather).

WHAT TO WEAR AND CARRY

T-shirts, shorts and training shoes are fine for summer rambles, but reserve clothing must also be carried in case the weather changes. And for routes over any rough and remote terrain you need:

Boots. Flexible soles are best, thick enough to cushion feet from stones and with cleated rubber Vibram treads. Also check: one-piece uppers; bellows tongue; D-rings and hooks for laces; and interior padding. Most vital of all is comfort.

Clothing. Wear thin layers to trap air in between: string vest, wool shirt, one or two lightweight jerseys. A proofed nylon anorak or cagoule (smock-length anorak) will keep off most rain like a 'shell', though even good ones leak to some extent. A zip right down the front helps ventilate you and prevents too much condensation building up on the inside of the garment. Also needed: wool hat to prevent 25 per cent heat loss; pair of mitts; climber's type breeches or long warm woollen pants (*not* jeans); long woollen socks; rainproof overtrousers; long zip-up snow gaiters.

Kendal mint cake and dried dates to be chewed throughout the day to give a steady source of energy and stave off any effects of hypothermia); flashlight (with spare bulb and battery); and whistle (for emergencies – six long blasts or torch flashes repeated after one minute).

Day sack. This small nylon rucksack with big top flap and padded shoulder straps is the ideal size for rambling – not too big. In it should be carried spare clothing and the following contents: Ordnance Survey map (1:50,000 is the most popular size); Silva Compass (see page 190); first-aid kit (bandage, lint, adhesive tape, dressings, safety pins, cotton wool, small tube of antiseptic ointment); Bivi Bag (500-gauge polythene survival bag which you can climb inside and sit out a blizzard or benightment); vacuum flask (hot drink); high-energy food (such as raisins, peanuts, chocolate,

THE RAMBLER'S COUNTRYSIDE CODE

Guard against starting a fire. Heaths, plantations, woodland and fell-side are highly inflammable.

Fasten all gates. Animals will always be drawn by an open gate, a risk to themselves, crops and traffic.

Keep dogs under proper control. Keep your dog on a lead wherever there is livestock about and on country roads.

Keep to paths across farmland. Recognised routes might be signposted 'public footpath' or 'bridleway'; with green/white metal pointers signifying the same; with the sign of a walking man; with painted coloured arrows; with splotches of coloured paint; with the acorn symbol of long-distance footpaths; or with cairns (heaps of stones). Always use gates and stiles even if your path detours to do so.

Leave no litter. Plastic bags can choke livestock – one example of how litter can be dangerous as well as unsightly.

Safeguard water supplies. Your path may cross a catchment area which supplies millions. Avoid polluting it. The same goes for cattle troughs.

Protect wild life, wild plants and trees. Wild life is best seen, not collected. To uproot flowers, carve trees and rocks or disturb birds and wild animals spoils other people's enjoyment and can be illegal as already explained.

Go carefully on country roads. High banks, blind bends, slow moving tractors or animals all offer risk. Walk facing oncoming traffic.

Respect the life of the countryside. Set a good example and try to fit in with the locality and locals of the countryside.

ally in poor weather.

South Downs Way: 80 miles (129km). The only long-distance path which is also a bridlepath throughout its length (apart from an optional section along the cliffs at Beachy Head). The route follows the relatively gentle grass-covered slopes along the ridge of the Downs – a route used since Neolithic times.

North Downs Way: 141 miles (227km). Another great chalk ridgeway but this time also incorporating the traditional Pilgrims Way to Canterbury. Good views into the Weald. The closest long-distance path to London.

Ridgeway: 85 miles (136km). This mostly follows the line of the most famous of ancient routeways – the Ridgeway, as it is known south of the Thames where it crosses the Berkshire Downs as a wide bridlepath, or the Icknield Way, as it is also known in the stretch across the Chilterns where it is mostly a footpath. Evidence of the route's importance in prehistoric times is abundant, especially near such places as Avebury and Uffington.

These official paths as yet have no equivalents in Scotland or Ireland. The difficulty of walking the paths varies. Paths through upland areas or along the coast are the most likely to suffer misty or foggy conditions, so care should be exercised and enough time allowed to seek overnight accommodation. In these conditions compasses are invaluable, particularly where paths strike out across empty moorland – see also page 190.

However, the paths are 'waymarked' with signposts or milestones to indicate directions where the route is not obvious or where it departs from another footpath. These signs are not always particularly conspicuous because the Countryside Commission is anxious to preserve the 'natural' state of the countryside that presumably also attracts walkers in the first place. But the acorn symbol is used on all signposts for long-distance paths, except on open moorland where cairns of stones have been constructed as landmarks.

Anyone tempted to pit their energies against the challenge of a long-distance path should remember the basic rule of never allowing their ambition to outrun their abilities. Clothes and equipment must also be chosen to match the route: what is sensible for a summer stroll along the South Downs Way would be madness at almost any time of the year for the higher reaches of the Pennine Way or Offa's Dyke Path, for instance.

Climbing: from roadside crags to the highest mountain peaks

Mountains offer to many people an experience which enriches their lives like no other recreation. There is the challenge of hard exercise, of obstacles met on the ascent and even on the descent when special care may be needed to avoid slipping on treacherous surfaces. There is also the satisfaction of seeing a new landscape or even of viewing a familiar landscape from a new angle. Those with special interest in geology, botany, indeed any field science, will see more than others, for mountains have forests and open moorlands as well as rock faces.

For the climber, as opposed to the fell-walker, mountains are all about facing problems: the better the problem, the more memorable the climb. Mountains pose such a variety of problems, however, that it takes time for the beginner to experience all the situations which threaten danger. And although you may show early promise as a rock climber on roadside crags, it is important to realise that hill walking, scrambling, route planning, navigation, bivouacking, scree running, river crossing, snow and ice climbing, traversing skylines and adapting to emergencies along the way are also part of climbing, too.

In all these situations the crux of the matter is the same: how, by knowing what you are about, can you exercise judgment and competence to tackle each new problem as it arises? To do so successfully and work your way to the top – and safely down again – is why climbers climb. The companionship involved, as partners on a climbing rope rely on each other completely during each ascent, is also an important element in climbing's appeal for many people.

Climbers tackle rock faces one at a time with the leader 'sharp-ending' routes which he knows from the appropriate climbing guidebook are within his capabilities. Paying out the nylon climbing rope around his back and through his 'burning gloves' – a friction brake to hold the leader if he falls – the second man is attached or 'belayed' to the crag wherever rock spikes, flakes and other anchorages accompany a suitable ledge or stance. To shorten any possible fall the leader clips his rope through 'running belays' as he progresses. These slings (rope loops) and karabiniers (metal clips) act as a safety pulley system if he did fall. On reaching the next available stance and belays the leader stops, ties himself to the rock and takes in the rope. Then putting it round his back he brings the second man up to his ledge. And so it goes on to the top of the crag.

Where to climb

There are thousands of rock faces in Britain ranging from tiny outcrops near most towns and cities to the great cliffs of North Wales, the Lake District, Scotland and Ireland. There are also sea cliffs from Land's End to the Orkneys which can offer superb climbing too. London has Harrison Rocks and High Rocks near Tunbridge Wells; Plymouth has the Dewerstone; Bristol has Avon Gorge and Cheddar Gorge; Leicester has Beacon Hill at Woodhouse Eaves and outcrops in Charnwood Forest; Liverpool has Helsby Rocks, Cheshire; Sheffield has Stanage Edge, Hathersage; Leeds has Almscliff Crag; Newcastle has Crag Lough near Hexham; Glasgow has 'The Cobbler' at Loch Lomond; and Dublin has Dalkey Quarry. All are examples of popular outcrops, their climbing as technically exacting as the crags of Snowdon, Scafell or Ben Nevis.

And it is on such low-level climbing that first ascents are best made – with an experienced climber as a companion. Mountain rock climbs can come later.

How to start climbing

Climbing courses are the safe way to begin. Many are run at mountain centres by local authorities. Climbing is on the curriculum at an increasing number of schools, too. Excellent courses are run by national Sports Councils and others. There are also climbing schools advertising in magazines like *Mountain* and *Climber & Rambler*. Run by expert climbers they provide bunkhouse accommodation, meals and climbing instruction. And in many areas there are British Mountaineering Council (BMC)-registered guides who can be engaged by the day to take you on climbs of appropriate difficulty.

Many tyros go on from their introductory course to join a climbing club. This gives continued opportunity to climb with experienced company, and the BMC will send details of local climbing clubs on request. Public libraries are another source of information, as are local climbing shops.

When to climb

Climb rock in summer, walk in winter – that could be the beginner's credo. Rock is always accessible, the routes always

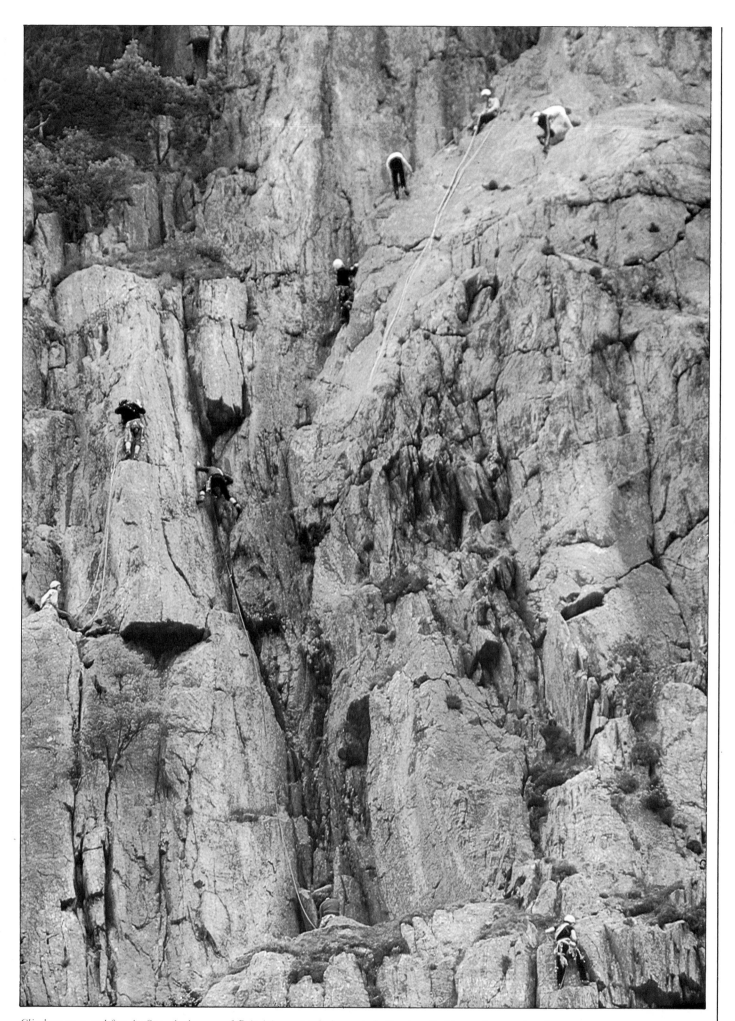

Climbers on a rockface in Snowdonia, one of Britain's most popular and challenging climbing and mountaineering areas

available, cleaned and tested by thousands who have gone before and documented in guidebooks. Rock climbs let you become used to exposure and climbing movement in relative safety. You learn to judge steepness and difficulty and learn rope handling proficiency the more crag routes you do.

Climbing steep snow and ice, however, is something else – the very stability of the stuff you are climbing is often uncertain at a time when you still lack the experience to tell good conditions from downright dangerous. Avalanches regularly take their toll on British mountains. So do poor snow and ice conditions when rock spikes or ice screw 'belays' used as anchorage points prove unsound and a falling climber can pull his companion bodily from the ice to which he was attached. Leave such winter routes until you have won experience on rock first, and also find experienced companions to partner you on snow and ice tremendously thrilling though they are. Even in Britain mountain climbs can pose problems which are alpine in scale, especially in bad weather and always in winter.

Safety in the mountains

Various rescue services are available in some major mountain areas, such as Snowdonia and the Lake District. Much of their brave enterprise should not be necessary. If conditions are bad, through mist or snow, it may be foolish to go forward. Some deaths are caused by hypothermia, probably through failure to carry an adequate supply of extra clothing. It is prudence, not weakness, to turn back, or even to have a walk in the valleys, if conditions are bad. In general it is wise to do most of the harder climbing early in the day, especially under warm conditions. An ascent of 1000ft (305m) or more in the late afternoon can be a severe test of stamina and in no circumstances should there be a long descent after dark.

Emphasis on 'solitude', so often given by those who write of mountains in romantic terms, is dangerous. Probably experienced people may safely go alone but only in areas where other people will be met. They should also tell someone where they are going and at what time they expect to return to their base, perhaps their car, hotel or camp site – some walkers in the Lake District leave such information in their cars. Good sense means recognition of dangers and provision for emergencies.

□ *Walking in winter: see page 217*

180

Angling: the most popular participant sport in Britain

Angling has been increasing in popularity steadily since the Second World War. Every week more people go fishing than watch soccer, the most popular spectator sport. They range from boys with their improvised rods and jam jars at the local canal to the lavishly-equipped syndicates who fish the salmon rivers of Scotland. Whoever they are, and wherever they fish, they are deemed to be 'anglers' if they go fishing at least six times a year.

There are broadly three types of angling – coarse fishing, game or fly fishing and sea fishing. The variety of angling is partly a consequence of the diversity of landscape since this is directly related to a diversity of waters; from fast-flowing upland streams to lowland meanders, the chalk streams of Hampshire to the land drains of the Fens. And, of course, there is the relatively small size of the British Isles and their location between the North Sea and the Atlantic Ocean.

Sea fishing is thus more readily available in Britain than most countries since few people live more than a half day's drive from the coast. Although coarse fishing is the most popular, largely because it is the most accessible, anglers are increasingly practising more than one type of fishing. As the close season for coarse fishing also roughly coincides with the open season for game fishing, angling is becoming a year-round activity.

In Great Britain especially angling is becoming big business, too, with a shoal of specialist magazines and books to cater for anglers of all types and abilities. There are national organisations, local clubs, angling classes and fishing holidays. Fishing tackle shops are a good starting point for would-be anglers, not only for the necessary equipment but as a source of information about fishing licences and day tickets. As with most sports it is possible to spend a small fortune on equipment but it is better to borrow or buy cheaply until satisfied that a particular form of angling really is for you. We describe here the basic characteristics of the three branches of angling – and what a beginner needs to know before embarking on any one of them. Fishing at sea involves particular risks. A 10-point safety code, covering equipment and boating lore, appears in the section on boating later in this chapter (see page 187). Tourists boards are good sources of information about angling.

Coarse Fishing

Coarse fishing is quite simply fishing for freshwater fish which are not members of the salmon family – that is to say, salmon and trout. It is carried out in rivers, lakes, ponds, reservoirs, gravel pits, canals and land drains all over the British Isles. Among the species which can be caught in these waters are the barbel, bleak, bream, carp, chub, dace, eel, gudgeon, perch, pike, roach, rudd, tench and zander. However, not every water is suitable for all these species. Some fish like fast-flowing waters while others prefer sluggish waters. Others favour gravel bottoms to muddy riverbeds.

Where to fish. Unfortunately you cannot just pick up a rod and line and fish anywhere you fancy. Coarse fisheries are controlled in one form or another so you have to have the appropriate permission. If you do not, then you could find yourself in trouble – possibly facing a fine from a magistrates' court.

Firstly, you require a rod licence in the same way that shotgun owners need gun licences. These licences are issued by the various Water Authorities but are generally most easily bought at local fishing tackle shops. These licences cost from £1 to £5 but they still do not entitle you to fish any of the waters within a water authority area; they simply mean you are allowed to use a rod. You still need permission to actually go out and fish.

Again this is quite easy to come by. The most popular way is to join a fishing club. Membership entitles you to fish any of the waters owned by the club. Furthermore it allows you to take part in matches organised by the club. If, however, you prefer to fish several waters then the best type to look for are day-ticket waters where you just pay a nominal fee for a day's fishing. Whatever your choice the best way of pursuing it is via a local tackle shop where they are normally only too pleased to advise on such matters.

When to fish. Fishing in most areas is not allowed while fish spawn. Any close season is decided by the Water Authorities but it is generally between March 15 and June 15.

What you will need. The basic tackle needed for a fishing trip is a rod and reel, line, floats, hooks, split-shot to weight your tackle, bait, a landing net and keepnet. Other accessories – rod rests, umbrella, holdall, etc – can be added later as you gain experience.

Rods. There are literally hundreds of various rods available for all types of

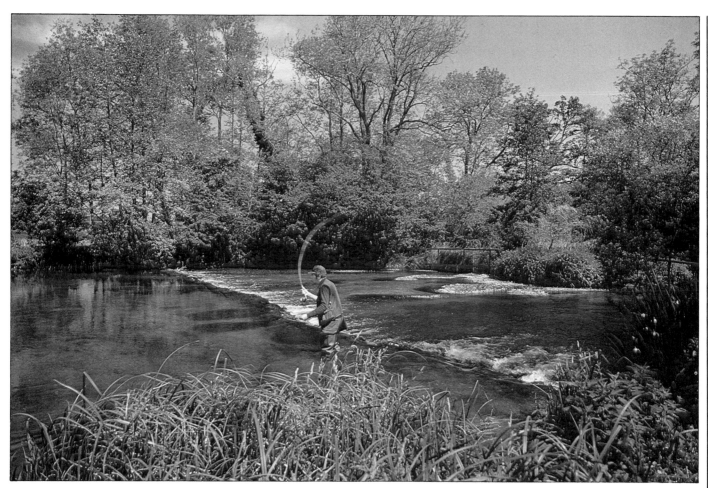

Fisherman at work: an angler casts his line in the River Kennet, Berkshire, amid idyllic surroundings on an early summer day

coarse fishing – float rods, leger rods, specialist rods for such fish as carp and pike. However, a beginner would be best off buying a 12 or 13ft (4m) float rod because much of his early fishing will most likely be float fishing.

This is just what it sounds like – a float is attached to the line and a bite is indicated by either the float sinking or lifting in the water. The float is 'cocked' by adding small weights (split-shot) to the line. Float fishing enables the angler to present his bait on the move at various depths at the same pace as the flow. The other type of fishing is 'legering'. Here special weights – the most common of which is the pear-shaped Arlesey bomb – are used to fish your bait still on the riverbed. Bite indication is shown by such tackle items as swingtips, quivertips, butt indicators or by simply watching the end of one's rod.

Reels. There are two main types – the fixed-spool and the centre-pin – but the former is the most popular, its major advantage over the centre-pin being that it allows long-distance casting.

Floats. To begin with you will need two types of float – one for still and slow moving waters and the other for medium to fast moving rivers. The antenna, with

its long thin tip and bulbous bottom, is the one for the first category. For faster waters you will require a streamlined float which has the majority of its buoyancy near the tip.

Which bait to use. Maggots in various colours and sizes are still the most common fishing bait around. However, there are many other baits which can be just as tempting. Among them are bread, worms, stewed wheat, hempseed, berries, cheese, luncheon meat, sweetcorn and so on. The list is endless because fish have been caught on just about everything that can be put on a hook.

Game Fishing

Game or fly fishing is regarded by many anglers as the finest and most exciting type of fishing in the world. And the species that have built up this reputation are the salmon and the trout. Years ago most of our game fishing was done on rivers, particularly in Scotland, Wales and Ireland. However, with the sudden upsurge of new trout-stocked reservoirs all over the British Isles, more and more people are taking it up.

Most trout fisheries are 'fly only', which means that you can only fish with an artificial fly and a proper fly line.

'Flies' are hooks dressed with feathers, fur, wool, tinsel or the like which, when tied, imitate a natural fly at some stage in its development. They can also represent other waterlife like shrimps, fish fry and beetles. Flies fished on the surface are known as 'dry flies'; those fished beneath the surface are referred to as 'wet flies'.

Where to fish. Salmon fishing is an expensive pastime and charges for visits to the top waters can be very high – even on a day-ticket basis, let alone a season. Some trout fishing is also expensive, but as it becomes more readily available it is also becoming somewhat cheaper, particularly at the new water authority reservoirs and purpose-built stillwater trout fisheries which now provide plenty of choice all over the country.

Most of these waters can be fished on a day-ticket basis for a few pounds at a time, but a few have a waiting list even for season tickets. The trout fisheries are often more expensive than the reservoirs but at least for the beginner there is the consolation of knowing he cannot be too far from trout. A third type of trout fishing is in rivers – either the rain-fed rivers of the north and west of Britain or the chalk streams of the south where fishing rights can cost up to £1000 a season for rivers such as the Test.

Nearly all fisheries have what is known as a 'limit bag'. If the limit is six, you must stop fishing as soon as you have caught six fish – or buy another ticket. As with coarse fishing you also need a general rod licence and again the local tackle shops can provide licences and general information about day or season tickets for game fishing in their area.

When to fish. The season begins around April 1 and ends around September 30, depending on where you live.

What you need. The beauty of fly fishing is that you do not have to kit yourself out with a lot of tackle. You simply need a rod, reel, line and flies. (Special clothing, like waders and fishing jackets, can be added later.)

Rods. These are hardly ever longer than 10ft (3m), except of course those used for salmon fishing on big rivers. The hollow fibreglass types are the most commonly used although carbon fibre rods are becoming increasingly popular. Their only disadvantage to the beginner is the cost – considerably more than fibreglass. (See below, under *Lines*, for the importance of matching rod and line and a description of the rating system.)

Reels. These need to be light. The $3\frac{1}{2}$in (9cm) diameter type costs only a few pounds and is ideal for the novice. Always make sure that your tackle is nicely balanced. Therefore if you buy the reel first, make sure you take it to the shop with you when you buy your first rod.

Lines. Fly casting is totally different to any methods used in sea or coarse fishing because there is no attached weight – ie a float or lead weight – to assist with the cast. It is quite obvious that a 'fly' weighs very little and is hardly likely to pull line from a reel. Therefore the fly line has to act as the weight.

As a result fly lines are thick and heavy compared with their sea and coarse counterparts. They are usually 30yds ($27\frac{1}{2}$m) long, thickest in the middle and taper off towards the ends. The way they are cast is much the same as the old coachman's whip. In other words the rod has to be used as a spring lifting loose line off the water, carrying it back over the angler's head, pausing while the line straightens out behind and then throwing the rod forward to send the line in the direction of the water (see illustration).

Lines come in different sizes because they have to match the various types of rod available. However, they are easily recognisable by a standard AFTM (Association of Fishing Tackle Manufacturers) rating. The rating is marked on line spools – AFTM7, for instance: the figure is based on the weight in grains of the first 30ft (9.1m) of line. The AFTM number is marked on the rod so if you have a number 7 rod – a good buy for beginners – then you need to have a number 7 line. The heaviest in common use is a number 9 while the lightest is a number 4.

The three basic types of fly-line – those that float, sink or only partly sink – are designed for fish feeding at different levels in the water. The beginner would do well to start with a floater – but do not economise on the quality of the line. A good one will last longer, cast more easily and float better.

What fly to use. Flies come in different types and sizes. 'Big lures', for instance, are streamers used for fishing big reservoirs but never for river or small still-water fishing. Sizes are identified by numbers and there are often maximum sizes specified for different locations such as reservoirs, rivers or small trout fisheries. There is not space here to go much beyond the fundamental distinction made at the beginning of this section, namely that 'dry flies' are used for fishing on the surface and 'wet flies' for fishing beneath the surface. But many of the subtleties which give such appeal to this branch of angling stem from the intricacies of the flies themselves.

Sea fishing

Most novice sea anglers get their early experience of this form of fishing from the beach or from piers and jetties. Such fishing is relatively inexpensive. Apart from the advantage of plenty of beach space in which to learn to cast there is the added bonus of being able to dig or collect free bait from the beach itself.

Boat angling is the alternative form of sea fishing but this can prove fairly expensive with the angler having to pay for boat fees and bait charges. If you are beach fishing you can also keep all that you catch, while some boat skippers may only allow you to keep just a few fish. For the skippers it is their living and they often sell catches to local markets or shops.

What you can catch. One exciting aspect of sea fishing is that you never know what you are going to catch. The movement of the various species of fish around the coastline means that the sea angler can expect variety during the year. Nor is there a close season for sea fishing which is another reason for its increasing popularity.

Cod and whiting are to be had from most sandy beaches in winter, with flat-fish, bass and thornback ray in summer. Piers and jetties will yield the same. Boat fishing is different, however, especially if you can fish the wrecks in the South West off Plymouth or the Irish coast. Wrecks are natural food larders for the big fish such as conger eel, ling, coalfish, pollack and cod. Hundreds of charter boats offer their services and the best way of finding them is by reading the classified pages of the national angling press. Shark fishing is particularly big business in the South-West with Looe the major centre.

What you will need. Unlike coarse fishing, you do not need licences and tickets to be able to go sea fishing. You simply need your tackle and bait – and a

---

The ones that didn't get away: some all-time record angling catches

More than 140 species are included in the anglers' hall of fame: a list of record weights and the (lucky?) anglers who caught them on rod and line in United Kingdom waters. In the 1979 list these ranged from a 851lb (386 kg) tunny caught by L. Mitchell Henry off Whitby, Yorkshire, in 1933 to a 4 dram (007 grammes) sea stickleback caught by Master Kevin Pilley at Poole Harbour, Dorset, in 1978. Records for ten of the more renowned species, if not necessarily the most frequently caught species, in the 1979 list were as below.

The record list is updated annually so if you want to claim a record – or obtain a copy of the full list and other information – contact the British Record (Rod-caught) Fish Committee, 5 Cowgate, Peterborough, Cambridgeshire. Claims for fish caught in the Irish Republic should be made to the Irish Specimen Fish Committee, Baenagowan, Mobhi Boreen, Glasnevin, Dublin 9.

* Different records exist for sea fish caught from boats and the shore; those listed here are the heaviest from either source.

Freshwater Fish	Sea Fish*
Carp 44lb (20 kg)	Bass 18lb 6oz (8.3 kg)
Pike 40lb (18 kg)	Cod 53lb (24 kg)
Roach 4lb 1oz (1.8 kg)	Haddock 13lb 11oz (6.2 kg)
Salmon 64lb (29 kg)	Halibut 212lb 4oz (96.2 kg)
Rainbow Trout $19\frac{1}{2}$lb (8.9 kg)	Mako shark 500lb (227 kg)

little luck. You can even stay ashore.

Rods. Beach fishing requires long casting if you are to land lots of fish. Therefore a long and powerful rod, or beachcaster as it is known, is necessary; hollow fibreglass around the 11 to 13ft (3.3–4m) mark is best. A good tackle shop will advise and generally allow you to try one or two.

While you may have to cast your bait at least 80 yards (73m) from the beach to find the feeding fish, with boat fishing it is generally a question of simply dropping your bait over the side of the boat. Therefore you do not need a particularly long rod – one between 6–7ft (2m) is quite sufficient.

Reels. Either fixed spool or multiplier reels can be used for fishing from the shore, but multiplier reels are the best bet when boat fishing. Fixed spools are much easier to cast since the multiplier may take a little time to master. However when you have mastered the multiplier, you will find that the reel creates a much smoother cast and therefore gives you the extra distance that is often required for successful sea fishing.

Whatever the choice make certain that your reel is capable of carrying at least 200yd (182m) of 20lb (9kg) breaking strain line for beach fishing or 200yd of 35 1lb (16kg) for boat fishing. Again a local tackle dealer is the best person to consult for advice.

Lead weights. Once you have bought your rod and reel you will need line, hooks, some swivels and a selection of lead weights. For beach fishing you will need weights of between 2–6oz (56–170gm) with spikes for fishing over sand, gravel or mud. For boat fishing you will need the much heavier stuff – from 4oz to 1½lb (113gm–0.7kg). The choice depends on where you are fishing, at what depths and in strong or slack tides.

Baits. Lugworm and ragworm, which can be easily dug from many beaches, are the most popular sea baits and will take most species of fish. However, other baits worth trying include the flesh of almost any fish but especially those with a high oil content such as mackerel and herring. Also used are shellfish, crab baits, squid and artificial lures; the latter range from small hooks dressed with coloured feathers which are intended to lure mackerel to large metal weights, known as pirks, which take specimen cod and ling. The angling press carry weekly guides to sea fishing telling you where the best areas or 'marks' are, what is being caught and which baits are proving deadly.

Riding: how to choose a riding school or pony trekking centre

Two million people ride regularly in the British Isles. Half of them are children. Most do not own horses but hire from riding stables. The horseback rush, which sprouted in the 1960s, has burst out in an epidemic of riding schools all over the country. Many suffer from economic problems and labour shortages which inevitably restrict individual attention to horses and clients. For the beginner, choosing the right school is the first crucial problem, as tough as buying a second-hand car if you are mechanically illiterate.

Do you really want to ride? The first question to ask yourself (or your child) is: do you really want to ride, and, if so, why? A summer day in open country might charm your great-aunt on to a horse; a sleeting winter one, necessary if you are to keep in practice, wouldn't. Ambitions such as foxhunting are inconvenient if you live in Central London.

The sport is physically demanding, time-consuming and fairly expensive. There is little point in taking up riding unless you have time for constant practice. Learning to ride takes time. Even once a week means slow progress, whereas once a fortnight – don't bother. Nor can you ride unless you are physically fit. Costs at riding schools vary according to whether or not lessons are shared and sometimes whether or not you have the chief instructor's attention. If subsequent enthusiasm impels you to buy a horse you will be in for £1000–£2000 a year, maybe even more, depending on where you keep the animal and what you want to use it for.

What to ask. While not guaranteeing a seat in the saddle of the gods, there are a number of ways of ensuring that you do not prostrate yourself before the riding boots of the local incompetent opportunist. Riding stables do exist – not many, but some – who will take you for the wrong sort of ride. Careful inquiry will provide a reasonable guarantee that a school, though not necessarily perfect, is at least worthy of your custom. First-class instruction in the early stages of riding is essential. If a school satisfies the following requirements it is likely to provide it:
1. Is it approved either by the British Horse Society or by the Association of British Riding Schools? It is well worth writing to these organisations – and its Irish equivalent – for their booklets of approved schools (addresses overleaf).

Neither the BHS nor the ABRS will sanction a riding school unless the school is licensed, has adequate insurance cover and has been examined for quality of instruction, condition of horses, and standards of safety, and both reserve the right to spot-check approved schools without prior warning to the proprietor. (It is possible that a perfectly good riding school may exist without being BHS or ABRS approved, but some non-approved stables have either failed to satisfy the inspectors or have not asked for approval because they know they will not get it.) Schools offering residential holidays or pony trekking should be approved (see overleaf). If they are not, clients may expect indifferent tuition, if any, and overworked and neglected mounts.

2. Can it produce evidence that it is licensed by the local authority? If not, it has failed to pass that authority's veterinary surgeon. This not only means that its horses are in inadequate condition but that it is probably not insured against accidents to its clients. A properly insured school will carry cover to a minimum of £250,000 per rider.

3. Does it require its clients to wear hard hats to protect their heads against falls? If not, it is not only irresponsible, since a fall on the head is the most dangerous of all riding accidents, but it is almost certainly uninsured because insurance companies like to safeguard themselves against claims for brain damage.

4. Has it got either an indoor school or a small, fenced paddock in which beginners can be taught to control their horses without being exposed to the dangers of traffic? Any responsible school will also try out new customers in these enclosed spaces before allowing them on the roads, no matter how great the client's claim to expertise.

5. Is the riding school convenient to your home? If not, getting there is going to be a nuisance. If several schools in your area fulfil these requirements, ask for personal opinions from people who use them – from other children as well as adults since they can be more honest in their judgments.

6. How many pupils in a class? More than eight riders in one class in a covered school or paddock is too many: how much of the instructor's attention could they receive? On the road the maximum string for *experienced* riders should not exceed a dozen, so beware of schools where 20 or so novices are exposed to the dangers of traffic.

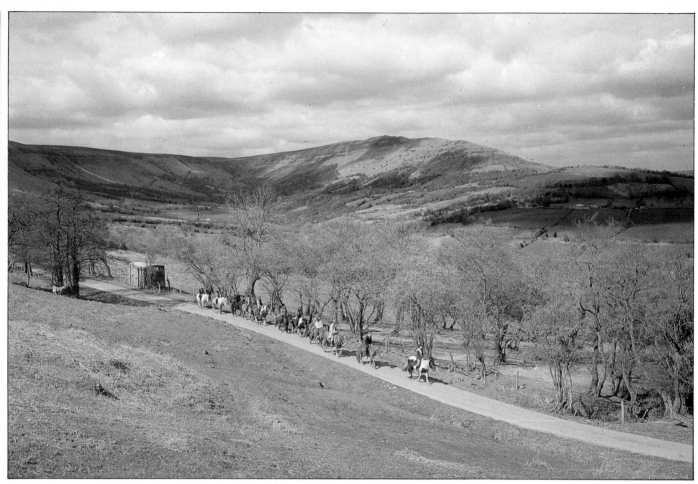

Children have always ridden ponies for obvious reasons of size. But pony trekking, as a sport or holiday activity, is relatively recent. There are now hundreds of centres offering pony trekking in the British Isles, especially in the upland areas such as above in the Olchon Valley of the Black Mountains in Wales.

For many people it is also their introduction to riding since the trekking itself is quite leisurely. All the rider normally has to do is to sit on his animal; the ponies are well used to walking in line with inexpert riders on their backs. They are often equally accustomed to the bridlepaths or old drove trails chosen by the trek guide or leader. But the treks can still be tiring so they are not recommended for children under 12 years of age.

Most centres operate between Easter and October and although one-week inclusive holidays are the normal minimum period, one-day treks are becoming increasingly common. Always choose a centre which has been officially approved: the Riding Holiday and Trekking Association of England, Wales, Scotland and Ireland run comprehensive schemes, often in conjunction with local tourist boards, while Ponies of Britain vets the standard of care for the animals.

Pony trekkers are accompanied by a guide, often with an assistant bringing up the rear. Ideally there should be no more than 12 riders in the string. Beginners usually go on short treks initially to build up confidence, but the distance to be covered in a day will rarely exceed 20 miles (32km). Some centres offer experienced riders 'trail riding', 'post trekking' or 'camping treks' which involve staying away from the centre overnight. These treks are much more rigorous, covering anything up to 25 miles a day.

It is not necessary to dress elaborately to go trekking but make sure you take warm, weatherproof clothing and strong shoes with heels. Riding hats can be hired or borrowed from the centre. Costs of trekking holidays vary greatly, largely according to the quality of accommodation. Often this is pretty basic. You may have to share a room – not with your pony, although you may have to help muck out his room, too.

It is generally possible to use layman's common sense to buttress the answers to these specific questions. You should obviously be wary of schools where instuctors are remiss enough to ride *inside* the pupil on roads; where pupils wear plimsolls or block heels while riding; where instructors shout (which may upset horses as well as human customers); and where the stables seem dirty and uncared for.

Having satisfied yourself as much as you reasonably can, it is time for a riding lesson. During this trial lesson you can establish whether you respect (important) and like (though this is not essential) the person who will be teaching you. Do not sign up for a course of lessons until you have tried and enjoyed riding. Likewise do not lash out on expensive clothing for your first lesson – see below.

What to wear. Riding is a physically demanding sport. It can be dangerous. It can be uncomfortable. It can hurt. In the early stages it is painful because you are having to use long-neglected (at best) muscles. If, in addition, your clothes rub, pinch, are too bulky, too tight, too hot or too cold, then you are on a crash course to misery.

Short-term gear. Safety and comfort are all that matter for the first few trial lessons. Essentials are a hard hat to protect your head. The best of these is not the pretty black velvet-covered peaked cap worn by show jumpers – it has a hard lining, but unless it fits perfectly, which is rare, it will usually fall off when you do. Much better is the really protective, inexpensive crash helmet or skull cap worn by jockeys and event riders.

Shoes should be lace-ups with plain leather soles, or the kind of rubber, smooth-soled riding boots which do double duty as elegant wellingtons. Stacked or block heels, corrugated soles or plimsolls are extremely dangerous because they can jam in the stirrups if you fall and may lead to you being dragged by the foot behind a panicking horse. Riders have been killed through wearing block heels.

Clothes should be close-fitting (a polo-necked sweater and windcheater, for example), not flapping about as this will impede your movement and may also frighten the horse. For trousers, avoid jeans which are stiff and pinch your legs excruciatingly against the stirrup leathers. Try a pair of soft trousers, corduroy or the like, and fold them into long, thick socks with the fold of the trousers lying on the outside of the leg so that the inside of the knee is spared from the rub of the trouser crease. Under the trousers wear tights for warmth (not cissy – jockeys always do), and bandage your legs from the calf to above the knee to safeguard against pinching. On a cold day, gloves are mandatory. Woolly ones will do, provided that they fit closely enough to allow each finger to move independently.

Long-term gear. If you decide to go on with riding, properly-fitting clothes will make your work much easier. Choose either ankle-length jodhpurs with leather jodhpur boots that cover and protect your ankles, or calf-length riding breeches with leather riding boots. Rubber boots are all right – but are cold in winter unless big enough to take two pairs of socks. The riding jacket should really fit so that your movements are unencumbered, or you could wear a lightweight windcheater over a sweater. String riding gloves help you to grip the reins when they are wet with rain or the horse's sweat, and never forget tights, undervests, woollen knickers if the weather calls for it. Above all, though, never forget the crash helmet.

Further information
National tourist boards publish lists of centres offering riding or trekking holidays; see appendix for details of the addresses and telephone numbers of the head offices of the tourist boards. Other sources of information on riding schools or trekking holidays include:
British Horse Society and the English Riding Holiday and Trekking Association, both based at the British Equestrian Centre, Kenilworth, Warwickshire;
Association of British Riding Schools, Chesham House, 56 Green End Road, Chesham, Surrey;
Ponies of Britain, Brookside Farm, Ascot, Berkshire;
Irish Horse Board, St Maelruan's, Tallaght, Co Dublin.

Boating: the many different ways of messing about on the water

Nobody in the British Isles lives far from water. This accessibility allied to increased affluence has encouraged a great growth in the popularity of all forms of boating in the last 20 years.

For people with a boat small enough to trail behind the family car, the choice of boating locations is almost infinite. For people without any nautical skills at all, hire boat fleets have expanded into a major holiday industry based on the easier waters of rivers, broads and canals. Even watching other people in their boats is attraction enough to draw large numbers of people to marinas and estuaries all around Britain.

Whatever the form of boating, it is an activity which offers the possibility of greater intimacy with the countryside. Here we examine what a beginner needs to know about starting to learn the three main types of boating: sailing, motor cruising and canoeing.

Sailing
Since the war sailing has changed from being a rich man's sport to one available to anybody with a few hundred pounds. Improvements in materials and technology have had a lot to do with it and the result is a new breed of cheaper, smaller, lighter and more mobile boats that can be kept at home.

Sailing dinghies
The simplest sailing boats are dinghies and most people who start the sport, especially those who start young, begin with dinghy sailing. But there are about 150,000 dinghies sailing in the British

Isles from over 100 different classes so the beginner needs to learn something about the sport before rushing off to buy his or her first boat.

Dinghy sailing is almost invariably based on a club because most owners race rather than potter, and all racing is club organised. Many clubs also have dinghy parks where members can safely keep their boats. But many restrict membership to owners of specific classes, which is another reason for not buying a boat before you have found a club.

Where to learn. The best way is through a Royal Yachting Association (RYA) approved sailing school. This will entail spending a week to get the RYA Dayboat Certificate. A few clubs offer instruction to members and their families, but these are mostly confined to the cadet classes for children. After a week at a sailing school, and having found your club, you will be able to decide what type of dinghy to buy. From there on progress is up to you and, to some extent, on how you fit in with the traditions and tempo of your club. The RYA booklet *Recognised Teaching Establishments* gives details of sailing schools and other organisations which run courses, and its publication code number G13 gives a complete list of 1500 affiliated clubs and sailing organisations in the United Kingdom. For the address of the RYA and other boating organisations, see page 188.

What to buy. If you are not interested in competitive sailing, but just want to buy a little boat and potter about on your own learning by your mistakes, buy a stable and slow general-purpose dinghy instead of an out-and-out racing ma-

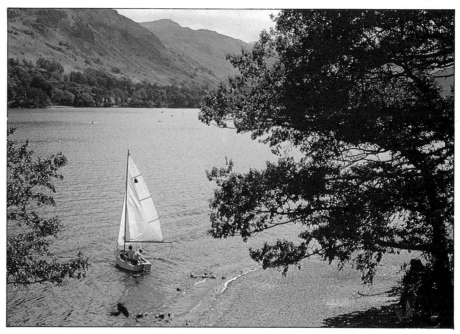

Sailing on the tranquil waters of Ullswater amid the mountain grandeur of the Lake District

chine. You might also be interested in joining the Dinghy Cruising Association, its title is self-explanatory. Whatever your choice of dinghy you will need a trailer to take it either to race meetings or on holiday, for instance. A wet suit is also essential in this country in the early and late season. And on all but the warmest days waterproof clothing is needed as protection against wind chill. A buoyancy aid when sailing in sheltered waters or a BSI-approved lifejacket in tidal or sea conditions is considered essential and is mandatory for all racing, and for children whenever and wherever they are on the water.

Sailing cruisers

Coastal and deep water cruising, to which most dinghy sailors eventually graduate as they get older and can afford the cost, is an altogether different game. Whereas the newcomer to dinghy sailing can think of getting afloat for as little as £500, the cruising enthusiast must start to think of at least £3000 for quite a small boat built and equipped to be suitable only for inshore cruising. Large boats now cost as much as small London houses, that is around £25,000 for a 30-footer suitable for long-distance cruising.

What to buy. Remember that the bigger a boat, the more crew will be needed to sail her. Remember, too, that it is not always easy to find enough compatible people who are all free at the same time to form a crew. On the other hand, the longer the waterline length of a boat the faster she will sail, and bigger boats tend to be more seaworthy than smaller boats. Size can also be equated with comfort when it comes to living on board. But if a boat is to be used largely for day sailing, the inconvenience of cramped accommodation never lasts long enough to spoil the fun. Other advantages of smaller boats are that they will go further inland to explore sheltered waters, can be sailed more easily single-handed and only need a small outboard instead of a more expensive inboard engine.

There are about 390 designs of sailing cruiser on the market ranging in size from 16ft (5m) 'Weekenders' (which are little more than day boats with a shelter) to 40ft (12m) ocean-going cruiser racers. Publications such as the practical Boat Owner *Buyer's Guide to Sailing Cruisers*, which is published each spring, give cross-referenced details and photographs of all the boats available. If you buy secondhand the boat should be subject to a survey, which may well call the seller's bluff and bring the price down consider-

ably. But it is often a better investment to spend more on a new boat; in the last decade new boats of quality have held their original price so that owners have at least got their capital back when trading in for a bigger boat. Boats can be bought as bare hulls for completion by the owner. But although this can save 50 per cent of the cost, the work will probably take much longer than you estimate.

Finally, however exciting the prospect of owning a boat, it is more economic to charter than to buy. That way you can sail better boats than you could afford to own, and you can choose a different cruising area every time. For details of charter yachts look in the classified advertisements of the yachting press, or write to the Yacht Charter Association.

Where to learn. It is better and quicker to invest in professional instruction than to rely on friends to teach you sailing. During the winter go to night school to learn navigation and then take a practical cruising course at an RYA-recognised school. At the end of a week, if you are fit and keen, you should achieve your Competent Crew Certificate. After a further week at sea on a practical course you can get your Day Skipper Certificate. You are then competent to take charge of a watch when cruising offshore, or to skipper a small cruiser on short coastal passages. During the next season spend at least one week, but preferably two, taking your turn as skipper on a charter yacht with a qualified instructor in charge. Then you should have enough knowledge and experience to command your own boat and crew. Schools with cruising courses and skippers who give instruction are advertised in the yachting press and are listed in the RYA publication *Practical Cruising Courses*.

Motor Cruising

Anybody who can drive a car can drive a motorboat – after a fashion. Unlike a sailing boat, a powered craft needs no special skills to get it moving. Nor, of course, are you so affected by tides and winds so that greater distances can generally be covered in less time. Another attraction to many people is that boats designed for inland waterways can be planned and furnished for comfort rather than speed or sea-keeping qualities. Seagoing motor cruisers, of course, must have sea-keeping capabilities.

But it does need a sound knowledge of pilotage and navigation, weather and sea conditions to go cruising at sea with any safety. It also requires more stamina to

cope with rough conditions in a motor cruiser, especially one with a high-speed planing hull, than it does in a sailing boat which rides the waves better and is steadied by its sails.

Personal clothing and safety gear are much the same as for sailing: good waterproofs, proper deck shoes, an ample supply of spare warm dry clothes, a BSI-approved lifejacket and safety harness.

The greatest motor boat activity is on the inland waterways. A recent survey estimated there were 44,000 motor vessels on the island waterways of the British Isles *excluding* the Broads, the Fens and the Shannon. On the Thames alone there were more than 1000 boats available for hire. Irish waters are generally less crowded than those of England and the Shannon in particular is an ideal cruising area served by several large hire fleets.

The cost of buying a boat as opposed to hiring one can be anything from £600 for a simple 15ft (4.5m) boat with a shelter (plus a further £600 for an outboard engine) to at least £15,000 for a 35ft (10.6m) canal cruiser equipped for living on board. Luxury cruising homes for inland waters and sleeping eight people can cost well over £50,000. One advantage of hiring a boat – other than avoiding this cost of purchase – is that hire boats are already licensed. All cruising on inland waterways has to be licensed – contact the British Waterways Board or the Irish Tourist Board for details about boat licensing, hiring etc. (addresses overleaf).

Canoeing

There are around 250,000 canoeists in the British Isles and, like other forms of boating, canoeing appeals to both the highly competitive or adventurous and those who enjoy being on the water for its own sake. For the former it is as skilled and energetic a sport as skiing. But for the majority, and probably for most beginners, the big attractions are canoe touring along inland waters and sea canoeing. Either way it is about the cheapest and most independently mobile way of getting afloat. When it is time to go home a canoe can be carried atop the smallest car.

There are canoeing waters in Great Britain and Ireland to suit all tastes and abilities. There is a legal right to navigate, and therefore to canoe, on nearly all tidal waters and a long-standing or statutory right on a number of rivers such as the Thames, Medway, Wye, Severn, the Stratford Avon, Trent, Great Ouse, Suffolk Stour and Spey. On other rivers licences are often granted to clubs by public and private owners. There are fewer restrictions on rivers in Ireland where the principal canoeing waters are the Erne, Shannon, Barrow, Blackwater, Suir, Nore and Slaney.

All canals and some canalised rivers require a licence before launching a canoe. Canals with their still water make an excellent nursery for beginners and can be used to link up with the Severn, Trent and Thames. On rivers where canoes are allowed it is possible to go where no boat can reach. The canoeist has a choice of probably thousands of miles of routes throughout the British Isles which can be explored by no other means, often not even on foot.

Canals are neither particularly wide nor deep, so they are reasonably safe for young teenagers even on their own. But beginners should always canoe in company, and sea canoeing should always be done in groups. At sea canoes can also go where boats dare not – among rocky islets, over shallows, and into caves. Sea kayaks are longer than touring canoes and have greater directional stability. They must be fitted with buoyancy –

30lb (13kg) at each end – and a lifejacket must always be worn.

Before going into any rough water or to sea in a canoe it is essential to have been taught how to handle the craft and particularly how to right it when it capsizes, which it surely will. The British and Irish Canoe Unions will supply lists of clubs to join and regional organisers who run their coaching scheme. Canoeing can also be learnt under the auspices of the Sports Councils which also runs sailing courses.

Safety on the water

Messing about in boats can be dangerous as well as fun. Every year people are drowned as a result of boating accidents. Every year people are rescued. Children are particularly vulnerable, of course, and in addition to equipping them with adequate safety aids (see below) their enthusiastic parents should remember that they will stand up to cold and wet less well than adults.

Boating takes so many different forms that it is difficult to devise one set of rules which embraces all types of water and types of craft from canoes to sea-going yachts. Nevertheless these 10 rules are always worth remembering:

1. In sheltered waters (canals, tideless reaches of rivers, small lakes and gravel pits) children must wear a BSI-standard buoyancy aid or life jacket at all times while on the water.

2. In tidal rivers, estuaries, inshore around the coast and on big lakes (eg, Lake Windermere) children must wear buoyancy aids or, preferably, life jackets at all times, and so should adults when underway.

3. Extra warm clothing should be carried even on warm days. If anybody gets wet and the sun goes in, wind chill can be dangerous.

4. All boats must have an alternative means of propulsion: oars for a small motor boat or dinghy, an outboard engine for a larger boat.

5. In coastal waters there must be sufficient lifejackets of a size to fit all members of the crew, and two lifebuoys available to throw overboard, one of which must have a water-activated light attached to it. Lifelines and safety harnesses should be available for crew working outside the cockpit in rough water.

6. Every boat must carry an adequate anchor.

7. Boats going to sea must have adequate means of communicating with other

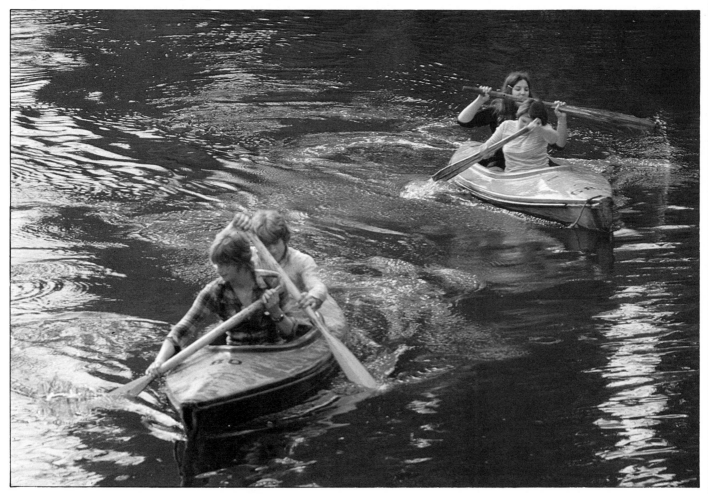

Canoeing: not only the cheapest way of getting afloat but also the only way to explore some of the most remote and beautiful waters in Britain

vessels or the shore if in distress – basically flares and smoke signals. Any boat going offshore should carry at least a small inflatable boat as a lifeboat; if going out further than three miles (4.8km) it should be a liferaft equipped with a survival pack and a radio to receive weather and shipping forecasts.

8. Small boats in any water should have sufficient built-in or installed buoyancy to keep them afloat when capsized or waterlogged, and no one should leave a capsized boat and try to swim to safety. A small boat, even upside down, is more visible than a person's head in the water, and always remember that even the strongest swimmer can be defeated by an adverse tide.

9. Boats with engines and galleys must carry adequate fire extinguishers, and all butane gas installations must be professionally installed, and containers vented outside the boat.

10. Good seamanship is good safety. A well-found and well-equipped boat, careful handling, and attention to weather are better safeguards than a lot of expensive safety equipment.

If you do get into difficulty at sea – or you see a boat in distress – contact the coastguard; they coordinate rescue services and alert shipping. If you have informed coastguards of your intended route before departure – a sensible precaution – do not forget to tell them when you arrive or else a search might be launched. The coastguards, like the RYA, publish various booklets on safety at sea.

Further information
National tourist boards and sports councils are good sources of information about holidays or courses in all forms of boating – see appendices. Other specialist organisations, including those referred to in the text above, are: Royal Yachting Association, Victoria Way, Woking, Surrey; Irish Yachting Association, 87 Upper George Street, Dun Laoghaire, Co Dublin; Yacht Charter Association Ltd., 33 Highfield Road, Lymington, Hampshire; British Waterways Board, Melbury House, Melbury Terrace, London NW1; Inland Waterways Association, 114 Regents Park Road, London NW1; British Canoe Union, Flexel House, 45 High Street, Addlestone, Weybridge, Surrey; and the Irish Canoe Union, Great Outdoors, Chatham Street, Dublin.

Country and Forest Parks: planning for leisure in the countryside

Individual concepts of leisure are as varied as the countryside itself. Not everybody wants to spend their holidays or weekends so actively as the practitioners of the sports discussed in preceding pages. For most people it is enough simply to be in the country with enough room for a picnic, the children to play safely and a gentle stroll. Of course, there should be pretty views and it would be nice if somehow you could know something of the countryside you are seeing. It is to help fulfil these quite modest ambitions – and to help the countryside itself – that a quiet revolution has been taking place throughout the British Isles.

The prime function of the countryside is as it always has been: to produce food. But today's city dwellers, ever more mobile, blessed with greater affluence and more leisure time than previous generations, look increasingly to the green fields to produce more than milk and potatoes.

Nowadays the rural areas serve a dual purpose. They are a giant playground, a place where batteries run down by the noise and pace of the urban rat-race may be re-charged with a breath of fresh country air. The result is that every weekend and all summer long the national parks and celebrated beauty spots are besieged and in some instances worn out by the sheer weight of visitors who, in all innocence, are to some extent participating in the destruction of the very landscapes they have come to see.

Clearly something needed to be done to ease the pressure where it was hurting most and reduce the impact of the lethal foot that is literally kicking some of the most beautiful bits of the British Isles to death. Artificial grass has had to be sown on the Pennines and a stretch of rubber matting laid near where the Pennine Way begins north of Edale, Derbyshire. One of the most positive responses to this challenge has been the emergence of the country park.

Just over a decade ago the country park concept was nothing more than an idea floated in a British Government report called *Leisure in the Countryside*. Today there are well over a 150 country parks flourishing in nearly every corner of England and Wales, and more parks are in the pipeline.

Such places had never existed before in the countryside. But they have been introduced with such little fuss and such modest publicity that many people are unaware of what has been achieved. Country parks are not half so wild or so big as the national parks which will be featured in Chapter 10. Nor are they so small and tame as a municipal recreation ground. Instead they fit somewhere between the two, with the accent on leisure rather than conservation.

They were designed to serve three basic purposes. Country parks would make it easier for town dwellers to enjoy the open air without travelling too far and adding to traffic congestion. They would ease the pressure on the more remote and solitary places. And above all, perhaps, in the words of the Government report, they would 'reduce the risk of damage to the countryside – aesthetic as well as physical which often comes about when people simply settle down for an hour or a day, where it suits them, somewhere "in the country" – to the inconvenience and indeed the expense of the countryman who lives there.'

A good country park will certainly be readily accessible for cars and pedestrians and you may be able to reach it by public transport. It will cover at least 25 acres (10 hectares) and may contain woods, open parkland or a stretch of water. It may even be on the coast.

Some country parks provide refreshment facilities, picnic sites, information centres and a warden service. All of them have car parks and toilets. There may be an admission fee or a charge for parking your car, and a few parks close during the winter, so try to check before setting out.

In some parks you can swim, sail, fish, or go horse-riding. Others offer the quieter pleasures of nature trails, gardens, ancient monuments and scenic viewpoints. The commonest type of park is the traditional parkland of a bygone ancestral estate, sometimes with the great house or castle still intact within the grounds, as at Elvaston Castle, near Derby. But there is no truly typical country park.

In landscape terms their range is immense; downs, cliffs, woods, moors, heaths – even reclaimed mineral workings, old gravel pits and derelict railway lines transformed with financial aid from the Countryside Commission. A few private individuals and non-public bodies such as the National Trust have established country parks, but so far most have been set up by local authorities.

In addition to the country parks in England and Wales there are vast forest parks. These are run, like those in Scot-

Deer graze in a country park of the 18th century: the grounds of Petworth Manor, Sussex: one of the first parks to be landscaped by Capability Brown

land (see below), by the Forestry Commission. Some of the parks are huge with more than a dozen areas within them laid out by the Commission as picnic areas, walks, trails or even special 'scenic drives'. Snowdonia is one such park. But there are also many smaller parks in both lowland and upland areas of England and Wales, often with information centres providing exhibitions about the ecology of the forests and details about the trails, etc.

In Scotland there are only a few country parks as yet. This is primarily because the pressures which led to the creation of the English and Welsh country parks have not yet made themselves felt to the same extent. North of the border, and particularly in the Highlands, the wild landscapes remain much as they were centuries ago. This is Britain's empty quarter, where there are often more sheep and deer than people, where cities are fewer, and even the industrial sprawl of Glasgow offers in-

stant release into the surrounding hills and sea lochs.

Nevertheless there is still a need to conserve, and in Scotland this has brought about the creation of forest parks and nature reserves. The forest parks include the beautiful Argyll and Queen Elizabeth forest parks, both within easy reach of Glasgow; the 135,000-acre (54,656 hectares) Glen Trool forest park with its lochs and falls and scimitar-horned wild goats; and the magnificent national forest park of Glen More at the foot of the Cairngorm mountains.

Scotland's nature reserves range in size and character from Rhum – an entire Hebridean island – to the mountain, moorland and relic pinewood reserves of Ben Eighe, Inverpolly, Cairngorm and Rannoch Moor, each one a refuge for wild cats, eagles and other Highland fauna. Conservation is paramount in these reserves, but many, like the forest parks, provide public access in the form of forest walks and nature trails.

Northern Ireland has only a handful of country parks but they include two of the finest in the British Isles. In Ness country park, Co Londonderry, the Burntollet River emerges from a narrow gorge called Shane's Leap and tumbles in a double cascade for nearly 40ft (12m), forming the highest falls in Ulster. And in the Castle Archdale forest and country park, Co Fermanagh, the shores of Lower Lough Erne are starred with the white flowers of grass of Parnassus.

Ulster also has a number of nature reserves open to the public, and nearly fifty state forests in the care of Northern Ireland's Forest Service, including over a dozen forest parks with nature trails, picnic sites, caravan sites and scenic drives. Ulster's first forest park, Tollymore, at the foot of the Mourne mountains, opened in 1955. Today over a million visits are made to Northern Ireland's forest parks each year.

The Republic of Ireland, too, has superb forest parks where visitors may walk, picnic, fish, swim or watch wildlife. For several years it has been the policy of the Republic's Forest and Wildlife Service to encourage the use of the state forests for leisure and recreation. Among them are the forest parks of Killykeen and Dun-a-Ri in Co Cavan, Lough Key in Co Roscommon, Guagan Barra in Co Cork, the John F. Kennedy park in Co Wexford, the Ards forest park on Sheephaven Bay in Co Donegal, and the Portumna forest park with its deer herds and wildfowl ponds in Co Galway. These are the major forest parks, but Ireland has another 250 woods and forests, great and small, all of them open to the public, and as romantic as their names: Three Rock Mountains, Pigeon Hole Wood, Kelly's Cave Wood, Cooleydoody.... Some historic estates in the Republic, such as Powerscourt at Enniskerry, 12 miles (19km) south of Dublin, are also open to the public and in Killarney, Co Kerry, magnificent Bourne Vincent national park covers several square miles.

Whatever other changes may alter the face of the countryside in coming decades, the country parks and forest parks of the British Isles are a welcome addition whose permanence seems assured by their popularity. A survey carried out by the Countryside Commission showed that on one Sunday in July well over 200,000 people visited the country parks of England and Wales.

Where to find the parks

Most country parks will be listed on a regional basis in the 1000 Days Out section of this book. Many of the more numerous forest parks, as well as nature reserves and trails, will also be featured in their appropriate regional sections.

A booklet listing country parks in England and Wales recognised by the Countryside Commission together with brief descriptions is obtainable post free from The Countryside Commission, John Dower House, Crescent Place, Cheltenham, Glos. GL50 3RA.
Other sources of information about country or forest parks are:
Northern Ireland Tourist Board, River House, 48 High Street, Belfast BR1 2DS.
A booklet called *The Open Forest* listing the state forests and forest parks of Ire-Forest and Wildlife Service, 22 Upper Merrion Street, Dublin 2, Ireland.
Scottish Tourist Board, 23 Ravelston Terrace, Edinburgh EH4 3EU.
Forestry Commission, 231 Corstorphine Road, Edinburgh EH12 7oT

Reading the Countryside
1: By Compass

Most people will not need a compass for a day out in the countryside. But it is an essential travelling companion if you wish to penetrate the wilderness areas that remain in the British Isles. These are invariably upland areas of moors and mountains where landmarks are fewest and severe weather conditions most common. These two characteristics make the Silva compass in particular as much a 'must' for the outdoors adventurer as the slide rule is for a mathematician. It cuts out errors in compass work and gives rapid results. It consists of three basic parts: a magnetic needle; a revolvable compass housing, its rim marked, N, S, E, W and with degrees from 0 to 360; and a clear plastic base plate marked with a Direction of Travel (DOT) arrow. The illustrations (below) show how it should be used.

Stage one. It is misty. Your route lies from X to the church in a straight line. Lay the compass on the map so one edge of the base plate touches both where you are now – and where you want to go – the DOT arrow pointing to the church.

Stage two. Turn the compass housing

rim until the 'orienting arrow' (printed on the base of this housing) points north on the map: ie, lies exactly parallel with the nearest map grid line and its arrow points towards the top of the map.

Stage three. Finally, in order to find the compass bearing – the number of degrees on the compass at which you will walk – check which degree mark on the compass housing rim touches the DOT arrow. Then allow for the magnetic variation. It is given on each OS map among the key to the symbols – the number of degrees deflected by the magnetic north pole (which moves about inside the Arctic circle) from the true north pole to which your map is drawn.

Let us say your original bearing is 35 degrees and the local magnetic variation is 10 degrees west from true north. So turn the compass housing until 45 degrees nudges the DOT arrow. Hold the compass base plate, pointing the DOT arrow away from you. Turn your body until the red magnetic needle points to north (360 degrees). Keeping the red needle here, walk slowly following the DOT arrow. And that, done carefully, will lead you to the church in mist.

How to use a compass to travel accurately to a church – see text above for explanation of each stage. Good map readers will know from the Ordnance Survey symbol that the church has a spire

Walkers on the Long Mynd, Shropshire; an upland thoroughfare since sheep droving days

2: By Maps

The countryside can be used and appreciated in many different ways, as this chapter has demonstrated. But one common factor that will always enhance enjoyment is an understanding of maps. Once you have mastered the language of maps you cannot understand how you could have previously visited the countryside without them.

There are maps for all occasions and all interests. Some people will use maps to discover minor roads for a day out in the car; others will seek a footpath for a ramble. Some maps are designed for planning long-distance journeys, others for tracking down remnants of the past. For a few people maps can even provide interesting reading in themselves.

'There are Ordnance Survey maps which one can sit down and read like a book for an hour on end, with growing pleasure and enjoyment,' wrote W.G. Hoskins in *The Making of the English Landscape*. (This classic text has a fascinating section in which Professor Hoskins recreates the history of one small part of England simply by discerning the clues in a map.)

Although most people will have somewhat humbler ambitions (and capabilities), understanding a map remains essentially the same question of interpreting the clues. First, though, there is the question of which map to buy.

Which map to choose

The need to choose the 'right' map for your purpose is illustrated by the three maps of the same area of South Devon shown overleaf. But even these three scales, with their clearly visible differences, do not exhaust the possibilities. Generally the most comprehensive and best value maps of Great Britain are provided by the Ordnance Survey – for Ireland, see below. Most others are poor copies, with the important exception of the half-inch to the mile (or 1:127,620 in metric scale) maps produced by Bartholomew and filling a major gap in the Ordnance Survey (OS) series.

Most maps are now produced in metric scales. This means that a map in the 1:50,000 series is drawn so that one centimetre on the map represents 50,000 centimetres or half a kilometre on the ground. A map in the 1:25,000 series has one centimetre on the map representing 25,000 centimetres and therefore shows an area in larger scale or greater detail.

The larger the scale the smaller is the area covered so that closely related to a map's scale is its purpose. No map can show all features of the landscape so most concentrate on a single theme, or at most, a group of themes. This is illustrated by summarising the features of the main Ordnance Survey maps available in Britain. In order of scale, from smallest to largest, these are:

1. The 1:625,000 scale. A Route Planning Map (one sheet covering all of Britain) is revised annually and is useful for touring. A Geological map of Britain (two sheets) is suitable for observing major geological features and other special maps at this scale include Iron Age, Roman and Dark Age Britain.

2. The 1:250,000 scale. Routemaster Series (nine sheets). Primarily road maps although mountains and woodland areas are also shown. A better buy, second-hand, are the superseded Quarter-Inch series maps which showed the countryside in more detail until their withdrawal in the late 1970s.

3. The 1:63,360 scale. The old one-inch to the mile series has been superseded by the metric 1:50,000 but is still used in 'Tourist Maps' for Exmoor, Dartmoor, Peak District, Lake District, North York Moors, Loch Lomond and the Trossachs, Ben Nevis and Glencoe, and the Cairngorms. For historical interest there are also reprints of the 19th century first edition one-inch maps published by David and Charles.

4. The 1:50,000 scale. In 204 sheets at roughly $1\frac{1}{4}$ inches to the mile these are useful for local touring by foot or car but lack detail. The 1:25,000 map is better for walkers, but the 1:50,000 series maps have become established as the most widely available and most widely used of all current OS maps. The larger scale enables greater clarity and detail than was possible in the old one-inch to the mile maps which they have replaced.

5. The 1:25,000 scale. Over 1000 sheets. Some are rather out of date but these are gradually being replaced by the double-size and more colourful Second Series. This scale, which provides an effective compromise between detail and area coverage, can be purchased in two forms: the standard or the 'Outdoor Leisure Map' which includes such extra information as camp or caravan sites, parking places, picnic spots, viewpoints and places of interest like ancient monuments. Outdoor Leisure Maps are available for such places as the Three Peaks, the English Lakes, the Wye Valley, Malham, the Brecon Beacons, Snowdonia, the South Pennines, Cairngorms, the Cuillins, Brighton and the Downs, Purbeck, and South Devon.

6. The 1:10,000, 1:2,500 and 1:1250 scales. For specialist use only and not generally recommended.

Maps in Ireland

Both the Republic and Northern Ireland have their own Ordnance Survey organisations. For the Wicklow area, covering the fine mountains to the north of Dublin, there is an excellent layered map on the 1 inch to 1 mile scale (1:63,360). Elsewhere in the Republic the most useful map is the $\frac{1}{2}$inch to 1 mile (1:126,720) series, based on earlier editions but with some recent additions.

Landforms represented by map contours. The diagrams have been slightly realigned from contour equivalents to maintain symmetry of the illustration

The Irish Tourist Board issues a motoring map indicating distances between towns and villages, plus areas of special scenic beauty.

Northern Ireland has a more modern cover of maps, with a 1:50,000 map like those of the OS in Great Britain currently in production. This is intended to replace the 1:63,360 maps. Motorists may also find the ¼inch to 1 mile Bartholomew maps useful.

How to read a map
Firstly, the scale should be noted and fully understood. It takes only a little practice to judge distances simply by looking at a map – once you know the key. The next step is to examine the content of the map more closely. These are the most important features:

The key explains all the symbols used on OS maps. It is not necessary to memorise these details (although this is often easily done) since all OS maps have a clearly laid out key and some maps will incorporate features which others lack. Use the key to pick out points that interest you.

The National Grid is explained on the keys of most small-scale OS maps although the detail provided varies. The grid is a framework of artificial lines spaced at one or 10 kilometre intervals, according to the scale of the map. These not only enable distance to be judged more easily (remembering that one kilometre is roughly equal to 0.6 miles) but more important means that places can be located with complete precision by stating their coordinates or numbers on the national grid. This is how to do it.

First, study the key. Look for the two grid letters which cover the part of the map for which you want to give a reference. For the 1:25,000 series it is simply the two letters in the map's overall code number – SY in the example opposite. For smaller-scale maps there may be several sets of letters, each covering part of the map, so use the key to find out where these sets begin and end.

Second, take the west edge of the kilometre square in which the point lies and read the large figures printed opposite this line on north or south margins – 08 for Otterton church, opposite page. Then estimate its position in tenths eastwards – 0 in this case.

Third, take the south edge of the kilometre square in which the point lies and read the large figures opposite this line on the east or west margins – 85 for Otterton church. Then estimate in tenths its position northwards of this line – in this case, 2.

This gives the full reference of SY 080852 which is accurate to within 100 metres. No other place within Britain has this reference – *if* the grid letters are included. If the letters are omitted, the numbers will recur at intervals of 100 kilometres. Obviously the grid is seen most clearly and used most easily on the larger scale maps where the key is also invariably fuller, too.

Contours show places of equal height above sea level (in feet or the metric equivalent according to the key). If in doubt a good rule of thumb is to multiply metres by three to get the measurement in feet. Closely spaced contours indicate steep slopes while a lack of contours indicates a plain, river valley or hill-top plateau. A good eye for contour patterns will reveal promising viewpoints: where closely spaced contours give way to few contours, for instance, or where closely spaced contours jut out into a valley and thus allow panoramic views. (Somewhat confusingly the 1:50,000 OS maps show contour values to the nearest metre but the vertical interval between contour lines remain at 50 *feet*.)

Special features are included in all but the smaller scale route-planning maps so that the locations of, say, battlegrounds, burial mounds or Roman roads can be found. (As indicated earlier specialist maps also exist for interests such as history, geology and leisure pursuits.)

How to use a map
Once you understand the language of maps, as explained above, a map can easily be used in the field to read the countryside itself. The first task is to 'set the map' in the direction you want to look at or view. It is unlikely that the view will be directly to the north-south angle of all maps, so the map should be turned round until the view seen corresponds with the orientation of the map. It usually helps if this is done at a viewpoint. The next task is to look for landmarks, for example, prominent churches, lines of pylons, notable hills, woodland, river valleys, lakes or the coast. The map can then be used to fill in the gaps between these obvious landmarks and so complete the landscape jigsaw. A final job is to check for further access to the next stopping point, and the most interesting way of getting there. Remember, that the most direct route may not be the most rewarding route, either by road or footpath. The map may reveal many interesting spots, not apparent on the ground.

1:250,000 map; sheet 8 in Routemaster Series

1:50,000 map; sheet 192

Below: 1:25,000 map; sheet SY 08/18

The three Ordnance Survey maps reproduced above show the same area of South Devon and illustrate how the scale of a map determines how much or how little is revealed about an area. All three maps clearly indicate the valley of the River Otter but which map can best be used for further exploration? From the 1:250,000 map the lack of details suggest that access to the coast from Otterton is impossible. But the 1:50,000 map and to an even greater extent the 1:25,000 map show not only roads leading to the coast but also a good network of footpaths.

The larger-scale maps also illustrate most of the points made in the general text on these pages. For instance, the closely-spaced contours west of Otterton suggest good views over the Otter valley (if also a steep climb). Further places of interest revealed only by the larger-scale maps include Bicton Gardens and the disused railway line. One common factor in all three maps, however, is the National Grid although it is read most easily and precisely on the 1:25,000 map. Otterton church is thus at SY080852 while the grid reference for Bicton House, north-west of Otterton, is SY071865 – see facing page for how to read the National Grid.

193

Gardens in the Countryside

Chapter Eight

There is no other area of the world where the garden is so enthusiastically worked, exhibited and celebrated as the British Isles. This passion has produced gardens which are unequalled anywhere such as the one shown here at Stourhead, Wiltshire. They have flourished because of a beneficial combination of climate and soils, a deep-seated compulsion to experiment and the wealth and resources of their creators. They reflect varying styles and great periods of history, and are open for all to see: some for only a few days a year, others virtually year round. In this chapter the evolution of the great country house garden, from the late Middle Ages to the present day, is described and its design and features explained. At the other end of the scale the origin and development of the cottage garden, for many the epitome of rural gardening, is unravelled

Sissinghurst Castle, Kent. A marriage of formality in design with informality of planting. In 1930 it was derelict. Now it is one of the great gardens

The great garden. It took history and talent to make it

To most people an English garden is a place of flowers. It may be a little lacking in design but makes amends with a rustic charm which is supposed to owe much to a long tradition of cottage gardening.

Yet experts have a totally different view of the great English contribution to the art of garden-making. For them it is the 18th century garden, wholly pictorial in conception and with a minimal requirement for flowers, which is supreme.

Fortunately, however, there are many different types of garden in the British Isles, for this is one art in which the British have proved to be unusually inventive. They have been encouraged to be so by an equable climate, a diverse geology, a love of travel and a fine independence of mind.

There is something else, too: the surprising fact that professionals have played a relatively small part in the story of garden-making. From quite early on the English seem to have concluded that however necessary it might be to employ master builders, surveyors and, as time went on, architects in the construction of their houses, anyone of average intelligence and good taste could design and

plant a garden. Freed of the disciplines of a profession they were ready for any experiment that seemed promising. This passionate interest has produced some of the finest gardens in the world.

The British emerged rather late from the Middle Ages and by the time they were ready to start garden-making in earnest the Italians had already brought the architectural garden to a degree of perfection which precluded further improvement. Naturally ideas were borrowed freely from them, and also from the French and Dutch who had already adapted Italian garden-making principles to their own requirements. The resulting 16th and 17th century gardens were formal and (see illustration overleaf) sometimes elaborate. Examples of them are to be seen at Hampton Court, Chatsworth, Edzell Castle and Pitmedden (reconstructed in the 1950s), the two last in Scotland, as well as some excellent reproductions at Blenheim Castle and at Powerscourt, Co Wicklow, Ireland.

But unlike the French, who stayed at home because their king liked to keep them safely under his eye at court, and the Italians who saw little need to travel since they already possessed the best, the British considered their education complete only after a grand tour across

Europe to see the wonders of Rome.

It was there that landscape, depicted by many artists, revealed itself to them in a new way. Not only was it beautiful, but it also afforded an alternative model for garden-making. It was from this that the English garden-makers invented a new style of their own where the natural beauty of the site was enhanced by planting. They were, in effect, contriving natural landscapes.

The conceptual leap from the formal, elaborate garden, acting as a buffer between house and wild countryside, to an 'improved' natural landscape sweeping right up to the house, still seems astonishing. Early in the 18th century Lord Burlington employed an artist, William Kent, to experiment in a more natural style of garden-making at Chiswick House; and in Yorkshire John Aislabie, in disgrace as a result of the South Sea Bubble financial crisis, consoled himself by making a formal water garden in an entirely informal setting at Studley Royal in the valley occupied by Fountains Abbey.

But the real revolutionary was Lord Carlisle at Castle Howard in north Yorkshire. Having engaged Sir John Vanbrugh to design a baroque palace, and the leading nursery firm of London and Wise to lay out an elaborate parterre to match it, he suddenly set off on an entirely different course. He began to dramatise the Yorkshire landscape with classical buildings, creating lakes and streams that appeared natural and building an elegant bridge, all for no reason other than they contributed to a picture that might have been devised by the landscape painter Claude Lorrain.

Very soon everyone who was anyone was doing much the same; Lord Cobham at Stowe, Colonel Dormer at Rousham, Henry Hoare at Stourhead and many more. By the middle of the century Lancelot (Capability) Brown, who had worked at Stowe, was setting up as a professional landscaper. In the next 35 years he made or altered about 200 gardens. Inevitably he had many imitators.

Classicism gave way to romanticism, with all the excesses of the gothic revival, plus a brief flirtation with Chinese art and architecture. Alton Towers in Staffordshire still shows this development at its maddest, although the immense growth of trees makes it difficult for visitors today to appreciate quite why J.C. Loudon, the Victorian garden writer and designer, should have described the emerging garden as 'in excessively bad taste, or rather, perhaps, as the work of a morbid imagination joined to a command of unlimited resources.'

In the great landscaped parks flowers were banished to the kitchen garden, and it was probably here that gardeners learned to mass them in long borders, as they still do on some old estates, particularly in Scotland at Williamston, Kincorth and Glen App Castle.

It was not until plant lovers at last revolted against this restriction, and declared that gardens should be designed for plants, that borders emerged from their exile among the vegetables and quickly became fashionable. So did terraces with multitudinous beds, the prime purpose of which was to display the vast numbers of half-hardy plants which gardeners were now able to raise in their greatly improved plant houses.

New plants were pouring into Europe from many parts of the world – pelargoniums from the Cape of Good Hope, fuchsias from South America and camellias from China and Japan – and there were no gardeners more eager to grow them than the British. The climate and geology of their islands combined to produce the varied conditions which made it possible to grow an astonishing range of these new introductions. In the mild coastal regions of the west, washed by the waters of the North Atlantic Drift, it was even possible to grow some of the more tender kinds out of doors. Magnificent collections were established in places as far apart as Tresco Abbey in the Isles of Scilly, Inverewe in north-west Scotland and Garinish Island in Bantry Bay, south-west Ireland.

Splendid conifers, many of them from America's north-west, inspired some landowners to plant collections in specially created pinetums; and when rhododendrons began to arrive from the Himalayas woodland gardens were created to give them the shade and shelter they enjoyed.

The interest in new species was so widespread that many garden owners subscribed to plant hunting expeditions, or even went to plant hunting themselves. They were so successful that they soon found themselves with more seedlings than they had room to accommodate. So gardens once again burst their boundaries and spread out into the countryside; not, this time, with the aim of creating idealised landscapes but of providing plants with conditions as much like those of their native habitats as possible.

The exuberant Victorians, having developed Switzerland as a winter playground, stayed on in summer to climb the mountains and were enraptured by the beauty of the alpine flora. Rock gardens, until then considered solely romantic features, took on a new role and were constructed to look like natural outcrops, and to provide the right conditions for the cultivation of rock plants.

The flowery English garden, with its supposed cottage ancestry, originated towards the close of the 19th century as part of the revolt against industrialisation and the return to traditional craftsmanship.

Although there was much talk about being guided by nature the new gardens were as highly organised as any which preceded them. Some were created by Edwin Lutyens assisted by Gertrude Jekyll, others by Harold Peto. One of the most beautiful and best preserved was made by an American amateur, Lawrence Johnston, at Hidcote Manor in the Cotswolds.

But the most popular of all came a little later and was the work of Vita Sackville-West and her husband, Sir Harold Nicolson. At Sissinghurst Castle in Kent they laid out a garden which might have been a text book illustration of the new ideals, summed up by its creator as being the maximum of formality in design combined with a high degree of informality in planting.

For possibly the first time flower-colour and leaf-texture received close attention and there was much discussion about the most felicitous associations of plants. Roses featured in many of these gardens, and although the old varieties were generally preferred, the public ignored these and took happily to the new races of perpetual flowering roses which were first produced in Britain towards the close of the 19th century. There is, as yet, little evidence that the spell of this kind of gardening has been broken.

Pitmedden Castle, Grampian, Scotland. An elegant reconstruction of a 17th century garden

Early formal. The house was nearly always by water, the garden small and intimate, like a courtyard – a protection from the surrounding wild countryside. Gardens were often attached to abbeys. The design was formal geometrical. Plants were grown primarily for their medicinal value or for fruit. Gradually these functional requirements gave way to more aesthetic considerations until this category overlapped with the Baroque. Characteristics were: mazes, labyrinths, gazebos or pavilions; square fishponds; carved wooden statues, often brightly painted; topiary; terraced walks. Flowerbeds became more elaborate, culminating in the 'knot garden' – raised beds made from lines of clipped shrubs, box, thrift or herbs with infillings of coloured earth, gravel, ornamental flowers and shrubs. Plants included mulberry bushes, martagon lilies, hornbeam, rosemary, gillyflowers, lavender and primroses.
Examples: Ham House, Richmond, Surrey; Edzell Castle, Angus, Scotland.

Baroque. Gardens were influenced by the flowering of the Renaissance in France and Italy. There was no longer the need for seclusion, gardens were more flamboyant, like a theatrical set, but still very rigid and formal and of an impressive size. Increased interest in horticulture popularised new species of trees and plants. The first botanic gardens were opened and also the first commercial nurseries. The main characteristics were avenues lined with hedges which fanned out, known as goose-feet or *pattes d'oie*. Beech hedges led the eye on to sculptures, temples and gently-playing fountains and long vistas. Topiary became commonplace but our native yew took the place of box which was very slow growing. Kitchen gardens were walled and separate from the main garden. Elaborate parterres – raised gardens, like embroidery, of plants, shrubs – took the place of knot gardens. There were geometric woods, grottoes and formal lakes.
Examples: Hampton Court, London; Cirencester Park, Gloucestershire.

English landscape. This revolt against the preceding formality was influenced by the 'new thinking' of philosophers, writers and particularly the 17th-century landscape painters, Salvator Rosa, Claude Lorrain and Poussin. Two main elements were involved. One was the 'picturesque' which was wild, rugged and romantic, ornamented with garden buildings. The second was the larger 'idealised' natural landscape. In both cases contours were altered, hills raised, valleys excavated, streams dammed to form lakes, and estate villages moved where they would not impair the view. William Kent was the pioneer designer of the period, followed by 'Capability' Brown and Humphry Repton. Thousands of acres were reclaimed from bog and scrub and turned into parkland. The sense of immense space could be deceptive. Landowners planted trees at their boundaries so that it was difficult to tell where the estate ended.
Examples: Petworth, West Sussex; Stourhead, Wiltshire.

Victorian formal. This marked the return to classical and geometric layouts. It was an eclectic style, fond of mass-produced 'Italian-style' ornaments and reproduction works of art. This period saw the rise of the suburban garden as the mercantile classes became increasingly affluent. They were encouraged by a new breed of writers and designers, like John Loudon and his wife Jane who published endless, comprehensive books for the new garden owners. There were many new discoveries: David Douglas went to America and brought back conifers which became popular with Victorians (Douglas Fir). Robert Fortune brought back plants from Japan and China: anemone, winter jasmine, weigela, bleeding heart, forsythia, primulas. Greenhouses, conservatories, orchids and ferneries became popular. The flowerbeds were elaborate and full of dazzling bedding plants. Lawnmowers took the place of the scythe.
Examples: Ascott, Buckinghamshire; Cliveden, Buckinghamshire.

Robinson/Jekyll. A violent reaction to mid-Victorian formality. Both William Robinson and Gertrude Jekyll loved wild woodland gardens which worked particularly well. in Surrey, hence the so-called 'Surrey School'. The movement coincided with the restoration and rehabilitation of long-neglected smaller country houses, farmhouses and cottages. Generally, elaborate geometrical beds full of half-hardy plants raised in greenhouses gave way to herbaceous plants in plain borders, creating the cottage garden effect. Robinson and Jekyll had great respect for country skills and village craftsmanship. There was a strong sense of colour, a back-to-nature effect, with flowers and foliage mixed together. Jekyll was famous for her grey-leaved plants. But there were a lot of other new plants for her disciples to take advantage of: camellias, magnolias and the old cottage garden plants which would flourish without further care or cost.
Examples: Barrington Court, Somerset; Wisley, Surrey.

20th-century gardens. No one style has yet emerged as representative of our own age but among the large gardens of large houses two are generally reckoned to be pre-eminent – Hidcote and Sissinghurst. The garden at Hidcote, fashioned by architect Major Lawrence Johnston, forms 'rooms' in a variety of colours and styles, each one a perfect garden in itself, with maybe a pool, garden house or other firm feature. Sissinghurst, which follows a similar pattern, was planned by Vita Sackville-West who described it as 'profusion even extravagance and exuberance within the confines of the utmost linear severity'. Sissinghurst is particularly famous for the 'White Garden' which is full of either white or grey plants. The abundance of styles mean that the gardens feature everything from waterfalls to topiary, avenues of trees to miniature cottage gardens, rose gardens to a wilderness for shrubs, in a changing, orderly procession.
Examples: Hidcote Manor, Gloucestershire; Sissinghurst Castle, Kent.

The cottage garden. It isn't as old as you think

The cottage garden is one of the sweet contentments of the countryside, very personal to those who plant and work it, admired and enjoyed by those who don't. It is small and informal, a patchwork glory of flowers, beds and meandering paths. Ramblers and climbers clothe its walls; roses are well-nigh obligatory round the door.

Nothing quite like it exists outside the British Isles and the picturesque face it presents to the world is re-inforced by the world's expectation, as presented on calendars, jig-saw puzzles and the lids of toffee tins, of what it should be.

Its reality is that it works and looks right, making a good marriage with every style of cottage building – cob and thatch, slate and stone, timber-frame, cobble flint. Cottages and their gardens happily accommodate to each other's character. A haphazard confusion of flowers – lupin, poppy, petunia, violet, periwinkle, hollyhock, nasturtiums, shrub roses, pansies – work well when perspectives are foreshortened and views confined.

All these 'cottagey' ingredients make a heady mix and reassuringly suggest a sense of timelessness, hint at days when life was simpler, enhance a feeling of long tradition. Which is all very comforting, save for one thing: the cottage garden as we know it today has no long tradition. It is a comparatively recent phenomenon which owes much to the urban dream of a little place in the country.

Hardly any of the plants mentioned above were introduced in Britain before 1800. Many other characteristic cottage garden subjects had not arrived by then either. The fleshy-leaved sedums did not appear from Japan until 1868.

Climbing roses such as Zéphirine Douhin and Madame Plantier had not been bred. Although the rose was popular long before the 1800s it was transformed by the introduction of remontant forms (those with the ability to bloom more than once in a year) from China at the end of the 18th and beginning of the 19th centuries. Hybrid Tea roses started to appear in the 1860s; the Floribundas came much later – in the 1920s.

Even the blowzy, large fruited gooseberry bush, serving as the cottager's clothes drier on which household cloths sweetened in the sun, did not appear until the 1840s, although the native shrub had been cultivated in English gardens since Tudor times.

Much that grows in the kitchen garden of the cottage is of modern origin. The cabbage patch had no Brussels Sprouts in it prior to the 19th century. Many of its standbys today were the exotic vegetables of yesterday imported from the New World – potatoes, French beans, sweet peppers, tomatoes and cultivated strawberries.

In any case it was not until after the Industrial Revolution that cottage dwellers had either the leisure or means to indulge in anything more ambitious than gardening for the table.

A growing market for food among the new urban populations improved produce prices. Alternative employment in the towns, with factories and mills competing for rural labour, helped improve hours and wages on the land. For the first time cottage dwellers were able to obtain some aesthetic pleasure from the larger plots which they had gained the right to cultivate centuries earlier in the turmoil following the Black Death when there was a critical shortage of rural labour, aggravated by frequent wars.

No one is really sure what the medieval forerunner of the cottage garden looked like. The domestic affairs of peasants did not merit much attention or illustration in manuscripts, and it is unwise to deduce too much from those references which do exist, since artists in those days tended to glamorise.

The plants available to the cottager were limited. One manuscript of 1440 lists just 78. Many of these were herbs which were essential in disguising the off-flavours of badly preserved meat and fish in the winter months. Their other use was medicinal.

The main preoccupation of the cottager was subsistence. Onions, leeks, spinach, cabbage, broad beans, turnips, parsnips, radishes and beetroot were all grown in Britain then. So were native fruits – apples, pears, damsons and plums. Some plots, or part of them, were probably given over to livestock: geese, ducks, hens, a sow and her litter and possibly a cow. Flowers, if grown, were probably planted at random among the vegetables. There were wild flowers in the garden hedge and at the base of trees and it seems likely that they were encouraged for their colour.

Yet it is possible that by 1580 the cottage garden could have grown many of the plants common to cottage gardens today. These plants were either native to the British Isles, introduced by the Romans and later invaders, or arrived with returning crusaders. Some were spin-offs of Europe's trade with the East for silks and spices.

Two hundred years later a vastly greater range of plants was available to gardeners. These came in the wake of the great voyages of discovery, of European settlement in India, Africa and the Americas and a developing sea trade with China and the Far East.

Initially, as rarities, they first graced the gardens of the great houses. But the natural spread of seed and gardeners taking cuttings for themselves took them into the cottage garden. Many of these plants, so common in today's cottage gardens, had never been seen in the British Isles before 1780. Until then hollyhocks were merely the weeds beneath which Moghul princes lost their polo balls. Red hot pokers were still to arrive from South Africa, so were phlox from North America.

Today's typical cottage garden has most of its roots in the 19th century. It was probably the growing middle class, armed with intellectual awareness and possessed of romantic notions, who played a greater role in the development of the cottage garden than the traditional cottage dwellers.

They shared the gentry's enthusiasms for the new plants which collectors were bringing back from all corners of the world. Their desire to outshine each other in the glory of their displays was fuelled further by the hybridising activities of plant breeders as the understanding of plant genetics increased.

Much of this effort was directed towards annual plants and many have changed almost beyond recognition. Popular varieties like petunias and French marigolds grow larger, flower earlier and last longer than their ancestors of a century ago.

It is a process which continues although it is regretted by some who feel that in increasing their showiness, breeders have sacrificed much of their simple cottage garden charm.

Top: Cottage garden and gardeners in the hamlet of Three Cups Corner, East Sussex. The photograph was taken in August
Bottom right: Haphazard glory of a village garden at Castle Combe, Wiltshire
Middle left: Topiary about to jump the wall at Cranham, Gloucestershire
Bottom left: Running water and a riot of shrubs at Lee Bay, north Devon

Alcove. A recess in a wall or hedge, frequently semi-circular in plan, used to house statuary or protect a seat. Such features have existed in gardens since Roman times.

ALCOVE AND KNOT GARDEN

Arbour. A shelter from breeze, sun or drizzle placed so that a fine view of the garden could be admired and solitude preserved. In the Middle Ages arbours were built from trellis, or poles, and tent canvas. More elaborate brick arbours were created by the Tudors. Solid timber and complicated wrought-iron structures came later.

ARBOUR

Belvedere. An open sided lookout commanding an impressive view of both garden and surrounding landscape. This was frequently in the form of a turret raised from a wall or above the roof of the main building.

Bosket. A well defined block of solid woodland planted with similar and uniform trees or shrubs used to provide a background to some sections of the garden and to hide others. Alleys were sometimes cut through them to create vistas; or wider, cleared areas formed outdoor rooms, like natural theatres, in which seats, ponds with fountains and other features were placed.

Bridges. These usually had minimal function but high aesthetic appeal, forming a feature in an open landscape garden, or drawing attention to a section of it. Most architects favoured the Palladian style with the bridge walkway covered by a portico supported on columns.

Cisterns. These large rainwater collecting butts, usually made of lead, often had intricate and attractive surface designs.

GREENHOUSE AND CISTERN

Clair-Voyee. A break in a boundary wall or hedge which gave longer views into the landscape. Sometimes complete lengths of boundary were replaced by elegant, free-standing wrought-iron screens. Simpler forms consist of grills covering perforations in the wall, or 'window' holes cut in hedges.

Conceits. Imaginative or eccentric superfluities, such as bridges over dry land or ponds on hill tops.

CLAIR-VOYEE. HA-HA. CONCEIT AND MAUSOLEUM

Conservatories. These glass structures were used initially to house delicate plants from abroad and were built to provide maximum light. They were increasingly used from the late 18th century onwards.

Dovecote. One of the oldest garden features with its origins in the practicalities of rural self-sufficiency. In the Middle Ages the cotes housed pigeons – up to a thousand or more birds in large ones – whose flesh provided food at the end of winter

DOVECOTE

when other meat was scarce. It was a way of benefitting from the birds which were eating fields crops anyway. Later the dovecote became a decorative feature with Fantails and Tumblers adding to the charm of the country house.

Exedras. Fairly large, semi-circular spaces, created by a

TEMPLE AND EXEDRA

hedge backed by taller trees, usually housing an ornament or statue. Much less intimate than alcoves.

Fish or Stew Ponds. Originally stocked with carp for the kitchen in medieval monasteries and manors. Now they often harbour decorative fish and water lilies.

Follies. Eccentric buildings-towers, pagodas, tumbling ruins – placed to increase the interest of a landscape and satisfy personal whims.

Gazebo. A two-storied garden house with windows on all sides which provided extensive views. Its architecture was often frivolous.

Grottoes. These were built to resemble natural caverns and were either dug into earth banks, excavated into rock faces or constructed in stone and covered with a mound of earth. They were often lined with shells and came to house zoological and geological collections in the 18th and 19th century. In summer they provided a cool halt during a warm walk.

GROTTO

Ha-Ha. A division between open parkland and garden. It could not be seen from the garden and prevented game and cattle from entering the garden area. It consisted of a wide ditch with a vertical wall on the garden side and a gentle slope up to ground level on the park side. Thus viewed from afar the Ha-Ha appeared to be no more than a slight undulation in the ground.

Ice House. A building with a well drained, underground chamber which was packed with snow in winter and remained very cold throughout the summer, permitting iced sorbets and drinks to be served in hot weather. To improve insulation it was surrounded by trees or tall shrubs and remained in shadow all day.

FOLLY AND MOUND

Features of the grand garden Many of the architectural features of the grand English garden reflect the elegant and leisured style of 18th century country house social life. Making a circuit of the grounds, or an expedition to one part of them, either

Knot Garden. This consisted of small, low-level hedges of clipped shrubs, such as box or yew, planted in various patterns. Sometimes, by clever arrangement and plant choice, the designs appeared to be formed from ribbons of plants tied into knots. The ground between was filled with ornamental flowers, coloured earths, gravels and crushed rock or even coal dust. These rock infillings add to the intricacy of the design and remain decorative during winter months. Knot gardens were usually surrounded by walls or hedges and were quite small.

Mausoleum. An impressive family tomb, frequently in the form of a classical temple, housing bronze or stone sarcophagi, or memorials to ancestors, favourite horses or hounds. Like many features of the great gardens they became popular during the 18th century, and were ideas which were imported by the gentry after having seen them during the Grand Tour.

Maze or Labyrinth. This was a complex network of paths, divided by wall-like hedges to form a labyrinth. It often led to a central arbour. In a true labyrinth the hedges were arched over the path to form a tunnel.

MAZE

Mount. A relic of the watch tower in the form of an artificially created mound providing a prospect of the world both within and without the walls of the park.

Obelisks and Columns. A popular and spectacular way of commemorating victories or defeats.

Orangerie. This was the first form of shelter provided for exotic plants in winter months. Architectural style and masonry was much more prominent than in the later glasshouse. They have existed since Tudor times. The first plants they protected were pruned orange

ORANGERIE

trees grown in wooden tubs which were put out to line paths and form groves in summer. In winter they were heated and their windows were sometimes covered with wooden boards.

Parterres. In the 17th century the parterre replaced the more intimate 16th century knot garden. This was much larger, more formally arranged and open to view from one facade of the house. Clipped grass, flowers and sometimes even water basins, separated the uniform designs indicated by the low clipped hedges.

PARTERRE

Patte D'Oie. A series of paths radiating fanwise like the toes of a goose from a single point.

Pavilion. This was the largest of garden houses, designed to provide comfortable alternative accommodation during the day, and occasionally at night, for

PAVILION

householders seeking a change of surroundings in an epoch when the difficulties of travel kept people at home much more.

Pergola. A fanciful development of the arbour built as a support for vines, trained fruit trees and roses. Extended into covered, or partially covered, walkways they were simply constructed in wooden trellis work. But more sophisticated pergolas combined brick or stone columns and timbers.

PERGOLA AND SUNKEN GARDEN

Topiary. The pruning of trees and shrubs into various shapes has attracted gardeners since Roman times. Yew and box are favourite subjects for sculpting geometric cones, pyramids, cubes, balls, or free forms resembling animals, ogres, men and gods.

TOPIARY

Pleached Alley. A path lined with trees which have been

pruned and trained to develop in a single direction to resemble a layered hedge.

PLEACHED ALLEY

Sunken Garden. An area at a lower level than the surrounding garden which gives a variety of contour. The sunken garden concentrated attention on the plants growing there, separating them from plantings in the rest of the garden. They were often sheltered so the blooms of favourite plants like roses kept longer.

Terrace. This was a level space skirting the house and acting as an open-air room to ease the transition from house to garden. Sometimes raised terraces created alongside boundary walls provided a change in perspective; and also gave a

TERRACE AND FISH POND

hanging garden effect, it being possible to walk at the level of the crowns of small trees planted alongside. Terraces were usually bordered by decorative balustrades of elegant masonry and ingenious and beautiful access stairways.

Temple. This was designed to be seen from afar, enhancing the classical aspects of the landscape. It was sometimes used as a mausoleum.

Trellis. Trellis was a simple interlaced diagonal or rectangular arrangement of thin wooden laths forming screens for climbing plants.

walking, riding or driving in a chaise, played a large part in the activities of the great houses. Walks and circuits were designed to include all manner of diversions: monuments and mausoleums, pavilions, arbours and gazebos, terraces and temples

Chapter Nine
Seasons in the Countryside

The British climate has an undeservedly bad reputation. It is hardly ever unbearably hot, seldom numbingly cold. Rain is distributed throughout the year and falls mostly gently with the characteristic lushness seen here near Newtown, Powys. Not for nothing did the Apollo 11 astronauts on their way to the moon in 1969 comment upon how green the British Isles seemed when viewed from space. It is the moderation of the British climate which has helped to give the countryside its distinctive qualities through the seasons

Forecast: a bright clear day as the cumulus and stratocumulus cloud begin to dissipate over the Lake District *Forecast: a summer's day*

The origins and characteristics of the British Isles climate

The British Isles do not have a climate dominated by reliable or immutable seasons such as the Indian monsoon or Canadian winter. Instead the weather is so unpredictable that Midsummer's Day can be colder than Christmas Day. Almost every year new climatic records are set as the weather varies, apparently dramatically, from day to day and year to year; the drought of 1976 being followed barely two years later by the long hard winter of 1978–9.

Yet over a 20-year period it is still possible to make broad generalisations about the British climate and to that extent one must distinguish between the terms 'climate' and 'weather'. It is the actual day-to-day weather over a long period that establishes an overall climate – and paradoxically it is the moderation and limited variation which in world terms are its prime characteristics.

A few comparisons will serve to illustrate its moderation. First, temperatures. Annual averages are only part of the story. Illinois in the USA and Kazakhstan in southern USSR have similar average temperatures to England, but they have much colder winters and hotter summers. It is when *variations* in temperature are considered that the special features of the British climate become apparent.

In a typical year the lowest temperature recorded anywhere in Britain will be about −18 degrees Centigrade (0° Fahrenheit) and the highest around 30°C (85°F). Yet the overall range of a typical year in north-east Siberia would be $1\frac{1}{2}$ times this maximum range for the whole of Britain. Throughout most of temperate Europe and North America the range of temperatures exceeds that of the British Isles.

Second, rain. The British climate is usually regarded as wet. Yet irrigation is often necessary for agricultural crops in the east and south-east of England, and London with 24in (61cm) of rain a year gets less than Rome or Nice. The average for England as a whole is 33in (84cm), is far less than New York's rainfall, while the average figure for Wales, Scotland and Ireland of about 50in (127cm) is roughly that of Sydney, Australia.

The catch, of course, is that rain in the British Isles falls comparatively lightly throughout the year. This means more wet weather and less sunshine. Nice, for example, has about 100 'rain days' (with a fall of a millimetre or more) in a year. Much of Britain has twice as many. But while the frequent cloudiness and rain may disappoint many holidaymakers it does not affect the gentleness of the British climate and the well-dispersed rainfall helps to make the countryside the glory that it is.

In one respect, however, the climate in many parts of Britain is not so moderate; its windiness. Around the coasts, particularly on the Atlantic seaboard, it is windy by any standards. One effect of the recurrent gales is obvious to the most casual observer even as far south as Cornwall. In places exposed to the full force of the winds from the sea, trees survive only in sheltered valleys or by cowering close to the ground, seeming to cringe at the memory of the wind on even the stillest day.

Friction with the ground always saps the strength of the wind so that inland Britain is not particularly windy. But on higher ground in Scotland and Northern England farmers have still found it necessary to counteract the wind by planting 'shelter belts' like the long strips of beech and pine that are such a feature of the Border landscape. And opposition to the destruction of so many hedges (see Chapter 10) is based partly on their value as wind breaks to protect crops and soil from wind erosion.

Latitude is a basic factor in shaping any climate since it largely determines the hours of sunshine and potential temperature range. But it is above all the Atlantic Ocean which gives the British climate its special characteristics. The temperature of the sea fluctuates with the seasons far less than that of the land, so that unless a major variation of the ocean currents were to occur – as has happened in colder centuries in the past – the sea is

Snowshill in the Cotswolds. Cumulus cloud sails across a blue sky with a chance of showers later in the day

a permanent force for moderation. Winds crossing water are affected by its temperature surprisingly quickly. A bitter wind from the Arctic may warm up 20 degrees (F) or so in a 24-hour journey from Iceland. Yet in summer air from the east, which is causing a heat wave in Germany, may arrive at the eastern coastline 10 degrees cooler as a result of its short passage across the North Sea.

Any large body of water has a moderating influence on climate, but in the North Atlantic there is the Gulf Stream as well. This derives its warmth from its origins as a westward moving current driven by the trade winds across the equatorial regions of the Atlantic Ocean. When it runs up against the land mass of South America this current splits into two parts, flowing north and south along the coast. The 'nose' of Brazil sends the greater part north where the waters pile up in the Gulf of Mexico. They emerge travelling north-east, again helped by the prevailing south-westerly winds towards Britain.

The warm waters of the North Atlantic Drift, as this part of the Gulf Stream is called, bring to the British Isles a climate that is remarkably mild for their latitude. Cornwall and County Kerry have average temperatures about 5.5°C (10°F) higher than the average for their latitudes, 50–52°N.

This is the reason why palm trees survive in parts of Scotland that are as far

north as Labrador, and the seas round Britain provide some of the warmest bathing in Europe north of the Mediterranean. The effects of the North Atlantic Drift are most marked in winter, when temperatures on the west coast of these islands are appreciably higher than those on the east coast.

A third great Atlantic influence on the British climate is the ocean's role as a prolific breeding ground for depressions. These depressions or cyclones are areas of low pressure which, with their cold and warm fronts, so dominate the weather charts which appear on television and in many newspapers. The weather associated with cyclones is broadly the opposite of that brought by anticyclones or areas of high pressure. In the simplest terms these are the characteristics and origins of these two systems:

Cyclones or depressions are areas of low pressure formed by the meeting of two or more air masses. When the warm air of one air mass meets the cold air of another their unequal characteristics lead to instability and the formation of cyclones with the original air masses over-running and undercutting each other at warm and cold fronts so that the lesser density of the warmer air brings this air mass to overlie the denser, colder air. These cyclones are in fact great circular storms, often a thousand miles or more across, which are driven by the prevailing westerly or south-westerly

wind in the upper air across the Atlantic to or near Britain. The actual weather caused by these cyclones varies even within the same cyclone, as illustrated overleaf. But it is these continually passing storms that are responsible for some of the prime characteristics of the British climate: the windiness of the coasts; the changeability of the weather from day to day; and the rain, since the winds are laden with moisture after travelling for thousands of miles over the Atlantic.

Anticyclones are areas of high pressure in which the air is stagnant or moving only slowly (in a clockwise direction). They are not the predominant feature of the British climate, but their influence is very strong since they 'steer' the depressions. There is also quite a high frequency of days in all seasons when anticyclones extend close to and partly over the British Isles. Whatever the season anticyclones bring settled weather for they are slow to develop, usually slow moving and slow to disperse. In summer this means high temperatures with usually minimal wind or clouds; in winter they can bring sharp frosts and persistent mists or fog. A strongly developing anticyclone will cause depressions either to break up or to change direction in order to avoid it.

The British climate is thus shaped by not only latitude but also this threefold effect of proximity to the Atlantic Ocean. But the weather in any one place within

Britain will be determined by other factors, notably height above sea level and longitude or, more specifically, distance from the continent.

Mountains have particularly important effects on local climate, notably on rainfall but also temperature. In parts of Snowdonia, the Lake District and Western Scotland the annual rainfall is around 200in (508cm), locally even more. Not much by world standards – at Cherrapunji, in the mountains of Assam, it can rain more than 1000in (2540cm) a year – but as much as ten times more than the driest parts of south-east England. Since most rain-bearing depressions arrive from the Atlantic, and most of Britain's mountains are in the west, this leads to a great drop in rainfall totals from west to east with inevitable consequences for agriculture.

There is also a natural decrease in temperatures as one goes further north. Coupled with the greater windiness of the north this accounts for the markedly more barren appearance of northern Scotland compared with, say, south-west England. More subtle, though, is the trend to greater 'continentality' from west to east. Continental climates are characterised by more extreme conditions, and one index of continentality is the difference between average temperatures in January and July. In south-east England, the part of the British Isles most

remote from oceanic influences, this is twice as great as in the Western Isles, where there may be little to choose between a mild day in the middle of winter and a bad one in high summer.

Ireland is the first landmass that many depressions encounter and rainfall is heavy on the western mountains. The number of rainy days varies from one in two in the east of Ireland to two in three in the west. In the inland districts sheltered by the mountains of Kerry, frosts are quite frequent though they seldom last as long as in England or Scotland. Snow is rare too, because of the warming influence of the North Atlantic Drift. Tree growth on exposed coasts is sparse but crops grow with luxuriance behind high walls and in the valleys, especially at Killarney, where there is rich and constant tree and plant growth.

Many factors, both global and local, thus combine to help shape the countryside – as explained alongside. They will continue to do so for the climate is continuously changing. There was, for instance, a Little Ice Age which was at its height in the 17th century when temperatures were on average a degree or so colder than today. There was a marked warming in the first 40 years of this century, although since about 1940 it has got a little colder.

Nobody really knows what will happen next. Climatic changes are imper-

ceptible in the short-term because of the much more prominent differences from one year to the next. Yet the implications of long-term changes are profound, particularly for agriculture if the growing season is curtailed, but also for the general water supply. There is now general agreement among climatologists that the climate over the last 30 years has got colder and that this 'cooling' is still continuing. Regions north of 50°N and especially the Arctic show the most significant changes. But the majority of climatologists are more worried by the possibility of a warming of the world climate which could shift crop belts and desert zones further north while raising sea levels with sometimes devastating effects as ice-caps melt.

One school of thought predicts as much as a 10 to 20°F warming over the next century simply as a result of the additional carbon dioxide man is adding to the atmosphere by burning fossil fuels. Others argue that this threat is unproven and claim that a one per cent increase in cloudiness would cancel out all the effects of extra carbon dioxide. It is an important but complex debate. And it is a fair bet that in the year 2000 climatologists will still be arguing about it, while as far as everyone else is concerned the British climate at least will be much the same as it always was: mild, damp and changeable.

Anatomy of a Depression

These illustrations (right) show how, and why, weather varies within an area covered by a depression, Air moves anticlockwise within a depression with 'fronts' forming between the masses of Tropical and Polar air of which the depression (or cyclone) is composed. At the warm front the Tropical air overrides Polar air whereas the cold front occurs where Polar air undercuts the Tropical air. An 'occluded' front occurs when a cold front 'overtakes' a warm front. Temperatures usually rise sharply at the warm front and fall at the cold front. Rainfall patterns are also different being more prolonged at the warm front although topographical features can cause considerable variation over land. Between the warm and cold fronts, particularly in the 'narrower' part of the warm sector, low clouds and drizzle are common. The weather associated with an occluded front is more or less a combination of the pre-warm frontal and post cold frontal weather, but sometimes heavy rain and thunderstorms.

| Winds in the warm air | Rain or snow area | ▲▲ Cold front | ▲■ Occluded front |
| Winds in the cold air | Cloud cover | ■■ Warm front | → Wind direction |

Cold air from the north overlaps warmer air from the south (top left) to cause warm and cold fronts (top centre) and finally an occluded front (top right). The weather associated with these fronts on a line from A to B is shown above

Source: Climate: present, past and future by H. H. Lamb. NB: maps should be inverted for southern hemisphere where cold air comes from south

How climate shapes the landscape

The effects of climate upon the landscape are both superficial and profound. It is the rain, day after day, month after month, which gives so much of the British Isles the green colour that is so vivid to foreigners. And it was the climate along with geology which helped to shape patterns of agriculture and settlement. One yardstick of climatic differences within Britain is the 'growing season' for plants. This is affected by both the north-south and west-east differences described earlier in this chapter (see map below).

It is in the mountains that the most striking effects of climate on landscape can be seen. One is the 'tree line'. There has been so much interference by man that it is difficult to find a true natural tree line in Britain, but it can still be seen where the Rothiemurchus forest struggles up to about 2000ft (610m) near Aviemore in north-eastern Scotland. This is about the limit anywhere in Britain, and in many places trees find it difficult to survive above 1500ft (457m) because of the wind. Considering the mildness of the climate the natural tree line is surprisingly low. In central Norway, for example, where the climate is much more severe, it is some 1500ft (457m) higher. Paradoxically it is the moderation of our climate that is responsible. Winter temperatures may be

(Source: Accumulated temperature maps of the British Isles, S. Gregory, 1954)

Key:
- 9 to 12
- 7 and 8
- 5 and 6
- No more than 4

How the growing season for plants varies within the British Isles. The length of this season is defined by the number of months (above) with a mean temperature above 6°C (42·8°F). Even within these four broad categories the length of the season will differ not only from year to year but also in intensity or range of temperatures. Topographical conditions, such as frost hollows or hilltops, also cause marked local divergences

Cumulus cloud developing over the hills near Troutbeck, Cumbria – see diagrams below

higher than in Norway, but lower summer temperatures make the growing season shorter.

At a height of 1800ft (549m), with temperatures on average 3–4°C (6–7°F) lower than at sea level, the growing season is some months shorter than in the lowlands, and this sets a limit on the greatest single influence on the making of the British landscape: human cultivation. Above 1800ft (549m) there are no crops, only very limited pasture for grazing sheep. Altitude even determines the times at which lambs are born, since this is timed to coincide with the renewed growth of the grass in spring. On the highest farms there may be no lambs until May, lower down they appear months earlier.

In some parts of the country – Dartmoor is an example – rainfall as well as temperature helps to fix the upper limits for agriculture. The higher ground is only workable if it has good natural drainage, artificial drainage being uneconomic. Therefore it may be the better drained side of a valley rather than the one facing south which is farmed.

The high rainfall of the uplands also helps to determine their character beyond the limits of agriculture. Where the underlying rocks are impervious to water, as they are over much of upland Britain and Ireland, peat bogs form on which few plants can survive. Even heather, a typical moorland plant, can be ousted here. Cotton grass is one of the few species that thrives. Yet a few

miles from the desolate tundra-like peat bogs of the Pennines, in the lowlands where the climate is warmer, drier and less windy and the soil fertile, delicate exotics are cultivated by gardeners. Like the geological landscape of Britain the climate is on the whole gentle, but exceptionally varied, providing sharp contrasts in a comparatively small area.

Cold air rises rapidly to cross hills or because of ground heating. Showers occur on upslopes. These can be heavy on the steeper slopes and near the tops of hills. Clouds disperse as descending air warms, though some local cloud can remain as a result of ground heating

Warm air also rises to cross hills but warm air masses aloft allow rising air currents less buoyancy. Only drizzle and fine rain fall, though this may be copious near the tops. Clouds disperse on lee side. See under 'Rain', p 211

Red sky at night . . .

There are dozens of proverbs for predicting the weather – hours, days, and even months ahead. Are they the distilled wisdom of centuries of shrewd weather observation, or merely old wives' tales? Here and there the old sayings are undoubtedly sound metereological observations.

'When clouds appear like rocks and towers, the earth's refreshed by frequent showers', for example, contains an accurate description of typical shower clouds. 'A northern *haar* brings fine weather from afar' is also often true: a *haar* (a sea mist on the North Sea coast of Scotland and northern England) is frequently a result of anticyclonic conditions, and if the mist clears a lovely day can follow.

'Mackerel sky, not long dry' also has some scientific basis. A striped 'mackerel' sky is often caused by ripples in the high level cloud sheet associated with an advancing front. Still higher-level veils of cloud ahead of a warm front can produce the halo round the moon which is popularly supposed to mean that rain is on the way.

'Red sky in the morning, shepherd's warning, red sky at night, sailor's delight' is more doubtful. It might have some justification in the fact that a red sky can be a result of the haze produced by good weather, anticyclonic conditions. Most of our bad weather comes from the west, where the sun sets, so a red sky at night may be a sign that there is nothing nasty in the offing. A red sky in the morning – to the east – provides no such assurance, though there is no particular reason why it should be a warning.

There could also be a grain of truth in such sayings as 'If Candlemas day (February 2) be fair and bright winter will have another fight, if Candlemas day be clouds and rain winter be gone and will not come again'. A mild anticyclonic break early in February often does develop later in the month to give a spell of cold weather, often when the same anticyclone moves further north and brings easterly winds to Britain.

Similarly the belief that a fine St. Swithin's day (July 15) means that the rest of the summer will be fine, and vice versa, is supported by the fact that summers do tend to settle into a pattern around the middle of July. So the weather around St. Swithin's day, though not necessarily on it, can provide a hint of what is to come.

The idea behind 'For every fog in March there'll be a frost in May' has actually been investigated by the British Meteorological Office and found to have some foundation in fact. Some professional meteorologists also think there is a connection between the phase of the moon and the weather, as in the saying 'The moon and the weather change together'.

Traditional weather lore often uses the state of trees and other plants to predict whole seasons ahead. A good show of holly berries, for example, is supposed to indicate a hard winter on the way. In 'Oak before the ash, we shall have a splash; ash before the oak, we shall have a soak' the time the oak and ash come into leaf is meant to show what the coming summer will be like. Yet another is 'Onion skin very thin, mild winter coming in. Onion skin thick and tough, coming winter cold and rough'.

It is just possible that there is a connection between the weather at different times of year which would marginally save such sayings from being so many old wives' tales. The number of holly berries, for example, might be due to a wet spring and wet springs might tend to be followed by cold winters. But the numerous holly berries during the run of exceptionally mild winters in the mid-1970s did not inspire confidence in their value in weather prediction.

Country weather lore, in fact, often has something in it, but not much. It is a rash farmer who plans his harvest around the weather on St. Swithin's day, and a rash holidaymaker who sets out for the coast believing that 'rain before seven' really would mean 'fine before eleven'.

The differing climatic worlds of Dartmoor and Torbay

Climatic differences, and especially their relationship to altitude, play an integral part in shaping the scenic contrasts of the British Isles. This can be seen in microcosm in the contrast between Torbay – and Dartmoor in Devon: a journey of around 25 miles (40km) from lush subtropical vegetation on the coastal lowlands to sub-arctic species on the uplands.

At Torre Abbey gardens exotic species can be observed in both the open and the palm houses. Torbay is sheltered from all but the severest winters and so it can support a wide range of sub-tropical vegetation. The most popular exotics are Eucalyptus and Acacias as well as the well-known palms. An interesting local

tree is the Evergreen Oak. (Even in Torbay, however, cold spells can occur and the winter of 1978–9 inflicted considerable damage.)

The road from Torbay to Dartmoor via Paignton and Totnes soon shows how vegetation deteriorates with rising altitude and distance from the sheltered coastline. An intermediate stage can be seen at Shinners Bridge. Looking north the mixed landscape of arable and pastoral farming, interspersed with a mixture of deciduous and coniferous woodland, reflects the normal progression of land use with increasing height from arable to pasture to woodland.

The road to New Bridge via Buckfastleigh and Ashburton travels upwards through first pasture and meadowland, and then woodland, before coming to the boundary of upland Dartmoor close to where it crosses the River Dart at New Bridge. Before the woodland gives way to the lower moorland vegetation of gorse and bracken it becomes poorer and thinner with the native birch, oak and hazel replacing the more luxuriant species found nearer the coast. But the decline is not solely due to altitude: the transition from the more fertile soil near the coast to the poor acid granites of Dartmoor is also a factor.

The drive from New Bridge to Princetown via Dartmeet and Two Bridges reveals not only the effect of altitude, but also the effect of local drainage conditions and man's attempt to modify the bleak Dartmoor climate. On the most exposed and wet sites only very poor vegetation can survive, but on the sheltered side of hills, or the lee side of shelter belts, or on freely drained sites, rich heather moorland or even cultivated fields can be seen.

Thus this short journey of such diverse vegetation illustrates very dramatically how patterns of agriculture and settlement can differ radically with very minor changes of climate. A slight deterioration would mean the elimination of all exotic species and much arable farming; a slight improvement could mean the reclamation of even upland tracts of Dartmoor to farmland.

Ten common phenomena of the climate in the British Isles

Cloud. The cooling of the air generally causes some of the water vapour in it to condense into a cloud of tiny droplets of water (or crystals of ice) which remain suspended in the air. Dust in the atmosphere plays a part in this process since the droplets of water tend to condense around a nucleus of solid matter. Clouds differ in appearance because they are formed in different ways – by rising air currents, cyclones or a combination of the two, for instance.

Dew. When the land cools at night this often causes condensation in the form of dew on soil or grass. When the point at which dew forms is below freezing point, the result is hoar frost.

Fog. Temperatures normally fall as altitude rises but the position is reversed on calm, clear nights. One consequence of this inversion of temperature, if the air is moist enough, is fog. Fog often forms first at valley bottoms where temperature inversion is most marked – see 'Frost hollows' below. Other places where fog forms first are over damp places such as marshes, wet fields and woodlands and where man adds moisture to the air, as in the exhausts of motor traffic. Occasionally, in still conditions, fog forms just along the roads or is thickest there. (See also: Sea Mists.)

Frost hollows. This is also a consequence of the inversion of temperature which occurs on calm, clear nights where hills surround substantial valleys. Cold air flows down the hillside during the night to accumulate at the valley bottom. As the air warms after dawn it rises and often mixes with cold air to form fog or low cloud. The effect of frost hollows on the landscape can be seen in areas like Kent and Worcestershire where orchards stick to valley sides where frost damage to the blossoms is less likely.

Rain. The droplets of water that make up clouds can unite to form larger drops which fall as rain (or, in the case of ice crystals, grow to form snowflakes). Rain can be caused in a number of ways. Cyclonic rain is produced by the low-pressure systems known as depressions described earlier; convection or convective rain is caused by warm moist air rising over hot ground; and relief rain occurs when damp air rises because of hills. Illustrations on page 209 show the different effects of warm and cold air passing over hills or mountains such as the Pennines.

As atmospheric pressure decreases with height, the air is rapidly cooled by expansion during its ascent. Whether the ascent of the air has been assisted by the wind being forced to rise over a ridge of hills or merely by the air coming over particularly hot land surfaces, the air can be cooled sufficiently by its ascent to produce a sharp, although usually short-lived, shower of rain or snow. Since temperatures of land surfaces rise during the day, showers are most likely to be frequent and heavy from midday onwards over strongly-heated plains and windward slopes or summits of hilly areas. In coastal areas they are likely to be much fewer, or not to occur at all, in the warm season. But in winter, when the sea is warmer than the land, shower activity is more frequent at sea or near the coast and rare inland.

Rainbow. This can be seen only when it is both sunny and wet. Rainbows are produced by the refraction and internal reflection of sunlight in minute droplets of water in the air.

Sea breezes. At sea level itself the sea is the major climatic influence: it is generally warmer than the land in the winter, and cooler in the summer. On warm summer days, therefore, as the land heats up and air begins to rise, cooler air from over the sea is sucked in to replace it, leading to sea breezes and often clear blue skies on the coast. Inland the moisture content of the sea breeze supplies the cloud development in the rising convection currents over the heated land, and sometimes plays an essential part in the thunderstorms that develop inland.

Sea mist. Fog can be caused by the mixing of warm and cold air and one instance of this breaks the general rule of warmth and sunshine at the seaside. The sea mist or haar is found most often on the east coast of England and Scotland in the early summer months when warm air from the continent travelling over the cold North Sea has been cooled so much that low cloud or fog is produced. As this air travels inland however, the warmer ground heats it up so that unbroken sunshine can then occur within 10 miles (16km) of the coast.

Thunderstorms. These are often violent over hills and mountains, but are probably most frequent and violent near rivers and lakes which ensure their moisture supply. Evaporation of moisture from the surface plays an important part in maintaining the essential moisture supply, the electrical charges being produced in the splitting of large raindrops in violently rising currents of air. Sometimes thunder and lightning are accompanied by hailstones, formed when raindrops are carried by a powerful updraught to levels where the air temperature is well below freezing point. Thunderstorms are a type of convection rainfall (see above) which occurs quite often in the British Isles, particularly in the summer, but which are more common in warmer climatic zones.

Winds. These have both global and local causes. Globally there are the great air masses and the depressions already described. Locally there are not only sea breezes but mountain and valley breezes which develop under much the same conditions. Cold mountain air descends into the valleys and plains during the night but in the daytime, since the mountains are first to be heated by the sun, warm air there rises causing a wind to blow from the valleys and plains towards the mountains.

Whatever the source or cause of a wind the recognised scale of measuring wind strength is the Beaufort Scale (below).

Beaufort Scale	Description	Speed metres per second	Observations
0	Calm	0–0.3	Smoke goes straight up
1	Light air	0.3–1.5	Drifting smoke; vanes still
2	Light breeze	1.6–3.3	Rustling leaves
3	Gentle breeze	3.4–5.4	Leaves and small twigs move
4	Moderate breeze	5.5–7.9	Small branches move; dust raised
5	Fresh breeze	8.0–10.7	Small trees sway
6	Strong breeze	10.8–13.8	Large branches move; singing telephone wires
7	Moderate gale	13.9–17.1	Whole trees in motion
8	Fresh gale	17.2–20.7	Walking difficult; whole trees sway
9	Strong gale	20.8–24.4	Chimney pots broken
10	Whole gale	24.5–28.4	Trees uprooted; much damage
11	Storm	28.5–33 5	Widespread damage
12	Hurricane*	over 33.5	Whole area laid waste

* Hurricanes are also known as typhoons, particularly in the Far East. They are both a consequence of cyclones which are more violent in tropical than temperature latitudes.

JANUARY

FEBRUARY

MAY

JUNE

SEPTEMBER

OCTOBER

This is one man's countryside, photographed each month for a year. It records not merely the passage of the seasons but less happily the march of electricity pylons across the landscape. The view looks north-west, from a height of about 800ft (244m) along the valley of the River Barle. At the very centre of the view, nestling between round-shouldered hills, is the Exmoor village of Dulverton, $3\frac{1}{2}$ miles (5.6km) away. The skyline, seven miles (11km) distant is Winsford Hill, maximum elevation

1275ft (389m) and true Exmoor.

If the man-made change to this particular view in the form of the pylons was the most enduring change that occurred in the 12 months, the changes wrought by the passage of the seasons were nonetheless dramatic. They were also unique for although every year people say that spring or summer is 'late' or 'early' there is never any fixed point when the four seasons begin or end.

They vary not only from year to year but also within Britain from area to area

in the same year. Although spring comes first to the south-west – because this is the area that benefits most from the warming effects of the North Atlantic Drift – the arrival of spring and the length of each season is closely related to the topographical features such as height above sea level, sheltered valleys and south-facing slopes. Even light sandy soils can make a local climate warmer.

If the seasons themselves are variable, so is the weather within each season. But here are the causes of the weather that is most characteristic of each season.

Spring. The land begins to get warmer than the surrounding sea so that rain starts to penetrate further inland to fall as April showers. Marked changes of temperature may occur with cold Polar airstreams dominant in some years giving late frosts and snow.

Summer. The best weather generally comes from a northwards extension of the Azores anticyclone. The combination of high pressure over the British Isles and light, warm and dry winds from the continent can produce a heatwave.

Autumn. From late August onwards the Azores 'high' becomes more variable in its behaviour and commonly sends off-shoots over Britain and Europe in September and early October. Ultimately an anticyclone establishes itself over Siberia and starts to intensify. This, in simplified terms, tends to bring the track of Atlantic depressions further south to produce autumn gales.

Winter. Sometimes British winters are continuously mild with a strong anti-cyclone near the Azores steering mild Atlantic air over the British Isles or an anticyclone over Eastern Europe steering southerly winds towards Britain. But the combination of high pressure over Scandinavia and a cyclone or low in the English Channel produces bitterly cold winds from the East. And where these meet moisture-laden air coming with a depression from the Atlantic, the result is snow. Similarly anticyclones over Greenland and Iceland send cold Arctic air towards the British Isles from the North.

Wildlife in the winter countryside

The inter-dependent worlds of nature are illustrated well by what can be observed – and not observed – during winter. It is a time of low sun and short days: in London the angle of the sun above the horizon at noon on December 21 is just 15° compared with 62° on June 21 and the day 7 hours 50 minutes long compared with 16 hours and 35 minutes.

The low sun and short days mean less energy for the plants and so less green leaf. Most woody plants shed their leaves while other plants die down to rootstock or underground tuber. Many survive the winter as seeds. And it is not only a matter of energy; drought can be a problem when water is locked up as ice in frozen soil. So the plants that retain their leaves tend to be those with thick, impervious skins such as pine, holly or ivy.

With leaves gone, the trees reveal their skeletons of trunk and branches. Each is distinctive. For instance, the ash, which is often the commonest field tree now that so many elms are dead, has the twigs of the bottom branches twisting upward at the end. Tree twigs with their late winter buds can also be as recognisable as leaves. Bark can be equally distinctive.

Without much plant life, insect life is also scarce. One exception is the winter moth which flies in December. The peacock butterfly and a few others hibernate, hidden in cracks in trees or in garden sheds; other butterflies pass the winter in the pupa stage. Many insects survive as eggs, aphids for example. Only the queen wasp survives, hibernating. Bees (Honey queen and workers) stay in the nest, living off honey stocks. Snails seal off their shells, and often congregate in groups. Communal winter dens of dormant, entwined adders have also sometimes been found. Frogs rest in the mud of the pond, while toads use holes in the soil. The danger to them all is a long, cold, snowless winter. Snow itself insulates – since it is mainly air (a foot of snow melts to an inch of water), and therefore protects the waiting life below.

Apart from the robin's sad little winter soliloquy, few birds sing. Natural food becomes scarce, and is even harder to find during a cold snap. This is the time for titbits of food. The greater the variety you put out, the more species you are likely to attract. The most regular visitors are robins, blue tits and great tits, starlings, blackbirds, song thrushes, hedge sparrows, chaffinches and greenfinches. But sometimes less common species such as siskins and marsh tits turn

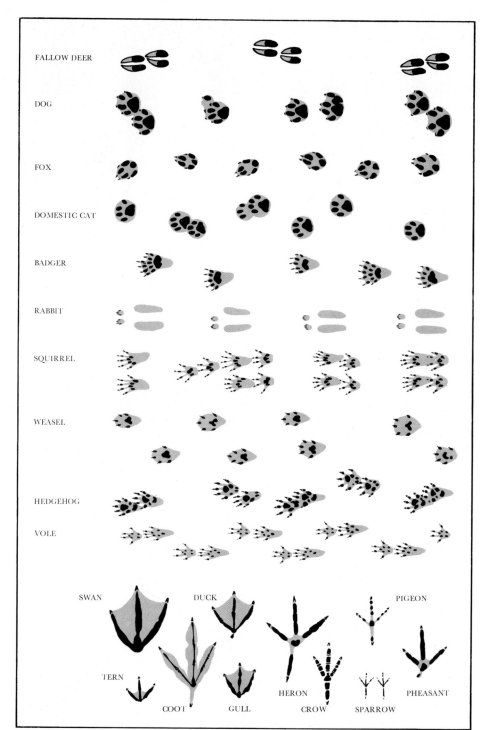

Animal and bird tracks in the snow: size and shape are the basis of identification

up, and in the extreme south and west of Britain you may even see a blackcap. This distinctive warbler is not rare but it is essentially a spring and summer visitor. However, some blackcaps have taken to over-wintering in the British Isles. Species such as starlings and hedge sparrows will peck happily at food put out on the lawn, but the acrobatic tits prefer hanging feeders topped up with nuts, while the robin and chaffinch are best served from a bird table.

Without plant or insect food, many birds leave Britain during the winter in search of warmer climates. But others, on the same quest, migrate to Britain – the

Greenland white-fronted geese that winter on the marshes around Wexford Harbour in Ireland and the dark-bellied Brent geese that fly into Essex from Siberia, for instance. Still more birds use Britain as a staging post in longer journeys while the behaviour of residents also changes, as described in Chapter Four.

Enough birds remain in the British Isles and enough large animals remain active to produce firm evidence of their existence in tracks across the snow. A thin layer of fine dry snow takes the best impression, though details fade and the tracks look larger as the edges melt. Tracks can also be found in the mud alongside a stream or on any soft ground where the minimal winter vegetation allows prints to be seen easily.

Even without a covering of snow the ploughed and bare fields can tell a story. Ploughing itself can bring to the surface scraps of tile, pottery and animal bone to indicate sites of former settlements. On pastureland lack of vegetation means that the ridge and furrow patterns of old strip farming can be seen more clearly, although snow also reveals these lines with great clarity. For those with the eyes to see the winter is alive with interest.

Walking in winter

Before you step out in winter remember that the landscape which has the beauty to entice also has the power to deceive and the power to kill. Even a gentle afternoon ramble can lead to a chilling shock. It can be made safe only by planning and applying some basic rules.

☐ Collect the right clothing and equipment (see Rambling, page 177) and break it in on short walks and rambles.

☐ Recruit some kindred spirits. In winter the balance favours the elements and companions help restore the odds.

☐ Plot your route – even for a stroll. Beside estimating your approximate speed, allow for fewer daylight hours. Start and finish than normal.

☐ Avoid steep grass above quarries, sea cliffs and other potential hazards. Proofed nylon waterproof clothing may be a hazard for its wearer and slide all too easily over the frozen grass as well as ice or snow; it is easy to slip and tumble out of control at high speed.

Snow and ice on mountains and wild moorland pose too much risk unless you have experience. You need to have learned the craft of climbing either from a course, or experience, or both. You need to know how to carry an ice axe, how to hold it, how to check a fall with it and how to cut steps. You must be able to navigate through mist so dense it merges with the snow to cause a 'white-out' and it is impossible to tell up from down without throwing snowballs ahead and spotting where they land. You need to be able to recognise the different types of snow and potential avalanche risks.

Pack your rucksack with care including food and a vacuum flask of hot soup or coffee. Fresh drinking water is difficult to find in winter; not only are pools and streams frozen solid, but taps and stand-pipes might be turned off in case they burst. Shops, cafes, pubs and hotels can be closed, too. Observe the 'Dos and

How to survive a blizzard in a 'snow hole'

Dont's' listed on page 177 and if unlucky enough to be caught in a blizzard in open country, dig a 'snow hole' and follow survival rules:

1 Get into the lee of any natural protection, like rocks or a wall.

2 Scoop a small cave or crater, depending on the firmness of the snow.

3 Put on all clothing except anorak.

4 Undo bootlaces, belts, cuffs and collars.

5 Make a seat from heather, maps, guidebook, towel, plastic food boxes, mug, water bottle, toilet paper and camera case.

6 Chew food from now on.

7 If no bivi bag (see page 177) sit on 'seat', put feet inside rucksack and put on anorak with arms inside (not in sleeves) and hold crotch or armpits; play pig-in-the-middle and huddle together.

8 If you have a bivi bag, climb into sleeping bag inside it. If no sleeping bag, sit in bivi bag on 'seat', feet inside rucksack and wear anorak as above. Pull bivi bag up over head and leave space for face.

9 Keep checking that your position is not restricting your circulation. Wriggle toes, move fingers and sing.

10 Wait until conditions improve (and probably daylight, too) and then move on without delay to notify anyone expecting you that you are alive and well.

The first signs of spring

There is a country saying: 'Spring has come when you can cover five daisies with your foot.' Each lengthening day of the new year weakens winter's grip as the earth tilts Britain closer to the sun. Soon, one by one, plants which have lain dormant through the dead mid-winter begin to grow again. Sap rises, buds swell; a miraculous built-in response to

the lengthening daylight hours and rising temperatures.

In the south and west, where spring comes first, wild flowers begin to bloom: snowdrops from January onwards, followed by coltsfoot, lesser celandine, delicate wood anemones and dog violets, the leafless pink spikes of butterbur, and most welcome of all, the sight of hedgebank primroses. The deciduous trees are also stirring. On the bare ash branches, sooty buds are prominent; on the horse chestnuts, every twig bears large and handsomely varnished 'sticky buds' (the toffee-brown resin protects the embryo leaves within from insects).

The fat, furry silver and yellow catkins of the pussy willow and the dusty gold 'lambs' tail' hazel catkins are among the first flowers to brave the early spring frosts. They are followed by sprays of blackthorn – the so-called 'blackthorn winter' – when white blossom spreads in snowflake drifts along the hedgerows before the leaves are out.

By early March the first butterflies are on the wing. These adults are survivors of over-wintering species – brimstones and small tortoiseshells – emerging from hibernation during the first warm days to lay the eggs from which the summer broods will be produced. The hedgehog uncurls to root and snuffle for food in the leaf litter of the hedge bottoms. In the woods, badgers, though not true hibernators, become increasingly more active. Mating hares can be seen running through the open fields.

With the approach of spring the great bird migrations begin again. In Scotland the hills are still piebald with snow when the yelping skeins of wild geese fly north to their Arctic breeding grounds and the ospreys return from Africa to take up residence again in the Highlands.

In the south, the first migrants to make themselves heard are usually the chiffchaff and willow warbler, but everywhere birds are beginning to sing, announcing territorial sovereignty over nesting areas. One of the earliest resident songsters is the mistle thrush – also known as the stormcock because of its habit of singing on blustery days.

Elsewhere, other nest-builders are busy, and the raucous clamour of village rookeries is one of the most characteristic sounds of imminent spring. But one voice is more eagerly awaited than any other: the haunting call of the cuckoo. For the cuckoo's arrival in early April after its marathon migration from Africa is a sure sign of winter's end.

Chapter Ten
The Future of the Countryside

The surrealist domes of the Fylingdales Ballistic Missile Early Warning Station in the North York
Moors National Park symbolise the profound changes which modern technology is bringing
to the rural landscapes of the British Isles. In this final chapter, part requiem, part eulogy,
we look at the vanishing countryside and at what is being saved for posterity

The face of the countryside is changing as never before. Every year thousands of acres of open land are commandeered to meet the growing demands of urban man; new roads, new houses, factories, airports, reservoirs, power stations; swelling the lost countryside of the British Isles already buried under brick and tarmac.

Elsewhere, quarries, gravel pits and coal mines blight the land. Motorways and massive pylons march across the fields with scant regard for their impact on the scenery.

And everywhere, land is being farmed more intensively. Hedgerows are grubbed out, woods cleared, wetlands drained, old pasture ploughed, leaving less room for wildlife. Habitats that might have taken a thousand years to evolve can now be bulldozed, burnt and ploughed in a day.

There has always been change in the countryside, but never at the speed with which it has been gathering momentum over the past three decades. And it is precisely this, the sheer pace and volume of change, its impact on cherished landscapes and fragile eco-systems, that is the cause of so much concern.

The result, especially in the farming lowlands of England and Wales, has been dramatic. The Countryside Commission has stated that the changes taking place there are as substantial as those that resulted from the enclosure movement of the 17th and 18th centuries.

Many familiar traditional features of the countryside are disappearing as the pace of progress quickens. Old farm buildings – relics of the days when life moved no faster than the steady stride of a heavy horse – are crumbling away. Clifftops, downs and heaths are increasingly being taken into cultivation – a controversial practice in areas valued for amenity and a disastrous one for wildlife. A recent review of the effects of modern farming carried out by the Nature Conservancy Council has revealed a serious loss of habitats, leading to alarming reductions in native wild plant and animal populations.

Stitch by stitch, the old tapestry of woods and spinneys, streams, hedgerows, ponds and ditches, is being unravelled, and replaced by a new countryside, more open, less diverse, and with fewer of those rich local flavours which add so much spice to the landscapes of the British Isles.

Yet the very fact that the vast majority of people in these islands are now urban dwellers renders the surviving countryside even more precious, and not just as land set aside for food production, even if that remains its paramount function. Today the countryside also provides fresh air, open space for recreation and escape from the cities, as well as those quieter, deeper pleasures that have inspired generations of poets, painters, writers and musicians.

Concern for the future of the countryside is widespread, and grows with every threat, real or imagined. But at least the case for conservation is now broadly accepted. National parks and nature reserves seek to protect the finest landscapes and wildlife habitats. Long-distance footpaths enshrine the freedom to ramble over miles of clifftops and open countryside. Historic castles, houses and gardens are preserved for public enjoyment, and dying villages re-vitalised.

Nevertheless, much remains to be done. Woods and hedgerows, heaths and marshes should be identified and managed for their landscape value, especially if they have an ecological or historic value. Even individual trees and odd corners of rough or boggy pasture may be evaluated for the way in which they add perspective and enrich the texture of the local scene.

More trees are desperately needed to fill the gaps left by decades of disease and neglect. Fertile land need not be used; the food it will produce is too precious. But most landscapes have odd corners where the plough cannot reach, and where trees could once again enhance the view.

Fifty years ago the countryside was far richer in terms of beauty and the sights and sounds of nature than it is now. Today's countryside still offers those pleasures in good measure, credit for which is at least partly due to the system of development control which has evolved in the British Isles and which, though far from perfect, has made possible the saving of a civilised environment.

But what of tomorrow's countryside? Without even greater commitment to conservation, at national and local level, the outlook is bleak and the Countryside Commission has issued a stark warning to the people of Britain. 'If we try hard we might sustain what we can now experience,' it says, 'but that will mean substantially multiplying our efforts as a nation. If we do no more than we are doing, much of the lowland countryside of England and Wales will become very dull to look at 50 years from now.'

Vanishing Britain

Country greenery no longer always means what it did: slow pace and leafy shade, the hum of insects, of birds in the hedgerows, meadows in flower. They are, all of them, harder to find, and green today can signify a monoculture prairie, ecologically barren, though green none the less.

The landscapes of the British Isles have changed, out of all recognition in some places, especially in lowland Britain. And a great deal of the change has taken place in the third quarter of this century.

There is no better example of what has vanished from the country scene than the pond. In yesterday's countryside you might have found a pond between every two or three fields. Today it is often hard to find one anywhere, even in the heart of the country.

The field pond is obsolete, and as it no longer serves a useful purpose, there is no reason for keeping it. Nowadays, pipes bring water to the cattle, and often the spring feeding the natural pond has dried up – the result of increasingly heavy extraction of local ground water.

All too often the village pond has suffered a similar fate; reduced by neglect to a rubbish-filled eyesore, then filled in to provide a new car park for the re-modelled village pub.

In its turn the vanishing pond has brought about a decline in formerly abundant creatures – the Common Frog, the Crested Newt – which thrived in its placid waters.

A far more conspicuous change has been the loss of trees, especially large trees, over much of the British scene. In many places they have already gone, and none so sorely mourned as the English Elm. For centuries this under-rated monarch of the vegetable kingdom, soaring in cumulus clouds of summer leaf, has sustained the illusion of England as a woodland country. Just over a decade ago, 23 million elms flourished south of a line from Birmingham to the Wash. Today $15\frac{1}{2}$ million of them are gone, laid low by a small beetle, *Scolytus scolytus*, carrier of the deadly Dutch elm disease, which is still laying waste to the land, leaving millions of dead and dying trees in its wake – a ghastly vision of winter-in-summer that will remain to haunt the English countryside for years to come. The only hope is that a series of hard winters will kill off the beetles and allow the remaining elms to regenerate.

Not even the comparatively modern concept of protected countryside is proof against drastic change. Exmoor national park has only been in existence for three decades, yet already one third of its moorland has gone under the plough. The same fate has overtaken the ancient sheepwalks and hill pastures of the southern chalk downs. And every acre lost means fewer wild orchids, fewer chalkland butterflies. Nor is it only wildlife that suffers. Modern farming has destroyed much of Britain's prehistoric past, especially Bronze Age barrows. They may still appear on the older Ordnance Survey one-inch maps, but many have vanished from the fields.

As if all this was not enough, development is depleting Britain's precious farmland at the rate of 50,000 (20,200 hectares) acres a year: new houses, new factories, new roads to add to the 210,000 miles (336,000km) of existing highways. Some 30,000 acres (12,120 hectares) of Britain are now solid motorway – and there is more to come. Every additional mile of six-lane super highway devours another 30 acres (12 hectares) of green land, for which motorway kestrels and grassy banks are but small compensation. Furthermore, each new mile of motorway requires 100,000 tons of aggregate, which in turn enlarges the quarries, causing them to bite deeper into the Mendip Hills and the national parklands of the Derbyshire Peak District and Yorkshire Dales.

It is difficult to be sure exactly how much countryside is being lost nationally. One estimate is that Britain 'loses out of green' an area the size of Berkshire every five years.

Hand in hand with mineral extraction goes pollution: streams are throttled with slurry and sediment, lifeless lagoons created. Yet to balance the picture it must also be said that recent years have seen a considerable improvement in the overall quality of Britain's inland waters: salmon can again survive in the River Thames, and Great Crested Grebes are colonising the disused and flooded gravel pits.

Everywhere land is taken out of green, covered with concrete, deep-ploughed or drenched with farm chemicals, it creates an environment that is fundamentally hostile to wild plants and creatures. Drop by drop, the wildlife heritage of the British Isles is being squeezed out of existence. The old way of farming, slow to change and more tolerant of nature, is being replaced by a more demanding economic regime in which agriculturally unproductive habitats such as moors, hedges and wetlands are seen as burdensome luxuries.

Wildlife can no longer be taken for granted because there is just not enough land to go round. One of the reasons that Otters are so rare in England now is that they cannot tolerate human disturbance.

As always, the deadliest foe is habitat destruction. Cover the Lancashire dunes with holiday camps and the mating rattle of the already endangered Natterjack Toad could become a voice of the past. Demolish an old barn and the Barn Owl is denied an ancestral nesting site. Improve an old meadow and the Cowslips will go.

Ancient meadows and pastures are especially vulnerable to change. The centuries-old mixtures of wild grasses and flowering plants have been replaced by laboratory-bred hybrid grasses, and the soil itself ploughed, drained, re-sown and treated with chemical fertilisers. In such new meadows, flowers are few: even Buttercups are becoming rare in some areas. The beautiful Fritillary is another flower now severely limited in distribution as a result of these changes.

Diversity of habitat in nature gives overall stability and safety to large populations of plants and animals with their complex and interwoven food webs. Only in those relic patches of wild or semi-wild habitat protected as nature reserves, official and unofficial, is that diversity being conserved for the future.

Of course, in some places wildlife is still abundant, but to seek it you must look to the more remote corners of the British Isles, to the wilder coasts and uplands of the north and west. Here you can still see Atlantic Seals and Peregrine Falcons. The Red Kite, though it breeds at only a handful of secret sites, appears secure in Wales. The handsome Kentish Glory moth will never fly again in Kent but it still survives in Scotland. The delicate Irish Lady's Tresses Orchid (an inhabitant of marshy, marginal pasture land) still flowers at a number of sites in Ireland.

Yet nowhere in the British Isles is so remote that it is not threatened by progress. In 1979, one small oil spill at Sullom Voe in the Shetlands killed nearly 4,000 seabirds, including 146 rare Great Northern Divers, a species with only a small European population. It also killed 15 Otters – the equivalent of the entire population of Norfolk. A year earlier a disaster caused heavy loss of human life and pollution at the oil terminal on Whiddy Island, Bantry Bay, Ireland.

Elsewhere, estuaries are threatened by the insatiable demands of industry and agriculture. The salt marshes of the Ribble estuary in Lancashire, a wintering ground of international importance for huge populations of wildfowl and wading birds, were rescued from an agricultural reclamation scheme only through last-minute intervention by the Nature Conservancy Council and the Royal Society for the Protection of Birds.

Human life, too, has changed dramatically in the countryside in no more than a couple of generations. The farm has lost all pretensions to self-sufficiency; it is now part of a national food enterprise. New agricultural buildings, which do not need planning permission and so can be any size and shape, are put up alongside centuries-old barns, which are unrepaired and allowed to rot. The few remaining windmills function for weekend visitors, if at all. Most traditional country crafts have withered away, though thatching thrives and adds to property values. And the blacksmith (really a farrier) lives on, but with a mobile workshop, servicing local riding stables or making artistic ironware for residents who have settled in modernised country cottages.

The great country houses and gardens of the British Isles are no longer the exclusive domain of the gentry. Lucky the squire in his manor, the lord in his hall who can support the burden of maintaining a stately home from his own resources. Nowadays most country house owners depend upon the paying public – some 20 million visitors a year – to preserve what has been called Britain's most important contribution to European civilisation. Many of the finest homes and gardens are now preserved by the National Trust, but 40 stand derelict and others face a similar fate.

The country church, pride and glory of so many villages, is also facing an uncertain future. Empty and redundant churches are becoming an all too familiar feature of the country scene. Some small chapels have been successfully converted into private dwellings, but what alternative use is there for a medieval church, repository of 900 years of village history with its tombs and monuments, leaning headstones, bells, bench-ends and stained glass windows? The problem of the medieval church is all the more acute because, as buildings, they are all slowly falling to pieces, a reflection of the fact that they were largely built within the same brief span of centuries. Even without a congregation, the parish church cannot be allowed to moulder away, yet who will pay for the enormous upkeep of what is, after all, part of a nationwide architectural heritage?

Organisations such as the Society for the Protection of Ancient Buildings and the Civic Trust have done much to restore old country buildings of all kinds. But whatever miracles can be worked with brick and stone and tile, the old social fabric of the village is harder to replace.

Cottages are greatly sought-after by retired city-dwellers, second home-owners and affluent commuters. The dwindling indigenous workforce, unable to afford the new inflated house prices, are forced into peripheral council estates. All over the country, village schools of the kind immortalised by Laurie Lee in *Cider With Rosie*, are closing, the children being bussed to the nearest town. And as often as not, the village shop is now part of a chain, indistinguishable from one county to another.

As the older village inhabitants die, the age-old rites and customs of country lore die with them. Who today would hope to cure whooping cough by passing the afflicted child under the belly of a piebald horse? Or cure warts with nine bramble leaves dipped in spring water? Yet these are not medieval customs conned from books; they were current practice in Cornwall earlier this century.

Today, freed from such ignorance and superstition, there is no doubt that country people live a better life. Nostalgia for the past should not obscure the fact that yesterday's countryside offered nothing to many but a life of hardship and grinding poverty. No-one should mourn the loss of country cottages which, though possibly picturesque, were often comfortless and unsanitary hovels.

So there are two sides to the story of the vanishing countryside; gains as well as losses. Derelict canals are being restored to life by dedicated groups of weekend volunteers. The folk music revival has rescued a rich haul of long-forgotten songs and ballads. Everywhere, new life is being breathed into old buildings. Conservation is a word on everybody's lips. And there have been some outstanding success stories.

At the beginning of this century, the Osprey, one of the world's most spectacular birds of prey, was driven from its breeding haunts in the Scottish High-

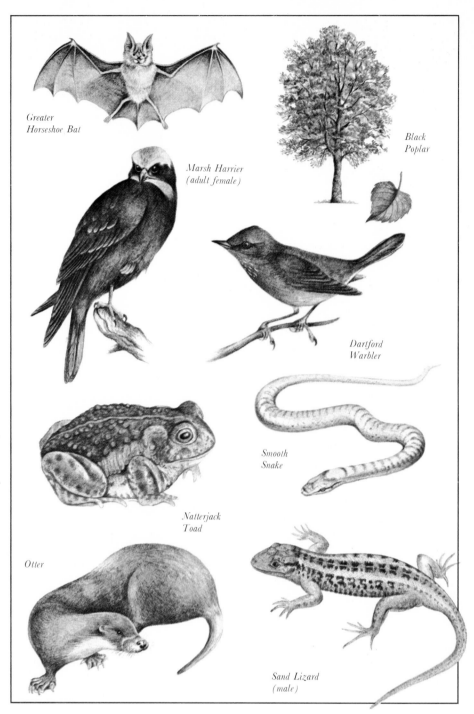

Wildlife in danger: all the species shown here are threatened with extinction

lands by human persecution. For fifty years the old eyries stood empty. It seemed as if the birds had gone for good, until one day the news came: the Ospreys were back. Protected by the Royal Society for the Protection of Birds, welcomed by a more enlightened public, the original home-coming pair and their offspring have now established a small but secure population of Scottish Ospreys which return every year to breed in the Highlands.

The return of the Osprey is a symbol of hope for the future of the countryside and its wildlife. Change in itself is not always harmful. The real task today is to recognise the speed of today's changes and

take steps early enough to protect those things that are treasured most, so that the best of yesterday's countryside may also belong to tomorrow.

Going – bats, toads, snakes, lizards
It is easy to arouse public sympathy for a bird as attractive as the Osprey. Not so for bats, reptiles and amphibians, which are more likely to cause a shudder than a smile. Yet the wildlife of the British Isles would be infinitely poorer without these fascinating creatures, some so rare they are protected by the Conservation of Wild Plants and Wild Creatures Act in Britain. They include the Greater Horse-shoe Bat, down from 7,000 in 1950 to a few hundred; the Natterjack Toad, more

Epitaph to the elm: one of the $15\frac{1}{2}$ million trees destroyed by Dutch elm disease

habitats are destroyed. There is concern for the Corncrake. In 1979 it was breeding in only a fifth of the sites logged a few years before. Hard winters and habitat loss have dealt the Dartford Warbler a double blow. A heathland species, it is now more or less confined to a few pairs in Hampshire and Dorset. Some common migrants are becoming scarcer. The Lesser Whitethroat has been hit by recent droughts in its sub-Saharan winter quarters. Many other migrants must run the gauntlet across Continental Europe, where millions of marksmen with shotguns lie in wait. But persecution has also left its mark in Britain, especially among birds of prey, and in particular upon the Marsh Harrier, now reduced to a handful of breeding pairs, and the even rarer Montagu's Harrier. Luckily, other species have been more fortunate. The Red Kite is holding its own in Wales. The Peregrine Falcon has recovered from the population crash of the late 1950s and early 1960s caused by pesticides. The Hen Harrier is steadily increasing its range and the Osprey is again breeding successfully in Scotland. Even the White-tailed Sea Eagle, absent from Britain since the First World War, could return. The Nature Conservancy Council is trying to re-introduce the species by raising and releasing birds from Norway on the Hebridean island reserve of Rhum.

Going – trees

Dutch elm disease has dealt the countryside a devastating blow from which it may never recover. To date, the plague has carried away at least $15\frac{1}{2}$ million of Britain's 23 million elms. Millions of other trees of all kinds suffered in the great drought of 1976. But while the elms perish in a blaze of national indignation, one of Britain's rarest native trees is passing away almost un-noticed. The Black Poplar (*Populus Nigra*), once a familiar sight in lowland Britain, is quietly dying for want of love. The last of these craggy giants are now so scattered they are simply too far apart to fertilise each other. Little more than a thousand remain, most of them already mature or beginning to die back. Unless the species is planted back into its natural flood plain habitat, the Black Poplar could die out within 50 years.

Oaks are also being lost. In some areas, half the oaks are over-mature and dying. The reasons here are more complex. Improved stream drainage can result in ground drought, which weakens the trees, which become vulnerable to dis-

numerous than the Common Toad in Victorian times; the harmless Smooth Snake and the Sand Lizard – heathland species gravely endangered by loss of habitat and heath fires. Today even the Common Frog is not common any more.

Going – animals

The Otter is now so rare that it is protected in England, Wales and Ireland (though not in Scotland, where it is more numerous). Norfolk, one of its former strongholds, now has only about 15 Otters left. The decline began in the 1960s. A combination of hard winters, hunting, disease and the effects of pesticides have all helped to bring about the Otter's disappearance from many rivers.

Increasing human disturbance and the clearing of river banks makes a comeback more difficult. Otters are shy animals. They need plenty of cover to lie up in during the day, and bankside trees (ash trees are the favourites) whose roots make a secure holt or den. Now that otter hunting is illegal in England and Wales, the future looks brighter. Special 'otter havens' have been set up on some rivers to help the Otter recolonise its old haunts.

Going – birds

Watching birds is a major pastime in the British Isles, and most species are loved and protected. Nevertheless, many birds are rare and becoming rarer as wild ease and careless stubble burning. Sick, stag-headed oaks now abound in the scenery of some counties.

The loss of so many trees brings other problems in its wake. It is creating a new countryside, more open, more threadbare, sometimes exposing unsightly modern development previously concealed by a screen of foliage.

That new treeless scene is here to stay, at least for the lifetime of anyone reading this book. To maintain any existing tree population requires six healthy saplings for each mature adult tree (disease and other hazards will claim the other five in time). Most areas have at best one sapling alive for each mature tree, and in some places the ratio is even worse.

The change brought about by the disappearance of these trees is all the more devastating in its impact upon the landscapes of lowland Britain because they were not clustered into dense woods. Most of them, the elms in particular, were strung out beside the lanes and along the hedgerows between the fields, or grouped in small clumps and spinneys, creating parkland vistas in all directions. Today many areas are losing not only their trees but their hedges too, as modern farming demands larger field units.

The Second World War is a good starting date to catalogue the decline, because at that time the British rural scene was in full maturity, a rich burgeoning based on centuries of slow change. Since then over half a million miles of hedgerows alive with flowers, butterflies and nesting birds have been lost – and are still being obliterated at the rate of 2,000 miles a year.

Nor can the remaining small woods and coppices be taken for granted. If they are not managed to provide timber, the land is more profitable when cleared of its broadleaved Oak and Hazel, and either ploughed or re-planted with fast-growing conifers.

In all, perhaps a third of the ancient hardwood woodlands have gone since the war, leaving less than nine per cent of the total land surface of Great Britain covered with trees. However, that does not mean new trees are not being planted. The Forestry Commission manages over 2 million acres (404,000 hectares) of productive forest – mainly conifers – and has begun to grant-aid the regeneration of the native Scots pine in the Scottish Highlands. The Countryside Commission is also helping amenity tree planting at the rate of around £1 million a year.

OBLONG WOODSIA
(Woodsia ilvensis

SOLDIER ORCHID
Orchis militaris

ALPINE SOW THISTLE
Cicerbita alpina

WILD GLADIOLUS
Gladiolus illyricus

MONKEY ORCHID
Orchis simia

MEZEREON
Daphne mezereum

BLUE HEATH
Phyllodoce caerulea

ALPINE WOODSIA
Woodsia alpina

GHOST ORCHID
Epipogium aphyllum

SPIKED SPEEDWELL
Veronica spicata

SNOWDON LILY
Lloydia serotina

SPRING GENTIAN
Gentiana verna

TEESDALE SANDWORT
Minuartia stricta

ALPINE GENTIAN
Gentiana nivalis

Of course the countryside changes. It cannot remain constant, a kind of giant open-air museum to preserve the past in perpetuity. That is generally accepted. After all, many of the hedges whose loss is mourned today were not growing 300 years ago, and it would be foolish to expect that every mile of hedgerow should be obstinately protected. What causes so much widespread public concern is the accelerating pace of change being imposed on the landscape by the new agriculture.

Going – prehistoric barrows

The practice of raising barrows, or burial mounds over the dead goes back to the Stone Age and continued into early Saxon times. Until recently there were at least 20,000 barrows in the British Isles, but most of them are concentrated on the chalk and limestone uplands where they are often vulnerable to ploughing. Many have been obliterated; others badly damaged. Of the 871 Bronze Age burial mounds recorded in South Dorset alone fewer than five per cent survive unscathed.

Going – cider orchards

Cider is the wine of the West Country, a golden, tipsy brew made from the fermented juice of sour apples. Sadly, the old cider orchards are following the heavy horse into oblivion. Relics of a bygone age when cider flowed freely in the harvest fields, most of them are long past their prime. Hoary with lichen, the oldest trees have stood since the reign of Edward VII. Every spring these octagenarian greybeards still glorify the landscape with pink and white blossom.

LADY'S SLIPPER
pripedium calceolus

KILLARNEY FERN
Trichomanes speciosum

RED HELLEBORINE
Cephalanthera rubra

TUFTED SAXIFRAGE
Saxifraga cespitosa

DROOPING SAXIFRAGE
Saxifraga cernua

CHEDDAR PINK
Dianthus gratian opolitanus

DIAPENSIA
Diapensia lapponica

But in September when the apples ripen they are left to rot where they fall, and every winter when the gales come, more trees are swept away, and are not replaced. The traditional orchard, its standard trees widely spaced at no more than 40 per acre, is no longer economic. Somerset has lost 1,000 acres (404 hectares) of cider orchards over the past decade, though paradoxically it now has twice as many trees. But the replacements are diminutive modern heavy-cropping bush varieties. The big old standard trees, varieties with splendidly Bacchanalian names like Hangydown, Brown Snout and Slack-ma-Girdle, become fewer with every passing year.

Going – wild flowers

Thirty years ago there was not overmuch concern about wild plants. Today, flowers are vanishing at such a rate that it has now been made illegal to uproot any wild plant in Britain without the permission of the owner of land. And for 21 of the rarest plants (listed below), even stricter rules apply. Removing *any part* of these 21 plants is an offence under the Conservation of Wild Creatures and Wild Plants Act of 1975. Tomorrow, even flowers like the common Cowslip – still locally abundant but going fast as old pastures are improved – could find themselves added to the endangered list, along with the rare but as yet unprotected Fritillary, Pasque Flower and Alpine Catchfly.

The following plants are protected by law in the United Kingdom under the Conservation of Wild Creatures and Wild Plants Act of 1975.

Oblong Woodsia (*Woodsia ilvensis*). Confined to four localities.

Soldier Orchid (*Orchis militaris*). Two sites only, in Suffolk and Chilterns.

Blue Heath (*Phyllodoce caerulea*). Sow of Atholl, Perthshire only.

Alpine Sow Thistle (*Cicerbita alpina*). On inaccessible ledges in one area of the Scottish Highlands.

Monkey Orchid (*Orchis simia*). Trio of sites in Kent, Chilterns.

Spiked Speedwell (*Veronica spicata*). Breckland, East Anglia.

Alpine Woodsia (*Woodsia alpina*). Rock crevices in 15 upland localities.

Alpine Gentian (*Gentiana nivalis*). A few Highland mountains.

Spring Gentian (*Gentiana verna*). Upper Teesdale.

Teesdale Sandwort (*Minuartia stricta*). Teesdale.

Ghost Orchid (*Epipogium aphyllum*). Few shady woods, Southern England.

Snowdon Lily (*Lloydia serotina*). Remote sites in Snowdonia.

Wild Gladiolus (*Gladiolus illyricus*). Few sites on Hampshire and Dorset heaths.

Mezereon (*Daphne mezereum*). Few areas of lime and chalk woodland.

Cheddar Pink (*Dianthus gratianopolitanus*). Cheddar Gorge, Somerset.

Drooping Saxifrage (*Saxifraga cernua*). On three Highland mountains only.

Lady's Slipper (*Cypripedium calceolus*). One secret site in Yorkshire.

Red helleborine (*Cephalanthera rubra*). Cotswold beechwoods.

Killarney Fern (*Trichomanes speciosum*). Handful of plants in south-west and north-west Britain.

Tufted Saxifrage (*Saxifraga cespitosa*). Some Highland rocks.

Diapensia (*Diapensia lapponica*). One hill-top in Inverness-shire.

Protecting a threatened heritage

The scenery of nearly one fifth of England and Wales (18.6 per cent to be precise) is protected by designation either as a national park or an 'Area of Outstanding Natural Beauty (AONB).

Scotland has neither national parks nor AONBs, partly because the development pressures on fine scenery north of the border have never been as great as in England and Wales, and partly because, on any reasonable aesthetic judgement, so much of Scotland would qualify as to render such designation meaningless. Instead Scotland has five National Park Direction Area Orders covering Loch Lomond and the Trossachs (320 square miles; 512 sq km); Glen Affric, Glen Cannich and Strathfarrar (260 square miles; 416 sq km); Ben Nevis, Glen Coe and Black Mount (610 square miles; 976 sq km); the Cairngorms (180 square miles; 288 sq km) and Loch Torridon, Loch Maree and Little Loch Broom (500 square miles; 800 sq km). Together these areas comprise six per cent of Scotland.

In these areas all proposals for development must be submitted to the Countryside Commission for Scotland which advises the Secretary of State for Scotland on their desirability. The Commission aims to keep development to a minimum.

Northern Ireland has no national parks, but has seven AONBs covering some 1000 square miles (1600 sq km) of magnificent countryside. They are: the Antrim Coast and Glens, North Derry, Sperrin Mountains, Lagan Valley, Strangford Lough, Mourne Mountains and South Armagh. Two more – Lough Erne and the Slieve Croob area (to be added to the Mourne Mountains) – are proposed.

The Republic of Ireland has plans to establish three national parks: Killarney (22 square miles; 35 sq km); Connemara (just under four square miles; six sq km); and Glenbeagh in Donegal (39 square miles; 62 sq km). These parks will be wholly owned by the state, and they have been defined more for historical reasons than through any policy of distinguishing outstanding areas of scenery. For in Ireland, as in Scotland, there is so much countryside which is wild and beautiful that a visitor might be forgiven for thinking that the entire Republic had been given national park status.

The seven English and three Welsh national parks remain in mainly private ownership although public bodies such as the Forestry Commission, the regional water authorities and the Ministry of Defence are major landowners in them. More compatible with their purpose, so is the National Trust, which controls nearly a quarter of the Lake District National Park. There is no general right of public access to the parks and they are in no sense wilderness areas (as, for instance in much of the admirable American park system) since in the British Isles true wilderness vanished long ago.

It is an old jest but a true one that the national parks of England and Wales are neither national nor parks. Yet the campaign to establish them was long and hard fought. It was launched by the Council for the Preservation (now Protection) of Rural England in 1929 with a memorandum to the Prime Minister. Determined, knowledgeable visionaries, the park protagonists were drawn from every walk of life, welded by a love of the countryside and a belief that without its conservation there would be nothing of man's natural world left to provide those things of deep human satisfaction which are being obliterated at an alarming rate from daily life: tranquillity, nature. uncluttered horizons, clean air, clear rivers, and freedom to roam.

People went to prison for a nation's right to climb Kinder Scout and roam the neighbouring Pennine moors. They challenged a land-owning few for access rights, organised weekend trespass hikes over privately-owned shooting preserves and sheep-grazing moorlands which drew thousands of participants.

In 1943 John Dower drew up his seminal report calling for the establishment of national parks and gave them shape in a definition which, though never enacted in so many words, remains their *raison d'être*. A national park, he said, should be: 'An extensive area of beautiful and relatively wild country in which, for the nation's benefit, and by appropriate national decision and action; the characteristic landscape beauty is strictly preserved, access and facilities for public open-air enjoyment are amply provided, wildlife and buildings and places of architectural and historic interest are suitably protected, while established farming use is effectively maintained.'

But it was not until 1949 – after yet another consideration of the whole issue (the Hobhouse Committee) – that the National Parks and Access to the Countryside Act, providing for the designation of both parks and AONBs, went on the statute book. And here the legislation fell far short of what John Dower and the other campaigners for national parks had sought. It failed to place the parks under the guardianship of a powerful executive national body. Instead it left them – as they still are today – to be largely administered by committees or boards of the local county councils.

The Countryside Commission has little more than an advisory role and has never been armed with enough legislative teeth to be an effective watchdog.

Both Dower and Hobhouse saw that there were large areas of outstandingly beautiful countryside which could not meet the Dower definition of a national park, being neither big enough or wild enough. For such landscapes the cumbersome accolade of the AONB was devised. AONBs are considered no less beautiful than the parks and require the same degree of protection. But the 1949 statute places less emphasis on providing public open-air enjoyment and no special administrative machinery.

Cinderellas the AONBs may be, both financially and administratively, but they cover much of the best countryside, for the Dower definition of national parks excluded the less wild areas of lowland Britain – Dorset is a perfect example – which are most typical of the English scene.

There are now 33 AONBs, covering about 5,600 square miles (8960 sq km) of England and Wales. At one end of the scale are remote and little visited areas such as the Solway Coast and the Lincolnshire Wolds which scarcely seem to have enough problems to deserve special protection. At the other are national and regional playgrounds like the Cotswolds and the Cornish coast – subject to intense pressure from holiday crowds and highly vulnerable therefore to commercial development.

By statute the parks had twin purposes, to protect 'natural beauty' (though in fact it was never wholly natural), and to provide for suitable recreation. The two aims inevitably got in each other's way as the number of visitors to them rose with increasing car ownership, shorter working hours and longer holidays. Eventually, in 1976 the Government decreed that where conservation and recreation prove incompatible, the former should prevail.

The parks are far from being the Arcadian retreats from the modern world which their founders originally

Above: the heathery Culter Hills of Strathclyde, Scotla of southern England.   Below right: the almost lun

North of the Border there are generally fewer pressures on fine scenery than in England. Below left: a new road cuts a broad swathe across the chalklands landscape of the china clay industry near St Austell, Cornwall. Locals call these white spoil tips 'the 'Cornish Alps'

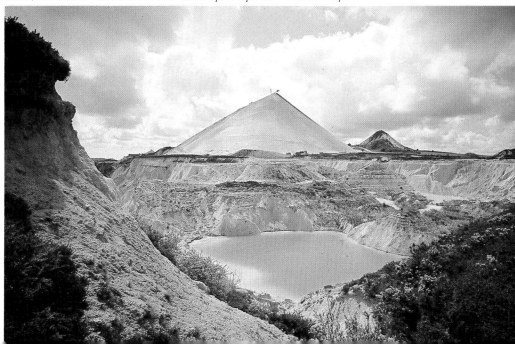

Conserving countryside for posterity: National Parks and 'Areas of Outstanding Natural Beauty' (see map) confer a measure of protection to the finest landscapes of England and Wales, and also Northern Ireland (inset). But they are still vulnerable.

Brecon Beacons; 519 square miles (830 sq km). Flat-topped mountains rising to close on 3000ft (923m). Geographically the nearest national park to London, but largely unthreatened by development. The valley of the Usk divides the Black Mountains area in the east from the main massif of the Beacons in the middle of the park and (confusingly) the Black Mountain in the west. All three outcrops share the same precipitous sandstone scarps, their severity modified by the sweeping curves of ice-hewn amphitheatres. To the north there are fine views over the Wye Valley and the soft knuckles of the hills that lead down to it.

Dartmoor; 365 square miles (584 sq km). The last wilderness of southern England. Tors, clitters, cleaves and combes – Dartmoor names for the granite outcrops, rock litter, gorges and river valleys – add drama to the park and underline its wild aspect, as do the quaking mires and tussock bogs. Many remains of ancient man, notably Bronze Age Grimspound. Modern man threatens. Almost the whole of the northern moor is a military training area.
Reservoirs and afforestation are changing both uplands and valleys, though a major reservoir scheme at Swincombe was defeated. Farmers increasingly seek to enclose the moor. Tourist traffic clogs the lanes in summer.

Exmoor; 265 square miles (425 sq km). Bare moorland skylines, plunging combes, huge hog-backed hills tumbling into the Bristol Channel. A wild park of bog and bracken and brawling streams, but vulnerable to change. The superb heather moorland, for the sake of which the park was designated, has shrunk from 60,000 acres (24,240 hectares) just after the war to barely 40,000 acres (16,160 hectares) today, through conversion to more intensive agricultural use rather than traditional sheep grazing.

Lake District; 866 square miles (1385 sq km). The biggest park and one of the most famous landscapes in the British Isles, unique in its mingling of great fells and still waters. Here the Lake poets launched the romantic movement and the area has continued to attract writers ever since. Today the main threat to Lakeland's beauty is its own popularity – resulting in damage through sheer numbers of visitors. The water authorities continue to cast covetous eyes at the natural lakes.

Northumberland; 398 square miles (636 sq km). Fifty miles (80km) of lonely, surging hill country stretching from the most dramatic length of the Roman Wall to the Scottish border near Kirk Yetholm (terminus of the Pennine Way). Contains the heathery Simonside hills and the round-topped Cheviots, bleakly beautiful, where there are more sheep than people. In the north the park is bisected by the Ministry of Defence Redesdale training area. Elsewhere afforestation is burying whole hills in conifers.

North York Moors; 553 square miles (888 sq km).
The biggest tract of heather in England. The main range, the Cleveland Hills, reaching 1490ft (458m) on wild Urra Moor, are flat-topped. The Cleveland Way path follows the northern scarp of these hills, leading eventually to a rugged coast of towering cliffs. For gentler views, the dales, notably Rosedale and Farndale are idyllic. Threats: potash mining near Whitby and loss of moorland to conifers and the plough.

Peak District; 542 square miles (867 sq km).
Britain's first national park and also the best run. Has its own financially independent planning board, internationally recognised for imaginative visitor management. Essential, this, because it is also the most visited park, wedged between the conurbations of Manchester and West Yorkshire. Geologically it is two areas, the gritstone moors and edges of the 'dark peak' and the romantic limestone dales of the 'white peak' in the south. Limestone and fluorspar extraction are the main threats.

Pembrokeshire Coast; 225 square miles (360 sq km).
The smallest park. No mountains here. Instead, one incomparable asset - 170 miles (272km) of majestic cliffscape rated among the finest coastlines in Europe – despite uncontrolled caravan sites and chalet developments. The cliffs are a paradise for birds – and bird-watchers. Skomer island (also in the park) is a national nature reserve open to the public, home of puffins, razorbills and

Manx shearwaters. And like all coasts, it is now prone to oil pollution, largely due to the oil terminal at Milford Haven.

Snowdonia; 845 square miles (1352 sq km).
The magnificent mountain fastness of North Wales, offering rock climbs whose challenge is out of all proportion to their height, lakes, woods, valleys, waterfalls and estuaries complete the picture. Quarries, power stations, afforestation and unsympathetic holiday developments mar parts of the park.

Yorkshire Dales; 680 square miles (1088 sq km).
Straddles England's spinal range, the Pennine Chain, offering visitors a choice of two worlds – the high and open striding fells, and the glorious dale bottoms with their sparkling becks and grey villages. The most spectacular countryside is the Three Peaks area (Whernside, Ingleborough and Pen-y-Ghent). Here quarrying has dug deep for limestone, and afforestation threatens.

North Derry
Rathlin Island
Antrim Coast and Glens
NORTHUMBERLAND
Northumberland Coast
Solway Coast
Strangford Lough
Sperrin Mountains
Lagan Valley
Mourne
Lecale Coast
South Armagh
LAKE DISTRICT
NORTH YORK MOORS
Arnside and Silverdale
YORKSHIRE DALES
Forest of Bowland
Anglesey
Lincolnshire Wolds
National Park
Area of Outstanding Natural Beauty
SNOWDONIA
PEAK DISTRICT
Norfolk Coast
Lleyn
Cannock Chase
Shropshire Hills
Suffolk Coast and Heaths
Wye Valley
BRECON BEACONS
Malvern Hills
Dedham Vale
PEMBROKESHIRE COAST
Cotswolds
Chilterns
Gower
Kent Downs
Mendip Hills
Surrey Hills
EXMOOR
North Wessex Downs
North Devon
East Hampshire
Quantock Hills
DARTMOOR
Sussex Downs
Chichester Harbour
Dorset
Isle of Wight
East Devon
South Hampshire Coast
Isles of Scilly
Cornwall
South Devon

tion of the old agricultural workforce. It is a rare discovery today to find a village where as many as a quarter of the population derive their income from the land. Nowadays the cottages are more likely to be inhabited by affluent incomers. The indigenous families whose names can be found on the headstones of the churchyard diminish every year. Such changes are inevitable – and not always for the worse. Many villages that were dying on their feet have been sympathetically renovated and the local communities revitalised. But the less fortunate villages – the smaller, more remote settlements – will almost certainly continue to wither away.

The countryside of the future will also have fewer wetlands, those areas of bog, marsh and fen beloved by naturalists, with their bitterns and reed beds and swallowtail butterflies. In Britain the acreage drained has multiplied six times since the early 1950's, from less than 50,000 acres (20,000 hectares) to more than a quarter of a million acres (101,000 hectares) a year. However, some of the best wet wild places should remain. The Ouse Washes in Bedfordshire, Hickling Broad and Horsey Mere in Norfolk, and the Dovey estuary and Borth Bog in Wales, Loch Druidibeg and Rannoch Moor in Scotland and Lough Neagh in Northern Ireland are among the wetlands designated for conservation.

Elsewhere, it is the plough that threatens the old-established rural landscapes. A quarter of the chalk downland of Dorset was ploughed in the 1950's and 1960's; half the pre-war total of downland in Wiltshire has now been ploughed; and three-quarters of the heathland in the Suffolk Coast and Heaths AONB has been converted into arable land or afforested since the 1920s.

Today there is some hope that these pressures are now being checked. The Ministry of Agriculture has begun to take a more critical line when considering the financial aid it gives to farmers for 'improvements'. In an outstanding case in 1978 grant aid for the draining of the 900 acres (363 hectares) of Amberley Wild Brooks in West Sussex was refused and a remarkable tract of near-fen at the foot of the South Downs saved. The Government is contemplating legislation which would enable national park authorities to make moorland conservation orders to stop the conversion of the remaining moors and compensate the affected farmer or landowner. This proposal was prompted by the catastrophic loss of moorland on Exmoor (see national parks, page 226). A report by Lord Porchester in 1977 said that the heartland of the moor should be preserved 'for all time'. The special significance of the proposed legislation is that it has the backing of the Ministry of Agriculture, whose traditional policy since the Second World War has been to encourage maximum food production regardless of its environmental effects, as well as that of the Department of the Environment.

However, there is little sign as yet that similar restraints will be applied to commercial forestry. It is true that the Forestry Commission (which runs the state-owned forests in Britain) and the bigger private forestry groups make commendable efforts to ensure that there is room for a varied wildlife in their forests, but the effect of mass afforestation on the open uplands – the only plantable land which does not eat too disastrously into the national agricultural estate – remains the same. The rate of afforestation in Britain has slowed somewhat in the last few years, but the Forestry Commission is still acquiring land at an average rate of over 50 square miles (80 sq km) a year.

So modern farming and forestry are mostly responsible for the future countryside being fashioned today, though urban sprawl, more strictly controlled in Britain, is still cited as the major threat to Ireland's rural acres.

Countryside conflicts which receive the most publicity often involve relatively small acreages, though their visual impact may be dramatic. The National Coal Board's controversial proposal to sink three new deep mines in the fertile Vale of Belvoir (mostly in Leicestershire) will be comparatively concentrated, though it will require pit-head installations and spoil tips. Perhaps more worrying to countryside conservation campaigners is the NCB's continued pressure – with Government backing – to expand open-cast coal production to 15 million tons a year from 10 million tons in 1975 when the target was set. This brings the spectre of strip-mining to hitherto unspoilt countryside far from the traditional coal-producing regions. Although the NCB has a good record for restoring worked out open-cast mines, the techniques are far less acceptable in agricultural areas which have not already been scarred and blackened by deep mining.

Another major consumer of open country if the British Isles opt for a nuclear future will be the rapid proliferation of associated power stations. For safety reasons they will need to be sited in remote locations, probably on the coast. Inevitably, such installations would reduce still further the dwindling miles of unspoilt coastline. They eat up land and are hard to hide. The Torness power station in East Lothian, for instance, will take more than 150 acres (60 hectares' of good farmland and require a network of giant pylon lines radiating from it.

On the other hand the roads programme has dwindled under a combination of economic stringency and effective criticism of the traffic forecasts on which it was based, though several major schemes are still under consideration.

Set against all these demands upon the countryside the forces for conservation seem puny by comparison. Yet they have their successes. Today wild life and wild places are cherished as never before. A new spirit of environmental awareness is in the air. Foul rivers are running clean again. Pioneers of conservation, among them the Nature Conservancy Council, the Countryside Commission and scores of voluntary amenity societies, are fighting to safeguard our finest landscapes, villages and wildlife habitats. The National Trust for England and Wales now owns and protects 628 square miles (1005 sq km) and has covenants safeguarding another 115 square miles (185 sq km). And whatever happens in the more fertile and heavily populated lowlands, huge expanses of peaceful and uncluttered landscape will remain inviolate for decades to come in the Welsh uplands, Scottish Highlands and the west of Ireland.

In the Scottish Highlands, especially in the west, many areas have lost almost all their population, and some have been taken over for forestry. Many of the crofts are deserted but some of the houses have been taken over as holiday cottages.

Although the west of Ireland resembles the west of Scotland, it has a far more numerous farming population, though even here, many old cottages have become holiday homes.

The sum total is a rich and heady mixture: osprey lochs and Cumbrian tarns; Dartmoor and the Brecon Beacons; Burren orchids, kingcup marsh; Norfolk flint and Skiddaw slate; Wicken Fen, Chesil Beach; scarp, swallet and gritstone edge, clint and cavern, drumlin, combe; tithe barn, henge, national park, heritage coast. . . . time has frayed the ancient fabric but the countryside of the British Isles still glitters with a green and irresistible magic.

Appendices

Acknowledgements

The contributors to this book are, appropriately, as diverse as the countryside itself. Some are academics who coped manfully with the journalistic pressures of short deadlines; some are journalists who were subject to academic scrutiny of the most rigorous kind. This fusion of skills was required, we believe, to bring before a wider public the knowledge which previously has been confined largely to specialist sources.

The names of our major contributors and consultants have been listed at the front of this book; those of the photographers and artists whose work appears in the book are given on p. 342. But the scale and complexity of the book is such that even these lengthy lists do not cover all the organisations and individuals to whom we are indebted.

In a few cases material first published in *The Sunday Times Magazine* has been reproduced in this book, although rarely in unaltered form. Such material includes contributions by Hunter Davies, a former editor of the Magazine, and Caroline Silver, equestrian correspondent of *The Sunday Times*. We would also like to acknowledge help from Roland Adburgham, Bill Cater, Noel Chanan, Veronica Horwell and George Rosie.

We are particularly grateful to John Fowles for his foreword. At his request the fee for this has been paid to the Kenneth Allsop Memorial Trust in aid of Steep Holme, the island in the Bristol Channel bought to commemorate Kenneth Allsop, broadcaster, author, dedicated conservationist and former Sunday Times journalist, who died in 1973.

Many specialist organisations helped us both compile the book and to check its accuracy. If any errors have survived a stringent series of checks and double-checks, then the responsibility lies with the book's editors rather than the following organisations whose help we now gratefully and gladly acknowledge: the Nature Conservancy Council; the Countryside Commission; the Royal Society for the Protection of Birds; the Council for the Protection of Rural England; the National Trust (and also the National Trust for Scotland); the Department of the Environment; the Ministry of Agriculture (especially Elizabeth Hoffman and her colleagues in the Economics Department); all the national park authorities; the Forestry Commission; the British Tourist Authority (in particular Barbara Feathers); the national tourist boards of England, Wales, Scotland, Northern Ireland and the Republic of Ireland; the regional tourist boards within England and Wales; the Meteorological Office; the Council for Small Industries in Rural Areas; the National Monuments Board; the Civic Trust; the WATCH environmental group; the National Farmers' Union; the National Farmers' Union of Scotland; the Irish Farmers' Association; the Ulster Farmers' Union; Massey-Ferguson (UK) Ltd; the Association of Agriculture; the Royal Highland Agricultural Society; Nottingham University School of Agriculture; the Irish Horse Board; the Irish Pig and Bacon Commission; the Shire Horse Society; the Agricultural Engineering Association; the Royal Agricultural Society of England; the Milk Marketing Board; the Cotswold Hybrid Pig Company; the National Pig Breeders' Association; University of Reading Museum of English Rural Life; the Countryside Museum; the Rare Breeds Survival Trust; the Geological Museum, Institute of Geological Sciences; the Royal Horticultural Society; Gascoigne, Gush and Dent Ltd; H.M. Coastguard; Royal National Lifeboat Institution; National Maritime Museum, Greenwich; Trinity House; Northern Lighthouses Board; Commissioner of Irish Lights; and the Irish Coastguard.

Many individuals within these organisations bore the brunt of our inquiries and we hope they will understand that lack of space inhibits a more personal acknowledgement. We would, however, especially wish to thank Michael Murless; John Habgood of the Norfolk Reed Growers' Association; thatchers W.R. Farman, Norfolk, and George Dray, Devon; wheat-straw grower David Hurford, Devon; blacksmiths H.G. Middleton and Sons, Devon; gamekeeper Alan Smith, Suffolk; Michael Leyburn; Hazel Waugh; Yvonne Adams; and Harold Hillier.

Clive Crook was greatly helped in the design of this book by Pedro Silmon. The diagrams and maps – unless otherwise stated – were the work of John Grimwade and David Worth. Additional picture research was provided by Anne Horton.

Inevitably a general book of this kind has drawn upon some information in specialist publications. Those which we have found most useful are listed in the bibliography on pages 339–341 and more specific acknowledgments are made in appropriate parts of the text. In particular we are grateful to Yale University Press for allowing us to reproduce on pages 80–85 the essay on country houses written by Mark Girouard for *The Sunday Times Magazine* but derived from his book, *Life in the English Country House*, first published in 1978. The maps on page 193 are reproduced by permission of the Ordnance Survey. The Saracen monument on pages 70–71 is by Mervyn Blatch from *Parish Churches of England in colour* (Blandford Press).

It is neither politeness nor duty which compels us to acknowledge the role of our publisher, Macdonald and Jane's. Without their imagination (and money) it would have been impossible to produce a book of either this scale or what we hope to be such high levels of art, photography and text; without their tolerance, as deadlines began to slip, quality would also have been impaired. Particular thanks are due to Susan Egerton-Jones and Alan Coombes.

Finally, but most important of all, is our debt to *The Sunday Times*. The book was only possible through the willingness of Harold Evans, the editor of *The Sunday Times*, and Ron Hall, the editor of the Magazine, to allow so many of their staff to be diverted to the project. We are also grateful for the help of Michael Rand, art director of *The Sunday Times Magazine*, and Robert Ducas, the head of the Times Newspapers office in New York. We hope that they, and all the other individuals and organisations whose help we have acknowledged here, believe the end-product to have been worth the effort.

Defenders of the Countryside

A guide to official and voluntary organisations concerned with the conservation of the countryside of the British Isles and its wildlife.

Official organisations

British Waterways Board Melbury House, Melbury Terrace, London NW1 6JX
Public body set up by the Transport Act 1962. The following year the Board took over the ownership of the nationalised inland waterways which it has managed ever since. These comprise some 2,000 miles of canals and navigable rivers – mostly in England but including several in Scotland and Wales.

Countryside Commission John Dower House, Crescent Place, Cheltenham, Glos., GL50 3RA
Principal statutory body concerned with country matters. Provides facilities for enjoyment of the countryside in England and Wales. Designates national parks and AONBs. Submits proposals for long-distance footpaths and bridleways. Encourages provision of country parks and picnic sites.
There is a separate Committee for Wales at 8 Broad Street, Newtown, Powys.

Countryside Commission for Scotland Battleby, Redgorton, Perth, PH1 3EW
Objects similar to those of the Countryside Commission.

Forestry Commission HQ: 231 Corstophine Road, Edinburgh, EH12 7AT. London Office: 25 Savile Row, London W1X 2AY Established 1919. Responsible for promoting the interests of forestry in Great Britain. The Commission has also developed the recreation potential of some of its forests, establishing forest parks to which the public are admitted.

Nature Conservancy Council 19/20 Belgrave Square, London SW1X 8PY
Established by the Nature Conservancy Council Act 1973, and taking over some of the functions of the Nature Conservancy, the Council is responsible for the conservation of flora, fauna, geological and geophysical features throughout Great Britain, and for establishing, maintaining and managing National Nature Reserves. At present the Council's 164 NNRs cover well over 300,000 acres. Land not being managed as a nature reserve but of special interest as a wildlife habitat can also be notified to a local planning authority as a 'Site of Special Scientific Interest' (SSSI). To date, over 3,356 SSSI's have been notified.

Water Space Amenity Commission 1 Queen Anne's gate, London SW1H 9BT
Established under the Water Act 1973. Forms a link between the national water and recreational interests.

Voluntary organisations

An Roinn Tailte Ant Seirbhis Foraoise & Fia-Dhulra (The Department of Fisheries, Forest and Wildlife Services) 22 Upper Merrion Street, Dublin 2

An Taisce (The National Trust for Ireland) 126 Lower Camden Street, Dublin 2

Association for the Preservation of Rural Scotland 20 Falkland Avenue, Newton Mearns, Renfrewshire, G77 5DR
Aims and activities similar to those of the CPRE.

Botanical Society of the British Isles c/o Dept of Botany, British Museum (Natural History), Cromwell Road, London SW7 5BD
Supports measures to conserve flowering plants and ferns. Publishes a code of conduct for the conservation of wild plants. Present membership: around 2,500.

British Butterfly Conservation Society Tudor

House, Quorn, Leicestershire LE12 8AD
Formed 1968. Promotes conservation of British butterflies. Present membership: around 1,350 – many of whom are actively engaged on carrying out habitat surveys for the Society.

British Mountaineering Council Crawford House, Precinct Centre, Booth Street East, Manchester M13 9RZ
Promotes the interests of British mountaineers and mountaineering in all its aspects, including access to climbing areas and conservation of mountain countryside.

British Naturalists' Association Willowfield, Boyneswood Road, Four Marks, Alton, Hants
Supports schemes for improvement of wildlife, and promotion and maintenance of national parks, nature reserves and conservation areas.

British Trust for Conservation Volunteers HQ: Zoological Gardens, Regent's Park, London NW1 4RY. Scottish Office of the National Conservation Corps: 70 Main Street, Doune, Perthshire
Runs and finances a voluntary field force, the National conservation Corps, composed of volunteers who devote spare time to practical conservation chores. They welcome volunteers from those who are physically fit and over 16 years of age.

British Trust for Ornithology Beech Grove, Tring, Hertfordshire
Promotes ornithology in the British Isles with particular emphasis on field work. Co-ordinates work of British bird observatories and bird-watchers in national surveys, nest records and bird censuses.

Civic Trust 17 Carlton House Terrace, London SW1 5AW
Founded 1957. Encourages the protection and improvement of the environment in town and country. Makes awards for good development. Has initiated hundreds of street improvement schemes. Encourages tree planting and removal of landscape eyesores. Administers the Architectural Heritage Fund, which provides loan capital to local building preservation trusts. Is prominent in promoting environmental legislation, such as the Civic Amenities Act 1967, which established for the first time the concept of the 'Conservation Area' as opposed to individual buildings.

Committee for Environmental Conservation (CoEnCo) 29–31 Greville Street, London EC1N 8AX
Formed 1969. Encourages the best use of natural resources. Considers matters of national importance affecting the environment by providing a forum at which problems may be examined by the major conservation organisations.

Commons, Open Spaces and Footpaths Preservation Society 166 Shaftesbury Avenue, London WC2H 8JH
Founded 1865. Aims to preserve commons (over 1½ million acres in Britain) and village greens for public use, to advise on the securing and preserving of public open spaces, to obtain public access to open country and to preserve footpaths and bridleways.

Conservation Society 12 London Street, Chertsey, Surrey KT16 8AA
Formed 1966. Aims at limitation of human population and introduction of national policies based on recognition of the finite extent of natural resources.

Council for National Parks 4 Hobart Place, London SW1W 0HY
Founded 1977. Composed of representatives from voluntary amenity, conservation and recreation bodies. Aims to preserve the natural beauty of National Parks.

Council for Nature Zoological gardens, Regent's Park, London NW1 4RY
Set up in 1958. Is the national representative body for the voluntary natural history movement in the UK. Has hundreds of associates and affiliated bodies including County Naturalists Trusts, field clubs, etc. By co-ordinating the efforts of thousands of naturalists it has become a potent force for nature conservation, active in advocating such measures as the Conservation of Wild Plants and Wild Creatures Act 1975.

Council for the Protection of Rural England (CPRE) 4 Hobart Place, London SW1W 0HY
Formed in 1926 to improve and protect the rural scenery and amenities of the English countryside. Keeps a close watch on legislation affecting the planning and protection of the countryside.

Council for the Protection of Rural Wales 14 Broad Street, Welshpool, Powys, SY21 7SD
Aims and activities similar to those of the CPRE.

Country Landowners' Association 16 Belgrave Square, London SW1X 8PQ
Formed 1907. Protects and promotes the interests of private owners of agricultural and rural land in England and Wales. Has more than 46,000 members – though half are owner-occupiers with less than 100 acres apiece.

County Naturalists Trusts
Every county in England and Wales has a Naturalists' Trust which establishes and manages nature reserves, organises meetings and visits for its members and publishes newsletters. Details of membership and addresses of the Trusts' Honorary Secretaries are available from the Society for the Promotion of Nature Conservation (SPNC), The Green, Nettleham, Lincoln, LN2 2NR.

Fauna Preservation Society Zoological Society of London, Regent's Park, London NW1 4RY
Founded 1903 to safeguard wild animals and their habitats throughout the world and to bring about the creation of more national parks for this purpose. Takes active interest in British Isles fauna and in 1977 played a major part in establishing otter havens in England and Wales.

Field Studies Council Director and Information Office: Preston Montford, Montford Bridge, Shrewsbury SY4 1HW. London Office: 9 Devereux Court, Strand, London WC2R J3R
An independent charity organisation encouraging the pursuit of field work and research in all branches of knowledge whose essential subject matter is out of doors. Runs wide range of courses at its own residential centres in England and Wales.

Friends of the Earth 9 Poland Street, London W1V 3DG
Founded in the UK in 1970 to urge understanding of the need for conservation and preservation of natural resources. Acts as a pressure group to promote environmentally sound legislation, the prevention of pollution and degradation of the environment.

Greenpeace Colombo Street, London SE1 8DP
International conservation body which supports vigorous policy of non-violent direct action in defence of the environment. Prominent in campaigns against nuclear energy, whaling, and the killing of grey seals in Scotland.

Irish Wildlife Conservancy c/o Royal Irish Academy, 19 Dawson Street, Dublin 2

Men of the Trees Crawley Down, Crawley, Sussex
Founded 1922. A charitable society advocating the planting and protection of trees in Britain and throughout the world.

National Trust 42 Queen Anne's Gate, London SW1H 9AS
Founded 1895. Owns and safeguards for the nation considerable areas of the most beautiful countryside in England, Wales and Northern Ireland, together with over 400 miles of unspoilt coast, 100 gardens and some 200 historic buildings open to visitors.

National Trust for Scotland 5 Charlotte Square, Edinburgh, EH2 4DU
Objects similar to those of the National Trust.

Otter Trust Earsham, near Bungay, Suffolk
Promotes the conservation of otters. Instrumental in setting up otter havens in England and Wales. Owns a 47-acre Norfolk fen where otters occur, in addition to the Trust's own 23-acre HQ at Earsham.

Ramblers' Association, 123 Wandsworth Road, London, SW8.
Founded 1935. Encourages rambling and mountaineering, care of the countryside, preservation of natural beauty, protection of footpaths, and provision of access to open country. Watchdog for ramblers' rights throughout Britain – including the 103,000 miles of public paths in England and Wales. Membership: 30,000.

Royal Society for the Protection of Birds HQ: The Lodge, Sandy, Bedfordshire, SG19 2DL
Founded 1889. Gained a Royal Charter in 1904. Seeks to encourage protection and conservation of wild birds. Manages over 70 reserves throughout the UK. Also investigates and combats contraventions of the protection of Birds Acts. Membership: well over 260,000.

Scottish Field Studies Council Forelands, 18 Marketgate, Crail, Fife, KY10 3TL
Educational body set up to provide teachers, students and amateurs with opportunities to increase their knowledge of countryside topics.

Scottish Rights of Way Society 32 Rutland Square, Edinburgh, EH1 2BZ
Aims to defend and acquire rights of way in Scotland.

Scottish Wildlife Trust 8 Dublin Street, Edinburgh, EH1 3PP
Set up in 1964 to prevent destruction of natural habitats and wildlife throughout Scotland. Has established over 40 nature reserves in past 12 years.

Society for the Promotion of Nature Conservation (Association of Nature Conservation Trusts) The Green, Nettleham, Lincoln, LN2 2NR
Voluntary organisation founded in 1912 and incorporated by Royal Charter in 1916. Promotes nature conservation and protection of flora and fauna by establishing nature reserves representing typical habitats. Acts as the National Association of the 40 County Conservation and Naturalists' Trusts, including the Scottish Wildlife Trust and the Ulster Trust for Nature Conservation. Total national membership stands at over 120,000. Over 1,000 nature reserves are owned, leased or managed by the Trust.

Society for the Protection of Ancient Buildings 55 Great Ormond Street, London WC1 N3J
Founded in 1877 by William Morris. Its main concern is the repair and protection of Britain's architectural heritage, both ecclesiastical and secular. Has been instrumental in preserving thousands of buildings, from barns and dovecotes to Fountains Abbey in Yorkshire.

The Soil Association Walnut Tree Manor, Haughley, Stowmarket, Suffolk 1P14 3RS
Founded 1946. Voluntary body which believes that organic husbandry is the best means of building up soil fertility to produce better crops of high nutritional value leading to better health.

Tree Council 35 Belgrave Square, London SW1X 8QN
Established 1974. Aims to promote the planting and good cultivation of trees in great Britain, and acts as a forum for organisations concerned with trees.

Ulster Trust for Nature Conservation, c/o Inver Cottage, 67 Huntley Road, Banbridge, Co Down.

Trees for Ireland 9th Floor, Fitswilton House, Wilton Place, Dublin 2

Watch c/o The Society for the Promotion of Nature Conservation, 22 The Green, Nettleham, Lincoln. The Watch Trust for Environment Education is a charity sponsored by the SPNC and The Sunday Times. Its objects are to educate young people in an understanding and appreciation of nature and the environment.

Wildfowl Trust The New Grounds, Slimbridge, Glos., GL2 7BT
Founded by Sir Peter Scott in 1946. The Trust is concerned with the study of wildfowl in the wild and in captivity. Maintains seven wildfowl reserves in England and Scotland, of which Slimbridge is the most famous.

Wildlife Youth Service of the World Wildlife Fund Wildlife, Wallington, Surrey

Encourages young people between the ages of 5 and 18 to play a greater part in nature conservation. Organises holiday adventure camps, field study projects, nature trails, film shows and lectures.

Woodland Trust Butterbrook, Harford, Ivybridge, Devon

Established as a registered charity in 1972. Aims to conserve, restore and re-establish trees (especially broadleaved trees), plants and all forms of wildlife in the UK.

World Wildlife Fund Panda House, 29 Greville Street, London EC1N 8AX

International charitable organisation founded in 1961. Primarily concerned with raising money for the conservation and safeguarding from extinction of particular species of wild animals and plants. In the past 17 years WWF has contributed £16 million to 2,000 conservation projects in 135 countries, including Britain.

In addition to the national organisations of Great Britain and Ireland there are countless smaller groups actively engaged in conservation at local and regional level. It is impossible to list them all here, but among the most vigorous are:—

Dartmoor Preservation Association 4 Oxford Gardens, Mannamead, Plymouth PL3 4SF

Founded 1882. Dedicated to preserving the wildness and true character of Dartmoor. Was successful in opposing the construction of a reservoir at Swincombe which would have drowned the wild heart of the moor.

The Exmoor Society Parish Rooms, Dulverton, Somerset

Technically a branch of the CPRE, but almost exclusively concerned with conservation of the Exmoor National Park. Set up in 1958 to fight (successfully) Forestry Commission proposals to afforest one of the wildest parts of Exmoor.

Friends of the Lake District Gowan Knott, Kendal Road, Staveley, Kendal, Cumbria LA8 9LP

Society of some 7,000 members whose special concern is to protect the landscape and natural beauty of the Lake District and Cumbria as a whole.

Society of Sussex Downsmen 93 Church Road, Hove, Sussex BN3 2BA

Founded 1923. Main objective is conservation of the Sussex Downs.

Further reading

Chapter 1
Britain before Man, Institute of Geological Sciences, HMSO.
Britain's Structure and Scenery, L.D. Stamp, Collins.
The Face of the Earth, G.H. Drury, Penguin.
Fenland: Its Ancient Past and Uncertain Future, Sir Harry Godwin, Cambridge University Press.
Fossils, H.H. Swinnerton, Collins.
Geology and Scenery in England and Wales, A.E. Trueman. Revised edition, J.B. Whittow and J.R. Hardy, Penguin.
Geology and Scenery in Ireland, J.B. Whittow, Penguin.
Geology and Scenery in Scotland, J.B. Whittow, Penguin.
On the Rocks – A Geology of Britain, Robert Muir Wood, BBC Publications.
Outline of Historical Geology, A.K. Wells and J.F. Kirkaldy, Murby.
Rocks, David Dineley, Collins.
Rocks and Pebbles, T.V. Østerguard and J.B. Whittow, Penguin.
The Story of the Earth, Institute of Geological Sciences, HMSO.
Organisations
Institute of Geological Sciences, Geological Museum, Exhibition Road, London SW7 2DE. Publications of the Institute are obtainable at the museum and HMSO. The museum also arranges a programme of lectures, films and field studies.

Chapter 2
Anglo-Saxon England and the Norman Conquest, H.R. Loyn, Longman
Deserted Medieval Villages, Maurice Beresford and J.G. Hurst, Lutterworth Press.
English Landscapes, W.G. Hoskins, BBC Publications.
Fields in the English Landscape, Christopher Taylor, Dent.
A Guide to Ancient Sites in Britain, Janet and Colin Bird, Paladin.
A Guide to the Prehistoric and Roman Monuments in England and Wales, Jacquetta Hawkes, Chatto and Windus.
Guide to Prehistoric England, N. Thomas, Batsford.
Guide to Prehistoric Scotland, R. Feachem, Batsford.
Handbook to the Roman Wall, J. Collingwood-Bruce, (12th edition by I.A. Richmond), Newcastle-on-Tyne.
The Industrial Archaeology of Britain, R. Buchanan, Pelican.
Ireland – A General and Regional Geography, T.W. Freeman, Methuen.
Iron Age Communities in Britain, Barry Cunliffe, Routledge and Kegan Paul.
Landscapes of Britain, Roy Milward and Adrian Robinson, David and Charles.
The Making of the English Landscape, W.G. Hoskins, Hodder and Stoughton/Penguin.
The Making of the English Landscape: series of county and regional surveys edited by W.G. Hoskins and Roy Milward, Hodder and Stoughton.
The Making of the Scottish Landscape, R.N. Millman, Batsford.
Medieval England: An Aerial Survey, M.W. Beresford and J.K. St Joseph, Cambridge University Press.
Medieval Monasteries of Great Britain, Lionel Butler and Christopher Given Wilson, Michael Joseph.
Prehistoric and Early Christian Ireland: A Guide, E.E. Evans, Batsford.
The Prehistoric Peoples of Scotland, S. Piggott, Routledge Kegan Paul.
The Reclamation of Exmoor Forest, C.S. Orwin and R.J. Sellick, David and Charles.
Roads and Tracks of Britain, Christopher Taylor, Dent.
Roman Britain, I.A. Richmond, Penguin.
Rural Settlement in England, Brian Roberts, Dawson and Archon/Penguin.
The Shell Book of Inland Waterways, H. McKnight, David and Charles.
Town and Country in Roman Britain, A.L.F. Rivet, Hutchinson.
The World's Landscapes – Ireland, A.R. Orme, Longman.
Organisations
The English Tourist Board, 4, Grosvenor Gardens, London SW1W 0DU. The board publishes a number of leaflets on various historic trails.
Roman Heritage Trails: A booklet 'Discover Roman Britain' has details of nine trails linking Roman sites. There are also leaflets on three of the trails which go into greater detail. These are the Brigantian (North), Coritanian (Midlands) and Saxon Forts Shore Trail (South East).
Norman Heritage Trails: 'Discover Norman Britain' details nine trails which cover nearly 200 Norman sites including cathedrals, churches, castles, museums, monuments and battle sites.
The Civil War Heritage Trail: a map-folder features over twenty civil war battle sites and places of interest in Bucks, Berks, Beds, Herts and Oxon.
Captain James Cook Heritage Trail: this trail is in a map-folder and takes the visitor on a tour of the north-east through some of the most scenic countryside in England.
Cassette Trails: The English Tourist Board produced three cassette tape trails for motorists. There are two in Northumbria: Trail One is Northumberland, Trail Two, County Durham. Both trails are about 250 miles (402km) long. The tapes give directional instructions, cover points of interest on route and present interviews with well-known local people. The third trail is in Somerset and North Devon and covers 150 miles (241km) of coastal scenery and moorland. The first two are obtainable from the Northumbria Tourist Board, 9, Osborne Terrace, Jesmond, Newcastle upon Tyne, Tyne and Wear, NE2 1NT: the third from the West Country Tourist Board, 37, Southernhay East, Exeter, Devon EX1 1QS.
Wales Tourist Board, Brunel House, 2 Fitzalan Road, Cardiff, CF2 1UY, publishes 'Wales, A Glimpse of the Past – A Tourist's Guide to the Industrial Trails, Slate Quarries, Mines and Mills'.
Scottish Tourist Board, 23 Ravelston Terrace, Edinburgh, EH4 3EU, publishes 'Scotland: In Famous Footsteps'. These trails are based on Mary Queen of Scots, Robert Bruce, Burns, Boswell and Johnson. The board also publishes 'Scotland 1001 Things to See'.

Chapter 3
Buildings of England (series) Nikolaus Pevsner, Penguin.
The Concise Oxford Dictionary of English Place Names, E. Eckwall, Oxford.
English Church Architecture through the Ages, Leonora and Walter Ison, Barker.
English Place Name Elements, A.H. Smith, Cambridge University Press.
English Villages, John Burke, Batsford.
English Villages, F.R. Banks, Batsford.
Historic English Inns, A.W. Coysh, David and Charles.
Houses in the Landscape, John and Jane Penoyre, Faber and Faber.
Inns and their Signs, E.R. Delderfield, David and Charles.
The Life and Sport of the Inn, M. Brander, Gentry Books.
Life in the English Country House: a Social and Architectural History, Mark Girouard, Yale University Press.
The Living Village, Paul Jennings, Hodder and Stoughton.
Market Towns of England, Gary Hogg, Batsford.

Ordnance Survey Place Names on Maps of Scotland and Wales, HMSO.
Patterns of English Building, Alec Clifton-Taylor, Faber and Faber.
Your House: the Outside View, John Prizeman, Hutchinson.
(Many books listed under Chapter Two are relevant to topics such as villages and market towns which are covered in Chapter Three.)

Chapter 4
Benningfield's Butterflies, Gordon Benningfield and Robert Goodden, Chatto and Windus.
The Birdlife of Britain, Philip Burton and Peter Hayman, Mitchell Beazley.
The Birds of Britain and Europe, Herman Heinzel, Richard Fitter and John Parslow, Collins.
Birds of the Wayside and Woodland, T.A. Coward, Frederick Warne.
British Birds of Prey, Leslie Brown, Collins.
The Broads, E.A. Ellis, Collins.
British and Irish Orchids, D.M. Turner Ettlinger, McMillan Press.
Butterflies, E.B. Ford, Collins.
The Concise British Flora in Colour, W. Keble Martin, Ebury Press and Michael Joseph.
The Englishman's Flora, Geoffrey Grigson, Paladin.
A Field Guide to the Birds of Britain and Europe, R. Peterson, G. Mountford and P.A.D. Hollom, Collins.
A Field Guide to the Butterflies of Britain and Europe, L.G. Higgins and N. Riley, Collins.
A Field Guide to the Insects of Britain and Northern Europe, M. Chinery, Collins.
A Field Guide to the Trees of Britain and Northern Europe, A. Mitchell, Collins.
Food for Free, Richard Mabey, Collins.
Grass and Grasslands, Ian Moore, Collins.
Grasses, C.E. Hubbard, Penguin.
Guide to the Mammals of Britain and Europe, Maurice Burton, Elsevier Phaidon.
Hedges, E. Pollard, M. Hooper and N.W. Moore, Collins.
Insect Natural History, A.D. Imms, Collins.
The International Book of Trees, Hugh Johnson, Mitchell Beazley.
Life in Lakes and Rivers, T.T. Macan and E.B. Worthington, Collins.
The Moths of the British Isles, R. South, Collins.
Mountain Flowers, John Raven and Max Walters, Collins.
Mushrooms and Toadstools, John Ramsbottom, Collins.
Mushrooms and Toadstools in Colour, Else and Hans Hvass, Blandford Press.
Natural History in the Highlands and Islands, F. Fraser Darling, Collins.
Nature Conservation in Britain, Dudley Stamp, Collins.
Trees, Woods and Man, H.L. Edlin, Collins.
The Unofficial Countryside, Richard Mabey, Collins.
Wild Flowers of Britain, Roger Phillips, Ward Lock.
The Wild Flowers of Britain and Northern Europe, Richard Fitter, Alastair Fitter and Marjorie Blamey, Collins.
Wild Flowers of Chalk and Limestone, J.E. Lousley, Collins.
Wild Orchids of Britain, V.S. Summerhayes, Collins.

Chapter 5
Agriculture, James A.S. Watson and James A. More, Oliver and Boyd.
British Agriculture, J. Donaldson, Atchley.
Craft Workshops in the English Countryside, Council for Small Industries in Rural Areas.
Crafts and Rural Industries – Wales, Wales Tourist Board.
Discovering Farm Museums and Farm Parks, Shirley Toulson, Shire Publications.

English Husbandry, Robert Trow Smith, Faber and Faber.
Farms and Farming, Rowland W. Purton, Routledge and Kegan Paul.
Farming for Profit, Keith Dexter and Derek Barber, Penguin.
Great Farmers, James A.S. Watson and May Elliott Hobbs, Faber and Faber.
New Agricultural Landscapes, Countryside Commission.
New Agricultural Landscapes: a discussion paper, Countryside Commission.
New Agricultural Landscapes: issues, objectives and action, Countryside Commission.
Pick Your Own – Where to Go, National Farmers' Union.
Stay on a Farm, British Tourist Authority.
Thatching and Thatched Buildings, Michael Billett, Robert Hale.
A Visitor's Guide to Scottish Craft Workshops, Scottish Development Agency, Small Business Division.
Organisations
The Association of Agriculture, Victoria Chambers, 16–20 Strutton Ground, London, SW1 publishes a monthly bulletin which lists farms holding open days from April to October.
Council for Small Industries in Rural Areas, Queen's House, Fish Row, Salisbury, Wiltshire SP1 1EX, publishes textbooks and information on many rural crafts.
The National Farmers' Union, Agriculture House, Knightsbridge, London SW1X 7NJ.
Scottish Development Agency, Small Business Division, 102 Telford Road, Edinburgh, EH4 2NP.

Chapter 6
Beaches and Coasts, C.A.M. King, Arnold.
Beside the Seaside, A. Smith, Allen and Unwin.
Book of the Seaside, Automobile Association, Drive Publications.
The Coast of England and Wales in Pictures, J.A. Steers, Cambridge University Press.
The Coastline of England and Wales, J.A. Steers, Cambridge University Press.
The Coastline of Scotland, J.A. Steers, Cambridge University Press.
The English Coast and the Coast of Wales, J.A. Steers, Collins/Fontana.
Flowers of the Coast, I. Hepburn, Collins.
The Hamlyn Guide to the Seashore and Shallow Seas of Britain and Europe, A.C. Campbell, Hamlyn.
Lighthouses of England and Wales, Derrick Jackson, David and Charles.
The Pebbles on the Beach, Clarence Ellis, Faber and Faber.
The Sea Coast, J.A. Steers, Collins.
The Sea Shore, C.M. Yonge, Collins.
Seashore Life, Gwynne Vevers, Blandford Press.

Chapter 7
Backpacking, Peter Lumley, Teach Yourself Books.
Backpacking in Britain, Robin Adshead and Derrick Booth, Kaye and Ward.
The Hike Book, Jack Cox, Lutterworth.
No Through Road, Automobile Association/Readers Digest.
Rambling and Youth Hostelling, Ramblers' Association and Youth Hostels Association, Know The Game Books.
The Walker's Handbook, H.D. Westcott, Penguin.
Walking, Hiking and Backpacking, Anthony Greenbank, Constable.

Classic Rock, Ken Wilson, Hart Davis, MacGibbon.
Climbing for Young People, Anthony Greenbank, Harrap.
Mountaineering, Alan Blackshaw, Kaye and Ward/Penguin.
Rock Climbing, Peter Livesey, EP Sport.

Safety on Mountains, Central Council for Physical Recreation, Mountain Leadership Training Board.
Where to Climb in the British Isles, E.C. Pyatt, Faber.

Fly Fishing, Maurice Wiggin, Teach Yourself Books.
The Pursuit of Stillwater Fish, Brian Clarke, A.C. Black.
Sea Angling, Trevor Housby, Teach Yourself Books.
Sea Angling for Beginners, Alan Young, Pan.
Where to Fish, The Field.

Better Riding, Lt. Colonel 'Bill' Ford, Kaye and Ward.
Eventing: the book of the three-day event, Caroline Silver, Collins.
Official Handbook, Association of British Riding Schools.
Where to Ride, British Horse Society.
Where to Ride in Ireland, Irish Horse Board.

The Beginner's Guide to Sailing, Donald Law, John Gifford.
Dinghy Sailing, Ken Duxbury, Pelham Books.
Family Cruising, T.L. Kinsey, Stanley Paul.
Sailing, Peter Heaton, Penguin.
Sailing, Robin Knox-Johnson, Collins.
Small Boat and Dinghy Sailing, John Chamier, Pelham Books.

The Beginner's Guide to Canoeing, Alan Byde, Pelham Books.
Know the Game – Kayak Canoeing, EP Publications.

Ordnance Survey Map Catalogue, HMSO.
Ordnance Survey Maps – a descriptive manual, J.B. Harley, HMSO.
Organisations
Backpackers Club, 20 St Michaels Road, Tilehurst, Reading, Berkshire.
Camping Club of Great Britain and Ireland Ltd, 11 Lower Grosvenor Place, London, SW1.
Country Commission for Scotland, Battleby, Redgorton, Perth.
Forestry Commission, 231 Corstophine Road, Edinburgh EH12 7AT. Publishes a wide variety of useful literature including 'See Your Forests' a series of complete guides to forest walks, picnic places, wayfaring, fishing and horse riding in forests in England, Wales and Scotland.
Girl Guides Association, 17–19 Buckingham Palace Road, London, SW1.
Outward Bound Trust, 14 Oxford Street, London W1.
The Ramblers' Association, 123 Wandsworth Road, London, SW8. Publishes lists of all path guides for ten regions.
Forest Service, Department of Agriculture, Dundonald House, Belfast BT4 3SB, publishes leaflets on forest parks and their facilities in Northern Ireland.
Forest and Wildlife Service, 22 Upper Merrion Street, Dublin 2, publishes 'The Open Forest – a guide to areas open to the public'. The booklet covers the forest parks of the Republic of Ireland.
Scottish Sports Council, 1 St Colme Street, Edinburgh.
The Scout Association, 25 Buckingham Palace Road, London SW1.
The Sports Council, 70 Brompton Road, London SW3.
Young Explorers' Trust, 238 Wellington Road South, Stockport.
Youth Hostels Association, Trevelyan House, 8 St Stephen's Mill, St Albans, Herts.
Irish Youth Hostels Association, 39 Mountjoy Square, Dublin 1.
Scottish Youth Hostels Association, 7 Glebe Crescent, Stirling FK8 2JA.
Royal Yachting Association, Victoria Way,

236

Woking, Surrey GU21 1EQ, publishes booklets on the following subjects: Motor Cruising Training Manual Basic Course; Motor Cruising Training Manual, Inland Waders; Motor Cruising Training Manual, Coastal Waters. The Association also has a 'Learn to Sail' list of establishments, sailing schools and clubs, including courses for power boat enthusiasts.

The British Canoe Union, Flexel House, 45 High Street, Addlestone, Weybridge, Surrey KT15 1JV, publishes a coaching handbook.

Inland Waterways Association, 114 Regents Park Road, London NW1.

Association of British Riding Schools, Chesham House, 56 Green End Road, Sawtry, Cambridgeshire PE17 5UY.

British Horse Society, National Equestrian Centre, Kenilworth, Warwickshire CV8 2LR.

Irish Federation of Sea Anglers, 137 Leinster Road, Rathmines, Dublin.

National Federation of Sea Anglers, 26 Downsview Crescent, Uckfield, Sussex.

Scottish Federation of Sea Anglers, 8 Frederick Street, Edinburgh.

Welsh Federation of Sea Anglers, 2 Coed Bach, Highlight Park, Barry, Glamorgan.

The Angler's Co-operative Association, Midland Bank Chambers, Westgate, Grantham. A body set up to fight pollution.

The National Anglers' Council, 5 Cowgate, Peterborough. The sport's main link with the Government. It is pledged to work with all other organisations for the benefit of angling.

The National Federation of Anglers, Haigh House, Green Lane, Derby. The biggest and most important national voice in coarse angling with a membership of around 500,000.

Chapter 8
AA Guide to Stately Homes, Museums, Castles and Gardens, Automobile Association.
The Flower Garden in England, Richard Gorer, Batsford/Royal Horticultural Society.
The Garden – a Celebration of One Thousand Years of British Gardening, John Harris (Ed), Mitchell Beazley.
The Garden: an Illustrated History, Julia S. Berrall, Penguin.
Garden Kalendar, Gilbert White, The Scolar Press.
The Gardens of Britain, a Series of Six Regional Guides, Batsford/Royal Horticultural Society.
Gardens of England and Wales Open to the Public, National Gardens Scheme.
Gardens to Visit, Gardeners' Sunday.
The Growth of Gardens, Richard Gorer, Faber and Faber.
Historic Houses, Castles and Gardens in Great Britain and Ireland, ABC Historic Publications.
Historic Houses and Gardens in Wales, Wales Tourist Board.
St Michael Book of Great Gardens in Britain, Peter Coates, Marks and Spencer.
Scotland's Gardens, Scotland's Gardens Scheme.
The Shell Guide to Gardens, Arthur Hellyer, Heinemann.
Visit an English Garden, English Tourist Board.
Organisations
Gardeners' Sunday, White Witches, Claygate Road, Dorking, Surrey.
National Gardens Scheme, 57 Lower Belgrave Street, London SW1W 0LR.
Scotland's Gardens Scheme, 26 Castle Terrace, Edinburgh EH1 2EL.
The Royal Horticultural Society, Horticultural Hall, Vincent Square, London SW1.

Chapter 9
Climate and the British Scene, Gordon Manley, Collins.
Climatological Atlas of the British Isles, HMSO.
The Drought in the South West, Frank Booker and James Mildren, Department of Economic History, University of Exeter, Exeter Industrial Archeology Group.
The English Climate, H.H. Lamb, English University Press.
Mammals of Britain: their tracks, travels and signs, M.J. Lawrence and R.W. Brown, Blandford.
Nature through the Seasons, Richard Adams and Max Hooper, Penguin.

Chapter 10
Countryside Planning, A.W. Gilg, David and Charles/Methuen.
Derelict Britain, J. Barr, Penguin.
The Destruction of the Country House, Roy Strong, Marcus Binney and John Harris, Thames and Hudson.
Epitaph for the Elm, Gerald Wilkinson, Hutchinson.
Green and Pleasant Land: Social Change in Rural England, Howard Newby, Hutchinson.
Man and Environment, Robert Arvill, Penguin.
New Lives, New Landscapes, Nan Fairbrother, The Architectural Press.
Policies for Landscape under Pressure, A.W. Gilg, Northgate Publishing.
Survival of the English Countryside, Victor Bonham-Carter, Hodder and Stoughton.
Tomorrow's Countryside, G. Christian, John Murray.
Tomorrow's Landscape, Sylvia Crowe, The Architectural Press.
Vanishing Britain, Roy Christian, David and Charles.
The Vanishing Wildlife of Britain, Brian Vesey-Fitzgerald, MacGibbon and Kee.

General
Akenfield, Ronald Blythe, Penguin.
Bartholomew Gazetteer of Britain, John Bartholomew.
Book of the Countryside, Automobile Association, Drive Publications.
The Country Diary of an Edwardian Lady, Edith Holden, Michael Joseph.
Discover Northern Ireland, Ernest Sandford, Northern Ireland Tourist Board.
The Highlands and Islands, F. Fraser Darling and J. Morton Boyd.
Historic Houses, Castles and Gardens, ABC Historic Publications.
Historic Monuments in the care of the State, HMSO.
In the Country, Kenneth Allsop, Hamish Hamilton.
Museums and Galleries in Great Britain and Ireland, ABC Historic Publications.
Nicholson's Guide to Great Britain, Robert Nicholson Publications.
The Past All Around Us, Readers' Digest.
Properties Open, National Trust.
The Shell Guides to England, Ireland, Scotland and Wales, Michael Joseph.
Stately Homes, Museums, Castles and gardens in Britain, Automobile Association.
A Walk along the Wall, Hunter Davies, Weidenfeld.
A Walk around the Lakes, Hunter Davies, Weidenfeld.
Organisations
The Geographical Association, 343 Fulwood Road, Sheffield S10 3BP. Publishes British Landscapes Through Maps series. Each booklet describes an area depicted on one or more Ordnance Survey Maps. Areas covered unclude Cornwall, Doncaster, Oxford and Newbury, East Kent, the Lake District, Strathpeffer and Inverness, Norwich, Fishguard and Pembroke, Snowdonia, Worcester District.

Tourist information

The tourist organisations listed below publish a wide range of literature and information on their respective countries and areas. 'Tourist Information Centres in England, Scotland, Wales and Northern Ireland' is a booklet which gives the addresses and telephone numbers of all the regional and local tourist information offices throughout the United Kingdom. It is published by the English Tourist Board.

British Tourist Authority, 64 St James's Street, London SW1A 1NF.

National Tourist Boards
English Tourist Board, 4 Grosvenor Gardens, London SW1W 0DU.
Irish Tourist Board, Baggot Street Bridge, Dublin 2.
Isle of Man Tourist Board, 13 Victoria Street, Douglas, Isle of Man.
Northern Ireland Tourist Board, River House, 48 High Street, Belfast BT1 2DS.
Scottish Tourist Board, 23 Ravelston Terrace, Edinburgh EH4 3EU.
Wales Tourist Board, Brunel House, 2 Fitzalan Road, Cardiff CF2 1UY.

Regional Tourist Boards (England)
Cumbria Tourist Board, Ellerthwaite, Windermere, Cumbria.
Northumbria Tourist Board, 9 Osborne Terrace, Jesmond, Newcastle upon Tyne, Tyne and Wear NE2 1NT.
North West Tourist Board, The Last Drop Village, Bromley Cross, Bolton, Lancashire BL7 9PZ.
Yorkshire and Humberside Tourist Board, 312 Tadcaster Road, York, North Yorkshire YO2 2HF.
Heart of England Tourist Board, PO Box 15, Worcester, Worcestershire WR1 2JT.
East Midlands Tourist Board, Bailgate, Lincoln, Lincolnshire LN1 3AR.
Thames and Chilterns Tourist Board, 8 The Market Place, Abingdon, Oxfordshire OX14 3HG.
East Anglia Tourist Board, 14 Museum Street, Ipswich, Suffolk 1PI 1HU.
London Tourist Board, 26 Grosvenor Gardens, London SW1 0DU.
West Country Tourist Board, Trinity Court, 37 Southernhay East, Exeter, Devon EX1 1QS.
Southern Tourist Board, Old Town Hall, Leigh Road, Eastleigh, Hampshire SO5 4DE and Isle of Wight Tourist Board, 21 High Street, Newport, Isle of Wight PO30 1JS.
South East England Tourist Board, Cheviot House, 4–6 Monson Road, Tunbridge Wells, Kent TN1 1NH.

Regional Tourist Boards (Wales)
Mid Wales Tourism Council, The Owain Glyndwr Centre, Machynlleth, Powys.
North Wales Tourism Council, Civic Centre, Colwyn Bay, Clwyd LL29 8AR.
South Wales Tourism Council, Darkgate, Carmarthen, Dyfed.

Regional Tourist Boards (Scotland)
Borders Regional Council, Tourism Division, Regional Headquarters, Newtown St. Boswells.
Central Regional Council, Tourism Department, Viewforth, Stirling FK8 2ET.
Dumfries and Galloway Tourist Association, Douglas House, Newton Stewart DG8 6DQ.

Fife Tourist Authority, Fife House, North Street, Glenrothes KY7 5LT.
Grampian Regional Council, The Leisure, Recreation and Tourism Department, Woodhill House, Ashgrove Road West, Aberdeen AB9 2LU.
Highlands and Islands Development Board, PO Box 7, Bridge House, Bank Street, Inverness.
Lothian Regional Council, Department of Recreation and Leisure, 40 Torphichen Street, Edinburgh EH3 8JJ.
Strathclyde Regional Council, Department of Leisure and Recreation, McIver House, Carogan Street, Glasgow G2 7QB.
Tayside Regional Council, Department of Recreation and Tourism, Tayside House, 26–28 Crichton Street, Dundee DD1 3RD.
Note: Some of the offices listed above answer written and/or telephone inquiries only.

Regional Tourist Boards
(Republic of Ireland)
Athlone, 17 Church Street.
Cashel, Town Hall.
Cork, Tourist House, Grand Parade.
Dublin, 14 Upper O'Connell Street and 51 Dawson Street.
Dun Laoghaire, 1 Clarinda Park North.
Ennis, Bank Place.
Galway, Aras Failte, Eyre Square.
Kilkenny, The Pabade.
Killarney, Town Hall.
Letterkenny, Derry Road.
Limerick, 62 O'Connell Street.
Mullingar, Dublin Road.
Nenagh, Kickham Street.
Skibbereen, 14/15 Main Street.
Sligo, Stephen Street.
Tralee, 32 The Mall.
Waterford, 41 The Quay.
Westport, The Mall.
Wexford, Crescent Quay.

Photographers and artists

Chapter 1
Photographs: 10 Institute of Geological Sciences. 12 (Top) Adam Woolfitt/Susan Griggs; (Bottom) J.W. Roberts. 13 Robert Freson. 15 Aerofilms. 16 (Top) Michael Sheil/Susan Griggs; (Bottom) Robert Freson. 17 Denis Waugh. 18, 19 IGS. 21 (Top) English Tourist Board; (Bottom left) Adam Woolfitt/Susan Griggs; (Bottom right) English Tourist Board. 22 David Reed. 24 Adam Woolfitt/Susan Griggs. 25 Michael Sheil/Susan Griggs. 26 Alan Le Garsmeur. 27 Denis Waugh.
Artwork: 11, 13, 14, 15, 17, 18, 19 John Grimwade. 20 David Worth. 22, 23 Michael Turner. 26 Dee McLean. 27, 28, 29, 31 Pavel Kostal/Artbag. 30 (Top) John Grimwade; (Bottom) Pavel Kostal/Artbag.

Chapter 2
Photographs: 32–33 Robert Freson. 34 Spectrum. 36 (Top left) Steve Herr; (Bottom left) Georg Gerster/John Hillelson. 36–7 Robert Freson. 38 David Reed. 38 Michael Sheil/Susan Griggs. 40–41 Donald McCullin. 41 David Lavender. 43 Bord Failte. 44 (Top left) Spectrum; (Middle) Aerofilms; (Bottom) Robert Freson. 45 (Top) Robert Freson; (Bottom) Denis Waugh. 46 Aerofilms. 47 John Prizeman. 49 (Top) Ken Griffiths; (Bottom) Robert Freson. 50 Michael Sheil/Susan Griggs. 52–3 Robert Freson. 54 (Top) Denis Waugh; (Bottom) Andy Williams/Robert Harding Associates.
Artwork: 39 David Worth. 46 Ken Lewis.

Chapter 3
Photographs: 56 7 Robert Freson. 58 (Top) Adam Woolfitt/Susan Griggs; (Bottom) Aerofilms. 59 Robert Freson. 60 (Top) Denis Waugh; (Bottom) Robert Freson. 61 (Top) Denis Waugh; (Bottom) English Tourist Board. 62 (Left) David Lavender; (Right) Robert Harding Associates. 63 Robert Freson. 64 Denis Waugh. 66 7 Robert Freson. 67 (Top) Adam Woolfitt/Susan Griggs; (Bottom) David Reed. 69 David Reed. 70 71 Edwin Smith; National Monuments Board; Oxford County Library. 72 Robert Freson. 74 David Reed. 75 Robert Freson. 76 7 John Prizeman. 78 Robert Freson. 79 Civic Trust. 80 Denis Waugh. 81 Yale University Press. 82 Malcolm Aird. 83 (Top) National Monuments Record; (Bottom left) Lucinda Lambton Library; (Bottom right) Nature Conservancy Council. 84 Country Life. 85 National Monuments Record.
Artwork: 64 5 David Baxter. 68 9 Ken Lewis.

Chapter 4
Photographs: 86, 87 Tony Evans. 90 Robert Freson. 113 Denis Waugh. 116 Ian Yeomans/Susan Griggs. 118 Mike Sheil/Susan Griggs.
Artwork: 88–89, 92 93 Peter Barratt, Artist Partners. 94 95 Josephine Ranking, Garden Studio. 96 97 Clare Martin. 98 99 Graham Allen, Linden Artists. 100 101 Norman Weaver, Artist Partners. 102 103 John Francis, Linden Artists. 104 105 Peter Barratt, Artist Partners. 106 107 Clare Martin. 109 John Francis, Linden Artists. 110 111 John Rignall, Linden Artists. 112 Phillip Rymer, Garden Studio. 114–115 Ian Garrard, Linden Artists. 116 117 John Francis, Linden Artists. 118 119 Richard Orr, Linden Artists.

Chapter 5
Photographs: 120, 121 David Lavender. 124 Adam Woolfitt/Susan Griggs. 125 (Top) Julian Calder/Susan Griggs; (Bottom) Adam Woolfitt/Susan Griggs. 127 Robert Freson. 128 David Lavender. 129 (Top) Donald McCullin; (Bottom) John Prizeman. 130 Pamela Toler. 133, 136 Ken Griffiths. 137 Denis Waugh. 138 Tony Evans. 140 (Top) Tony Evans; (Middle) Noel Chanan; (Bottom) Adam Woolfitt/Susan Griggs. 141 Ken Griffiths. 142, 143 Robert Freson. 144 (Top) Denis Waugh; (Bottom) Tony Evans.
Artwork: 122, 123 Ken Lewis. 130 David Penny. 132, 133, 134 Jake Tebbit. 135 Hargrave Hands. 139 Ken Lewis.

Chapter 6
Photographs: 146, 147 Robert Freson. 148, 149 (Above left) David Lavender; (Above right) Aerofilms; (Bottom) Robert Freson. 150 David Reed. 151 Don McCullin. 152 Adam Woolfitt/Susan Griggs. 154 Don McCullin. 155 John Whittow. 156 Aerofilms. 157 (Top) Robert Freson; (Bottom) Richard Shirtcliffe. 158 Robert Freson. 159 Aerofilms. 161, 162 David Reed. 163 Robert Freson. 165 Tony Evans. 171 IGS.
Artwork: 152 John Grimwade. 153 David Worth. 156 (Top) John Grimwade; (Bottom) David Worth. 158, 159, 160 David Worth. 163 John Grimwade. 164, 165 David Worth. 166, 167, 168, 169, 170 Gillian Platt, Garden Studio. 171 IGS.

Chapter 7
Photographs: 172–3 Ken Griffiths. 174 Robert Freson. 176, 179 Robert Freson. 181 Donald McCullin. 184 Spectrum. 185 Adam Woolfitt/Susan Griggs. 187, 189 Robert Freson. 191 Robert Freson.
Artwork: 198 199 Diane Tippell.

Chapter 8
Photographs: 194, 195 Robert Freson. 196 Robert Freson. 197 Arthur Hellyer. 201 (Top) Ken Griffiths; (Bottom left) Robert Freson; (Middle right) David Lavender; (Bottom right) Robert Freson.

Chapter 9
Photographs: 204 5 Robert Freson. 206 7 Adam Woolfitt/Susan Griggs. 209 Denis Waugh. 212 3 Noel Chanan.

Artwork: 208, 209, 214 David Worth. 215 John Grimwade.

Chapter 10
Photographs: 216–7 Robert Freson. 221 Tony Evans. 224–5 (Top) Tony Evans; (Bottom left) Robert Freson; (Bottom right) Adam Woolfitt/Susan Griggs. 228–9 Denis Waugh.
Artwork: 222 223 Janet Marsh.

Index

Numerals in ordinary type refer to page numbers of the main text. Numerals in *italics* refer to the page numbers of captions.

244

Numerals in ordinary type refer to page numbers of the main text. Numerals in *italics* refer to the page numbers of captions.

Numerals in ordinary type refer to page numbers of the main text. Numerals in *italics* refer to the page numbers of captions.

Numerals in ordinary type refer to page numbers of the main text. Numerals in *italics* refer to the page numbers of captions.